Mr. Ben F. Kyser
1528 B St NW
Miami, OK 74354

PUBLISH GLAD TIDINGS

PUBLISH GLAD TIDINGS

READINGS IN EARLY LATTER DAY SAINT SOURCES

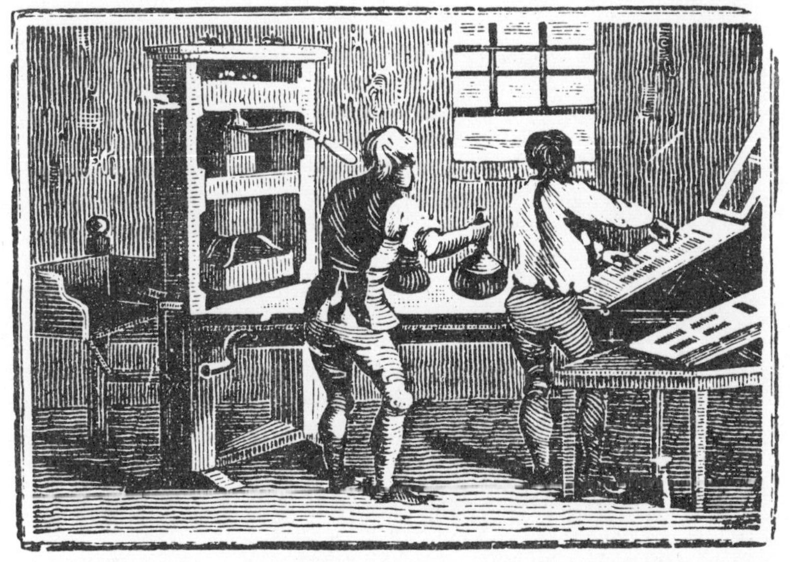

SELECTED AND EDITED BY WAYNE HAM

HERALD PUBLISHING HOUSE

FOREWORD

One of the important admonitions to modern mankind through the prophet of the Restoration, Joseph Smith, Jr., is to "Remember that the worth of souls is great in the sight of God." Though these words were uttered in 1829, the emphasis is appropriate for the latter part of the twentieth century. In a day of great emphasis on things, technical procedures, data, and material wealth, it is appropriate for us to be reminded that the great value among all values is personality. We who believe that man is made in God's image have sufficient reason also to believe that persons are to be valued for their own sakes.

It is in this spirit that we read with appreciation those descriptions of life in the early years of the Restoration movement by which we come to understand our spiritual heroes as persons. Our faith in God is strengthened as we recognize that the spiritual heritage which is so dear to us arises out of the lives of people who are struggling with some of the same problems and questions with which we struggle. Their circumstances were different, but their basic needs were much the same as ours. Their experience not only contributed to their growing· understanding but becomes the foundation upon which our expanding insights must stand.

These excerpts from the early publications of the church dramatically describe the problems and persecutions of the Saints, their search for a place for peaceful settlement, the development of theological speculations about marriage and ordinances for the dead, and the conditions under which Nauvoo was finally abandoned.

We commend to the reader particularly careful consideration of Chapter 7 in which Brother Ham deals with significant aspects of our interpretations of history. Our spiritual forebears were people subject to the problems and weaknesses that all human beings are plagued with. But God worked with them and through them in spite of everything. If we are faithful and responsive he will also work with us and through us both for our own blessing and the blessing of others.

THE FIRST PRESIDENCY

CONTENTS

The misspelling and typographical errors in the excerpts from the various periodicals of the early Restoration movement are found in the original publications. No attempt to correct them has been made.

O Zion, haste, thy mission high fulfilling,
To tell to all the world that God is light,
That he who made all nations is not willing
One soul should perish, lost in shades of night.
Publish glad tidings, tidings of peace,
Tidings of Jesus, redemption, and release.

—MARY A. THOMSON

Chapter 1

THE PAST IS EVER WITH US

Sometime ago I visited a woman whose life seemingly had been caught in a web of tragic experiences. Her latest tragedy was the loss of her teen-age son, from whom she had been estranged. I went to comfort her, but found that she had stoically faced her situation and had already come to terms with the tragic circumstances. At one point in our conversation she stated, "Life goes on just the same. As for my son, I will remember much of the good about him, a little of the bad, and some things I will forget altogether. I will grieve, to be sure, but life will go on."

Many times since then, as I have watched our people struggle with the meaning of our movement's history, I have thought of her remarks. In remembering our past, we tend to be especially conscious of the noble achievements and successes of our spiritual forebears. We have also been honest enough to permit our pride to be tempered by a little bit of awareness of times and situations in our history of which we have cause not to be so proud. But, then on other occasions, we have repressed, or at least refused to acknowledge, much that would perhaps be quite apparent to the historian who might more objectively view the historical processes in which the Restoration movement has been caught up. In this study we are affirming the need to be open to all the recorded details of our movement's beginnings and development, whether or not they support our preconceived notions about how things must have been. In other words, the times in which we live now demand that we be historians, rather than apologists, in our care and keeping of the artifacts of our past and in our consideration of their meaning for our present.

This, of course, is easier said than done because of the nature of historical studies. History has been described as an enormous jigsaw puzzle with a lot of missing parts. The reason is that many raw, undifferentiated events and happenings are experienced by persons but are not captured for the future by being recorded in print. Much of life's occurrences go unnoticed, at least beyond the moment of their actual occurrence. Life, in a sense, is like a motion picure in which only a few frames are made into stills to be preserved in someone's archives. Yet even if all happenings could somehow be recorded in chronological order of their occurrence, this would not in and of itself constitute history, for history is more than the sum of all happenings. History is the remembered past, coherently reconstructed—happenings in meaningful relationship.

The historian himself is involved in the setting forth of history, as he brings a sense of order to the data that is available to him for consideration. The historian selects his material from a vast array of data available. Admittedly his organization of the data is affected by his viewpoint, his perspective, his appreciations, and his dislikes. This is why historical happenings constantly need to be reviewed and re-evaluated, especially as new data about them become known. The function of the historian, then, is not to defend or condemn the past but rather to seek to understand it so that it may become a kcy to the understanding of the present and to the opening up of the future. For this reason, Cicero said, "To be ignorant of the past is to remain a child." Those who do not know their past are often condemned to repeat the mistakes of the past.

A sense of historical presence may often be felt in primary sources, or documents, as well as in secondhand, previously digested accounts. By reading a newspaper of a century ago, we can get the flavor of the times, a sense of what the people were thinking and feeling and concerned about. Of course, even primary sources need to be evaluated with care since they sometimes emerged in the climate of controversy and were carefully stated to make a particular point, often at the expense of some known facts or values. For example, early literature about the Latter Day Saints tends to fall into one of two camps. Either it is of the nature of exposé, in which the demonic elements of the movements are held up to light and gloated over, or it is apologetic, attempting to justify the Saints even to the point of making angels or superheroes of them. Both sides have at times made absolute claims for the correctness of their observations, unwilling to confess that all human historical inquiry is touched by finitude and therefore by ambiguity and ignorance. In our day, however, there is to be found a serious attempt to detach our past from the unrealistic claims of both those who assumed the Saints could do no wrong and those vitriolic critics who thought the Saints could do no right. Increasing numbers of modern Latter Day Saints are willing to see the coming forth and development of the Restoration movement in the context of the story of Christianity and the mainstream of American frontier history, where it can be better understood and appreciated.

Not all are so happy with our current openness to historical inquiry, however. Paul Edwards speaks with some validity when he states, "We want a historian's office because churches have historian's offices, but we do not want historians. Antiquarians, yes, with their collections of baptism statistics and the hairs in Joseph's beard, but not historical investigation, collections, and interpretation." But the winds of change are blowing everywhere, even through our dusty archives and vaults, and they are bringing to us a new sense of urgency for the task of understanding who we are as a people by understanding who our fathers were and why they were as they were. Our understanding of our role in Christian mission, our comprehension of the task that God has set before the church, are more clearly seen when we can face *and accept* our history honestly and without apology. Nothing is so sure as change in our world, and our view of the changes occurring throughout our history as our people responded creatively to the changing world about them will encourage us and free us to be responsive to the kinds of changes called for to meet the challenge of ministry to the world of the twentieth century.

To be capable of a truly creative response to our present, we need to eliminate some of the obstacles that hinder us from confronting our past. Some of our people are still acutely sensitive to the kind of historical probing that might bring a corrective view to bear upon long cherished myths and half-truths concerning our past. Our ideas may come to fit us like an old suit of clothes or an old pair of shoes, and it may be painful to have to break in some new ones. Another problem is the notion entertained by some people to the effect that the Saints of earlier days thought and felt about things exactly as we do. Or to put it another way, unless we think and feel about things exactly as they did, we have allowed a degree of apostasy to creep into our lives. But this is just not so. Our spiritual forebears, the Latter Day Saints of the 1830's, lived in a thought world different from the one we inhabit. Life in an agrarian, frontier society before the invention of electric lights, automobiles, and atomic bombs was vastly different in many ways from life in an urbanized, technological world of the late twentieth century.

The nature of life, of course, conditions the kind of response that is drawn forth from persons, and it does much to shape and mold the kinds of thoughts we think and the concerns we feel. For example, when some modern Latter Day Saints first hear of Joseph Smith's attempts to locate buried treasure with the aid of a "seer stone" during his adolescence, their faith may be shaken. But we must recognize that Joseph Smith, as any of us, was a product of his times, and his times were replete with this sort of activity. Notice how Fawn Brodie treats this incident.

> Crystal-gazing is an old profession and has been an honored one. Egyptians stared into a pool of ink, the Greeks into a mirror,

the Aztecs into a quartz crystal, and Europeans into a sword blade or glass of sherry—any translucent surface that made the eyes blur with long gazing. When Joseph Smith first began to use his seer or "peep" stone, he employed the folklore familiar to rural America. The details of his rituals and incantations are unimportant because they were commonplace, and Joseph gave up money-digging when he was twenty-one for a profession far more exciting.*

It should be clear that many of our difficulties in accepting our own history are due to our lack of a sense of the context out of which it has emerged. No movement arises in a vacuum nor can it remain untouched by the course of events in the world in which it has come forth. Every human institution, including the church, draws heavily upon the ethos of the times in which it struggles to express its mission. The church and its surrounding culture interact upon one another, with much give and take. Yet in days past we have often tried to talk of church history without any recognition of or interest in the larger cultural situation in which the Restoration movement developed. Today, perhaps, we are more willing to admit the great extent to which the concerns and questions of the nineteenth-century American frontier shaped the early theology and polity of the movement.

This frees us to consider what form our theology and polity must take *today* in order to adequately fulfill our God-given mission in the world in our time. The hold of absolutes upon us has disintegrated; we can now, with some measure of ease, witness to the relativity of the human situation. We are then able to assume a new posture toward and appreciation for social change, recognizing that God is continually breaking open new ground before us and calling us forth into the future. We once again become the people of the exodus, free to move in history wherever God summons

---

* Fawn Brodie, *No Man Knows My History,* p. 21. Copyright 1945 by Alfred A. Knopf, Inc. Used by permission.

us. We can self-consciously assume the role of history-makers, not just history-observers.

In our preparation for the march ahead, we are prepared best by knowing clearly who we are as a people and the route that our pilgrimage has taken us up to this point of time. As a small step in our journey of understanding, we will here become acquainted with some of the early, official publications that were published during the days of the founding prophet, Joseph Smith, Jr. We will confine our reading of early sources to the following:

> *The Evening and the Morning Star,* a monthly periodical published at Independence, Missouri, from June 1832 to July 1833 with W. W. Phelps as editor (14 issues) and continued at Kirtland, Ohio, from December 1833 to September 1834 with Oliver Cowdery as editor (10 issues). These 24 issues were revised and reprinted at Kirtland between January 1835 and October 1836.

> *Latter Day Saints' Messenger and Advocate,* a monthly periodical published at Kirtland, Ohio, from October 1834 to September 1837 with Oliver Cowdery, John Whitmer, and W. A. Cowdery each serving as editor for a period.

> *Elders' Journal of the Church of Latter Day Saints,* four issues only, published at Kirtland in October and November of 1837 and at Far West, Missouri, in July and August of 1838, with Joseph Smith, Jr., editing.

> *Times and Seasons,* published monthly, then semimonthly, at Nauvoo, Illinois, from November 1839 until February 1846 with a number of men doing the editorial work, including Ebenezer Robinson, Don Carlos Smith, R. B. Thompson, Joseph Smith, Jr., and John Taylor.

Another journal worthy of note was begun in this early period of church history, the *Millennial Star,* published in England from May 1840 on. We will limit our study, however, to those official publications of the church produced under the immediate watchcare of the president of the church, and thus we will not consider the *Millennial Star.*

Only brief excerpts from these periodicals can be reprinted here, yet we hope that these extracts will reflect the spirit and viewpoints of the total publication. Those portions that have been selected have been chosen primarily to give insight into the pervasive thought and ethos of the time. Many short passages are presented not necessarily because of historical significance but because of their "human interest" qualities. Many other items could have been selected with equal justification.

The chronology involved is one of publication. Thus we will have articles concerning the beginnings of the Restoration movement in the order in which they appeared in print rather than in the order in which they happened. The commentaries that introduce the selections from the various periodicals are not intended to detail the period or to give the complete background of the situation being discussed, but merely to help set the writings in a context that will assist understanding. It is our hope that we can all gain a better understanding of the early Restoration church by reading from periodicals that were so dear to the hearts of those who banded together in the 1830's and -40's for the sake of establishing the long-awaited kingdom.

Chapter 2

THE SETTING AND THE CONTEXT

On April 6, 1830, six young men met together under the direction of Joseph Smith, Jr., and Oliver Cowdery to organize the "Church of Christ." As they met in the John Whitmer home at Fayette, New York, they were participating in an activity that was neither unique nor unprecedented. Others in that general region had felt compelled to give expression to the spirit of religious quest abroad in the land by reforming old religious institutions or creating new ones. This was an era of schism and reformulation, affecting the largest of denominations and the smallest of sects. Of the many religious groups emerging in the Great Lakes region in the first half of the nineteenth century, few were to survive and still fewer were to make such an impact upon America's history as did those who called themselves Latter Day Saints.

This was a day of tension between the *fact* of the diversity of the religious scene and the *ideal* of institutional and doctrinal unity. Between 1814 and 1830 the Methodists split into four denominations, and the Baptist movement saw the rise of Free-Will Baptists, Hardshell Baptists, Reformed Baptists, and Seventh-day Baptists. Everywhere church groups were splintering, sometimes over doctrine or regional differences among their membership or ethnic origins, and yet most were concerned that the church of Jesus Christ be unified in its witness to the world.

This was a day for experimentation in utopian community building. The vision of the just society stimulated many idealists to band together for the practice of religious socialism based on the principle of Christian love. Some of the best known communitarian experiments attracting attention during this period were the following: the Amana Society, also called the "Community of True Inspiration," with its belief in contemporary revelation and common property; the Shakers, or the "United Society of Believers," in which celibacy was encouraged and all property was held in common; the Oneida Community, also called "Perfectionists," with common property and a complex marriage system that was commonly interpreted as free love; the Ephrata Community, or "The Order of the Solitary," with all property held in common, and with celibacy required; the Harmonists, involving 140 families, with vows of celibacy; the Robert Owen Community, best known for its stand against using machinery and its stipulation that children be reared by the community after they were two years of age. Many other groups were founded, flourished briefly, then disappeared. Few made any lasting impact. Almost all were concerned at some level with the questions of ownership of property and the relationship of the sexes. Small wonder, then, that the community of Latter Day Saints at Kirtland in the 1830's was widely considered, with all its talk of Zion, to be just one of several *communitarian* experiments on the Western Reserve.

At frequent intervals teachers and "prophets" would rise up here and there on the frontier to embody in a dramatic way the religious concerns of the day. Most of them merely proclaimed in a charismatic way the kinds of notions that were already widely believed. For example, the nearness of the approaching end of the present age was a common assumption. There are probably some in every generation who feel that it will be given to them to witness the culmination of all history, but in the early nineteenth century this belief was prevalent among many Protestant Christian groups. Thus when William Miller, a Baptist minister, began teaching that Jesus would soon come to usher in the millennium, he was preaching a message that was already familiar to many. By arithmetical calculations based upon biblical prophecy, he determined that the date of the Second Advent would be March 1843. As the time approached, thousands of his followers auctioned off their property, bought ascension robes, and gathered in hillside communities in order to be ready to be caught up with the Lord in glory when he returned. But the expected date came and went. With some refiguring, a new date was set, and then finally another. While many were disillusioned with the calculations, only a few totally lost their expectations concerning the imminence of the Lord's appearance. In time the scattered remnants of Miller's followers, under the vigorous leadership of Ellen White and others, founded the Seventh-Day Adventist Church.

A hotly debated issue of the early nineteenth century had to do with how the divine authority of the church had been preserved for the contemporary generation, and in fact who possessed that authority in its highest expression. Basically three arguments were set forth, each one championed by a set of churches and sects. One approach pointed to apostolic succession, in which it was conjectured that an unbroken line of authority had passed from Christ to his apostles and finally to us through the apostles' successors, seen as bishops or congregations or elders depending upon which religious group was making the claims; others opted for the continuance of authority through the Reformation, affirming first the continuity of the Christian witness through the stream of history but judging the original institution to have become tarnished with the passage of time to the point that an institutional housecleaning was needed; another group contended that merely cleaning up and patching up the old institution was not sufficient in that essentially a new start was needed, in this case a restoration of primitive Christianity in our day. The signs of the presence of the authority of God were generally interpreted to reside in the priestly leadership of men of God, or in doctrine rightly interpreted, or in miracles, or in special revelations that set the group apart from other fellowships with supposedly lesser understandings of divine truth. Some groups tried to combine several of these features to bolster their claims to authoritative ministry. In the midst of all of this competition, we find patterns developing in which minor as well as major differences of belief and practice are accentuated, with a resultant submergence, at least on the part of some groups, of the sense of a common Christian tradition and history that undergirded and nurtured and sustained all the competing groups.

For many sensitive Christians the tendency toward splintering and schism in the church led all the more to a desire for a united, authoritative church that would express the essential unity of all who claimed to live under the rule of Jesus Christ. Ironically, many groups arose to provide that ecumenical focus around which Christendom could unite, only to create another sect or denomination to add to the complexity of the situation. Perhaps the best example of trying to recover a base for Christian unity is the Disciples of Christ movement. This group grew out of the conviction that only a recapturing of the essence of the undivided, primitive Christian community of faith would suffice for drawing the scattered churches together. The spiritual pilgrimage of Thomas Campbell and his son Alexander led them from conservative Presbyterianism, where ministerial authority rested with a ruling body of elders, to Baptist congregationalism, where authority resided in the consent of the congregation, and finally to a totally new formulation of the church. Eventually the "disciples" under Campbell in Ohio united with the "Christians" under Barton W. Stone in Kentucky to form the Churches of Christ (Disciples). Many persons responded enthusiastically to their affirmation of a restoration of primitive Christianity in our day and to their attempts to stimulate the essence of the New Testament community. Actually, many religious groups made claims to more nearly conforming to the doctrines and practices and organizational setup of the New Testament church than did their rivals. And so for many, one of the major issues to be faced was the question, "Where is the church of Christ most perfectly embodied among all of the many sects and denominations?"

20

Into this milieu came the Joseph Smith family from New England. This family was typical of the New Englanders moving west into upstate New York and the Western Reserve. Hounded by business failures in Vermont and New Hampshire, the Smiths decided to seek their fortune in the great land that was now opening up in the frontier regions of the young country. And so Joseph Smith, Sr., Lucy Mack Smith, and their eight children emigrated to the Palmyra region. Though poor when arriving in Palmyra, the senior Smith was able to hire himself and his sons out for labor, eventually saving enough for an initial down payment on a one-hundred-acre farm in the area. As was the case with almost everyone in the area, members of the Smith family received very little formal education. Joseph, Jr., we may surmise, had only a few years of schooling in Palmyra. In his later years, Joseph could read fairly well, but his writing skills were minimal, with him depending heavily on scribes except for personal letters. Yet in spite of his lack of schooling, this young man was obviously rich in imagination and ingenuity, and extremely dexterous at making a creative response to whatever circumstances happened to thrust themselves upon him. His interests and concerns ranged widely over a number of areas, such that even in his early years his family felt that he would someday make history rather than merely coast through it unnoticed.

Latter Day Saints point out that Joseph Smith was quick to respond to a certain spiritual stimulation that set him upon his life's work at an early age. Nevertheless, we would expect that to some extent his everyday thoughts and concerns would be shaped by the environmental forces that were ever impinging upon him. Much of his ministry reflects a faithful response to the cultural situation in which he found himself and in which he was called to serve. Let us look at some of the major forces affecting his life and the lives of his contemporaries. First of all, this was a robust period of expansion, a day of invention, an era of road and canal building, when the boundaries of nature and nation were being pushed back by enthusiastic pioneers. This was a day in which an abundant faith in and optimism about the future of the American nation were everywhere apparent, a sense of manifest destiny, a notion that divine Providence was directing the course of the nation's development. This sense of destiny did not lessen political disputes and regional controversies, however. For example, the issue of states' rights was being debated at length, thus the seeming hesitancy of the federal government to intervene in the Missouri versus the Latter Day Saints difficulties in the 1830's. Slavery was also a disruptive issue that split the nation into hostile factions. The Missouri Compromise of 1820, in which Missouri entered the Union as a slave state and Maine came in as a free state, assured Missouri of being a "hot spot" when the Saints, many of whom had abolitionist tendencies, began to arrive in 1831. Even in the realm of religious needs, there were deep rifts in the nation. In the upper New York State region, the opening of the Erie Canal in 1825 caused an influx of Roman Catholic and "freethinker" immigrants into an area that had been solidly Protestant. The way these newcomers seemed to flaunt the notion of temperance concerning "distilled spirits" and the way they violated the rather puritanical observance of the sabbath that was normal to those parts caused a scandal among the old-timers. Even the Protestants found themselves at odds among themselves on many occasions as doctrinal issues came to the fore, often in times of revival.

There was a series of crests in religious zeal in the nation beginning with the First Awakening in colonial times under the leadership of Jonathan Edwards and other evangelists. Yet the close of the Revolutionary War found religious affiliation and church attendance at an all-time low, with only one out of twenty having membership in a church. Various causes can be cited: the geographic and cultural separation of the American churches from their parent bodies in the Old World, with a resultant lack of local leadership; the distresses and social confusion inherent in the struggle to create a new,

22

unified nation from a complexity of war-torn fragments; and the westerly exodus into vast, unchurched or underchurched areas of the west. With the separation of church and state in America, religious affiliation was placed on the basis of voluntary consent. Since no church had the means to coerce people into the ranks of the faithful, persuasion became the methodology, resulting in an evangelistic rivalry that found its most pervasive expression in revivalism, camp-meeting style. Revivalism often appealed to the emotions, depending upon vivid images of some future hell and heaven to stimulate response. The signs of salvation, often interpreted in terms of tangible actions, were emphasized so that the presence of the Holy Spirit in a meeting was most convincingly demonstrated, it was thought, by such activities as speaking in a sort of gibberish, weeping, or undergoing convulsive jerks in various parts of the body, sometimes resulting in a trance-like state similar to that induced by shock.

On the eastern seaboard, the revival was generally characterized by a calm, quiet spirit, but in the west excesses abounded. Some denominations were at times willing to cooperate to present a united front in the preaching ministries, but they were usually careful to approach the sacramental services of baptism and Holy Communion with separate observances. We know little about what occurred in the revivalistic camp meetings that swept across upstate New York at regular intervals, but we may assume that on occasion they reached in intensity the wildly emotional revivals characterized by great excitement and strange manifestations that were experienced in Kentucky and Tennessee at the beginning of the nineteenth century. Many of the revivalists, in catering to the concerns of their clients, put their emphasis upon a personal experience with God either by ecstatic vision, mystical illumination, or miraculous signs. Others stressed their millennialistic view that the time of the end had arrived and a new age of prosperity and peace would shortly be ushered in by the return of Christ to the earth. Adequate preparation for an encounter with God or for the advent of the Lord was seen in terms of believing the right doctrine, joining the right church, and refraining from bad habits.

Western New York, settled primarily by "Yankees" from New England, witnessed one religious revival after another in rapid sequence. For this reason, this area has been labeled the "burnt-over district." In the 1820's Bible-thumping itinerant preachers poured into the area with their scriptures and tracts, ministering to the needs and whims of the Bible-minded inhabitants who invariably held to literal approach to scripture. The completion of the Erie Canal opened the floodgate to more immigration, this time not of such a homogeneous type, though the majority were still New England Protestants seeking prosperity in a rapidly developing land. As they arrived, they too, as the earlier settlers had done, viewed with awe the nearby Indian burial mounds and told one another tales that excited their imagination concerning the ancient inhabitants of the land. They too adopted similar attitudes concerning slavery (they were against it) and Masonry. The anti-Masonic agitation became so strong in 1826 that it reached near hysteria. They too assumed the imminent second coming of Christ, and the "burnt-over district" then became a center of the Adventist craze. It was also in this region that the Fox sisters were convinced that the spirits of the departed walked the lonely country roads at night and returned on occasion to bring good or ill to those whom they singled out for attention.

All in all, the atmosphere of the locale and the times made it possible for young Joseph Smith to present his claims of divine inspiration and angelic visitations without having everyone laugh in his face. Indeed, many who were searching for a faith that would satisfy their religious needs were anxious to follow a prophet who spoke in the name of God and labored under His command. Many also were ripe for the message of the Book of Mormon, which seemed to readily provide an answer to many of the questions that perplexed

24

the people of that day. Thus the church arose out of the "burnt-over district." But it was not destined to remain there or to die there as so many other religious experiments had done. Given the westering spirit of the pioneers who comprised the church's early membership, it seemed natural that the church leaders themselves should gravitate toward the Western Reserve, and even beyond that to the outposts of civilization on the borders of Kansas territory. It was no surprise when the Prophet announced that there on the far western frontier, in the heartland of the American continent, was the center place of Zion, where the people of God would gather to bring forth His kingdom out of brick, wood, and stone and repentant lives.

Organizing the Church, April 6, 1830

Chapter 3

THE EVENING AND THE MORNING STAR

Recorded in Joseph Smith's Journal under the date September 1831 is the following:

> A conference was held in which Brother William W. Phelps was instructed to stop at Cincinnati on his way to Missouri and purchase a press and type for the purpose of establishing and publishing a monthly paper at Independence, Jackson County, Missouri, to be called the *Evening and Morning Star*.

This recommendation of the conference, which convened at Hiram, Ohio, arose out of a felt need for suitable material for evangelistic work and also for a vehicle by which the membership of the newly organized church could be informed of their duties and responsibilities. Such a proposal constituted a big step for such a small band of people, and evidenced their supreme confidence in the success of their missionary appeal. And so with a press from Cincinnati and paper from Wheeling, in the western part of Virginia, W. W. Phelps, poet and journalist from New York State, set up a printing shop in a two-story brick building on Liberty Street near the center of Independence. This printing office was 120 miles farther west than any other in the United States at that time, the closest press being the one at Columbia, Missouri, in Boone County. Independence, though a village less than a decade old, was rapidly becoming a frontier boom town, an important supply center and jumping-off point for the Santa Fe Trail.

In February a prospectus for the newspaper was published. According to this rather lengthy document, *The Evening and the Morning Star* was intended to

> unfold the meaning of revelations of God from earliest times til the present. . . . In the fear of Him, and to spread the truth

Independence, Missouri, about 1830

William Wine Phelps, editor and poet

among all nations, kindreds, tongues and people, this paper is sent
forth, that a wicked world may know that Jesus Christ the Redeemer who shall come to Zion will soon appear.

Brother Phelps also indicated that the periodical would
carry "certain information that will benefit the Saints
temporally as well as spiritually without interfering with
politics, broils, or the gainsaying of the world." The title was
seen as significant in that the evening star symbolized the
forerunner of the night of the end while the morning star
represented the dawn of the day of redemption.

Much of the editor's time was consumed with compiling
the revelations for publication in the Book of Commandments and with supervising the preparation of the *Upper Missouri Advertiser*, a weekly newspaper devoted to general and
secular news. Nevertheless, by June of 1832 the first number
of *The Evening and the Morning Star* was off the press, the
first paper published in Jackson County as well as the first
for the Restoration movement.

This first issue was an eight-page sheet, royal quarto size,
with printing matter of each page measuring 8¼ by 11 inches.
The pattern of content and format was set for future issues.
The primary purpose of the *Star* was immediately seen to be
the advocacy and defense of the newly established church.
This paper would be the means of disseminating the revelations of the Prophet, articles on church doctrine, reports of
the elders from the mission field, news from abroad, hymns
and poems, and much miscellaneous matter.

The immediate reaction of the church members was joy
and pride in this accomplishment. Joseph Smith records the
arrival of the first issue in Kirtland, Ohio:

> In July we received the first number of the *Evening and Morn-
> ing Star* which was a joyous treat to the saints. Delightful, indeed,
> was it to contemplate that the little band of brethren had become
> so large and grown so strong in so short a space as to be able to
> issue a paper of their own, which contained not only some of the
> revelations, but other information also which would gratify and
> enlighten the humble inquirer after truth

As succeeding issues appeared, however, some of the original joy became tinged with muted, then vocal, criticism. To be sure, the editor could often be faulted for the recurrent gloomy talk of plagues and pestilences, poor choice of subject matter, and failure to inform the reader concerning the movement's beginnings (a nonmember would have very little context provided in which to understand the development of the church). In addition, a certain turgid style of writing, all too common in the journalism of that day, rendered reading at times a most difficult task. After several issues had appeared, the Prophet found it necessary to write from Kirtland to reprove the editor:

> We wish you to render the *Star* as interesting as possible, setting forth the rise, progress, and faith of the church as well as the doctrine; for if you do not render it more interesting than at present, it will fall, and the church suffer a great loss thereby.

Whether or not Brother Phelps got the point of the Prophet's barbs is difficult to tell when scanning succeeding issues.

In all, fourteen issues were published in Independence, the last one dated June 1833. By then, the Saints were profoundly alienated from the area's original settlers and were beginning to sense that open hostilities were likely to erupt at any time. An article in the *Star* entitled "Free People of Color" was the spark that ignited the powder keg (see page 50). In the wake of the violent reaction that followed, four or five hundred persons razed the printing office and home of the printer, scattering the press and strewing the galley sheets of the *Book of Commandments* in the streets. In frontier America destroying the press of the opponents was a common method used by an aroused mob to show displeasure for the group sponsoring the press. Later the scattered press was reassembled and used during the next half century to publish papers in Liberty and St. Joseph, Missouri, and in Colorado.

30

But this was not the end of *The Evening and the Morning Star*. In December of 1833 publication of the *Star* was resumed at Kirtland, Ohio, with Oliver Cowdery as editor. A four-article series on "The Outrage in Jackson County" chronicled in detail the grievances of the Saints expelled from Jackson County. Ten issues were printed at Kirtland, the last one dated September 1834. By then the leaders of the church were ready to begin an entirely new periodical which they entitled *Messenger and Advocate*. But the contribution of the first paper to the church's developing self-identity cannot be easily dismissed. In a very fluid time of church organization and doctrinal development, the *Star* served as an instrument of unifying the church around the revelations of the young prophet and the doctrines emphasized by the careful selection of the editor.

THE REVELATIONS

Twenty sections of our present-day Doctrine and Covenants were printed in their entirety (Doctrine and Covenants 1, 17, 20, 26, 28, 36, 38, 45, 46, 49, 50, 59, 61, 63, 65, 68, 72, 76, 82, 108). Four sections appear in part (42, 43, 58, 85). One portion of a letter from the Prophet to the editor was phrased in such a way as to permit the Saints to consider it a revelatory message. For this reason the Church of Jesus Christ of Latter-day Saints has published it in its Doctrine and Covenants as Section 85. The basic concern of this instruction was the law of consecration, under which the Missouri Saints were struggling to live, and particularly the question of what should be done about those who refused to observe this law. The standards of holiness and spiritual perfection demanded of the Saints in this article constituted a challenge that very few could meet. The portion in bold type has become Utah Doctrine and Covenants 85.

LET EVERY MAN LEARN HIS DUTY

Every man ought to know his duty to God and man; especially the saint that has the benefit of revelation to guide him: he ought to know his duty, not only to say, but to do in all things. He ought to practice holiness before the Lord, that he may be counted worthy of an inheritance in Zion, and meet his Savior in peace.

Every soul that comes up to Zion for an inheritance, for the present, must prepare temporally and spiritually. He should settle all his concerns with the world, and owe no man: he should overcome the world, and be ready, when he arrives at the place of gathering, to consecrate all to the Lord, through whom the Lord has appointed for that purpose, that he may be prepared to keep the commandments, and do the will of his heavenly Father: otherwise he may not hold communion with the brethren: nor can he expect an inheritance, according to the regulations and order of the church.

While the gathering is sounded, that Israel may come in from his long dispersion, and also, as many of the Gentiles as will, the invitation is free, but unless the articles and covenants, the law and regulation; yea, verily all the commandments, are kept, all is vain. The Lord has order, and many that may come to the land of Zion, for an inheritance, without obeying all the requirements of the Lord, will be weighed in the balances and found wanting. It is not every one that says Lord, Lord, that shall abide the day of tithing. Every soul that is saved in the celestial kingdom, will be saved by its own faith and works: therefore, how necessary it is, that the saints should keep all the commandments, that others seeing a good example, may go and do likewise. If any should ask what is my duty? Let him read: To love the Lord supremely: To love his neighbor as himself: To consecrate all to the Lord: To be faithful to the end, and, above all, to have charity. A saint must be holy, or he cannot have a portion in the holy city.

Again: Let all things be in order. Let every one that quits the world for the sake of eternal life, act consistent in every thing: by obeying the commandments; by paying his just debts; by taking care of his property, if any, if not, by assisting others to do so: not hurrying up to Zion with some and leaving some to whet the appetite of an over anxious world. The Lord is never in a hurry, but gives every thing its proper proportion of time. Be cleanly; no matter what condition yours may be, cleanliness is a virtue, that will be required in Zion. Heaven shines with glory, and the Lord clothes his angels with *White Robes*: How necessary, then, that his saints should be decent.

In relation to consecrating, and continuing worthy, and faithful to the end, we make the following extract of a letter:—

It is the duty of the Lord's clerk, whom he has appointed, to keep a history, and a general church record of all things, that transpire in Zion, and of all those who consecrate properties and receive inheritances, legally from the bishop; and also, their manner of life, and their faith and works: and also, of all the apostates, who apostatize after receiving their inheritance.

It is contrary to the will and commandment of God, that those who receive not their inheritance by consecration, agreeable to his law, which he has given, that he may tithe his people to prepare them against the day of vengeance and burning, should have their names enrolled with the people of God; neither is their genealogy to be kept, or to be had where it may be found on any of the records, or histories of the church: their names shall not be found, neither the names of their fathers, or the names of their children, written in the book of the law of God, saith the Lord of Hosts; yea, thus saith the still small voice, which whispereth through and pierceth all things: and often times it maketh my bones to quake while it maketh manifest, saying:—And it shall come to pass, that I the Lord God will send one mighty and strong, holding the sceptre of power in his hand, clothed with light for a covering, whose mouth shall utter words, eternal words, while his bowels shall be a fountain of truth, to set in order the house of God, and to arrange by lot the inheritance of the saints, whose names are found, and the names of their fathers, and of their children, enrolled in the book of the law of God: while that man who was called of God, and appointed, that putteth forth his hand to steady the ark of God, shall fall by the shaft of death, like as a tree that is smitten by the vivid shaft of lightning; and all they who are not found written in the book of remembrance, shall find none inheritance in that day, but they shall be cut asunder and their portion shall be appointed them among unbelievers, where there is wailing and gnashing of teeth. These things I say not of myself, therefore, as the Lord speaketh he will also fulfil.

And they who are of the High Priesthood, whose names are not found written in the book of the law, or that are found to have apostatized, or to have been cut off out of the church, as well as the lesser Priesthood; or the members, in that day, shall not find an inheritance among the saints of the most High: therefore, it shall be done unto them as unto the children of the priests, as it is written in the second chapter, and 61st and 62nd verses of Ezra: And of the children of the priests: the children of Habaiah, the children of Koz, the children of Barzillai: which took a wife of the daughters of Barzillai the Gileadite, and was called after their name: These sought their register among those that were reckoned by genealogy, but they were not found: therefore were they, as polluted, put from the priesthood.

—January 1833, page 61.

DOCTRINAL ARTICLES

Within two years after its founding, the church already had a complex "oral tradition" of theology that derived heavily from the kinds of scriptural concerns being discussed at some length in upper New York State and the Ohio region. Now, with the advent of a Latter Day Saint press, these theological concerns were focused and crystallized in printed form. In most cases, the phraseology was heavy with biblical images and reflected an unremitting literal interpretation of scripture, as was common in most of the sects and churches of that day. Some articles are almost entirely direct quotes or paraphrases of biblical passages. We can expect most of the unidentified doctrinal writings to have come from the pen of W. W. Phelps.

Note how "preachy" in tone this first excerpt is as it lays stress upon moral uprightness and the necessity to live as an example of saintly conduct.

To the Church of Christ Abroad in the Earth

It is the duty of the Church of Christ, in Zion, to stand as an ensign to all nations, that the Lord hath set his hand the second time to restore the house of Israel to the lands of their inheritance &c.; and it behooves the members of this Church, to manifest before the world by a godly walk; by a noble example, as well as by stering precept; by prudence in living; by plainness in dress, by industry; by economy; by faith and works, and above all, by solemnity, humility and patience, that this is a day of warning and not a day of many words.

This being the order in Zion, how much more necessary is it, that the Churches of Christ, which have not yet come up to this land, should show the world, by well ordered conduct in all things, that they are the children of the living God! It is all important: and the salvation of many souls, depends upon their faultless example. They will, therefore, knowing that the Lord will suddenly come to his temple, do their part in preparing the way, by observing the Sabbath-day and keep it holy: by teaching their children the gospel and learning them to pray; by avoiding extremes in all matters; by shunning every appearance of evil; by studying to be approved, and doing unto others, as they would have others do unto them; by bearing trouble and persecution patiently, without a murmur, knowing, that Michael, the arch angle, when contending with the devil, be disputed about the body of Moses, durst not bring against him a railing accusation, but said, The Lord rebuke thee. They will not only set an example worthy of imitation, but they will let their light so shine as that others, seeing, may go and do likewise. Example is the great thing that defies the world with all its vain glory; by letting their moderation be known unto all men, both in dress and in living; in words and in deeds; in watching and in praying; in love and in labor, and in works as well as in faith, they preach the world a lecture, they set the enquirer a sample, and teach all Christendom a lesson, that studied preaching and pulpit eloquence have failed to accomplish.

—June 1832, page 6.

The following article is an attempt to provide some guidelines for "gathering" to Jackson County. Note first in the preamble, the justification presented for latter-day revelation. Here we see a reaction against the bibliolatry of the day; this bibliolatry grew out of a posture toward the Bible in which it was viewed as a final and absolute arbiter of value for all ages. As the advice concerning removal to Jackson County is given, we can sense something of the frustration that Edward Partridge, bishop in Zion, must have been feeling as he attempted to settle newly arrived church members, introduce them to the law of consecration, and mete out to them their inheritance.

THE ELDERS IN THE LAND OF ZION
TO THE CHURCH OF CHRIST SCATTERED ABROAD

Brethren, We think it proper to give you some general information respecting the present state of the church in Zion, and also

35

the work of the gathering. Notwithstanding that nearly all christendom doubt the propriety of receiving revelations for the government of the church of Christ in this age, and generally adopt the Scriptures of the old and new testament as the only rule of faith and practice, yet we believe, from the Scriptures of truth, that to every church in the past ages, which the Lord recognized to be his, he gave revelations wisely calculated to govern them in the peculiar situation and circumstances under which they were placed, and to enable them by authority to do the peculiar work which they were to perform. The Bible contains revelations given at different times to different people, under different circumstances, as will be seen by editorial articles in this paper. The old world was destroyed for rejecting the revelations of God, given to them through Noah. The Israelites were destroyed in the wilderness for dispising the revelations given to them through Moses; and Christ said that the world, in the days of the apostles, should be condemned for not receiving the word of God through them: thus we see that the judgments of God in the past ages have come upon the people, not so much for neglecting the revelations given to their forefathers, as for rejecting those given immediately to themselves. Of the blessings of heaven it may be said, they have always rested upon the heads of those to whom they were promised: Therefore, seeing that it not only was, but as long as God remains the same, always will be the privelige of the true church to receive revelations, containing blessings and cursings, peculiarly adapted to itself as a church. . . . And now brethren, if we wish for blessings upon this church, we must walk humble before the Lord, and observe to keep all his commandments. Notwithstanding the work of the gathering will be accomplished, we believe, in a speedy manner, yet the Lord has commanded that it shall not be done in haste, nor by flight, but that all things shall be prepared before you; and for this purpose he has made it the duty of the Bishop or Agent in the land of Zion, to make known, from time to time, the priveleges of the land, to the conferences, which may determine and make known how many can be accommodated. And the saints will remember that the Bishop in the land of Zion, will not receive any, as wise stewards, without they bring a recommend from the Bishop in Ohio, or from three elders. The elders therefore, will be careful not to recommend and send up churches to this place, without first receiving information from the Bishop in Ohio, or in the land of Zion, that they can be accommodated when they arrive, so as to be settled without confusion, which would produce pestilence. Therefore, if a church is desirous to come to the land of Zion, we would recommend, that first, by letter or otherwise, they make known their desires and their situation to the Bishop in Ohio, or in the land of Zion, and receive information from them before they start. Brethren will perceive as well as we, that where churches of fifty or a hundred souls each, are coming to the land of Zion from different parts of the nation, and, as soon will be the case, from different nations, without a knowledge of each other, they would, when they arrive, be in a state of confusion, and labor under many disadvantages, which might be avoided by strictly observing the rules and regulations of the church. Moreover by being in haste, and forcing the sale of property, unreasonable sacrifices have been made, and although this is a day of sacrifice and tithing, yet to make lavish and unreasonable sacrifices, is not well pleasing in the sight of the Lord.

—July 1832, page 13.

The early Saints shared with other sectarian groups a love of speculating about the end of the present age, which was judged to be imminent. In the following we find an attempt to "hurry" the Second Coming by recalculating the time of the Creation. The implied assumption is that the world will end exactly 6000 years after it was created. While such arithmetical calculations may seem tedious to the modern mind, it provided excitement on many a lonely evening in the backlands of frontier America.

PRESENT AGE OF THE WORLD.

There are so many different opinions upon, as well as various periods to the age of the world, that we fear the truth of the matter will be believed by few. Whether by the commentators upon the sacred writings, or by the clergy, the term of four thousand and four years, was put down as the exact time from the beginning till the birth of the Savior, we shall not pretend to say, but content ourselves by stating, that 4004 years, which is the present Christian calculation, added to the current year of our Lord, makes but 5836 years since the commencement of time in this world. But upon collecting the passed periods that the Lord has been pleased to measure out to his servants, by the prophets, we find a very different amount of years from the beginning. We compute thus:

Chapters.			Years.
Gen.	5 & 8.	From Adam to the end of the flood, ...	1656
”	11.	From the flood to Abram, ...	292
”	21.	From Abram to Isaac, ...	100
”	25.	From Isaac to Jacob, ...	60
”	47.	From Jacob's birth to his entering Egypt, . . .	130
Ex.	12.	The children of Israel in Egypt, ...	430
		From their departure out of Egypt till the birth of the Savior, ...	1491
		Years before Christ, ...	4159
		Since his birth, ...	1832
		From the begining till now, ...	5991
		Deduct, ...	5836
		Difference, ...	155

Here we have more than a century and a half difference on a subject of the utmost importance to the human family; and that, too, from the word of the Lord: And how comes this, asks the humble enquirer, I thought the spirit of God taught his disciples alike in all ages, and in all things? Be patient, beloved reader, and you shall know where the error comes from. The different parcels of time, from the creation till Jacob told Pharaoh the days of his pilgrimage were 130 years, are just as explicit as words at full length can make them; and he that will, may add the years of each man from birth to birth, till he comes to Jacob's pilgrimage, when he entered Egypt, and he will find 2238 years. Very well, but notwithstanding the word of the Lord says, in several places, that the children of Israel sojourned in Egypt four hundred and thirty years, in words at full length, yet all christendom reject the account, and declare that the said 430 years commenced when Abram departed from Ur in Chaldea, leaving Israel in Egypt but 220 years; and some have actually had the presumptuous audacity, to endeavor to strengthen this calculation, by quoting Paul's words in the third chapter of Gallatians: The covenant, that was *confirmed* before of God in Christ, the law, which was four hundred and thirty years after, can not disannul, that it should make the promise of none affect. Now let us search out the word confirm, and we shall learn that Paul allowed the children of Israel to be in Egypt 430 years, according to the record of the prophets. The 105th Psalm says, O ye seed of Abraham his servant, ye children of Jacob his chosen: He is the Lord our God; his judgments are in all the earth: He hath remembered his covenant to a thousand generations; which he made with Abraham, and his oath unto Isaac, *confirmed* the same unto Jacob for a law, and to Israel for an everlasting covenant. He that believes the bible, knows that God made a covenant with Abraham; and said to Isaac, I will perform the oath which I sware unto Abraham thy father, and when the same God spoke to Jacob saying, Fear not to go down into Egypt—I will surly bring yon up again, in addition to the promise before, that, in him and his seed should all the families of the earth be blessed, he has the confirmation, that Paul when he used *confirm* had no reference to the time when God *made* the *covenant* with Abraham. Besides the prophetic declaration that the seed of Abraham should be a stranger in a land not theirs; and they should be afflicted 400 years (Gen. 15.) Stephen says, in the 7th chapter of Acts, that they were evil entreated that length of time, which just agrees with the general account, that about 30 years after Jacob went into the land of Goshen a new king rose up, who began to torment Israel and to increase the tale of his labor, which lasted four hundred years!

The objection to this account of time, is, like others against the scripture, made by man upon the supposition, that if Levi begat Kohath, and Kohath begat Amram, and Amram begat Moses, there could not have been 430 years, as the age of man at that day rarely exceeded 120 or 130 years.

As there is but one place, as we recollect, that carries an idea tha Moses was the SON of Amram, if the world will furnish us with The Book of the Kings of Israel and Judah, mentioned in the 9th chapter of I Chronicles, wherein the genealogies of the fathers of Israel were regularly kept we will endeavor to explain the secret: so we add 430 years to the last sum, and it makes 2668, years when God brought Israel out of bondage.

From this till the Savior came, are 1491 years: Divided thus: To the commencement of Soloman's Temple, 480, as mentioned in the 6th chapter of the first book of Kings. From thence to the Babylonish captivity of the Jews, are 411 years, drawn from the different reigns of the varous Kings. In this account, we think there is a small difference, not to exceed 8 or 10 years; we take the least. From the Babylonish captivity till the birth of the Savior, not only the scripture and commentators, but the Book of Mormon also, agree in 600 years; which three sums, added to 2668, give an aggregate of four thousand one hundred and fifty five years to the commencement of this present era.

We will remark here, that years cannot be calculated by generations: For the 1948 years from Adam to Abraham included 20 generations: 97¼ years to a generation in all, but before the flood about 165 years. From Abraham to Christ were 42 generations, 2211 years; which would give about 52 2/3 years to a generation: But as the sacred writer divided the said 2211 years into three portions of fourteen generations each: We have, from Abraham to David, 1126 years; equal to 80 1/2 years to a generation. From David to the captivity at Babylon, 485 years; equal to 34 2/3 years to a generation: And from the captivity to the birth of Christ, 600 years: equal to 42 1/3 years to a generation. Wherefore, he that is wise will watch the signs, without measuring the length of a generation.

As no serious objections have been made to the current account of time, called the christian era, we shall not only suppose it correct, but set it down so, at 1832, and, with the old and new eras, we have Five thousand nine hundred and ninety one years; leaving the world NINE years from the begining of the seven thousandth year, or sabbath of creation: But as all have the privilege of ascertaining such facts for themselves, we ask no man to take our word for the age of the world; the word of the Lord is enough, and whether it be 160, or only 9 years to the morning of the Great Day, is not so much matter, as the solemn reality—Are we ready?

—August 1832, pages 21-22.

In the January 1833 issue the editor (we must assume him to be the author) greets the new year with the confidence that the Lord is visiting the earth in judgment. Listen to the kinds of proof cited.

But stop, and let us reflect, that although almost six thousand years have witnessed the mighty and many scenes which have happened or been acted on earth, few men, since Israel became a chosen nation of the Lord, have lived to see an hundred New-Years: and, that, from the signs of the times, and the convultions of nations, notwithstanding about one third of this century has already been numbered among departed years, very few, if any, in their present existence, will behold the New-Year of nine-teen hundred! The destroying angel is on the earth, scattering the pestilence where the Lord will, and as some of the inhabitants are swept away by this unseen power, the residue seem to harden their hearts and forget that now is the time when all flesh is grass: The Journal of Commerce thus sums up the amount of the cholera in New-York: "COST OF THE CHOLERA.—It appears from a report recently submitted to the Board of Assistant Aldermen, that the expense of the city government on account of the cholera, amounted to $100,000. But this is a small matter in comparison with the damage occasioned by the derangement and suspension of business, the quarantining of our vessels wherever they went, the expence of sickness and flight, and the host of other inconveniences to which the calamity gave rise. Leaving out of the account, all higher considerations, such as the loss of life and the sundering of earthly ties, an assessment of $1,000,000 upon our inhabitants, (perhaps we should say two millions,) would have been a cheap purchase of exemption from the scourge.

It is surprising how soon the effects of this calamity disappear. The pecuniary sufferings is no longer visible—the 6400 persons deceased since the first of July are not missed by the public—the 3000 dram shops are again in full action—the Theaters, Distilleries, and other engines of destruction, are plied as warmly as ever.

This is the reign of error, and a day of trouble, and we caution the disciples of the blessed Savior, to be aware and not asset or write, things as truth without evidence, or a knowledge of their own. The present generation is very much given to lying, and, as a natural consequence, a lie will be believed and circulated by ten persons, where the truth can scarcely be heard by one. Good is seemingly, perished among all nations, and men's hearts fail them, while looking for those things which are about to take place on the earth. No man can calculate from last year's experience, and say, as it was in eighteen hundred and thirty-two, it will be in eighteen hundred and thirty-three: For the Lord is exerting the powers of heaven, and will, ere long, shake terribly the earth; yea, his arrows are shot to the ends of it, and all flesh will know, that he hath put forth his hand to rebuke the world for its pollutions, and abominations.

In proof of this the saints are gathering home to the land of Zion, that they may be ready to meet the Lord when he comes suddenly to his temple. And besides this, the Spirit of the Lord, as it were, works upon the great men of the earth, to hasten the work of the gathering, in its time. The President of the United States, in relation to the remnants of Joseph, thus speaks in his last Message: I am happy to inform you, that the wise and humane policy of transferring from the Eastern to the Western side of the Mississippi, the remnants of our aboriginal tribes, with their own consent and upon just terms, has been steadily pursued, and is approaching, I trust, its consummation. By reference to the report of the Secretary of War, and to the documents submitted with it, you will see the progress which has been made since your last session, in the arrangement of the various matters connected with our Indian relations. With one exception, every subject involving any question of conflicting jurisdiction, or of peculiar difficulty, has been happily disposed of and the conviction evidently gains ground among the Indians, that their removal to the country assigned by the United States for their permanent residence, furnishes the only hope of their ultimate prosperity.

This is true, and we can only say, verily all things move to further the work of the Lord: and now to conclude, we can say as we did at the beginning, many years have rolled away, since the Morning Stars sang together, but few more shall pass, till the Sons of God will shout for joy! The Lord will come the second time: The Lord will bring again Zion! Let earth rejoice, and let all things, even the bells upon the horses, be HOLINESS TO THE LORD.

—January 1833, page 63.

The following article is more of the nature of historical review but it does reveal the theological categories in which the early members viewed the coming forth and early development of the Restoration church.

Other than references to the founding of the church in previously printed revelations, this is the first attempt to systematically set down some historical data concerning the earliest days of the young church. Part of the reason for publishing this account was to refute certain allegations made about the corporate life of the Saints, including the rumor that they were engaged in a social experiment involving having property and wives in common.

RISE AND PROGRESS OF THE CHURCH OF CHRIST.

Having promised in our last number, something on the rise and progress of the church of Christ, we commence with the intention of giving a relation of a few facts, as they have occurred since the church was organized in eighteen hundred and thirty. We shall be brief in this article, as we design to give from time to time the progress of this church, for the benefit of inquirers as well as the satisfaction of those who believe.

Soon after the book of Mormon came forth, containing the fulness of the gospel of Jesus Christ, the church was organized on the sixth of April, in Manchester; soon after, a branch was established in Fayette, and the June following, another in Colesville, New York.

We shall not give, at this time, the particulars attending the organization of these branches of the church; neither shall we publish in this, the account of the persecution of those who were then called and authorized to preach the everlasting gospel. Twenty more were added to the church in Manchester and Fayette, in the month of April; and on the 28th of June, thirteen were baptized in Colesville: and of these we can say as Paul said of the five hundred who saw the Savior after he had risen from the dead: The greater part remain unto this present, but some are fallen asleep. In October [1830], the number of disciples had increased to between seventy and eighty, when four of the elders started for the west, and founded a branch of the church at Kirtland, Ohio, around which many have since arisen.

These first four, having added one to their number, proceeded to the west, after having baptized one hundred and thirty disciples in less than four weeks and ordained four of them elders, and finally stopped in the western bounds of the state of Missouri, having been preserved by the hand of the Lord, and directed by his Spirit.

In the winter [1831], the church in the state of New York, after a commandment had been received from the Lord, began to prepare to remove to the state of Ohio. The following is a part of the revelation referred to above: And that ye might escape the power of the enemy, and be gathered unto me a righteous people without spot and blameless: wherefore for this cause I gave unto you the commandment that ye should go to the Ohio; and there I will give unto you my law, and there you shall be endowed with power from on high, and from thence, whomsoever I will shall go forth unto all nations, and it shall be told them what they shall do, for I have a great work laid up in store: for Israel shall be saved, and I will lead them whithersoever I will, and no power shall stay my hand.

In the spring the greater part of the disciples who were in New York, removed to the Ohio. In June, the word having been preached in many places and hundreds having been baptized, a number of the elders, by the commandment of the Lord, journeyed west, proclaiming the gospel and bearing testimony of the work of the Lord in these last days; saying none other things than that which the prophets and apostles had written, and that which was taught them by the Comforter, by the prayer of faith, as the Lord had said. Many gladly received the word and were baptized, so that branches of the church were built up in many places, notwithstanding the opposition with which the elders were often met.

Indeed we have the testimony before our eyes of the faithfulness with which they discharged their duty in publishing salvation to their fellow men. Many have already come up to the land of Zion who were fruits of their labors; and by what we can learn from time to time, we are reminded of the parable of the seed, for we are certain that much of it has fallen on good ground: and we are sure, having the testimony in our hearts, that these faithful elders, although often fateagued and wearied with the length of their journey, will at the last day receive a crown of eternal life, and joy unspeakable in the everlasting kingdom of God and the Lamb, with those that they were the means of turning from darkness to light. And while reflecting on this subject, a few words from Daniel seems to be applicable: And they that be wise shall shine as the brightness of the firmament; and they that turn many to righteousness, as the stars forever and ever. For the word of the Lord to them has thus far been verified, which says: Let them go two by two, and thus let them preach by the way in every congregation, baptizing by water, and the laying on of the hands by the water's edge: for thus saith the Lord, I will cut my work short in righteousness: for the days cometh that I will send forth judgment unto victory.

In July they began to arrive in the western boundaries of Missouri, and shortly after, a branch of the church from colesville, New York, came on by water, and thus the gathering commenced.

From this time, the progress of the church though gradual, has been more than many of great faith had anticipated. Many churches have been built up in different states, and some hundreds of members have come up to this land, and are striving to keep the commandments of the Lord, that they may be prepared, whether in life or in death, to meet him when he comes in his glory with all his holy angels.

It may be proper to say, as we have often said before, that this church is taught by the revelations of the Lord, in all things, as they have been received from time to time from the days of Adam, until now. And it is really a matter of joy to see how fast the work of the gathering is continuing amid the discouragements, persecutions, and false statements of the world.

It has been reported that the church had settled in this country, and were living as one family. This is not so.

The faith of the church has greatly increased in these first three years of its existance, in these last days. Much is said at home and abroad about Mormonites, as the world has seen fit to call the diciples of Jesus Christ, but wherever the gospel has been truly set forth; wherever the book of Mormon has been fully explained and understood, and wherever men have listened with unprejudiced minds to learn the truth for the purpose of escaping the desolations and calamities which are already abroad in the earth, there the Lord has borne record of his own work by his Spirit.

While the gifts in many instances have been manifested beyond doubt, in healing the sick, &c. some have doubted and some have believed, as in the days of the apostles; and even from the beginning this has been the case more or less, and will be till satan is bound.

We promised to correct as many falsehoods as we could, that were in circulation. In this article we have commenced, but upon looking at some of the late misrepresentations that have found their way to the public, we think the best method will be for us to continue an account of the rise and progress of the church, and publish the truth as we have done; for, of all the statements that have been published in the newspapers of the day concerning this church, not one has reached us but what in a greater or less degree was untrue; and what adds more to our astonishment, is, that these publications came from those who proffess the religion of Christ. By this however we do not intend to cast any reflections, for we remember the example of our Lord, who, when he was reviled, reviled not again.

The progress of the church has been great, and while we witness the spread of the work, knowing it is of God, we are willing to give the world all the light we can that will lead them to salvation.

—April 1833, page 84.

45

The early church's millennialistic perspective is readily apparent in this simple recapping of the great events of history.

GREAT EVENTS

In the first thousand years, was witnessed the fall of man; the building up of Zion, when Enoch with all his people, walked with God three hundred and sixty five years on earth, and then were taken up into heaven.

In the second thousand years, the world was deluged with a flood for its wickedness; the tower was built that man might go to heaven; the language was confounded; the earth divided into continents and oceans; the people scattered upon the face of the whole earth; and America was peopled by the Jaredites.

In the third thousand years, Pharaoh and his host were swallowed up in the Red Sea; Israel, the chosen of the Lord, was overshadowed by his glory in a cloud by day, and a pillar of fire by night; and the building of the temple of the Lord at Jerusalem.

In the fourth thousand years, the ten tribes of Israel were led away captive out of the land of Canaan, and taken to a place by the hand of the Lord that has not yet been discovered by the Gentiles; the Jaredites were destroyed because of their wickedness; Lehi was guided by the matchless power of God to this continent.

In the fifth thousand years, the Savior of the world was born, crucified, and rose again from the dead; the most of the apostles were slain for preaching the gospel; and Jerusalem was destroyed.

In the sixth thousand years, America, the land of liberty, choice above all others, was settled by the Gentiles; the fulness of the gospel of Jesus Christ came forth in the book of Mormon, the church established, and the gathering of the saints, commenced, preparatory to the second coming of their Lord, that in the seventh thousand years the earth may rest.

—June 1833, page 102.

In the summer of 1833 relations between church members and original settlers had deteriorated to the point of open hostility. Theological and cultural differences between the two groups were too deep to afford any sort of reconciliation. One of the Saints' bitter opponents, a certain Reverend Pixley, wrote a tract entitled "Beware of False Prophets," which he distributed widely in Independence in order to urge the settlers to drive the Saints from their midst. As an answer to the tract, *The Evening and the Morning Star* published an article of the same title, contrasting the marks of false prophets and those of true ones. While making no direct allusion to Pixley's tract, the *Star* editorial fixes many of the marks of false prophets on the priests and ministers of the times who, "while clinging to forms of godliness, were denying the power thereof."

BEWARE OF FALSE PROPHETS

Our object in quoting this caution of our blessed Savior, is to give the saints and the world, inasmuch as the inhabitants thereof wish to enter in at the door and be saved, a few hints relative to false prophets.

There have been, are, and will be, till the Lord comes, false prophets, that have tried to, and would if possible, but it is not possible, deceive the very elect.

Jesus said, Beware of false prophets, which come to you in sheep's clothing, but inwardly they are ravening wolves. Ye shall know them by their fruits.

To come to the point, there were to be many that should deceive many in the last days: such as Paul said should be lovers of themselves, covetous, boasters, proud, blasphemers, false accusers, incontinent, dispisers of those that are good; lovers of pleasure more than lovers of God, having a form of godliness, but denying the power thereof. . . .

When men, who pretend to be shepherds of the Lord's sheep, without authority, rail against the word of the Lord, or endeavor to warp its meaning to fit some peculiar notion, which will never extend farther than to gain the esteem and goods of this world, we say, Beware of false prophets, which come to you in sheep's clothing.

When men, as servants of the Lord, under the sacred name of religion instead of building up the church of Christ, by preaching baptism for the remission of sins, and the gift of the Holy Ghost, by the laying on of the hands, with a promise of eternal life, by keeping all the commandments of the Lord, and continuing faithful to the end, are building up mite societies, temperence societies, missionary societies, bible societies, or any other societies wherein the scribes and pharisees sit in Moses' seat; or wherein money is the principal means of urging on the work of the Lord, (as it is termed) seeing that the blessed Savior never taught any such things as the gospel, or as an appendage to it, we exclaim, Beware of false prophets, which come to you in sheep's clothing, but inwardly they are ravening wolves. . . .

Lest we should offend any of the disciples of Christ, or even tire the patience of any, that are earnestly seeking the kingdom of our Redeemer and its righteousness, we will say something about true prophets.

The only way of ascertaining a true prophet, is to compare his prophecies with the ancient word of God, and see if they agree, and it is not possible that the Lord will suffer FALSE prophets, to bring forth the truth, moved upon by the Holy Ghost, for it is written that the Holy Ghost dwelleth not in unholy temples. By their fruits shall they be known.

When, therefore any man, no matter who, or how high his standing may be, utters, or publishes, any thing that afterwards proves to be untrue, he is a false prophet. And if he does it uncalled for, for the sake of injuring his fellow-beings, or for the sake of gain, or to deceive any man, by putting a false coloring upon a matter of religion, to lead astray or prejudice the minds of any, to hinder them from receiving the truth, wo unto him, he is a false prophet and will have his part with the beast in the lake of fire and brimstone, where their worm dieth not and the fire is not quenched!

Truth is light, and needs no art to recommend it to the soul that loves the Lord: A wise man is choice of his heart, but the fool exposes his to the world, and is not the better for it. Here then we can say, where we find a person uttering, or publishing, what he does not know to be a truth, merely to make a noise, whereby the least saint on earth might be offended, beware of

false prophets, lest you have a portion with them, in the lake of
fire and brimstone where their worm dieth not and the fire is not
quenched.

Brethren in the church of Christ, did you ever hear of a true
prophet, that persecuted any one for his religion, whether pure or
of man? Did you ever hear, or have you ever read of a true
prophet, that spake evil of any man, or that would lie to further
the cause of God, or any thing else? If you have, brethren, then
has the hypocrite an excuse for leaving his own fault unexposed,
and, publishing his neighbor's to the world!

Then has the false prophet an opportunity to plead his right to
send his lying words abroad, that he may obtain the praise and
glory of this world, and deceive the simple.

But this is not so; what is good comes from the Lord, and
what is evil comes from satan: therefore brethren, when any man,
priest or prophet, minister or member, walks after the image of
his own god, which is in the image and likeness of the word, and
is filled with evil contentions, mark that man, for his heart is not
right before the Lord, and his soul without repentance, will have
a part in the lake of fire and brimstone, where their worm dieth
not and the fire is not quenched.

Brethren, when a man who obeys the ordinances of the Lord,
preaches, prophecies, utters or publishes, any thing that will make
men better; any thing that will guide men in the path of eternal
life; any thing that will promote the fulness of the gospel of Jesus
Christ, showing by a godly walk, and a holy conversation, that he
is meek and humble; and witnessing unto the world that he is
willing to leave father and mother, wife and children, houses and
lands, for the sake of his Savior, follow his example, for his end
will be peace, and his glory eternal in the presence of God.

–July 1833, page 105.

The original settlers had come to Jackson County largely
from Tennessee and Kentucky. Many of them were slave
owners: in fact, the population of Missouri in 1830 was more
than one-fifth slave. The Saints, on the other hand, had come
largely from New York and Ohio—free states—and were

suspected of harboring abolitionist sentiments. When the *Star's* editor heard that a handful of free blacks had been converted to the church in the East and were attempting to emigrate to Jackson County, he hastened to publish a reprint of a Missouri statute forbidding their entry without a certificate of citizenship from another state.

FREE PEOPLE OF COLOR

To prevent any misunderstanding among the churches abroad, respecting Free people of color, who may think of coming to the western boundaries of Missouri, as members of the church, we quote the following clauses from the Laws of Missouri.

"*Section.* 4. Be it further enacted, That hereafter no free negro or mulatto, other than a citizen of some one of the United States, shall come into or settle in this state under any pretext whatever; and upon complaint made to any justice of the peace, that such person is in his county, contrary to the provisions of this section, he shall cause such person to be brought before him. And if upon examination, it shall appear that such person is a free negro or mulatto, and that he hath come into this state after the passage of this act, and such person shall not produce a cerificate, attested by the seal of some court of record in some one of the United States, evidencing that he is a citizen of such state, the justice shall command him forthwith to depart from this state; and in case such negro or mulatto shall not depart from the state within thirty days after being commanded so to do as aforesaid, any justice of the peace, upon complaint thereof to him made may cause such person to be brought before him, and may commit him to the common goal of the county in which he may be found, until the next term of the circuit court to be holden in such county. And the said court shall cause such person to be brought before them, and examine into the cause of commitment; and if it shall appear that such person came into the state contrary to the provisions of this act, and continued therein after being commanded to depart as aforesaid, such court may sentence such person to receive ten lashes on his or her bare back, and order him to depart the state; and if he or she shall not depart, the same proceedings shall be had and punishment inflicted, as often as may be necessary, until such person shall depart the state.

Section. 5. Be it further enacted, That if any person shall, after the taking effect of this act, bring into this state any free negro or mulatto, not having in his possesion a certificate of citizenship as required by this act, [he or she] shall forfeit and pay, for every person so brought, the sum of five hundred dollars, to be recovered by action of debt in the name of the state, to the use of the university, in any court having competent jurisdiction; in which action the defendant may be held to bail, of right, and without affidavit; and it shall be the duty of the attorney-general or circuit attorney of the district in which any person so offending may be found, immediately upon information given of such offence, to commence and prosecute an action as aforesaid."

Slaves are real estate in this and other states, and wisdom would dictate great care among the branches of the church of Christ, on this subject. So long as we have no special rule in the church, as to people of color, let prudence guide; and while they, as well as we, are in the hands of a merciful God, we say: Shun every appearance of evil.

While on the subject of law, it may not be amiss to quote some of the Constitution of Missouri. It shows a liberality of opinion of the great men of the west, and will vie with that of any other state. It is good; it is just, and it is the citizens' right.

"1. That all men have a natural and indefeasible right to worship Almighty God according to the dictates of their own consciences; that no man can be compelled to erect, support or attend any place of worship, or to maintain any minister of the gospel or teacher of religion; that no human authority can control or interfere with the rights of conscience; that no person can ever be hurt, molested or restrained in his religious professions or sentiments, if he do not disturb others in their religious worship:

5. That no person, on account of his religious opinions, can be rendered ineligible to any office of trust or profit under this state; that no preference can ever be given by law to any sect or mode of worship; and that no religious corporation can ever be established in this state."

—July 1833, page 109.

The immediate reaction of the settlers was to interpret the newspaper item as "inviting free negroes and mulattoes from other states to become 'Mormons,' and remove and settle among us." Nothing was quite so threatening to slave holders as to have free black men around to stimulate their slaves' interest in personal freedom.

Trying to further clarify his position, W. W. Phelps hurriedly printed an "extra" in the form of a handbill for quick circulation. The portion of this extra that appears to exclude black people from church membership must be seen as the personal opinion of the editor, and not official church policy.

The Evening and Morning Star EXTRA

Having learned with extreme regret, that an article entitled, "Free People of Color," in the last number of the *Star,* has been misunderstood, we feel in duty bound to state, in this Extra, that our intention was not only to stop free people of color from emigrating to this state, but to prevent them from being admitted as members of the Church.

On the second column of the one hundred and eleventh page of the same paper, may be found this paragraph:—"Our brethren will find an extract of the law of this state, relative to free people of color, on another page of this paper. Great care should be taken on this point. The Saints must shun every appearance of evil. As to slaves, we have nothing to say; in connection with the wonderful events of this age much is doing towards abolishing slavery, and colonizing the blacks in Africa."

We often lament the situation of our sister states in the south, and we fear, lest, as has been the case, the blacks should rise and spill innocent blood, for they are ignorant, and a little may lead them to disturb the peace of society. To be short, we are opposed to having free people of color admitted into the state; and we say, that none will be admitted into the Church; for we are determined to obey the laws and constitutions of our country, that we may have that protection which the sons of liberty inherit from the legacy of Washington through the favorable auspices of a Jefferson and Jackson.

SCRIPTURAL ARTICLES

A few extracts from the Bible appear without comment in the pages of *The Evening and the Morning Star*, apparently reflecting the editor's idea of what was edifying for the Saints to read. On at least one occasion, there is an attempt to provide an exegetical interpretation for a passage of scripture, namely the third chapter of Hosea (July 1832, page 6).

An "extract from the Prophecy of Enoch," which later became Genesis 7 in the Inspired Version, appears for the first time in the August 1832 issue.

A short quotation from the apocryphal addendum to the Book of Esther, is printed without any explanation of purpose.

THE BOOK OF ESTHER.

In the remainder of the book of Esther, which the ancient men of the world, put down as doubtful, may be found the following:

Then Mardocheus said, God hath done these things.

For I remember a dream which I saw concerning these matters, and nothing thereof hath failed.

A little fountain became a river, and there was light, and the sun, and much water: this river is Esther, whom the king married, and made queen.

And the two dragons are I and Aman.

And the nations were those that were assembled to destroy the name of the Jews: and my nation is this Israel, which cried to God, and were saved: for the Lord hath saved his people, and the Lord hath delivered us from all those evils, and God hath wrought signs and great wonders, which have not been done among the Gentiles.

Therefore hath he made two lots, one for the people of God, and another for all the Gentiles.

And these two lots came at the hour, and time, and day of judgment, before God among all nations.

—January 1833, page 62.

As would be expected, many sections of the Book of Mormon are reprinted in the *Star*, once again the choice of passages apparently reflecting the editor's interest and concerns. A long article explaining what the Book of Mormon is appears in the January 1833 issue. Appended to this article, which quotes extensively from the book itself, are the statements of the "Three Witnesses" and the "Eight Witnesses."

Succeeding articles attempted to muster proof for the Book of Mormon. The following examples of this apologetic writing will appear rather weak, but it should be remembered that an elaborate system of "archaeological evidence" had not been assembled.

DISCOVERY OF ANCIENT RUINS IN CENTRAL AMERICA.

A late number of the London Literary Gazette, contains a letter from Lieut. Col. Galindo, at Peten, in Central America, giving some idea of those antiquities which rescue ancient America from the charge of barbarism. These ruins extend for more than twenty miles, and must anciently have embraced a city and its suburbs. The principal edifice is supposed to have been a palace, formed of two rows of galleries, eight feet wide, separated by walls a yard thick; the height of the walls to the eaves is nine feet, and thence three yards more to the top. The stones of which all the edifices are built, are about eighteen inches long, nine broad and two thick, cemented by morter. The front of the palace contained five lofty and wide doors. Numerous statues of stone are scattered about. In another building, which Col. G. calls the study, are numerous full length figures, of about six feet high, some of them holding naked infants on their right arms, and not in the manner of the modern Indian woman, who always set their children astride on their hips. A place of religious worship and a prison, complete the list of buildings enumerated by Col. G.

"The whole of the ruins," says Col. G. are buried in a thick forest, and months might be delightfully employed in exploring them. I have seen sufficient to ascertain the high civilization of the former inhabitants, and that they possessed the art of representing sounds by signs, with which I have hitherto believed no Americans previous to the conquest were acquainted."—"The neighboring country for many leagues distant, contains remains of the ancient labors of its people, bridges, reservoirs, monumental inscriptions, subterraneous edifices, &c." "Every thing bears testimony that these surprising people were not physically dissimilar from the present Indians; but their civilization far surpassed that of the Mexicans and Peruvians; they must have existed long prior to the fourteenth century."

REMARKS.—We are glad to see the proof begin to come, of the original or ancient inhabitants of this continent. It is good testimony in favor of the book of Mormon, and the book of Mormon is good testimony that such things as cities and civilization, "prior to the fourteenth century," existed in America. Helaman, in the book of Mormon, gives the following very interesting account of the people who lived upon this continent, before the birth of the Savior.

And now it came to pass in the forty and third year of the reign of the Judges, there was no contention among the people of Nephi, save it were a little pride which was in the church, which did cause some little dissensions among the people, which affairs were settled in the ending of the forty and third year.

And there was no contention among the people in the forty and fourth year; neither was there much contention in the forty and fifth year.

And it came to pass in the forty and sixth, yea, there were much contentions and many dissensions; in the which there were an exceeding great many which departed out of the land of Zarahemla, and went forth unto the land northward, to inherit the land; and they did travel to an exceeding great distance, insomuch that they came to large bodies of water, and many rivers; yea, and even they did spread forth into all parts of the land, into whatever parts it had not been rendered desolate, and without timber, because of the many inhabitants which had before inherited the land.

And now no part of the land was desolate, save it were for timber, &c.; but because of the greatness of the destruction of the people which had before inhabited the land, it was called desolate.

And there being but little timber upon the face of the land, nevertheless the people which went forth, became exceeding expert in the working of cement; therefore they did build houses of cement, in the which they did dwell.

And it came to pass that they did multiply and spread, and did go forth from the land southward, to the land northward, and did spread insomuch that they began to cover the face of the whole earth, from the sea south, to the sea north, from the sea west, to the sea east.

And the people which were in the land northward, did dwell in tents, and in houses of cement, and they did suffer whatsoever tree should spring up upon the face of the land, that it should grow up, that in time they might have timber to build their houses, yea, their cities, and their temples, and their synagogues, and their sanctuaries, and all manner of their buildings.

—February 1833, page 71.

GOOD PROOF

No people that have lived on this continent, since the flood, understood many of the arts and sciences, better than the Jaredites and Nephites, whose brief history is sketched in the book of Mormon. The facts following, from the Star in the West, is not only proof of their skill, but it is good proof, to those that want evidence, that the book of Mormon, IS TRUE.

In Rowan County, (N.C.) on the summit level of a piece of table land, in the first settlement of that section of the new world, a stone house was found completely imbeded in the earth—even the funnel of the chimney was covered by the growth of the earth. This relic of antiquity, was discovered by one of the early planters in plowing up a piece of land. Finding some stone on a particular part of his farm, in a position which seemed to indicate the work of art, he fell to removing the same, and soon he was taking off the funnel of a stone chimney. This circumstance excited the curiosity of the neighboring planters, who met and agreed to examine the edifice by excavating the earth from the stone wall. They soon found that the chimney was attached to a large stone house; by tracing the angles of the same, and digging to the very foundation, they found its dimentions to be 23 feet 11 inches, by 36 feet 3 inches, with a wall 15 feet in height, constructed with doors and windows according to the strict rules of architecture. At the foundation of this ancient edifice, which appeared to be built with must taste, was found relics of house-hold furniture, such as broken pieces of earthen pots, & c. which showed the arts of civilized life were well understood by the inhabitants of this antique dwelling place of human beings.

In Cincinnati, when excavating the earth, at the first settlement of that place, 27 feet below the surface was found an arti-

ficial peach and pear, cut out of stone, with a complete imitation
of the stem and blossom end, which proved beyond the possibility of a doubt, that the skill of some human being had been
exerted in imitation of nature's beautiful works.

—June 1833, page 99.

In the June 1833 issue, there is the announced intention to
publish the whole Book of Mormon in segments. Chapter 1 (I
Nephi 1:1-74) is introduced thusly:

THE BOOK OF MORMON

Notwithstanding the church of Christ has received the fulness
of the gospel from the book of Mormon, and every member as a
true disciple of the blessed Savior, studies it as a heavenly treasure, yet few, very few of our fellow men in the world, know any
thing about the merits of this sacred volume. We therefore, have
concluded to commence its publication in the Star, and shall
continue from number to number until it is finished.

By this means the world will have an opportunity to read for
themselves and prepare for the great days to come. By this means
those who are seeking for truth can find it, and compare the book
of Mormon with the Bible, and witness the great doings of the
Lord in these last days, in bringing forth his everlasting covenant
for the gathering of his elect, and the restoration of the tribes,
and scattered remnants of Israel from the four quarters of the
earth.

We have again inserted the articles and covenants according to
our promise in a previous number, for the benefit of our brethren
abroad who have not the first number of the first volume. As
there were, some errors which had got into them by transcribing,
we have since obtained the original copy and made the necessary
corrections.

—June 1833, page 98.

The next (and last) issue of the *Star*, however, reveals a re-
versal of policy.

In our last number, we commenced the publication of the book of Mormon, but having altered our calculation, it is stopped. Our reason is, that, at no very distant period, we shall print the book of Mormon and the Testament, and bind them in one volume: therefore to continue it in the Star would be superfluous.

—July 1833, page 109.

LETTERS

W. W. Phelps soon discovered that it was easier to get news of the world than it was to get news of the church. For this ecclesiastical news he was dependent upon letters from Kirtland and from elders on missions. And so we find this plea:

One of the commandments says, My servants who are abroad in the earth, shall send forth the account of their stewardships to the land of Zion, for Zion shall be a seat, and a place to receive, and to do all these things: Wherefore we would remind the elders at a distance, to send forth, to the Editor of the Star, post paid, all matters connected with their mission, embracing historical facts, the number of sheaves the faithful laborers are blessed with, and all else, that may be well-pleasing in the sight of him who said, What thou seest, write in a book.

—August 1832, page 23.

To bolster his request, in the next issue the lead article is "Writing Letters," in which the following practical pointers are given:

The Art of writing is one of the greatest blessings we enjoy. To cultivate it is our duty, and to use it is our privilege. By these means the thoughts of the heart can act without the body, and the mind can speak without the head, while thousands of miles apart, and for ages after the flesh has mouldered back to its mother dust. . . . Beloved brethren, before we can teach the world how to do right, we must be able to do so ourselves: Therefore, in the love of him who is altogether lovely, whose yoke is easy, and whose burden is light, who spake as never man spake, let us offer a few ideas on this important subject, for the consideration of such as mean to love their neighbors as themselves, for the sake of righteousness and eternal life.

1. Never write a letter to friend or foe, unless you have business which can not be done as well in some other way; or, unless you have news to communicate, that is worth time and money. In this way you will increase confidence and save postage.

2. Never write any thing in a letter to friend or foe, that you are afraid to read to friend or foe, for letters from a distance, especially one or two thousand miles, are sought for with great anxiety; and, as no one is a judge of men and things, you are liable to misrepresent yours If, your country, your friends, and your enemies, and put in the mouth of the honest, as well as the dishonest, a lie, which truth, in her gradual but virtuous way, may not contradict till your head is under the silent clods of the valley.

3. Never write any thing but truth, for truth is heavenly, and like the sun, is alwas bright, and proves itself, without logic, without reasons, without witnesses, and never fails. Truth is of the Lord and will prevail.

4. Never reprove a friend or foe for faults in a letter, except by revelation; for in the first place, your private intentions, be they ever so good, are liable to become public, because, all letters may be broken open, and your opinion only on one side of the question, can be scattered to the four winds, and he to whom you meant good, receives evil; and you are not benefited. Again, we can hardly find a language, written or spoken, on earth, at this time, that will convey the true meaning of the heart to the understanding of another; and you are liable to be misunderstood, and to give unpleasant feelings; and you merely to use a simile, bleed an old sore, by probing it for proud flesh, when it only wanted a little oil from the hand of the good Samaritan, in person, to heal it. . . .

5. Never write what you would be ashamed to have printed; or, what might offend the chastest ear, or hurt the softest heart. . . .

As to the church, this being a day of warning and not a day of many words, let them that wish to communicate, or instruct, whether high or low, whether male or female, whether parent or child, whether master or servant, whether teacher or member, whether elder or high priest, come to this conclusion, That the eyes of God are upon them, and that what they do is for eternity; for God shall bring every work into judgment, with every secret thing; whether it be good, or whether it be evil: and therefore, to obey the commandments, of the Lord, and to set an example in all things, worthy of imitation by the world; knowing that in the midst of counsellors there is safety; with the light of revelation shining around them, as the sun in his strength; while the tidings from heaven to the faithful, is, Peace on earth, and good will to men; while the spirit of Christ directs them to pray for the angels to look upon. Begin to think right and your thoughts may be worth saving: begin to speak truth in all things, and your words may be powerful; so much so, that you can exclaim like Job: O that my words were now written! O that they were printed in a book! We can not close this essay without saying, Brethren! live for Jesus, for he lives for you: Children! live for Jesus, for he lives for you: And whatever you write, let it be—the truth: in fact and in very deed, let your yea be yea, and your nay be nay, and then, when letters are written by you, from Zion to the world, the spirit of the Lord will bear record, that they are true: and if letters from abroad, are written by the disciples, to Zion, the spirit of the Lord will bear record, that they are true, and the glory of God will be in Zion. Again, should hypocrites or sinners, write, either to or from Zion, and not write the truth, their own words may condemn them: Their own letters can be sent back, either way, as witnesses of their folly now, and remain as testimony against them, when the Lord comes out of his place to punish the inhabitants of the earth for their iniquity.

—September 1832, page 25.

In response to some letters inquiring how the church fares in Independence, we have this response:

THE GATHERING.

There is a great anxiety manifested to learn how the church of Christ prospers, since it commenced settling in the western part of the state of Missouri. To satisfy this inquiry, and more especially to publish the truth upon this great subject, that none may be deceived by flying reports, we shall endeavor to give all the information in our possession. Since the gathering commenced, which is a little over a year, the number of the disciples which have come from the east, and which have been baptized in this region, is   465
    Children and those not members, about   345
    Total   810

This little flock, which is now enjoying the glorious privileges and blessings of the everlasting gospel, preparatory to the second coming of the Savior, have, as it were, almost simultaneously come together from New England, New York, Pennsylvania, Ohio, Indiana, Illinois, Tennessee and Missouri, to worship God and keep his commandments, on the land of their inheritance.—So far, the disciples have been highly favored; coming, as most of them have, from different climates, and changing, as is necessarily the case, their modes of living, undergoing the troubles and hardships of a long and tedious journey, and planting themselves down without the conveniences and even necessaries, which most of them have been used to, it is certainly a matter of great joy, if not a miracle, that they are generally so healthy, so industrious, so thriving, and more than all, so contented to love the Lord and their neighbors as themselves. Reports, to be sure, have been circulated, that so many were moving in, that a famine must succeed, and some starve to death; perhaps a few believed so, but in the joyful language of the Psalmist we can exclaim: We have been young, and now are old; yet have we not seen the righteous forsaken, nor his seed begging bread. The great consolation is, the promises of the Lord never fail; nor is his store-house ever empty. Virtue, honesty, diligence, industry, economy, and patience, added to that pure religion, and undefiled before God and the Father: To visit the fatherless and widows in their affliction, and to keep himself unspotted from the world, bring about the purposes of God, in their eternal salvation, and blesses the contrite soul with a sweet consolation and a prospect before it, that the world, with all its alluring, but vanishing appearances, can neither give nor take. We admit that the flowing together of so many saints has the appearance of a meeting of strangers; but as they already begin to grow in grace and in the knowledge of the Lord, the world may witness that it is the preparation of Israel to meet his God. As the prophet said, Zion is a wilderness, but with faithful hearts raised to God, the wilderness will soon blossom as the rose, and, as the prospect brightens, we look forward with joy to the day when Zion shall arise and put on her beautiful garments and become the joy of the world.

Amid all things, for it is appointed for all once to die, twelve persons have died since the emigration commenced to this land: that is, nine here, and three upon the way. There have been solemnized six marriages.

Our news from abroad is cheering. The harvest is truly abundant, but the laborers are few.—New churches have been built up in Missouri; in Illinois; at Fulton, near Cincinnati, Ohio· at

Guyandotte, Virginia; in Spafford, Onondaga Co. at Tompkins, Delaware Co. and at Essex Co. N. York; at Benson, North Troy, and Charleston, Vermont; at Bath, New Hampshire; in N. Rowley and Boston, Massachusetts, and how many in other places we can not say: while we look at the distress of nations, and hear how the judgments of God sweep off the inhabitants of the earth, we must exclaim, The Lord is making a short work. It was but two years last April, since the church of Christ was organized, by special revelation; now branches are rising up in almost every state in the Union, which, willing to overcome the world for the sake of Christ, the Redeemer, will come to Zion, and assist in enlarging her borders; and stretching forth the curtains of her habitations: No weapon that is formed against thee shall prosper; and every tongue which shall rise against thee in judgment, thou shalt condemn. This is the heritage of the servants of the Lord, and their righteousness is of me, saith the Lord.

—November 1832, pages 45-46.

Another plea for letters appeared in the March 1833 issue. From then on, there seems to be an ample supply of reports from the mission field. Here are a few extracts:

Bath, New Hampshire, January 23, 1833.

Dear brethren, we have traveled in the states of Pennsylvania, New Jersey, New York, Vermont, New Hampshire, Massachusetts and Connecticut; and we baptized four in Blakely, Pennsylvania; and also my brother on Long Island; eight in Madison, Connecticut; twenty in Bath, New Hampshire; twenty seven in Charleston Vermont; and eighteen in Troy, Vermont. We went to a conference which was held in Spafford, New York, on the tenth of November, where brother Lyman (Johnson) baptized eight: he then, in company with brother Hazen Aldrich, started for Ohio; and I, in company with brother William Snow, started for Bath and Charleston, and baptized twelve by the way.

We have ordained several elders, since last February, and they bid fair to be faithful, and may do much good.

Brother Orson (J.) has returned from Missouri.

Brother Hazen has baptized four in Colebrook, New Hampshire. There are calls on the right hand and on the left, for faithful laborers in this region. Your brother in Christ,

ORSON PRATT.
—March 1833, page 78.

Extract of a letter from one of our correspondents, dated at Piqua, Ohio,

February 13, 1833.

Dear Sir: Your letter of January 22, was very thankfully received last evening, by myself and many persons with whom the Indians were acquainted. I am truly glad to hear from them: they were, many of them, as fine people as I wish to travel with. I expect to come through your Village again in July or August, with the remaining few of the Shawnees, who reside at Waghpaghkonnetta. It is thought they will leave here about the first of June. There are about ninety people of them in all, and if they start at that time they will arrive at the Kansas about the time named above.

I read your letter to two of the Chiefs who were in town today, and they were very much pleased to hear that their brothers were well, and pleased with their new homes. Their old Interpreter (Jo. Parks) left this place for Washington City today to try to obtain deeds for some lands he had granted to him by the Indian Nation. When he returns, which will be in about four weeks, he will commence getting ready to move, for he goes with them: he intends settling in the Indian country, of the Kansas River.

Respectfully, Yours, &c.
—March 1833, page 79.

Pontiac, Michigan Territory, February 16, 1833.

Dear Sir: I am requested by brother Jared Carter, an elder in the church of Christ, to inform you, that he will pay one dollar over to the bishop in Kirtland, and wishes you to send the Evening and the Morning Star, directing it to Jeremiah Curtis, Pontiac, Oakland County, Michigan Territory. Brother Carter has been laboring in the ministry for about five weeks past, in this county, and his labors have been blest by God, to a goodly degree; he has baptized 22 persons and received them into the church of Christ, myself, and wife, are two of the above named members, for which I desire to bless the Lord. He has ordained me an elder in the church of Christ, and I earnestly desire that God will bless me, and make me faithful, to become an instrument in his hands in building up his church and kingdom in this region.

63

There is a great opposition to this cause in this section of country, but I hope and trust, that the Lord, will over rule and glorify his name, & subdue the hearts of his people, and make them obedient to his will.

I have been travelling with brother Carter, for two weeks past; I find him to be a faithfull servant of our Lord and Master. When I view the dealings of God, towards me, I feel to adore his great and holy name, that he has opened my eyes to see the wondrous things of his kingdom, which he has commenced in these last days.

I have been a proffessor of the christian religion for twenty seven years, and stood among the sects, but never, until about four weeks past, have I been brought to see the errors which the different sects embrace.

Be pleased to except these few lines from a brother in the church of Christ with you, & laborer in the same great cause; although I am not personally acquainted with you, yet my heart feels to unite with you in the same great cause of our great Redeemer.

I hope, if God shall see fit to spare my life, I shall see you in Zion before long, and converse with you upon things appertaining to the kingdom of Christ.

From your brother in the Lord.

SAMUEL BENT.
—April 1833, page 88.

EXTRACT OF A LETTER.

Rutland, Pa. March 19, 1833.

Dear Brethren in Zion, peace from God the Father and our Lord Jesus Christ, be with you all. I rejoice much for what my ears hear and my eyes see, of the rising and spreading glory of Zion in these last days.

As the mild rays of the sun, poured forth upon the earth, causes vegetation to spring up, even so the rays that shine from Zion's hill, upon a benighted world, cause the fruits of righteousness to put forth in many parts of our land: And while we are yet struggling in the midst of spiritual Babylon, to save our souls, and them that hear us, it rejoices our hearts & feasts our souls, to hear through the medium of your Star, the success of our brethren who are also laboring in the vineyard, and have sent up their accounts to the land of Zion,

Now, inasmuch as it is requested in your paper, that the elders abroad should do thus, we, therefore take this opportunity to inform you, that we, through the grace of God, have shared a measure of the blessing shed forth in his new and everlasting covenant. About forty five have been baptized into the church where I live. Some have set out for the land of Zion, and nearly all the rest are ready to go up this spring.

I was baptized one year ago from last June, and after a close trial of about three weeks respecting the revelations and the gathering to Zion, my mind became clear, and I was ordained an elder in the church of Christ.

In the fall following, I went with brothers Potter and Bowen to Shaftsbury Vermont where a few received the work. In the winter several of us went to Mendon, New York, and the work of the Lord commenced here. From thence we went to Warsaw, then to Lake Erie, and home by the way of Angelica, preaching the word, and blessed be the name of the Lord, signs followed them that believed, insomuch that some who were sick was healed, and some spake with tongues and glorified God.

Last summer four of us from Rutland, and two from Mendon, went to this province of Upper Canada. We landed at Kingston, and labored at Ernest town and its vicinity. Here thousands flocked to hear the strange news; even so that the houses could not contain the multitude, and we had to repair to the groves. Hundreds were searching the scriptures to see if these things were so. Many were partly convinced, and some were wholly, so, when we left, and a small church was founded there. We have heard since we came away, that the cause of the Lord was prospering in that region.

Brother Miller, an elder that has travelled with me in the two last routes, has baptized about twenty. I have baptized, in all, thirty-five; nine in Rutland and Sullivan; four in Columbia; seven in Troy and three in Canton, Pennsylvania; five in Shaftsbury, Vermont; one in Chenango, and one in Mendon, New York, and five in Ernest town, Upper Canada.

We have labored under some disadvantage, not having instructions till within a few months past, respecting this great work, other than the Articles book of Mormon, and the Comforter. But we remember, that where much is given, much is required, and where little is given, little is required: Therefore by the grace of God, we mean to improve the talent, or talents that we have received, that we may gain other talents: Hence we would call upon our brethren in Zion, from whence the light is to flow, and the law is to proceed, to remember us in Babylon, and let the strong bare the infirmities of the weak. Pray the heavenly Father to open an effectual door for us, to make our escape from the midst of spiritual wickedness, to the place of the name of the Lord of Hosts, the mount Zion.

We rejoice that the time has come, that the Lord has set his hand again the second time to gather his elect. That he has already set up the ensign and lifted the standard for the gathering of the nations; that the covenants and promises made to the fathers, concerning the remnants of his people, might be fulfilled.

And above all, we have great reason to rejoice, that we, as Gentiles, have the privilege of receiving the light manifested for their restoration; and by entering into the covenant, we may become the spiritual children of Abraham, and with Israel partake of the fatness and the fulness of the olive tree.

We long to see the time when we can see the tribes of Israel's remnants, coming up to Zion with songs of everlasting joy; we long to see the time when Jacob's face will no longer wax pale; when the bride shall be adorned and ready for the Bridegroom; and finally, we long to see the time, when Jesus shall come in the clouds of heaven, with power and great glory, and be admired by all his saints.

Your brethren in the Lord,

ELIEL STRONG,
ELEAZER MILLER.

—May 1833, pages 94-95.

SELECTIONS

"Under the head of Selections, we intend to furnish the disciples with well-written articles from celebrated authors, that they may be enabled to judge between right and wrong; between the church of Christ and the church of man, and set an example worthy of imitation." This is the stated purpose for the reprint of passages from books of various topics. A wide variety of interests and concerns is apparent in the choice of selections. An article on Nero's persecution of the early Christians (June 1832, page 3) was obviously intended to boost the morale of the Saints who were even then beginning to feel the sting of active prejudice and hostility. Persecution was seen as a badge of true discipleship. Selections dealing with "The Simplicity of the Sacred Writers" (July 1832, page 4) and "The Valley of the Jordan, and the Dead Sea" (August 1832, page 4) can readily be seen as supplying material to quench a thirsting after information on religious themes. Other articles of more general interest, such as "Description of Lake Superior" (November 1832, page 8), seem to be more of the nature of "fillers."

On occasion a selection from some exterior source is quoted, followed by some remarks, often of a moralizing kind, from the pen of the editor. Notice how Brother Phelps takes a simple, exaggerated report of a bee colony and turns it into a platform for mentioning the Book of Mormon and an excuse for upbraiding his generation for lack of belief.

A BEE STORY.

A friend told me the other day a bee story, and were he not a man on whose word I can strictly rely, I should set it down as a real Munchausen. Such as it is you shall have it.

In Wythe county, in Virginia, in a spur of the Alleghany Mountains, called the 'Tobacco Row,' is a perpendicular ledge of rock fronting the southeast, about fifty feet high—an open sunny situation. About thirty feet from the base, a horrizontal crack or fissure opens in the rock, from half an inch to six inches in width, and extending near eighty feet in length. How deep this fissure extends into the mountain is not known, as no one has ever examined it. This fissure is full of bees! Their numbers are so great, that in the summer time they hang out in huge clusters for several feet, above and below the fissure, in its whole length. A short distance above are two other cracks, containing earth, in which grow some little chinquapin bushes, and these are covered with the bees. They frequently go off in huge swarms, like a barrel or hogshead in bulk, and are often compelled to return, finding no place large enough to contain them. In the spring, previous to commencing their labors, the dead bees, remnants of comb, and cleanings of the habitation which are brought out and dropped by them, make a winrow of a foot in height the whole length of the opening.

My informant saw it in the month of June, when immense numbers of bees were out on the surface, making great patches of rock black with their swarming masses. The oldest inhabitants say that the first settlers found the bees there, and the Indians told them that their oldest traditions knew nothing of its origin. 'It was always there.'

No one has ever been found bold enough to attempt its plunder, or to examine the place where they are. It is in fact too dangerous an enterprise to meddle with.

If these facts be so, and I cannot doubt it, does it not form rather a new feature from that generally received in the history of the bee? By the way, I fear that I am going to have all this bee discussion to myself. But we'll see.

Do none of the correspondents of the American Farmer live near this great bee hive? If so I should be much gratified to hear further about it.–(Gen. Farmer.)   ULMUS.

REMARKS.–To them that believe in the revelations of the Lord, this bee story is no great mystery. The bees may have been there more than three thousand years. When Jared and his brother came from the tower of Babel, to settle the continent of America, they brought bees, as it is written in the book of Ether: And they did also lay snares and catch fowls of the air; and they did also prepare a vessel, in the which they did carry with them the fish of the waters: and they did also carry with them deseret, which, by interpretation, is a honey bee: and thus they did carry with them swarms of bees, and all manner of that which was upon the face of the land, seeds of every kind.

What a pity it is that man has strayed so far from the knowledge of the Lord! Created as he was in the image of his Maker, an agent unto himself, and capable, by obeying the commandments of the Lord of receiving the Holy Ghost, which bringeth all things to remembrance, he might let his understanding reach to heaven, and never be at a loss for the truth; but alas he trusts in his own wisdom, and scarcely arrives at certainty.

Before the flood, bees might have been in every part of the world, but since Noah left them on the other side of the Atlantic, unless brought by man they would not have been able to cross it.

–July 1833, page 107.

NEWS FROM THE OUTSIDE WORLD

> Under the head, also, of Worldly Matters, shall be given, as far as our limits may permit, such items of general news, as may enable the saints to know the condition of the world. We, therefore, can not be responsible for the errors that may be in the articles or items, but shall endeavor, at all times, to give correct information, praying to God continually for his Spirit to guide us to all truth."

Knowing the unreliability of much that passed for news, Brother Phelps adds, "In giving the News of the world, we take it as we find it, and will not be responsible for its truth."

Most of the news seemingly was selected to show that the signs of the end of the age were breaking in upon all the peoples of the world—wars, plagues, earthquakes, deterioration of law and order, and so on.

On a rare occasion there is a subtle touch of humor displayed, as for example, in this news item: "Robert Dale Owen, the free thinker, who was in favor of free intercourse independent of matrimony, has lately been married" (June 1832, page 7).

More often, the news is given, often with editorial comment, to hammer home the theme that the Lord's Coming was near at hand.

FOREIGN NEWS

It is a day of strange appearances. Every thing indicates something more than meets the eye. Every nation is opening events, which astonish mankind: Even the heart of man begins to melt at the prospect before it. The unquenchable thirst for news; the continuity of emigration; the wars and rumors of wars, with many other signs of the distress of nations, from the old world, (as it is called across the Ocean) whispers so loud to the understanding, that he that runs may read the label on the Eastern sky: The end is nigh. France is filled with a spirit of rebellion, and when the Cholera was sweeping its thousands, mobs were collecting to slay their tens of thousands. While the hospitals were crowded with the sick, and the groans of the dying filled the air.

the fashionable French were holding Cholera Balls and dancing at the judgments of the almighty. In England, where an anxious multitude have been waiting for Reformation in goverment for years, disappointment is distruction. The house of Lords has rejected the Reform bill, and the proud hearted Englishman says—Reform or Revolution! No stop there: for the sound comes across the Atlantic. Reform or ruin! All the Kingdoms of the East seem to be preparing to act the part allotted to them, when the Lord rebukes the nations. As on a morning of some, great festival, the church bell, the cannon, the small arms, the music, and the cheers of the multitude, arouse all to what is going on, and thunders to man: Behold the day! so also earthquakes wars, and rumors of wars, the distress of nations, the constant tide of emigration to the West, the wide spreading ravages of the Cholera Morbus, and the joy of the Saints of God as they come out of Babylon, alarms the world, and whispers to every mortal, watch ye, for the time is at hand for the second coming of Jesus Christ, the Redeemer of Israel, with peace on earth and good will to man. Watch the signs of his coming, that ye be not deceived.

—July 1832, page 14.

A matter on everyone's mind was the cholera outbreak that was spreading rapidly in many parts of the world. The *Star* relayed to the Saints some of the facts and statistics concerning the ravages of this dread disease.

HORRORS OF THE CHOLERA MORBUS.

We have witnessed in our days the birth of a new pestilence, which, in the short space of fourteen years, has desolated the fairest portion of the globe, and swept off at least fifty millions of our race. It has mastered every variety of climate, surmounted every natural barrier, conquered every people. It has not, like the simoon blasted life, and then passed away; the cholera, like small-pox or plague, takes root in the soil which it has once possessed. The circumstances under which the individual is attacked are no less appalling than the history of the progress and mortality of the disease. In one man says an eye witness, the prostration of strength was so great that he could hardly move a limb, though he had been but fifteen minuits before in perfect health, and actively employed in his business of a gardener. A Lascar in the service of an officer was seized in the act of picking

70

up his rice, previous to going out to cut grass close to his master's feet, and being unable to call for assistance, he was observed by an other person at a distance from him, picking up small stones and pitching them towards him, for the purpose of attracting his notice. This man died in an hour. It is no wonder that the approach of such a pestilence has struck the deepest terror into every community.

The origin of this disease is not known. It broke out at Jessore, about a hundred miles south east of Calcutta, in August, 1817. "Spreading from village to village, and destroying thousands of the inhabitants, it reached Calcutta early in September. It then spread into other parts of the country, taking different places in succession; and at length it appeared in the grand army, and eventually extending over a large portion of Hindostan." In Bassora, which contained 60,000 inhabitants, in fourteen days it destroyed from 15,000 to 18,000 persons. In seven months, it had extended from Caramania to Judea, over a space of not less than a hundred leagues, and reached the shores of the Mediterranean. But it was introduced into Europe at the mouth of the Volga on the Caspian Sea, in 1830.—[London Quarterly Review.]

—July 1832, page 15.

THE CHOLERA.

This desolating sickness is spreading steadily over the United States. The account of its ravages, in many places, we cannot give: The whole number of cases in New-York, to July 31, is—3731. Deaths—1520.

No man can stop the work of the Lord, for God rules the pestilence, and the pestilence rules men. Oceans, sentinels, and forts, may hinder men, or money may bribe, but when the pestilence rides on the wings of the wind, the ocean is no barrier; the sentinel has no power; the fort is no obstacle, and money has no value: the destroying angel goes, waving the banner of death over all; and who shall escape his pointed arrow? Not he that could brave death at the cannon's mouth, but shrink at the sound of the cholera; not he that worshiped his god in some stately chapel, every sabbath till the cholera comes, and then flees for his life; no; none but him that trusts in God, shall be able to stand when a thousand shall fall at his side, and ten thousand at his right hand, by the noisome pestilence.

—August 1832, page 17.

On occasions statistics were given to feed the Saints' prejudices about those outside the fold. Note, for example, the blatant anti-Catholic slant of the following table of figures:

FOREIGN STATISTICS.

Inhabitants of Sicily,	1,780,000
Ecclesiastics,	300,000
Monks,	1,117
Income of the clergy in Spain,	$71,040,000
Government Tax, in 1799,	$24,420,000
Clergy loaned government in 16 years,	£1,890,000
Received from the people in the same time,	£195,000,000
Extraordinary exactions, same time,	£56,000,000
Number of Priests,	200,000
Number of beggars—nearly,	300,000

Ignorance among the lower classes keeps Spain bound with the fetters of a tyranic Priesthood.

—September 1832, page 31.

Occasionally some sensationalism crept into the reporting, which then, as now, was bound to excite one's curiosity. Imagine the fodder for imagination that this news release would provide, especially for the young children.

THE PLAGUE OF FIERY SERPENTS.

The following is an extract of a letter dated, Bassorah, the 25 of August, 1831, and received in Calcutta by an Armenian gentleman:—"Almost every country in these regions of the globe has been visited by a dreadful visitor of Providence.—You must have been, long before this, informed of the many calamities that have befallen the devoted city of Bagdad, and the places adjacent to it. News had also been received from Hanadan, or the ancient Ecbatana, of the occurrence of another natural calamity in that place. The city is described to be literally infested with a species of fiery serpents, the bite of which is followed by immediate madness, which in the course of a very short time terminates in the death of the sufferer.—The streets of the town are said to be choked with dead bodies, which are fed upon by dogs and jackals! The inhabitants are seized with consternation and trepidation, not knowing where to fly from the anger of the Almighty."—[India Gazette, December 23rd.]

Earthquake.—A letter from Smyrna says, "The earthquake which we felt here on the 9th of March, has been very destructive at some places in the interior of Antolia, a few days' journey to the coast of Smyrna. At Ballagda, a town about forty leagues from Smyrna, four minarets and twenty houses were overturned. The small village of Eldrick, one hour's journey from Ballagda, consisting of 40 or 50 houses, was entirely destroyed. A large village called Ienidje, in which there were 2 or 300 houses, also suffered a great deal, as did two other villages within two hours distance of Ballagda. At Degniztu, five or six leagues distant from that town, half the houses and the walls of the ancient fortress tumbled down. In fine, the calamity was general along a line of from 8 to ten leagues, and in addition to an extensive destruction of property, a great number of persons lost their lives.

—October 1832, page 37.

News was culled from many domestic and foreign newspapers, and often the date of occurrence was not cited. Thus the news items could be many months old by the time they came to the attention of the Saints. But many of the church members, especially those in outlying frontier settlements, depended upon the *Star* to bring the news of the world to them, and to interpret that news in light of the church's understanding of God's plan for the world.

HYMNS

Of the eight pages in the first issue of *The Evening and the Morning Star*, one page was devoted to hymns "selected and prepared for the Church of Christ, in the last days." Of the six hymns in this first issue, only two are retained in the hymnody of the church, "Redeemer of Israel," and John Newton's famous hymn, "Glorious Things of Thee Are Spoken."

Some of the hymns that appeared in the *Star* were the original creations of Latter Day Saint authors, with, we may assume, W. W. Phelps receiving most of the laurels. Others were reprints of popular hymns of the day, while still others were adaptations of already existent hymns. Some adaptations involved merely the change of a phrase here and there;

others were a complete rewrite. For example, notice how W. W. Phelps altered Joseph Swain's hymn to make it one of the most beloved hymns of the Restoration movement.

O Thou, in whose presence
   my soul takes delight,
On whom in affliction I call,
   My comfort by day,
and my song in the night,
My hope, my salvation, my all!

Where doest Thou, dear Shepherd,
   resort with Thy sheep,
To feed them in pastures of love?
Say, why in the valley of death
   should I weep,
Or alone in this wilderness rove?

O why should I wander an alien
   from Thee,
Or cry in the desert for bread?
Thy foes will rejoice when my
   sorrows they see,
And smile at the tears I have shed.

Restore, my dear Saviour, the light
   of Thy face;
Thy soul-cheering comfort impart;
And let the sweet tokens of
   pardoning grace
Bring joy to my desolate heart.

Redeemer of Israel,
   our only delight,
On whom for a blessing we call,
Our shadow by day
   and our pillar by night,
Our King, our Companion, our All!

We know he is coming to gather
   his sheep
And plant them in Zion in love;
For why in the valley of death
   should they weep
Or alone in the wilderness rove?

How long we have wandered as
   strangers in sin
And cried in the desert for thee!
Our foes have rejoiced when our
   sorrows they've seen,
But Israel will shortly be free.

As children of Zion, good tidings
   for us,
The tokens already appear;
Fear not, and be just, for the
   kingdom is ours,
And the hour of redemption is near.

Brother Phelps added a stanza to affirm his personal faith. Very early this fifth stanza was dropped. To many it suggested a sense of unchristian arrogance.

The secret of Heaven,
   The mystry below,
That many have sought for so long
We know that we know
   For the spirit of Christ,
Tells his servants they cannot be wrong.

—June 1832, page 8.

74

The hymns were, by modern poetic standards, of uneven quality with most of them not surviving to our day because of lack of literary merit. Here are a few stanzas of the "Pilgrims' Hymn."

> Go on, dear pilgrims, while below,
>   In wisdom's paths of peace,
> Determined nothing else to know,
>   But Jesus' righteousness.
>
> Do like the Savior, follow him,
>   He in this world has been,
> And oft revil'd, but like a lamb,
>   Did ne'er revile again.
>
> O take the pattern he has given,
>   Seek first the things of worth,
> And learn the only way to heaven,
>   Is—worship God on earth.
>
> Soon we shall reach the promis'd land,
>   With all the ransom'd race
> And meet with Enoch's perfect band,
>   To sing redeeming grace.
>
> When we've been there a thousand years,
>   Bright shining as the Sun.
> We've no less days to sing God's praise,
>   Than when we first began.
>
> —July 1832, page 16.

Several hymns focused on the Book of Mormon, as does this one:

> An angel came down from the mansions of glory,
> And told that a record was hid in Cumorah,
> Containing the fulness of Jesus's gospel;
> And also the cov'nant to gather his people.
>   O Israel! O Israel!
>   In all your abidings,
>   Prepare for your Lord
>   When you hear these glad tidings.

A heavenly treasure; a book full of merit;
It speaks from the dust, by the power of the Spirit;
A voice from the Savior that saints can rely on,
To prepare for the day when he brings again Zion.
    O Israel! O Israel!
       In all your abidings,
     Prepare for your Lord
       When you hear these glad tidings.

Listen O isles, and give ear ev'ry nation,
For great things await you in this generation:
The kingdom of Jesus, in Zion, shall flourish;
The righteous will gather: the wicked must perish.
    O Israel! O Israel!
       In all your abidings,
     Prepare for your Lord
       When you hear these glad tidings.

—February 1833, page 72.

A hymn that has been preserved in Mormon hymnody but ignored by the Reorganization is the following:

HOME

Now let us rejoice in the day of salvation,
   No longer as strangers on earth need we roam;
Good tidings are sounding to us and each nation,
   And shortly the hour of redemption will come:

When all that we promis'd the saints will be given,
And none will molest them from morn until even,
And earth will appear as the garden of Eden,
   And Jesus will say to all Israel: Come home!

In faith we'll rely on the arm of Jehovah,
   To guide through these last days of trouble and gloom;
And after the scourges and harvest are over,
   We'll rise with the just, when the Savior doth come:

Then all that was promis'd the saints will be given,
And they will be crown'd as the angel of heaven:
And earth will appear as the garden of Eden,
   And Christ and his people will ever be one.

—March 1833, page 80.

The hymns are usually too long to sing in our worship services today. One hymn, "Age After Age Has Roll'd Away" (May 1833, page 8) has a record twenty-three stanzas.

The final page of the last issue of the Independence *Star* is closed with a "Song of Zion" in which the praise of God is proclaimed with majestic imagery.

SONG OF ZION.

The great and glorious gospel light,
Has usher'd forthinto my sight,
Which in my soul I have receiv'd,
From death and bondage being freed

With saints below and saints above.
I'll join to praise the God I love;
Like Enoch too, I will proclaim,
A loud Hosanna to his name.

Hosanna, let the echo fly
From pole to pole, from sky to sky,
And saints and angels, join to sing,
Till all eternity shall ring.

Hosanna, let the voice extend,
Till time shall cease, and have an end;
Till all the throngs of heav'n above,
Shall join the saints in songs of love.

Hosanna, let the trump of God,
Proclaim his wonders far abroad,
And earth, and air, and skies, and seas,
Conspire to sound aloud his praise.

—July 1833, page 112.

MISCELLANEOUS MATTER

The *Star's* editor had on hand a variety of fillers to help use up space when the copy for the various articles did not completely fill the allotted pages. Some of these fillers were lifted from other newspapers; some were announcements concerning *Star* distribution or reports on the postmarks of recent letters to the *Star*; some were proverbial gems of wisdom. Given below is a cross section of the type of fillers tucked in here or there to eliminate bare white space.

> The commerce of the west, dependent on the river Ohio and its tributary streams, gives employment of 190 steam boats, 5,000 flat boats and arks, and not less than 10,000 men and boys.

—June 1832, page 5.

> It has lately been discovered that the best paper for wrappers, writing, and printing, may be produced from wood shavings, boiled in mineral or vegetable alkali. One hundred pounds of wood and twelve pounds of alkali will produce a ream of paper.—(London paper.)

—June 1832, page 5.

> Every person that will procure ten subscribers for the Star, and transmit to us, free of postage, $10, (U. S. paper.) shall be entitled to a paper per. an. gratis. In all cases, payment must be made to us through the post office, or to an authorized agent, before the Star will be forwarded.

—June 1832, page 6.

> Notwithstanding the Month of May was wet and cold, the weather, for some time past, has been such, that the prospect of the farmer is fair, and we have hopes of good crops.

—July 1832, page 14.

> The frontier Indian war continues. There have been several killed on both sides. The government of the United States has appropriated $300,000 for this purpose, and we may calculate, the war will be prosecuted vigorously as far as necessary.

—July 1832, page 14.

> A correspondent of the Nat. Intelligencer, among the many preventives against the Cholera, says:—God will hear, if man will pray. This we endorse as truth.

—July 1832, page 16.

A great man with the Lord, is what the world would call a
poor wretch, or he is of no note. Thus the simple confound the
wise.

—July 1832, page 16.

The Providence (R. I.) American, gives the names, ages and
residence of thirty-seven Revolutionary Soldiers, who were present at the recent celebration of our National Independence in
that city. The oldest was 94 and the youngest 62. At the celebration in 1830 says the American, 76 Revolutionary Soldiers were
present; and in 1831, 53. In a few years more, those last remains
of Revolutionary glory will live only in the memories of their
countrymen.

—August 1832, page 21.

The prophet told the truth, when, prophesying of the last
days, he said, The good is perished out of the earth; for so it is.
Christ's disciples were nick-named CHRISTIANS, in the meridian
of time; and his disciples, are now called MORMONITES without
authority or provocation, by the sectarian papers, as well as the
political; not, however, with an intimation to follow the Savior's
golden rule, or to teach mankind, to embrace Paul's more excellent way! Let brotherly love continue.

—August 1832, page 23.

The editor of this paper, husked, of this season's growth, ripe
corn on the 28 July last; some of which has been planted for a
second crop, and is coming on finely.

—August 1832, page 23.

REMEDY FOR VOMITING.—Common Coffee—Prepare it in
the following manner;—Roast half a pint of Indian corn in an iron
pan or kettle, free from any grease; stir it steadily until it is so
brown as to be nearly black; grind or powder it. To one tea cup
of the corn powder, pour a pint of boiling water—let it boil five
minutes in a clean tin vessel, then stiring it, and give half a tea-cup
full without milk; and if it is vomited once, give the other half
cup which is usually suffcent.
This receipt cures nine times out of ten, and is valuable as it
enables the stomach to retain medicine.—(Alb. Jour.)

—September 1832, page 31.

A very sick infant was lately found in Philadelphia, whose mother had died of cholera, and the father was "bringing it up on apples and whisky." The latter article was doubtless the favorite of the father.

—October 1832, page 39.

The first impression of a drunkard is a grin, the last a gasp; sizzled, he imagines himself a prince; sober, he finds he is only a pauper.

—October 1832, page 39.

The Spanish slave vessels, bound to Cuba, with 989 slaves, have been lately captured by British cruisers and carried into Nassau.

—October 1832, page 39.

The present season has been remarkable for the abundance of venomous reptiles, which are to be found in the pastures and fields in many towns in the vicinity of Salem, Massachusetts.

—October 1832, page 40.

Supposing the earth to contain 800,000,000 of inhabitants, the cholera has already swept off more than a 16th of them.

—November 1832, page 48.

One good rule to live by, is to talk little: hear much, and reflect upon every thing you have done during the day, and then ask the Lord to forgive your trespasses as you forgive those that trespass against you.

—December 1832, page 56.

Our accounts of the ravages of the cholera, in the south-western states, exceeds any thing of last year. We shall notice the subject in our next.

—July 1833, page 111.

There was no "next," at least from Independence. The mob had done its work well and Brother Phelps's Independence-based *Evening and the Morning Star* passed into history.

The mob tarring and feathering
Joseph Smith, from the print made about 1850

Chapter 4

MESSENGER AND ADVOCATE

With the "outrage in Missouri" uppermost in mind, the church leaders in Kirtland turned their attention to the most effective means of reestablishing contact with church members scattered throughout the country. The *Evening and the Morning Star* had served this function well. Even before the invasion of the printing office by the hostile mob, plans had been laid to establish a newspaper to service church interests at Kirtland. The name had already been selected as noted in this explanation given in the *Star*.

> As the Evening and Morning Star was designed to be published at Missouri, it was considered that another name would be more appropriate for a paper in this place (Kirtland), consequently, as the name of this Church has lately been entitled the Church of the Latter-day Saints, and since it is destined, at least for a season, to bear reproach and stigma of this world, it is no more than just that a paper disseminating the doctrines believed by the same, and advocating its character and rights should be entitled *The Latter Day Saints' Messenger and Advocate*.

> —September 1834, page 185.

It seemed prudent, in view of the Missouri debacle, to hasten the formation of a printing company in Kirtland, and so in September 1833 the church authorities met in council and resolved to purchase another press. The plan was to publish the *Messenger and Advocate* and the *Star* simultaneously until the *Star* could be transferred to its former location.

As preparations for the new newspaper were carried on, some objectives for this official publication were articulated by church leaders, namely, *not* to air grievances and grudges but rather to spike false rumors causing dissension in the ranks of the church; to provide a forum for letters and reports by which the Saints could be informed of the conditions of the church members expelled from Jackson County and now residing in the northern counties of that state; and also to give information to the membership and interested investigators concerning the rise and progress of the church, and to apprise them of current developments through missionary reports and conference minutes.

In spite of the sense of urgency felt by the church leaders, the first issue of the *Messenger and Advocate* was not ready until October of 1834. From then on it continued regularly as a monthly periodical for three years, the last issue appearing in September of 1837. Over this period of time almost six hundred pages of reading matter were presented to the Saints for their enjoyment, enlightenment, and edification. The *Star*'s subscription list was to provide the basis for the *Messenger and Advocate's* support but it was hoped that many more subscribers would send their one dollar per year fee as the church grew in number and influence. Many of the same problems that slowed up the initial appearance of the paper—shortage of newsprint, inexperience of the editors and printers, failure of contributors to meet deadlines—were to hound the editors for the total life of the paper. Several apologies were printed, with some attempts to justify the delay. Note the following in the first issue:

> *An apology.*—This No. of the Messenger and Advocate has been delayed beyond the time we had designed issuing it, in consequence of our *necessary* abscence to the West, with a detention on the water of five days and nights longer than we had anticipated. We therefore excuse ourselves, because the delay was order by HIM who "holds the winds."
>
> —October 1834, page 11.

Three men served as editors, first Oliver Cowdery, the "second elder" of the church, from October 1834 to May 1835; John Whitmer, "church historian," from June 1835 to

March 1836; Oliver Cowdery again from April 1836 to February 1837; concluding with the services of W. A. Cowdery, from February to September of 1837. A change in form from the *Star*'s format occurred—the *Messenger and Advocate* was to be in octavo form rather than quarto size (that is, eight sheets were to be cut from the large leaf of paper rather than four), presumably for greater convenience in binding. Even more important, perhaps, was the change in content and tone. Far fewer prophesies of gloom haunted its pages. For example, the cholera is scarcely mentioned at all in the *Messenger and Advocate* whereas Editor Phelps of the *Star* at times seemed obsessed with it. Even admitting a decline in the incidence of the cholera, the general fear of a renewed outbreak was ever present, and so the *Messenger and Advocate*'s silence is something of a mystery.

In actuality, there was noticeable difference of concern and style evident among the *Advocate*'s three editors. For example, selections from non-Latter Day Saint writings and news from the secular world were all but ignored until W. A. Cowdery took the reins. This final editor was also perhaps the most courageous of the three in facing, rather than evading, the big issues confronting the church, as witness his probing questions and comments about the Kirtland Safety Society (See page 157).

Launched under somewhat difficult circumstances, the *Messenger and Advocate* survived in the midst of one of the most critical periods in the nation's history without giving any indication at all of the turbulence of the times. This paper also presided over one of the most creative periods of Latter Day Saint history, an era which saw the organization of the high quorums, the publication of the Doctrine and Covenants, the beginning of the School of the Elders, the completion of the Kirtland Temple, the acquisition of some Egyptian scrolls which later became the basis for the Book of Abraham, the financial fiasco of the Kirtland Safety Society, and the first overseas mission of the church—and yet its coverage of these important incidents in church history is at best only spotty. It seems a bit strange that the bank failure could be given a fairly extensive airing, and yet the organization of the Quorum of Twelve and the Quorum of Seventy isn't even noted. In spite of some of these more obvious omissions, the *Messenger and Advocate* is one of our best sources for understanding the developments that were transpiring during this volatile period of church history.

THE DEVELOPING DOCTRINE

The first "epitome of faith" of the Restoration movement was penned by editor Oliver Cowdery as he attempted to set forth the principles to which his paper was committed. In his "Address" in the first issue, we find:

> We believe in God, and his Son Jesus Christ. We believe that God, from the beginning, revealed himself to man; and that whenever he has had a people on earth, he always has revealed himself to them by the Holy Ghost, the ministering of angels, or his own voice. We do not believe that he ever had a church on earth without revealing himself to that church: consequently, there were apostles, prophets, evangelists, pastors, and teachers, in the same.— We believe that God is the same in all ages; and that it requires the same holiness, purity, and religion, to save a man *now,* as it did anciently; and that, as He is no respecter of persons, always has, and always will reveal himself to men when they call upon him.
>
> We believe that God has revealed himself to men in this age, and commenced to raise up a church preparatory to his second advent, when he will come in the clouds of heaven with power and great glory.
>
> We believe that the popular religious theories of the day are incorrect; that they are without parallel in the revelations of God, as sanctioned by him; and that however faithfully they may be adhered to, or however zealously and warmly they may be defended, they will never stand the strict scrutiny of the word of life.
>
> We believe that all men are born free and equal; that no man, combination of men, or government of men, have power or authority to compel or force others to embrace any system of religion, or religious creed, or to use force or violence to prevent

others from enjoying their own opinions, or practicing the same, so long as they do not molest or disturb others in theirs, in a manner to deprive them of their privileges as free citizens—or of worshiping God as they choose, and that any attempt to the contrary is an assumption unwarrantable in the revelations of heaven, and strikes at the root of civil liberty, and is a subvertion of all equitable principles between man and man.

We believe that God has set his hand the second time to recover the remnant of his people, Israel; and that the time is near when he will bring them from the four winds, with songs of everlasting joy, and reinstate them upon their own lands which he gave their fathers by covenant.

And further: We believe in embracing good wherever it may be found; of proving all things, and holding fast that which is righteous.

—October 1834, page 2.

Three articles—"Millennium," "Faith of the Church," and "The Gospel"—had been run serially in the *Evening and the Morning Star* and were then continued in the *Messenger and Advocate*. The author is later revealed to be Sidney Rigdon, a counselor to the Prophet. Several other doctrinal topics were treated by Brother Rigdon, as we shall note later on.

The May 1835 issue carried an announcement concerning the soon-to-be-published Doctrine and Covenants, in which would appear certain lectures "delivered before a THEO-LOGICAL class in this place last winter." Two of these lectures, the fifth and sixth, were printed in this issue of the *Messenger and Advocate* with this introduction:

In giving the following lectures we have thought best to insert the catechism, that the reader may fully understand the manner in which this science was taught. It was found, that by annexing a catechism to the lectures as they were presented, the class made greater progress than otherwise; and in consequence of the additional scripture proofs, it was preserved in compiling.

LECTURE FIFTH.

1 In our former lectures we treated of the being, character, perfections and attributes of God. What we mean by perfections,

is, the perfections which belong to all the attributes of his nature.
We shall, in this lecture speak of the Godhead: we mean the
Father, Son and Holy Spirit.

2 There are two personages who constitute the great, matchless, governing and supreme power over all things—by whom all
things were created and made, that are created and made,
whether visible or invisible: whether in heaven, on earth, or in the
earth, under the earth, or throughout the immensity of space—
They are the Father and the Son: The Father being a personage
of spirit, glory and power: possessing all perfection and fulness:
The Son, who was in the bosom of the Father, a personage of
tabernacle, made, or fashioned like unto man, or being in the
form and likeness of man, or, rather, man was formed after his
likeness, and in his image;—he is also the express image and likeness of the personage of the Father: possessing all the fulness of
the Father, or, the same fulness with the Father; being begotten
of him, and was ordained from before the foundation of the
world to be a propitiation for the sins of all those who should
believe on his name, and is called the Son because of the flesh
—and descended in suffering below that which man can suffer, or,
in other words, suffered greater sufferings, and was exposed to
more powerful contradictions than any man can be. But notwithstanding all this, he kept the law of God, and remained without
sin: Showing thereby that it is in the power of man to keep the
law and remain also without sin. And also, that by him a righteous judgment might come upon all flesh, & that all who walk
not in the law of God, may justly be condemned by the law, and
have no excuse for their sins. . . .

3 From the foregoing account of the Godhead, which is
given in his revelations, the Saints have a sure foundation laid for
the exercise of faith unto life and salvation, through the atonement and mediation of Jesus Christ, by whose blood they have a
forgiveness of sins, and also, a sure reward laid up for them in
heaven, even that of partaking of the fulness of the Father and
the Son, through the Spirit. As the Son partakes of the fulness of
the Father through the Spirit, so the saints are, by the same
Spirit, to be partakers of the same fulness, to enjoy the same
glory; for as the Father and the Son are one, so in like manner the
saints are to be one in them, through the love of the Father, the
mediation of Jesus Christ, and the gift of the Holy Spirit, they are
to be heirs of God and joint heirs with Jesus Christ.

Question. Of what do the foregoing lectures treat?

Answer. Of the being, perfections and attributes of the Deity.

Q. What are we to understand by the perfections of the Deity?

A. The perfections which belong to his attributes.

Q. How many personages are there in the Godhead?

A. Two: the Father and the Son.

Q. How do you prove that there are two personages in the Godhead?

A. By the Scriptures. Gen. 1:26. And the Lord God said unto the Only Begotten who was with him from the beginning, Let us make man in our image, after our likeness:—and it was done. Gen. 2:22. And the Lord God said unto the Only Begotten, Behold, the man is become as one of us: to know good and evil. John, 17:5. And now, O Father, glorify thou me with thine own self with the glory which I had with thee before the world was.

Q. What is the Father?

A. He is a personage of glory and of power. . . .

Q. What is the Son?

A. First, he is a personage of tabernacle.

Q. How do you prove it?

A. John 14:9, 10, 11, Jesus says unto him, Have I been so long time with you, and yet have you not known me, Philip? He that has seen me has seen the Father; and how do you say then, Show us the Father? Do you not believe, that I am in the Father, and the Father in me? The words that I speak unto you, I speak not of myself: but the Father that dwells in me, he does the works. Believe me that I am in the Father, and the Father in me. . . .

Q. Does the believer in Christ Jesus, through the gift of the Spirit, become one with the Father and the Son, as the Father and the Son are one?

A. They do. John 17:20, 21. Neither pray I for these (the apostles) alone; but for them also who shall believe on me through their word; that they all may be one; as thou, Father, art in me, and I in thee, that they also may be one in us, that the world may believe that thou hast sent me.

Q. Does the foregoing account of the Godhead lay a sure foundation for the exercise of faith in him unto life and salvation?

A. It does.

Q. How do you prove it?

A. By the third paragraph of this lecture. . . .

LECTURE SIXTH.

1 Having treated, in the preceding lectures, of the ideas of the character, perfections and attributes of God, we next proceed to treat of the knowledge which persons must have, that the course of life which they pursue is according to the will of God, in order that they may be enabled to exercise faith in him unto life and salvation.

2 This knowledge supplies an important place in revealed religion; for it was by reason of it that the ancients were enabled to endure as seeing him who is invisible. An actual knowledge of any person that the course of life which he pursues is according to the will of God, is essentially necessary to enable him to have that confidence in God, without which no person can obtain eternal life. It was this that enabled the ancient saints to endure all their afflictions and persecutions, and to take joyfully the spoiling of their goods, knowing, (not believing merely,) that they had a more enduring substance. Heb. 10:34.

3 Having the assurance that they were pursuing a course which was agreeable to the will of God, they were enabled to take, not only the spoiling of their goods, and the wasting of their substance, joyfully, but also to suffer death in its most horrid forms; knowing, (not merely believing,) that when this earthly house of their tabernacle was dissolved, they had a building of God, a house not made with hands, eternal in the heavens. Second Cor. 5:1.

4 Such was and always will be the situation of the saints of God, that unless they have an actual knowledge that the course they are pursuing is according to the will of God, they will grow weary in their minds and faint. . . .

5 For a man to lay down his all, his character and reputation, his honor and applause, his good name among men, his houses, his lands, his brothers and sisters, his wife and children, and even his own life also, counting all things but filth and dross for the excellency of the knowledge of Jesus Christ, requires more than mere belief, or supposition that he is doing the will of God, but actual knowledge: realizing, that when these sufferings are ended he will enter into eternal rest, and be a partaker of the glory of God.

6 For unless a person does know that he is walking according to the will of God, it would be offering an insult to the dignity of the Creator, were he to say that he would be a partaker of his glory when he should be done with the things of this life. But

when he has this knowledge, and most assuredly knows that he is doing the will of God, his confidence can be equally strong that he will be a partaker of the glory of God.

7 Let us here observe, that a religion that does not require the sacrifice of all things, never has power sufficient to produce the faith necessary unto life and salvation. . . .

8 It is in vain for persons to fancy to themselves that they are heirs with those, or can be heirs with them, who have offered their all in sacrifice, and by this means obtained faith in God and favor with him so as to obtain eternal life, unless they in like manner offer unto him the same sacrifice, and through that offering obtain the knowledge that they are accepted of him.

9 It was in offering sacrifices that Abel, the first martyr, obtained knowledge that he was accepted of God. . . .

10 Those, then, who make the sacrifice will have the testimony that their course is pleasing in the sight of God, and those who have this testimony will have faith to lay hold on eternal life, and will be enabled, through faith, to endure unto the end, and receive the crown that is laid up for them that love the appearing of our Lord Jesus Christ. . . .

11 All the saints of whom we have account in all the revelations of God which are extant, obtained the knowledge which they had of their acceptance in his sight, through the sacrifice which they offered unto him: and thro' the knowledge thus obtained, their faith became sufficiently strong to lay hold upon the promise of eternal life, and to endure as seeing him who is invisible; and were enabled, through faith, to combat the powers of darkness, contend against the wiles of the adversary, overcome the world, and obtain the end of their faith, even the salvation of their souls.

12 But those who have not made this sacrifice to God, do not know that the course which they pursue is well pleasing in his sight; for whatever may be their belief or their opinion, it is a matter of doubt and uncertainty in their mind; and where doubt and uncertainty are, there faith is not, nor can it be. For doubt and faith do not exist in the same person at the same time. So that persons whose minds are under doubts and fears cannot have unshaken confidence, and where unshaken confidence is not, there faith is weak, and where faith is weak, the persons will not be able to contend against all the opposition, tribulations and afflictions which they will have to encounter in order to be heirs of God, and joint heirs with Christ Jesus; and they will grow weary in their minds, and the adversary will have power over them and destroy them.

Note. This lecture is so plain, and the facts set forth so self-evident, that it is deemed unnecessary to form a catechism upon it: the student is therefore instructed to commit the whole to memory.

—May 1835, pages 122-126.

Whether these lectures were solely the work of Joseph Smith or the composite effort of several persons is nowhere made clear.

The Prophet actually contributed very few articles to the *Messenger and Advocate*, only four letters, one business document (Articles of Agreement of the Kirtland Safety Society), and one set of conference minutes. About one third of his first letter "to the elders of the church of Latter Day Saints" consisted of biblical quotations. Here are some points he wanted to stress:

> After so long a time, and after so many things having been said, I feel it my duty to drop a few hints, that, perhaps, the elders, traveling through the world to warn the inhabitants of the earth to flee the wrath to come, and save themselves from this untoward generation, may be aided in a measure, in doctrine, and in the way of their duty. I have been laboring in this cause for eight years, during which time I have traveled much, and have had much experience. I removed from Seneca county, N. Y. to Geauga county, Ohio, in February, 1831.
>
> Having received, by an heavenly vision, a commandment, in June following, to take my journey to the western boundaries of the State of Missouri, and there designate the very spot, which was to be the central spot, for the commencement of the gathering together of those who embrace the fulness of the everlasting gospel—I accordingly undertook the journey with certain ones of my brethren, and, after a long and tedious journey, suffering many privations and hardships, I arrived in Jackson county Missouri; and, after viewing the country, seeking diligently at the hand of God, he manifested himself unto me, and designated to me and others, the very spot upon which he designed to commence the work of the gathering, and the upbuilding of an holy city, which should be called Zion:—Zion because it is to be a place of righteousness, and all who build thereon, are to worship

the true and living God—and all believe in one doctrine even the doctrine of our Lord and Savior Jesus Christ. . . . After having ascertained the very spot, and having the happiness of seeing quite a number of the families of my brethren, comfortably situated upon the land, I took leave of them, and journeyed back to Ohio, and used every influence and argument, that lay in my power, to get those who believe in the everlasting covenant, whose circumstances would admit, and whose families were willing to remove to the place which I now designated to be the land of Zion: And thus the sound of the gathering, and of the doctrine, went abroad into the world; and many we have reason to fear, having a zeal not according to knowledge, not understanding the pure principles of the doctrine of the church, have no doubt, in the heat of enthusiasm, taught and said many things which are derogatory to the genuine character and principles of the church, and for these things we are heartily sorry, and would apologize if an apology would do any good.

But we pause here and offer a remark upon the saying which we learn has gone abroad, and has been handled in a manner detrimental to the cause of truth, by saying, "that in preaching the doctrine of gathering, we break up families, and give license for men to leave their families; women their husbands; children their parents, and slaves their masters, thereby deranging the order, and breaking up the harmony and peace of society." We shall here show our faith, and thereby, as we humbly trust, put an end to these faults, and wicked misrepresentations, which have caused, we have every reason to believe, thousands to think they were doing God's service, when they were persecuting the children of God: whereas, if they could have enjoyed the true light, and had a just understanding of our principles, they would have embraced them with all their hearts, and been rejoicing in the love of the truth.

And now to show our doctrine on this subject, we shall commence with the first principles of the gospel, which are repentance, and baptism for the remission of sins, and the gift of the Holy Ghost by the laying on of the hands. . . .

But we discover, in order to be benefitted by the doctrine of repentance, we must believe in obtaining the remission of sins. And in order to obtain the remission of sins, we must believe in the doctrine of baptism, in the name of the Lord Jesus Christ. And if we believe in baptism for the remission of sins, we may expect a fulfilment of the promise of the Holy Ghost: for the promise extends to all whom the Lord our God shall call.

—September 1835, pages 179-181.

Sidney Rigdon postulates a view concerning "the Ancient Order of Things" which has been widely believed among Latter Day Saints since his time. The Disciples movement and a few other smaller groups were also stressing the need for "restoration" of the primitive Christian gospel.

The ancient order of things has engrossed the attention of the religious public to some extent in modern times, and has given rise to many parties and sects in the so called christian world; each one in their turn supposing that they had the ancient order of things among them, and had come to the standard of righteousness set up in the scriptures, and representing other religious denominations as having come short of the glory of God, and as not having come to the standard of truth, or else they had departed from it. . . .

What I understand by the ancient order of things, as used in modern dialect, is the order of things revealed in the bible, and taught to mankind by the holy prophets and apostles, who were divinely inspired to teach them the way of life and salvation. If I am correct in this conclusion the only way to settle the question about this order of things is to have recourse to the book, and let it speak for itself, and set forth the ancient order of things, as the holy prophets and apostles declared it, by he spirit of inspiration.

I conclude, and I think correctly too, that it requires the entire order of things established by the Savior of the world, to constitute the ancient order of things, and not a part of it only. . . .

There is this peculiarity about the works of God, that to add to them is to injure them: and so it is to take from them. All the ingenuity of the world combined could not add any thing to the structure of the human body without injuring it; neither could they take any thing from it without doing it an injury; it is best just as it is; so is all the other works of God, in the spiritual as well as the natural kingdom; they are best as God formed them; to alter them any way is to make them worse instead of better.

The order of things which God established for the salvation of man, which is called in modern dialect, the ancient order of things, is in every respect calculated to produce the effect for which it was intended, that is to save men, and in order that men might be saved, it was necessary that an order of things should be established, beginning with apostles, and then to have prophets, and then evangelists, and after that pastors, teachers, &c. with gifts healings, miracles, tongues, interpretation of tongues, as an established order to continue as long as the Lord our God should call men to be his sons, and women to be his daughters. . . .

In the whole history of this religion as set forth in the scriptures, its order was the same; it produced the same effect among all people, whether they were Scythian, Barbarian, bond or free, Jew or Gentile, Greek or Roman, it mattered not what they were; for in this respect, there was neither Greek nor Jew, bond nor free, male nor female; but they were all one in Christ Jesus, and the same blessing belonged to all, and the same fruits followed all, and the order was the same, whether it was in Africa, Asia, or Europe, and that so perfectly so as to establish this fact forever, that the Lord has but one order of things, and that all other orders are not of him, and where this order of things is not found, there the Lord's order is not. This then is the ancient order of things, if we mean by the ancient order of things, the order of things laid down in the scriptures. . . .

All other order of things beside this are human orders, and not divine orders, and all other teachers are human teachers; for no teacher can be found in the world, of whom God approves but one who has obtained his office by reason of an apostle, whom God first called, and through him others were called,—we do not mean a dead apostle but a living one; for whenever there ceases to be apostles on earth, then the order of God has ceased, and the order of men, or devils, or of both has got its place.

—September 1835, pages 182-185.

Another subject little spoken of in our day but fiercely debated then is that of "Christian perfection." The early Methodists considered this doctrine one of their "distinctive" beliefs. Here we have Sidney Rigdon addressing himself to this topic in the following manner:

PERFECTION.

Christian perfection, so called, is a subject which has engrosed the attention of the religious public in the different ages of the world in no small degree. It was, if we may credit the sacred writers, a subject which was called forth as early as we have any account of the revelations of God: and from that to the present, whether the world has been in a state of apostacy, or whether it has not, the subject of christian perfection has been one which has called forth a pretty large share of public discussion.

94

There can be little doubt, but those who were under the immediate influence of divine revelation, and received constant communication from the Deity on all subjects in any degree affecting their salvation, understood this subject much better than those who were in a state of apostacy; as they had all the opportunities that any mortals could have to settle all questions in relation to their religion: indeed the sacred writers speak of it as a subject which was well understood among the saints of their day; as at no time have they proposed it as a subject of discussion, and given us a formal investigation of it, as they have other subjects which were matters of controversy among the saints; but spake, and wrote, of it as of a matter which was well understood among them all. . . .

How hard must it be for a person who denies christian perfection, to understand what the Savior meant, when he said be ye perfect &c? When he firmly believes that it is impossible for any person to be so: he cannot think that the Savior said any thing wrong; but comes to the conclusion that he cannot understand him, there is some mystery about his sayings, some how or other. The man never seems to reflect for a moment that the error may be in his sentiments, and the difficulty arises from his having embraced sentiments which are not according to godliness; but perfectly satisfied with his religion, he comes to the conclusion that there is some thing wrapped up in these very plain sayings, which cannot be easily understood, and there he leaves the matter.

And those who profess to believe in perfection among the saints, find some difficulty also; for the Savior seems to push the subject a little farther than they can go. To require of the saints to be perfect, is what they believe in; but for him to say that they must be perfect, as their father in heaven is perfect, is a little beyond the faith of those who believe in perfection, and they also come to the conclusion that there is some little mystery some where about the savior's saying. . . .

When we speak of perfection, we mean to be understood that a perfect thing cannot be improved. There is perfection in mechanics, when a machise is so constructed, that it cannot be improved, or made better, we call it a perfect machine. We say of the *human* system it is perfect; because we cannot suggest an improvement in any part of it, it is brought to as high a state as it can, being the contrivance of infinite wisdom, and if we were to say that the great Jehovah could not improve it, we think we should not insult him.

We say of God, he is perfect. And why? because his nature
cannot be improved; and because he possesses all things of which
his nature is capable. When we speak of a perfect religion, we
mean that the religion is in every respect adapted to the wants,
and necessities, of those for whom it is designed. It expands the
human mind until it can expand no more, and then supplies it
with all it is capable of enjoying. So that the enjoyment is in
every way suited to the capacity of the persons who possess it;
insomuch, that even God himself could not expand the human
mind any more, nor give it one enjoyment which it does not
possess, This done, the religion is perfect; but without this, it is
not.

For a person to be perfect before God, is for him to have his
mind expanded until it can be expanded no more, and then to
enjoy all things which it is capable of enjoying. This would be
perfection, and thus a man would be perfect as his father in
heaven is perfect. And until this takes place, in vain may the
religious world talk about perfection. . . .

We think this subject is easy of understanding, if we are willing
to let our religion fall a prey to it; for such will be the case with
the whole sectarian world, if the bible is to be our guide. Perfection then, is perfection, and nothing else but perfection, is perfection. When a person or thing is perfect, it is perfect, and when
it is not perfect, it is not perfect. When any thing can be improved, it is not perfect. When any scheme which is designed for
the benefit of men can be bettered, it is not perfect, perfection
reaches beyond improvement.

—May 1836, pages 310-311.

For a person to be an heir of God, and a joint heir with Christ
Jesus, would be to endow him with the powers of the great God;
for how can any person be an heir of God, and yet never partake
of either his power or glory; where would his heirship be?—a mere
fiction, as bad as a Methodist God, without either body or parts.
If a person is ever an heir of God, he will partake of his glory; and
this he cannot do, unless he first partakes of his power. Or if a
person is ever a joint heir with Christ Jesus, he will be so by
reason of his partaking of the same power and glory: And the
Savior said of himself that, "all power is given unto me, in heaven
and on earth."—Now may I not ask, with propriety, can a person
be a joint heir with him who has *all* power in heaven and on
earth, and yet have *no* power in heaven nor on earth. This would

be too paradoxical for any rational being to pretend to believe. For any rational being must know, that for a person to be a joint heir with another, requires nothing less than to equally partake of the power, by which that other person partook of, and enjoyed his heirship; for if he did not he never could be heir with him. . . .

When the scriptures speak of making the saints "heirs of God, and joint heirs with Christ Jesus;" they surely take into consideration what will be necessary to do it, and if so, the thing proposed to men in the religion of heaven is, to put them in possession of the power, the wisdom and the knowledge, sufficient to make them heirs of God, and joint heirs with Christ Jesus. If a person is to partake of only part of the heirship of Christ, then, part of his qualifications will be sufficient; but if he is to be a joint heir, and be an equal partaker with Christ, then, nothing short of the same powers which Christ possesses, will enable him to do it. . . .

A few more words about the former day saints, and the sects of this generation, and I have done for the present. It is this, either the saints of former days were more than perfect (and that is impossible) or else the sects of this day are infinitely short of it. The former day saints could by their faith stop the mouths of lions, quench the violence of fire, escape the edge of the sword, put the armies of the aliens to flight, receive their dead children to life again, heal the sick, cast out devils, speak with tongues, interpret tongues, prophecy, dream dreams, see visions, &c. &c. I say then either the exercise of these powers among the former day saints was more than perfection, or else the sects of these days are no where near to perfection neither are they making the least advances towards it, and which of the two it is, I will leave a candid public to judge.

—November 1836, pages 406-408.

In July 1836 Apostle Orson Hyde takes up the pen to issue "A Prophetic Warning: To all the Churches, of every sect and denomination, and to every individual into whose hands it may fall." This may well give us an excellent example of how the rationale for the coming forth of the Restoration was set forth for unbelievers in order to persuade them of the validity of the Latter Day Saints' position. These excerpts represent about one-half of the entire document, which Hyde released in a large handbill during a missionary campaign at Toronto.

97

Forasmuch as many have taken in hand to set forth or order a declaration of those things which are most assuredly believed among us, and which must shortly come to pass: It seemeth good unto me, and also unto the Holy Spirit, to write unto you, that you may know of a certainty, your standing and relation to God; and also of the times and seasons of the fulfilment of the words of his servants, the Prophets. . . .

In the first place, let me ask: Have the founders of the christian system foretold an apostacy of the church from the true order of worship? They certainly have. Paul says, 2 Thess. 2, 3. "Let no man deceive you by any means; for *that day* shall not come except there come a falling away first, and that man of sin be revealed, the son of perdition, &c.". . .

I will now present the Gentile churches before the glass of the holy scriptures, and see if they possess the same form and beauty now, that they did Eighteen Hundred years ago. When Jesus gave his disciples their last commission to go forth into all the world to preach the gospel, he said unto them: "These signs shall follow them that believe. In my name shall they cast out devils; they shall speak with new tongues; they shall take up serpents: and if they drink any deadly thing, it shall not hurt them; they shall lay their hands upon the sick, and they shall receover." It appears that this miraculous power did, and ever will continue with *true believers:* for the same Being who said, "These signs shall follow them that believe," also said, "Though the heavens and the earth pass away. yet my words shall not fail." It is very readily discovered why the above signs do not follow pretended believers; because Jesus never said they should. . . .

God will soon begin to manifest his sore displeasure to this generation, and to our own country, by vexation and desolating wars; bloody! bloody in the extreme! The war cloud will arise from an unexpected quarter. The hearts of many, in authority, shall faint, because they shall not know what measure to adopt to avert the calamitics of war; so complicated and perplexing shall be the state of affairs at that crisis. Thus will the wicked shortly slay the wicked, except they like the people of Nineveh, speedily repent of their sins which have ascended up, with offence, before the Most High. Wo! wo! unto them, saith the Lord, who preach for hire, and pervert the ways of truth. Wo! to them who suffer themselves to be led by the precepts of men, contrary to that which they know to be written in the oracles of truth: they for shall perish! Wo be unto him who drinketh strong drink, and taketh the name of God in vain! . . .

The prime cause of all these calamities coming on the earth, is: the apostacy of the church. If the church was all righteous, they could save the nations from destruction. But the salt has lost its savor; and all men seem determined to pursue their own course. The eyes of Jehovah have not been closed upon the scenes of most abandoned wickedness which have been committed by the world: (The church not being free from the charges.) He has looked down and beheld all your scenes of revelling and drunkenness. . . .

When Jesus appears in the clouds of heaven, the saints who have slept, will arise from their graves; and those who are living will be changed speedily, and all be caught up to meet the Lord in the air. Then shall all the wicked, who have escaped the former judgments, be consumed, root and branch. Then shall the earth be cleansed from pollution; and the Lord descend upon it, and all the saints with him, to reign a thousand years while satan is bound. Then will the saints inherit this promise: "Blessed are the meek, for they shall inherit the earth.". . .

Now, therefore, the word of the Lord is unto all people: Repent! Repent! and be baptized in water for the remission of sins; in the name and by the authority of the Lord Jesus Christ; and you shall receive the gift of the Holy Ghost, by the laying on of the hands of him who is ordained and sealed unto that power. There is no class of people exempt from the requirement; but it is in force upon all alike; who have not already obeyed it. Then miraculous signs shall follow you. Pray, therefore, that God may send unto you some servant of his, who is authorized from on high, to administer to you the ordinances of the gospel. Except you do this, you cannot enjoy the *celestial* glory: But must fall victims to the messengers of destruction, which God will soon send upon the earth.

Now to conclude: I am sensible that I have written in great plainness; and some may consider me quite presumptuous. But I have nothing to retract. "What I have written, I have written;" and that too, under a sense of duty which has been impressed upon me, from the highest authority of which I have any knowledge. The fulfilment of the foregoing predictions, will convince this generation that I have not been presumptuous.

May the great Creator of the Universe, have mercy upon a fallen and perishing world!

—July 1836, pages 342-346.

The gathering of Israel back to its homeland was another theme that occupied the thoughts of many persons in the early nineteenth century. Identifying his sources as reason, analogy, and revelation, an author who signs himself as W, expounds on this topic. W might have been John Whitmer or F. G. Williams, a member of the First Presidency.

> The subject of the gathering of Israel from his long dispersion in the last days, has become a fruitful theme of theological disquisition among all believers in divine revelation. The pulpit and the press have teemed with arguments on the subject drawn from the sacred writings to elucidate different doctrines and support entirely different opinions. Perhaps, there is no one great and important event treated with that clearness and precision by all the ancient prophets, that we find on the subject of the gathering of Israel, and yet so much diversity of sentiment obtain, as now obtains on that subject. . . .
>
> I believe that the subject of the gathering not only affects the Jews, or direct lineal descendants of Abraham, but every nation, kindred, tongue and people under the whole heaven, and that the prophets meant as they have said, that there is no private interpretation to their expressions, but when speaking on that subject, they are to be understood literally. . . .
>
> Jeremiah who prophesied 628 years before the coming of Christ, records the word of the Lord through him in the 23d chap. and 3d ver. of his prophecy, thus: I will gather the remnant of my flock out of all countries whither I have driven them; and will bring them again to their folds and they shall be fruitful and increase. Chap. 31st, 6, 7, 8 and 9 verses read thus: For there shall be a day that the watchman upon mount Ephraim shall cry arise ye and let us go up to Zion, unto the Lord our God. For thus saith the Lord; sing with gladness for Jacob, and shout among the chief of the nations; publish ye, praise ye, say O Lord save thy people the remnant of Israel. Behold I will bring them from the north country and gather them from the coasts of the earth, and with them the blind and the lame, the woman with child, & her that travaileth with child together. . . .
>
> Two ideas strike the mind as matters of fact on casting the eye over the above quotations from the sacred writings. And first, the Babylonish captivity affected only the two tribes of Judah and Benjamin. The other ten tribes having been carried into captivity by Salmanassar, king of Assyria, 115 years before the Babylonish captivity by Nebuchadnezzar the king of Babylon. Second: On

100

looking at these scriptures, it is plainly discoverable, that the prophet mentions the whole house of Israel; and sometimes Ephraim and Judah are particularized as heads of tribes. Now we will mention one fact more for the consideration of all. Ephraim constituted one of the ten tribes, who have never yet been returned, therefore the return of Judah and Benjamin from the Babylonish captivity could not be a fulfilment of the prophecies quoted. I will still adduce another proof to those in any degree acquainted with history; viz. The prophets in those passages, have promised more real happiness than Judah and Benjamin have ever realized, consequently we conclude it follows, that from these considerations, Israel is not yet gathered, but will be gathered according to the predictions of those holy men whose words we have quoted. . . .

To those who are willing to admit that the Jews or children of Israel are to be gathered as the Lord has said, but deny that this gathering affects the Gentiles, we will suggest a few queries. And first, In what part of the volume of inspiration is to be found a covenant, or the copy of a covenant, that the Lord made with the Gentiles as a party abstract from the Jews, or the seed of Abraham: We wait for a reply. None can be given, because none can be found. Then have the Gentiles no promise left them. Seperate from Israel they have none. The Lord said to Abraham, in thee and in thy seed shall all the families of the earth be blessed. This St. Paul said was preaching the gospel to him, and it will readily be acknowledged, that it always requires a belief in, and an obedience to that gospel, before either Jew or Gentile could be benefitted by it. Is it not plain that both must comply with all the requirements of it in order to be benefitted by it? Most certainly you will admit it. Then we further ask, has the Lord any other scheme of saving men but by the gospel? Certainly not any. . . .

We might adduce much valid testimony of a positive command of God by revelation to gather in these last days, but, to the saints it would be unnecessary; for the reason that they are not only taught it by revelation but by the spirit and living instrnction. So that to them any farther argument would be superfluous.

It is humbly hoped that those who deny any revelation in this day and age of the world, will carefully examine the testimony and arguments drawn from the ancient scriptures, divest themselves of all tradition, and preconceived opinion and then judge of the plain matter of fact before them.

—September 1836, pages 369-372.

Some of the animosity toward fellow Christians which caused Sidney Rigdon to make many enemies on the Ohio frontier is manifest in his discussion of "The Latter Day Glory," in which "priests and drunkards, deacons and scoundrel, professors and thieves" are taken to task for not accepting the beliefs of the Saints.

> The subject of the latter day glory, has produced as much speculation among professed believers in the bible, perhaps, as any other which is supposed to have been a subject of revelation. Every new sect in religion which has made its appearance, has been supposed by its founders, to be the sect which is to lead the world to the full blaze of the latter day glory: and every sect in all sectariandom supposes, that when the latter day glory comes they will be the principal or prevailing party. . . .
>
> We, in modern times, speak of the exertions of the ancients to usher in this day, as the greatest folly, and even wickedness. For it is a fact of great notoriety, that the generations back for many centuries, felt as much zeal in the ushering in of the latter day glory, and as much interest in that day, as we in modern times feel; and used as great exertions to bring it about: but they differed widely with us as to the means by which it was to be accomplished. For instance, Peter the hermit thought that the only way by which this day was to be ushered in, was by taking the holy land (as it was called) and dispossessing the infidels who then held it, and thereby prepare the way for the coming of the Son of man. And in the greatness of his zeal to accomplish so laudable an object, he went through all Europe proclaiming the coming of the Son of man, and the necessity for all christian kings to arouse, and prepare his way, by rescuing the holy land out of the hands of the barbarians, that the Son of man might come again to his own inheritance.
>
> And such was the effect of his zeal, that all Europe was litterally electrified: the kings were aroused to put their armies into requisition; and army after army marched off into Asia, to redeem the holy land. In history, their armies are known by the name of crusaders. And after much fighting and blood shed, they finally succeeded in getting possession of the holy land; but the Son of man not coming according to their expectations, the land finally rolled back again into the hands of unbelievers, and remains so to this day. . . .
>
> It is the belief in the coming of the Son of man and in the glory which shall follow that is the spur to all the efforts of the

religious communities of the present day. The great exertions which are made to excite revivals of religion, and bring mankind under the dominion of some religious party or other, is in view of the near approach of the latter day glory, and the coming of the Son of man. All the missionary schemes of the age are founded on the belief of it. The attempts which are making to convert the heathen on every continent, and in the islands of the sea, grow out of this belief. The cry of Millenium is heard all over the land, and men are required to use all their exertions to usher in the glory of the last days, by converting the world, as they call it, so that the knowledge of God may cover the earth, as the waters do the sea, and the testimony of the prophets not fail. . . .

It is in relation to these things that the church of the Latter Day Saints has been so shamefully abused and belied, by all these parties both Jews and gentiles, reformers and non-reformers, (not even excepting the pious A. Campbell and old Clapp, his Sanco Panza, and the *will-making* A. Bently, one of his flunkies:) not that they do not believe in the second coming of the Savior, and in the glory that shall follow; but because they differ from all the other parties about the means by which the Savior will prepare the way of his second coming, and what the glory will be which will follow.

The Latter Day Saints believe that Christ will prepare the way of his coming by raising up and inspiring apostles, prophets, evangelists, pastors and teachers, and under their ministry restore again to his saints all the gifts of the church as in days of old.— And the glory which shall follow, will consist in the increase of faith on the earth, by which men shall obtain revelations, visions, the ministering of angels, and the manifestations of the Savior himself; so that the saints shall know that he lives, and shall each one know it for himself, and not for another; and these blessings will gradually multiply and increase, until they will have power to behold the Father of glory; and spiritual gifts through faith will so greatly increase, until every individual saint shall have power to behold the face of God in the flesh, as did Moses and others in days of old, until the prophecy of Isaiah shall be literally fulfilled, that the knowledge of God will cover the earth as the waters do the sea.

The Latter Day Saints further believe that previous to Christ's coming, and at the time of his coming, he will cut off and consign to the perdition of ungodly men, the before mentioned motley gang of professers, and nonprofessers, priests and drunkards, deacons and scoundrels, professers and thieves, as being of their father the devil, and materials suitable for his kingdom, and there

103

will none be able to stand in this great and notable day of the
Lord, except such as have obtained like precious faith with the
apostles, and have power over all things this side the celestial
world; among whom all the spiritual gifts are found that ever
were known among men, and if these gifts never return to the
world, God will come and smite the whole earth with a curse, and
not one will escape.

Such is the faith of the Latter Day Saints, and for this their
belief, earth and hell have combined for their overthrow: the
devil and his emisaries on earth, the priests of all denominations,
have used their utmost exertions, but their exertions have been
vain for the truth prevails exceedingly, far beyond the expectations of any of the saints. . . .

For believing these things, and acting accordingly, the saints
have been made to feel the hand of persecution from this ungodly
generation which is fast ripening for the damnation of hell; for
the saints have began to gather together, in spite of all the lying
priests there are this side the perdition of ungodly men, (and this
is only such as are in the flesh) until they shall all have come from
one end of heaven to the other, and not one left in all nations,
tongues, languages and kindreds, under heaven, and then, and not
till then will Christ come and the glory will follow.

—November 1836, pages 401-404.

CHURCH HISTORY

The earliest attempt to publish an account of the origin of
the church appeared in the *Messenger and Advocate* as a
series of eight letters written by Oliver Cowdery. In some
ways this is a disappointing effort. So many digressions are
indulged in that only small portions of the letters actually
discuss the announced topic. Also, we are informed that the
author intends to give us "a full history of the rise of the
church of the Latter Day Saints, and the most interesting
parts of its progress . . . until the time when the church was
driven from Jackson County Missouri by lawless banditti."
And yet the series is discontinued eight letters later at the
point where Joseph Smith has just married Emma Hale, three
years before the organization of the church.

104

That our narrative may be correct, and particularly the introduction, it is proper to inform our patrons, that our brother J.
SMITH jr. has offered to assist us. Indeed, there are many items
connected with the fore part of this subject that render his labor
indispensible. With his labor and with authentic documents now
in our possession, we hope to render this a pleasing and agreeable
narrative, well worth the examination and perusal of the
Saints. . . . (*Editor's comment*)

Near the time of the setting of the Sun, Sabbath evening, April
5th, 1829, my natural eyes, for the frist time beheld this brother.
He then resided in Harmony, Susquehanna county Penn. On Monday the 6th, I assisted him in arranging some business of a
temporal nature, and on Tuesday the 7th, commenced to write
the book of Mormon. These were days never to be forgotten—to
sit under the sound of a voice dictated by the *inspiration* of
heaven, awakened the utmost gratitude of this bosom!

After writing the account given of the Savior's ministry to the
remnant of the seed of Jacob, upon this continent, it was easily
to be seen, as the prophet said would be, that darkness covered
the earth and gross darkness the minds of the people. On reflecting further, it was as easily to be seen, that amid the great strife
and noise concerning religion, none had authority from God to
administer the ordinances of the gospel. For, the question might
be asked, have men authority to administer in the name of Christ,
who deny revelations? when *his* testimony is no less than the
spirit of prophecy? and his religion based, built, and sustained by
immediate revelations in all ages of the world, when he has had a
people on earth? If these facts were buried, and carefully con-
cealed by men whose craft would have been in danger, if once
permitted to shine in the faces of men, they were no longer to us;
and we only waited for the commandment to be given, "Arise
and be baptized."

This was not long desired before it was realized. The Lord,
who is rich in mercy, and ever willing to answer the consistent
prayer of the humble, after we had called upon him in a fervent
manner, aside from the abodes of men, condescended to manifest
to us his will. On a sudden, as from the midst of eternity, the
voice of the Redeemer spake peace to us, while the vail was
parted and the angel of God came down clothed with glory, and
delivered the anxiously looked for message, and the keys of the
gospel of repentance!—What joy! what wonder! what amazement!
While the world were racked and distracted—while millions were
grouping as the blind for the wall, and while all men were resting

upon uncertainty, as a general mass, our eyes beheld—our ears
heard. As in the "blaze of day;" yes, more—above the glitter of
the May Sun beam, which then shed its brillancy over the face of
nature! Then his voice, though mild, pierced to the center, and
his words, "I am thy fellow servant," dispelled every fear. We
listened—we gazed—we admired! 'Twas the voice of the angel
from glory—'twas a message from the Most High! and as we heard
we rejoiced, while his love enkindled upon our souls, and we were
rapt in the vision of the Almighty! Where was room for doubt?
No where: uncertainty had fled, doubt had sunk, no more to rise,
while fiction and deception had fled forever!

But, dear brother think, further think for a moment, what joy
filled our hearts and with what surprise we must have bowed, (for
who would not have bowed the knee for such a blessing?) when
we received under his hand the holy priesthood, as he said, "upon
you my fellow servants, in the name of Messiah I confer this
priesthood and this authority, which shall remain upon earth,
that the sons of Levi may yet offer an offering unto the Lord in
righteousness!"...
Brother O: Cowdery:

Having learned from the first No. of the Messenger and Advocate, that you were, not only about to "give a history of the
rise and progress of the church of the Latter Day Saints;" but
that said "history would necessarily embrace my life and character," I have been induced to give you the time and place of my
birth; as I have learned that many of the opposers of those
principles which I have held forth to the world, profess a personal
acquaintance with me, though when in my presence, represent me
to be another person in age, education, and stature, from what I
am.

I was born, (according to the record of the same, kept by my
parents,) in the town of Sharon, Windsor Co. Vt. on the 23rd of
December, 1805.

At the age of ten my father's family removed to Palmyra, N.
Y. where, and in the vicinity of which, I lived, or made it my
place of residence, until I was twenty one—the latter part, in the
town of Manchester.

During this time as is common to most, or all youths, I fell
into many vices and follies: but as my accusers are, and have been
forward to accuse me of being guilty of gross and outragious
violations of the peace and good order of the community, I take
the occasion to remark that, though, as I have said above, "as is
common to most, or all youths, I fell into many vices and fol-

Oliver Cowdery, editor

Joseph Smith reading the Bible

lies," I have not, neither can it be sustained, in truth, been guilty of wronging or injuring any man or society of men; and those imperfections to which I alude, and for which I have often had occasion to lament, were a light, and too often, vain mind, exhibiting a foolish and trifling conversation. . . .

By giving the above a place in your valuable paper, you will confer a lasting favor upon myself, as an individual, and as I humbly hope, subserve the cause of righteousness.

I am, with feelings of esteem, your fellow laborer in the gospel of our Lord. . . .

JOSEPH SMITH jr.

You will recollect that I informed you, in my letter published in the first No. of the Messenger and Advocate, that this history would necessarily embrace the life and character of our esteemed friend and brother, J. SMITH JR. one of the presidents of this church, and for information on that part of the subject, I refer you to his communication of the same, published in this paper. I shall, therefore, pass over that, till I come to the 15th year of his life.

It is necessary to premise this account by relating the situation of the public mind relative to religion, at this time: One Mr. Lane, a presiding Elder of the Methodist church, visited Palmyra, and vicinity. Elder Lane was a tallented man possessing a good share of literary endowments, and apparent humility. There was a great awakening, or excitement raised on the subject of religion, and much enquiry for the word of life. Large additions were made to the Methodist, Presbyterian, and Baptist churches.—Mr. Lane's manner of communication was peculiarly calculated to awaken the intellect of the hearer, and arouse the sinner to look about him for safety—much good instruction was always drawn from his discourses on the scriptures, and in common with others, our brother's mind became awakened.

For a length of time the reformation seemed to move in a harmonious manner, but, as the *excitement* ceased, or those who had expressed anxieties, had professed a belief in the pardoning influence and condescension of the Savior, a general struggle was made by the leading characters of the different sects, for pros-eyltes. Then strife seemed to take the place of that apparent union and harmony which had previously characterized the moves and exhortations of the old professors, and a cry—I am right—you are wrong—was introduced in their stead.

In this general strife for followers, his mother, one sister, and two of his natural brothers, were persuaded to unite with the Presbyterians. . . .

In this situation where could he go? If he went to one he was told they were right, and all others were wrong—If to another, the same was heard from those: All professed to be the true church; and if not they were certainly hypocritical, because, if I am presented with a system of religion, and enquire of my teacher whether it is correct, and he informs me that he is not certain, he acknowledges at once that he is teaching without authority, and acting without a commission! . . .

You will recollect that I mentioned the time of a religious excitement, in Palmyra and vicinity to have been in the 15th year of our brother J. Smith Jr's, age—that was an error in the type—it should have been in the 17th.—You will please remember this correction, as it will be necessary for the full understanding of what will follow in time. This would bring the date down to the year 1823. . . .

But if others were not benefited, our brother was urged forward and strengthened in the determination to know for himself of the certainty and reality of pure and holy religion.—And it is only necessary for me to say, that while this excitement continued, he continued to call upon the Lord in secret for a full manifestation of divine approbation, and for, to him, the all important information, if a Supreme being did exist, to have an assurance that he was accepted of him. . . .

On the evening of the 21st of September, 1823, previous to retiring to rest, our brother's mind was unusually wrought up on the subject which had so long agitated his mind—his heart was drawn out in fervent prayer, and his whole soul was so lost to every thing of a temporal nature, that earth, to him, had lost its claims, and all he desired was to be prepared in heart to commune with some kind messenger who could communicate to him the desired information of his acceptance with God.

At length the family retired, and he, as usual, bent his way, though in silence, where others might have rested their weary frames "locked fast in sleep's embrace;" but repose had fled, and accustomed slumber had spread her refreshing hand over others beside him—he continued still to pray—his heart though once hard and obdurate, was softened, and that mind which had often fitted, like the "wild bird of passage," had settled upon a determined basis not to be decoyed or driven from its purpose.

In this situation hours passed unnumbered—how many or how few I know not, neither is he able to inform me; but supposes it must have been eleven or twelve, and perhaps later, as the noise and bustle of the family, in retiring, had long since ceased.—While continuing in prayer for a manifestation in some way that his sins were forgiven; endeavoring to exercise faith in the scriptures, on a sudden a light like that of day, only of a purer and far more glorious appearance and brightness, burst into the room—Indeed, to use his own description, the first sight was as though the house was filled with consuming and unquenchable fire. This sudden appearance of a light so bright, as must naturally be expected, occasioned a shock or sensation, visible to the extremities of the body. It was, however, followed with a calmness and serenity of mind, and an overwhelming rapture of joy that surpassed understanding, and in a moment a personage stood before him. . . .The stature of this personage was a little above the common size of men in this age; his garment was perfectly white, and had the appearance of being without seam.

Though fear was banished from his heart, yet his surprise was no less when he heard him declare himself to be a messenger sent by a commandment of the Lord, to deliver a special message, and to witness to him that his sins were forgiven, and that his prayers were heard; and that the scriptures might be fulfilled, which say—"God has chosen the foolish things of the world to confound the things which are mighty. . . .

"This cannot be brought about until first certain preparatory things are accomplished, for so has the Lord purposed in his own mind. He has therefore, chosen you as an instrument in his hand to bring to light that which shall perform his acts, his strange act, and bring to pass a marvelous work and a wonder. Wherever the sound shall go it shall cause the ears of men to tingle, and wherever it shall be proclaimed, the pure in heart shall rejoice, while those who draw near to God with their mouths, and honor him with their lips, while their hearts are far from him, will seek its overthrow, and the destruction of those by whose hands it is carried. Therefore, marvel not if your name is made a derision, and had as a by-word among such, if you are the instrument in bringing it, by the gift of God, to the knowledge of the people."

He then proceeded and gave a general account of the promises made to the fathers, and also gave a history of the aborigines of this country, and said they were literal descendants of Abraham. He represented them as once being an enlightened and intelligent people, possessing a correct knowledge of the gospel, and the plan of restoration and redemption. He said this history was written and deposited not far from that place, and that it was our brother's privilege, if obedient to the commandments of the Lord, to obtain, and translate the same by the means of the Urim and Thummim, which were deposited for that purpose with the record. . . .

While describing the place where the record was deposited, he gave a minute relation of it, and the vision of his mind being opened at the same time, he was permitted to view it critically; and previously being acquainted with the place, he was able to follow the direction of the vision, afterward, according to the voice of the angel, and obtain the book. . . .

Far from this; for the vision was renewed twice before morning, unfolding farther and still farther the mysteries of godliness and those things to come. In the morning he went to his labor as usual, but soon the vision of the heavenly messenger was renewed, instructing him to go immediately and view those things of which he had been informed, with a promise that he should obtain them if he followed the directions and went with an eye single to the glory of God.

Accordingly he repaired to the place which had thus been described. . . .

After arriving at the repository, a little exertion in removing the soil from the edges of the top of the box, and a light pry, brought to his natural vision its contents. No sooner did he behold this sacred treasure than his hopes were renewed, and he supposed his success certain; and without first attempting to take it from its long place of deposit, he thought, perhaps, there might be something more equally as valuable, and to take only the plates, might give others an opportinity of obtaining the remainder, which could be secure, would still add to his store of wealth. These, in short, were his reflections, without once thinking of the solemn instruction of the heavenly messenger, that all must be done with an express view of glorifying God.

On attempting to take possession of the record a shock was produced upon his system, by an invisible power, which deprived him, in a measure, of his natural strength. He desisted for an instant, and then made another attempt, but was more sensibly shocked than before. What was the occasion of this he knew not—*there* was the pure unsullied record, as had been described—he had heard of the power of enchantment, and a thousand like stories, which held the hidden treasures of the earth, and supposed that physical exertion and personal strength was only necessary to enable him to yet obtain the object of his wish. He therefore made the third attempt with an increased exertion, when his strength failed him more than at either of the former times, and without premeditating he exclaimed, "Why can I not

112

obtain this book?" "Because you have not kept the commandments of the Lord," answered a voice, within a seeming short distance. He looked, and to his astonishment, there stood the angel who had previously given him the directions concerning this matter. . . .

At that instant he looked to the Lord in prayer, and as he prayed darkness began to disperse from his mind and his soul was lit up as it was the evening before, and he was filled with the Holy Spirit; and again did the Lord manifest his condescension and mercy: the heavens were opened and the glory of the Lord shone round about and rested upon him. While he thus stood gazing and admiring, the angel said, "Look!" and as he thus spake he beheld the prince of darkness, surrounded by his innumerable train of associates. All this passed before him, and the heavenly messenger said, "All this is shown, the good and the evil, the holy and impure, the glory of God and the power of darkness, that you may know hereafter the two powers and never be influenced or overcome by that wicked one. Behold, whatever entices and leads to good and to do good, is of God, and whatever does not is of that wicked one. . . .

From this time to September, 1827, few occurences worthy of note, transpired. As a fact to be expected, nothing of importance could be recorded concerning a generation in darkness.—In the mean time our brother of whom I have been speaking, passed the time as others, in laboring for his support. But in consequence of certain false and slanderous reports which have been circulated, justice would require me to say something upon the private life of one whose character has been so shamefully traduced. By some he is said to have been a lazy, idle, vicious, profligate fellow. These I am prepared to contradict, and that too by the testimony of *many* persons with whom I have been intimately acquainted, and know to be individuals of the strictest veracity, and unquestionable integrity. All these strictly and virtually agree in saying, that he was an honest, upright, virtuous, and faithfully industrious young man. And those who say to the contrary can be influenced by no other motive than to destroy the reputation of one who never injured any man in either property or person. . . .

Soon after this visit to Cumorah, a gentleman from the south part of the State, (Chenango County,) employed our brother as a common laborer, and accordingly he visited that section of the country; and had he not been accused of digging down all, or nearly so, the mountains of Susquehannah, or causing others to do it by some art of nicromancy, I should leave this, for the present, unnoticed. You will remember, in the mean time, that those who seek to vilify his character, say that he has always been notorious for his idleness. This gentlemean, whose name is Stowel, resided in the town of Bainbridge, on or near the head waters of the Susquehannah river. Some forty miles south, or down the river, in the town of Harmony, Susquehannah county, Pa. is said to be a cave or subterraneous recess, whether entirely formed by art or not I am unimformed, neither does this matter; but such is said to be the case,—where a company of Spaniards, a long time since, when the country was uninhabited by white settlers, excavated from the bowels of the earth ore, and coined a large quantity of money; after which they secured the cavity and evacuated, leaving a part still in the cave, purposing to return at some distant period. . . .Enough however, was credited of the Spaniard's story, to excite the belief of many that there was a fine sum of the precious metal lying coined in this subterraneous vault, among whom was our employer; and accordingly our brother was required to spend a few months with some others in excavating the earth, in pursuit of this treasure.

While employed here he became acquainted with the family of Isaac Hale, of whom you read in several of the productions of those who have sought to destroy the validity of the book of Mormon. It may be necessary hereafter, to refer you more particularly to the conduct of this family, as their influence has been considerably exerted to destroy the reputation of our brother, probably because he married a daughter of the same, contrary to some of their wishes, and in connection with this, to certain statements of some others of the inhabitants of that section of country. But in saying this I do not wish to be understood as uttering aught against Mrs. Smith, (formerly Emma Hale.) She has most certainly evidenced a decidedly correct mind and uncommon ability of talent and judgment, in a manifest willingness to fulfill, on her part, that passage in sacred writ,—"and they twain shall be one flesh."—by accompanying her husband, against the wishes and advice of her relatives, to a land of strangers: and however I may deprecate their actions, can say in justice, *her* character stands as fair for morality, piety and virtue, as any in the world. . . .The translator of the book of Mormon is worthy the appellation of a seer and a prophet of the Lord. In this I do not pretend that he is not a man subject to passion like other men, beset with infirmities and encompassed with weaknesses; but if he is, all men were so before him, and a pretence to the contrary would argue a more than mortal, which would at once destroy the whole system of the religion of the Lord Jesus; for he

anciently chose the weak to overcome the strong, the foolish to
confound the wise, (I mean considered so by this world,) and by
the foolishness of preaching to save those who believe.

On the private character of our brother I need add nothing
further, at present, previous to his obtaining the records of the
Nephites, only that while in that country, some very officious
person complained of him as a disorderly person, and brought
him before the authorities of the county; but there being no
cause of action he was honorably acquited. From this time forward he continued to receive instructions concerning the coming
forth of the fulness of the gospel, from the mouth of the heavenly messenger, until he was directed to visit again the place where
the records was deposited.

REPORTS FROM MISSOURI

The failure of the first Latter Day Saint colony in Independence disturbed many church members who found themselves wondering how God's plan for his people could be so
easily thwarted. It was a common assumption, then, that the
exile from Jackson County must be only a brief one, and that
the Saints would soon return to Independence from the
counties to the north to reclaim their inheritance. The whole
church eagerly sought any news from the Missouri Saints. W.
W. Phelps wrote several letters from Liberty, Missouri, but,
other than giving a description of the land and the Indians of
that region, he occupied himself primarily with doctrinal
discourses on a variety of topics. In the following excerpts we
gain some insight into life on the Missouri plains in 1834.

To begin my subject—I shall give a few sketches of the country
often called the Upper Missouri; situated in the borders of the
vast prairies of the Great West. Very little difference is percep-
tible, in the upper counties of Missouri, in soil, productions, settlements, or society. If there be an exception, it must be in the
position and soil of Jackson. The appearance, soil and productions of Lafayette, Saline, Van Buren, Ray, Clinton, and Clay
counties, are so near alike, that I can only say there may be a
preference, but no difference. These counties, in general have a
tolerable rich soil, composed of clay, fine sand, and black mold,

115

especially upon the prairies. The cultivated produce consists chiefly of small quantities of wheat, large quantities of corn, some oats, hemp, cattle, horses, a few sheep, hogs, in scores, and a variety of vegitables, but not to any extent.—Sweet potatoes, cotton, tobacco, and perhaps other plants, grow, in fair seasons, very well.

The face of the country is somewhat rolling, though not hilly, and, owing to the great deapth of soil, the branches, or brooks, are worked out and present ugly ravines from ten to fifty feet deep; one of the great causes why the Missouri is ever rily. Every rain starts the mud. . . .

The climate is mild and delightful nearly three quarters of the year; and, being situated about an equal distance from the Atlantic and Pacific oceans, as well as from the Allegany and Rocky mountains, in near 39 degrees of north latitude, and between 16 and 17 degrees of west longitude, it certainly affords the pleasing hope of becoming as good a spot as there will be on the globe, when the wolf shall lie down with the lamb. The coldest weather comes in December and January, with, hardly ever two day's sleighing: so that sleighs and bells are among the unmentionables of this great center of North America.—February is not unfrequently a mild month, and March so much so, that potatoes planted the latter part of it, are sometimes digable the last of May. April though it has some frost, is the opening season for business, for gardens, for corn, and, in fact, for every thing for summer crops, if you wish a good yield. The spring is often wet, and the summer warm and dry. The fall beautiful. As the October frosts change the green strenght of summer into golden age, the Indians begin their fall hunt, and fire the prairies, till the western world becomes so full of smoke, that, as it eventually spreads by the fall winds, for all I know, it makes the "smoky days," or "Indian summer," throughout the continent.

The wild game is an important link to the living of many in the west. In the inhabited sections, however, it grows "less plenty;" and where the hunter could once drop the huge buffalo, the surly bear, the stately elk, the sly beaver, and the proud swan, he can now find difficulty in bringing down the deer, the wolf, the fox, the turkey, the goose, the brandt, the duck, &c. while the squirrels, rabbits, raccoons, and many other small animals sport as they please. . . .

Among the serpents, the rattle snake, and the copper head are the worst, though not very plenty. That bird, whose image, if not worshipped, has more adorers in this nation than the Lord of

116

glory, for it stands alike in the gold eagle, and silver dollar, and pearches as gracefully on the soldier's cap, as on the officer's hat, and appears larger upon the sign of a tavern, than upon the seal of the United States,—I mean the *American Eagle* is a commoner among the great ones of the west.

—November 1834, pages 22, 23.

Notwithstanding, this great country may be ranked as a part of the realm of the United States, yet, the title to the land, is held by the Indians that hunt upon it; or, at least, the most of it, is theirs; and as the general government, has already commenced gathering and settling the various tribes upon the south-eastern limits of this grand region, I shall be justified on that point, and because we have the word of the Lord, that these Indians are a remnant of the seed of Joseph, I certainly shall write truth, on another point, when I call it THE LAND OF ISRAEL. Time will tell whether the United States will be so humane as to gather all the wandering tribes of the forest, and extinguish their title to such lands as they do not want. If the government should succeed in its philanthropic operation to ameliorate the condition of the Indians, and honorably purchase much of their land; if the Lord should permit timber to grow upon the prairies, like corn stalks upon the cultivated fields, so that towns and cities might speckle the west as they now do the east, still, when "Jacob takes root," according to the prediction of Isaiah, "and blossoms and buds and fills the face of the world with fruit," this country will then be *The Land of Israel.*

I should do injustice to the subject, were I to omit a notice of the Indians that inhabit the territory, of which I am writing. When I was at the garrison, I saw a noble looking, portly Indian, dressed and harnessed in fine style for hunting, and for the life of me, I could not help composing the following lines for

THE RED MAN.

O stop and tell me, Red Man,
    Who are ye? why you roam?
And how you get your living?
    Have you no God,—no home?

With stature straight and portly,
    And decked in native pride,
With feathers, paints, and broaches,
    He willingly replied:—

"I once was *pleasant Ephraim,*
        "When Jacob for me pray'd;
"But oh! how blessings vanish,
        "When man from God has stray'd!

"Before your nation knew us,
        "Some thousand moons ago,
"Our fathers fell in darkness,
        "And wander'd to and fro.

"And long they've liv'd by hunting,
        "Instead of work and arts,
"And so our race has dwindled
        "To idle Indian hearts.

"Yet hope within us lingers,
        "As if the Spirit spoke:—
'He'll come for your redemption,
        'And break your Gentile yoke:

'And all your captive brothers,
        'From every clime shall come,
'And quit their savage customs,
        'To live with God at home.'

"Then joy will fill our bosoms,
        "And blessings crown our days,
"To live in pure religion,
        "And sing our Maker's praise."

Now, to my story again. Besides the Delawares, Shawnees, Kickapoos, Wyandots, Pottowattomies, Senecas, Osages, Choctaws, Cherokees, Kaskaskies, Kansas, &c. &c. which our nation and the missionaries are domesticating as they are gathered, upon the southern limits of the land of Israel, the Pawnees, the Sioux, the Rickarees, the Mandans, the Nespersces, the Blackfeet, the Sacs, the Foxes, and many other tribes, rove and hunt from prairie to prairie, from river to river, from hill to hill, and from mountain to mountain, and live, and are blessed before the face of heaven daily as well as their cotemporary whites; and, perhaps I may add, are as justifiable before God, as any people on the globe, called *heathens.* No church bell from its elevated steeple, rings "Go to meeting; it is Sunday," while a dozen lesser ones, for stages and Steam boats, peal a ding-dong "for parties of pleasure, as a holiday," among these rude sons of the west.—And it is a difficult matter to make one soul of them believe the Great Spirit ever said, *"Remember the Sabbath day to keep it holy,"* while they know, that the majority of the white nation, use it for a holiday. No politicians boast of freedom and equal rights, while thousands are imprisoned for debt, or are in bondage: No; when the tribes are at peace, the Indian is free; his land is free; his game is free; his time is free, and all is free.

—December 1834, pages 33-34.

After maintaining a long silence concerning the situation in Missouri, the August 1836 issue devotes over half its space to an extensive report of a new set of problems there, as evident in the following excerpts.

We have recently perused with intense interest and deep feeling, the report of a committee of vigilance appointed on the seventh of May last at a meeting of the citizens of Jackson county, Missouri, relative to the course they recommend to their constituents to be pursued towards our brethren, in case they attempt to come into that county to form a settlement, or to possess their own property.

It will be recollected that our brethren went into that county, purchased land, formed a settlement, established a printing press and a store of Merchant goods, and were proceeding peaceably and quietly in the lawful enjoyment of their rights as citizens of these United States. It will also be recollected that they were forcibly driven from their purchased possessions by a ruthless mob in the inclement season of the year, November, 1833, and left without any covering but the open canopy of heaven. It will also be borne in mind, that many of their dwellings were thrown down—much, and in some instances all their property destroyed; and they driven from the county to perish with cold or famine, or to seek relief as mendicants among the hospitable of the county of Clay.—These acts, though thrilling to the heart of the philanthropist, and black as the character of their projectors are, light in comparison with the sable shade that yet remains to fill up the interstices of the great outline, and complete the picture! Yes, reader, they proceeded further. They not only destroyed property, and drove off peaceable citizens from their own dwellings, but they threatened life! Aye would to heaven they had done no more!— They unmercifully beat some, and deliberately killed others! (a few only.) . . .

119

We have read a copy of their manifesto, and it is not even there asserted, though teeming with falsehoods as black as the hearts of their fabricators or the father of lies himself, that they had either law or constitution to warrant them in their hellish procedure. What then, you will ask, was the cause? We say simply because our brethren took the liberty guaranteed to all citizens of these United States to think differently from the professing christian world in matters of religion. This was not avowed as the cause in their manifesto, because it was matter of fact, and with this they had but little to do. But that it was the *real* cause you will believe when we say that when six of our brethren were in the hands of this lawless banditti, as a condition of peace and friendship offered them, they must renounce their religious belief, and all would be well.—This they peremptorily refused. The only alternatives they had then left, were death, immediate death, or leave the county. . . .

If our brethren had been guilty of some offence or misdemeanor, prejudicial to the feelings or best interests of their supercilious neighbors, what should be done? The case is a plain one: if it were a breach of the law, the law was open and as said one anciently, there were deputies let them implead one another; and as we have before said, the law, the officers and the power were in the hands of our enemies.

Has the liberty of speech, the liberty of the press, the liberty of conscience, become odious to this religious generation? Is the foundation of all liberty, civil and religious to be sapped and the beautiful superstructure erected thereon by our fathers to be razed to the ground to gratify whom? the whole community beside our brethren? no, a lawless, ruthless, perjured banditti and their accomplices in bigotry, guilt and crime. These same monsters in human shape not content with the blood of a part of our brethren and with inflicting one vital stab to the constitution and laws of our country, seem eager to reek their hands in the heart's blood of the remainder, and end their satanic career only with their final extermination. They have said they would not stop while a single Mormon's foot pressed their soil. Have our brethren attempted to drive them from their houses or their lands? have they attempted to urge their claim to any except that to which they had been seized by honest right of fair purchase? We fearlessly say no. . . .May the Lord deliver us from the power of such men and the malevolent influence of their religion.

We say further, that all such as are the aidors, abettors or apologists for such conduct or such characters as have signed the

120

first or last manifesto of the Jackson county *mob,* are participators in their guilt and crime.

—August 1836, pages 361-364.

In his December 1836 editorial, "The Closing Year,"
Oliver Cowdery makes a report referring to the new settlement at Far West.

The affairs of the church in the west have been very distressing: Men, women and children, have been so much and so long
exposed to the inclemency of the weather, that sickness, with a
number of deaths, have followed. Our enemies here, and the
enemies of truth, righteousness and justice, have acted their part
in this tragedy. From time to time has the country, where our
brethren have lived, been flooded with false statements concerning *our* situation and acts; and the people of the west, not suspecting the design, have been thrown into commotion, and ready
to believe it their duty to raise the oppressing hand of persecution, and drive our friends from the face of society. And even
during the past summer, our friends were obliged to forego some
of the most sacred rights guaranteed in the constitution and laws
of our country; to save the effusion of blood. . . .
We are happy to have it in our power to say, now, that from
the last accounts, health was restoring to that afflicted people.
They have made purchases in a new place, and many families are
already prepared for the winter: in all probability, they have
made such an arrangement, and have cultivated that friendly
understanding with their neighbors, that they will now be permitted to gather by themselves and form a community of their
own. This we are willing for, and would rather choose than they
should live in the midst of confusion and war; but we regret that
men are so destitute of righteous principles that they will vilify
the innocent, and cause strangers to become alarmed for their
own safety so much as to wish our friends from among them.

—December 1836, page 427.

An optimistic report is issued the following month:

From information, both written and oral, we feel warranted in
saying that our brethren in the far West, who have so long been
afflicted and driven without a peaceable dwelling place, are now

121

permitted to live quietly as other citizens: We hope they are grateful to God for all the benefits he bestows upon them or permits them to enjoy.—We also hope, they have that self respect, which will commend them to the favor and respect of all worthy citizens, and evince to intelligent men that the blessings of peace and the peaceable privileges of citizenship, are not received by them as a boon from their neighbors, but as a constitutional right. A salubrious climate, good water, cheap land, and a fertile soil, are among the inducements to the husbandman to emigrate to that delightful country.

—January 1837, page 447.

A short announcement of peaceful and prosperous conditions at Far West appears in the June 1837 issue:

For the information of our brethren generally we say, from the latest intelligence we have received; that our brethren are fast settling in a new county set off from the North part of Ray, that they have 2 county Judges 14 justices of the peace and one Post Master appointed from among their number. They have appointed a building committee and are making their arrangement to build a house of worship. Subscriptions are collecting for the building. Their county is called Caldwell, and their city or centre and the name of their Post Office are called "Far West." It is said to be fertile, with a salubrious climate and that the brethren are rapidly gathering in from all parts of the country. Our brethren and the Missourians are at peace for ought we know. Indeed we hope better things than to hear of any disturbance, since they settled in their present location by the mutual consent of a committee, representing some of the people of Clay County, and a majority of our brethren in the same place.

—June 1837, page 519.

A letter from W. W. Phelps tells of the beginning phase of temple building at Far West. A few indications of the trouble to come are given as well.

Far West. May 7, 1837.

Dear Brother in the Lord,

Permit me to drop you a few lines to show you our progress temporally and spiritually. A multiplicity of business has prevented me from writing much the year past, but the greatness of our doings and the importance of the occasion require a recital to you for your consolation.—Monday the 3rd of July, was a great and glorious day in Far West; more than fifteen hundred saints assembled in this place, and, at ½ past 8 in the morning, after a prayer, singing, and an address, proceeded to break the ground for the Lord's House; the day was beautiful, the Spirit of the Lord was with us, a cellar for this great edifice, 110 long by 80 broad was nearly finished: on Tuesday the fourth, we had a large meeting and several of the Missourians were baptized: Our meetings, held in the open prairie, or, in fact larger than they were in Kirtland when I was there. We have more or less to bless, confirm and, baptize every Sabath.

This same day our school section was sold at auction, and although entirely a prairie, it brought, on a years credit, from 3 ½ to $10,20 an acre, making our first school fund $5070!! Land can not be had round town now much less than $10 per acre.

Our numbers increase daily, and, notwithstanding the season has been cold and backward, no one has lacked a meal, or went hungry. Provisions to be sure have risen, but not as high as our accounts say they are abroad.

Public notice has been given by the *mob* in Davis county, north of us, for the Mormons to leave that county by the first of August, and go into Caldwell. Our enemies will not slumber, till Satan knows the bigness of his lot.

Our town gains some, we have about one hundred buildings, 8 of which are stores. If the brethren abroad are wise, and will come on with means, and help enter the land and populate the Co. and build the Lord's House, we shall soon have one of the most precious spots on the Globe. God grant that it may be so. Of late we receive but little news from you: and we think much of that is exaggerated.

As ever,

W. W. PHELPS.

N. B. Please say in your Messenger: "A Post office has been established at *Far West,* Caldwell County, Missouri. Our brethren will now have a chance to write to their friends."

—July 1837, page 529.

MISSION REPORTS

If the *Star* had difficulty securing missionary reports, the *Messenger and Advocate* certainly did not. Out of a large bulk of information sent in by correspondents in the mission field, the following are selected as fairly representative of the labors of those expending themselves to spread the message of the Restoration.

I left Clay co. Mo. the last of Aug. Since that time I have preached to many congregations, mostly in villages; however I have baptized but few—I was unable to travel and preach for several weeks last fall in consequence of sickness.

I baptized three at Sugar Creek Ia.—the church in that place numbers nineteen. Two in the village of Terrehaut Ia. and seven in Campbell co. Kentucky, eight miles from Cincinnati: the church in that place now numbers eighteen.

Give my respects to all enquiring brethren and especially to my aged parents if they are living in that place.

I remain your brother

in the gospel.
O. PRATT

P. S. *March* 4th.

Since writing the above we have preached three times in Cincinnati, three times in Fulton, and three times in the village of Commingsville, 6 miles from the city. We have had large congregations and many are astonished at the doctrine—some believe, many disbelieve, and others obey.—We have this day baptized two who reside in Cincinnati.

There are now 22 or 23 members of this church in Fulton and Cincinnati. We expect to leave this place soon for the village of Batavia about 20 miles distant.

Brother Barns and myself preached twice in the court house at Brookville, Indiana—we were kindly received by the people of that village, and were solicited to tarry longer, but we could not conveniently: it was the first time the people in that place had heard concerning the principles of our faith, and it was somewhat marvellous to them, perhaps rendered more so in consequence of a short debate which lasted about three or four hours, principally upon the second coming of Christ.

The debate of which I speak was between myself and a preacher of the Universalist order (Mr. St. Johns,) the people were very well satisfied and were desirous to know more concerning the doctrine.

—March 1835, pages 89-90.

Huntsburgh, O. April 16th, 1835.
Bro. O. Cowdry,—

Having just returned from a most interesting meeting, where baptizing was attended to, and while the curtains of night are drawn around me and I am seated in the friendly family circle with some beloved brethren, although it is snowing quite fast and is very cold, especially considering the season of the year, while musing and meditating on the past, a thought suggested itself, that, probably, a few lines from me would not be uninteresting to the readers of your most *valuable* paper.—During last summer and fall elders Joel Johnson and Oliver Granger visited this neighborhood and preached a number of times. They baptized none in this town, but elder J. preached also, in the town north of this and baptized three or four.

I first visited this place in December last, and stayed one week, during which I preached sometimes, twice a day, and the truth took hold on the hearts of many, and six of the number came out and declared it openly by obedience. Since that time I have occasionly been here and declared to them the things which I most assuredly believee, and I always found that there were some who were honest in heart and ready to obey the truth.—The church or the number of *saints* here at present is twenty seven, and there are a number more believing and others seriously inquiring. May the Lord grant great prosperity to the cause of truth.

On the 21st of March I attended an appointment at the center of this town, in the midst of a society commonly called Campbellites, and the truth comeing so near them it roused up thos whose craft was in danger, and I received a challenge to hold a public discussion with a Mr. J. M. Tracy, who, in his note to me, pledged himself to prove that "the book of Mormon was not a divine revelation." I have been informed that Mr. T. was formerly a Universalist preacher, but becoming tired of their principles or society, I know not which, latterly some of the Campbellites in Huntsburgh have hired him to preach for them. I accepted his offer, and on the 27th of March we met and the debate continued two days, about eight hours each, the parties speaking alternately thirty minutes. When the interview closed a majority of the con-

125

gregation arose, by an anxious urgency on the part of Mr. T. to testify thereby that they did not believe in the divinity of the book of Mormon. But when I asked them if they had been convinced that it was false by Mr. Tracy's arguments, (if I might call them such,) there was not one to answer—"Yes."

Whether good has resulted from that discusion can only be known by the effects produced. As soon as the debate closed I went immediately to the water and baptized two—it being Saturday. On Sunday President J.—Smith Jr. delivered a discourse in the same house of about three hour's length, and on Monday morning four more came forward and, "were buried with Christ by baptism;" and were confirmed by the laying on of hands, in order that, "they might put off the old man with his deeds and arise and walk in newness of life."

Since I have been here this time, more have been received into the church. Thus you see that *truth is powerful and will prevail.*
—April 1835, page 102.

Elder W. Parish writes: Kirtland, Aug. 13, 1835. "Dear Brother in Christ:—I am happy to inform you, that through the blessing of God, I have returned from my mission in the South, in company with Seth Utley, a visiting brother from the church in West Tenn. and in the enjoyment of common health. The Lord in his goodness has smiled upon us and crowned our labors beyond our anticipation.—On the 23rd of July last, after delivering a lecture on the subject of the gospel, to a large and respectable congregation, assembled on the banks of the Tennessee River, I opened the door for baptism and received one member: I then took the parting hand with my brethren and sisters, (who were overwhelmed in tears,) commending them to God in the name of Jesus Christ.—The church in that vicinity consists of 86 members, organized into six branches which I left under the superintendance of Elder W. Woodruff. Brother D. W. Patten and myself, I believe, were the first that opened the gospe kingdom in the western district of Tennessee, in the month of October last; the adversary and his votaries were immediately disturbed; the heathen raged, and the people imagined many vain things; but the honest in heart have, and will believe, and obey; and mighty truth will triumph, and roll on until Christ's kingdom becomes universal. I expect when God calls upon the South to give up, that many will come with songs of everlasting joy to rejoice with me, and all the saints in the kingdom of our heavenly Father. Even so let it be. Amen."
—August 1835, pages 167-168.

126

Kirtland, Sept. 17, 1835.

After a short illness, of which I am recovering, I would inform you, that since I wrote from Green county, Ia. I have labored about six weeks in that place, for the good of my fellow men. When I came to Eel River church in said county, I found a small band of Latter Day Saints, say ten in number, somewhat weak in the faith. There had been once a large church here, but the greater part of the members had removed to Missouri; so that the remaining few were like sheep without a shepherd. During my short stay here I baptized 18, and ordained one teacher. The brethren desire if any travelling elder passes that way he would call and tarry a season. I have been engaged in my mission, since I left home last fall, nearly ten months.

G. M. HINKEL.
—September 1835, page 186.

Kirtland, May 26, 1836.

Dear brother Cowdery:

Sir, having just returned from a short mission in Upper Canada, I take the liberty of addressing a few lines to you for insertion in the Messenger and Advocate, praying that it may be edifying to the readers of that useful and interesting paper.

I left Kirtland April 5th, in company with elders, O. Pratt and F. Nickerson; and after a long and tedious journey, through mud and rain, we arrived in Upper Canada, where I took leave of the other two brethren, and persued my course for Toronto, the capital of the Province, at which place I arrived on the 19th of April. I sought in vain for a chapel, court-house or other public building, in which to preach, all being closed against me.—At length one or two private dwellings were opened freely, where I commenced, and continued preaching, until it was no longer practicable for want of sufficient room to accommodate the multitude, when I commenced preaching on the steps of a private dwelling: two rooms of the house were first filled, and then a large door-yard. This place was situated in the midst of the city so that many thousands could hear. I continued several sabbath days to hold forth the word of life to multitudes. I also continued preaching both in the city and country daily: In the country, we were under the necessity of opening large barns in order to accommodate the people. Many who were greatly rejoiced at first, soon began to search for truth with all diligence, by night and day, insomuch that sleep departed for a season from our eyes, and sometimes, daylight dawned in the East before we retired to

127

rest. Our meetings were sometimes disturbed by Rev. gentlemen
of the clergy; among them was the Rev. Mr. Evens, Editor of the
Christian Guardian, and others who attended with a design to
prove the Book of Mormon an imposition and myself an imposter. I refused to hear them at ten, or eleven o'clock at night, in
a crowded private dwelling, without order or moderators; but I
offered to meet any, or all of them on fair grounds, if they would
open any public building, appoint moderators to keep order and
give me half of the time, I pledged myself under these circumstances, to sustain the Book of Mormon with all the evidence
they could the Bible, but they very prudently refused. . . . At 4
o'clock P.M. a multitude assembled a the barn, I then replied
publicly to the Rev. gentlemen's arguments of the preceding evening. After I closed my discourse, we went to the water and I
baptized nine persons, who, apparently, came with contrite
spirits, believing with all their hearts; expressing a full determination to serve the Lord to the end.—The next day being Sunday,
May 22d, the numbers of those who had been baptized having
increased to twenty five, and brethren O. Pratt and F. Nickerson
being present and assisting, we laid our hands upon them and
confirmed them in the name of the Lord Jesus, for the gift of the
Holy Ghost. In the ordinances of the day, we were blessed with
joy and peace and with the powers of the Holy Ghost. Thus grew
the word of God and prevailed mightily. May the Lord bless them
and add to their numbers, daily, such as shall be saved.

Yours in the bonds of the everlasting covenant.
To the Editor of the   }
Messenger & advocate.} P. P. Pratt.

—May 1836, pages 318-320.

The venerable Patriarch of our church Joseph Smith. sen. and
Elder John Smith set out on a mission from this place, May 10th,
to visit some of the branches of the church south of this, to
regulate them and set in order the things that were wanting; they
returned again on the 18th, being absent but eight days, during
which time they either baptized, or witnessed the baptism of 16,
and 95 received their patriarchal blessing. Although their stay was
necessarily short, yet the Lord of the harvest appeared to crown
their labors with abundant success, and a number, from a thorough conviction of the error of their former ways, followed them
home and were baptized in this place, on the next Sabbath after
their return. Thus we see, that when men, (and they are but men)
go forth clothed with authority from on high, and the ancient

order of things is being established according to the word of God, the honest in heart see it, and know it, and prejudice and error give way before the light of truth and reason. While we are penning this article, these aged fathers are about to set out on a mission to the East. We most devoutly pray the Lord to be with them and bless them. We also entreat our brethren in the Eastern churches to receive them cordially, entertain them hospitably, and above all, to appreciate their instructions. The Lord, for his Son's sake preserve them in health and strength and return them to the bosom of their families and the church in this place in peace.

—June 1836, page 331.

Kirtland, Nov. 26, 1836.
President O. Cowdery, Dear brother,

Perhaps it would not be altogether uninteresting to our friends abroad, to give them a brief sketch of my travels in the ministry, and travels since I left Kirtland, in May, 1834; at which time I joined the saints to go up to Zion, for the purpose of visiting our brethren in their afflictions. I deem it unnecessary to give an account of my travels while journeying to that place; suffice it to say, that after I arrived in Missouri, I spent the summer and fall in laboring with my hands. On the 5th of Nov. 1834, I was ordained to the office of a priest, under the hand of elder S. Carter, and sent forth in my weakness to proclaim the first principles of the gospel. After receiving some advice from bishop Partridge, I left Clay county, Missouri, on the 13th of January, 1835, in company with elder Henry Brown, for the purpose of preaching the gospel in the south country. We first visited Jackson county, the only success we met with, was to procure a few signers to the petition to the Governor of Missouri, for redress of wrongs done to the saints, who inhabited that county: and we felt to rejoice in the privilege of bowing the knee on that land, to worship the God of Israel, although, at the same time it was polluted by wicked and ungodly men.

From hence we passed into the territory of the Arkansas, and traveled through an extent of country where the fulness of the gospel had never been proclaimed by the Latter Day Saints. Many parts of the country we visited was but thinly inhabited, as we found in it places from 20 to 50 miles between dwelling houses, in which places was frequently the wide prairies, inhabited only by the bounding deer, and prouling wolf which are very numerous. Some parts of the Arkansas was considerably populous; and

129

wherever we found inhabitants, we did not shun to preach the word unto them as we had opportunity, either in the family circle or in the public assembly. Elder Brown, having been absent from his family for some length of time, felt it his duty to return; we travelled with speed through the country, consequently we had not time to establish churches in that region; yet I trust our labors were not in vain: the minds of many were awakened to enquire into the work, prejudice removed, and the way opened for those who may visit that country in future. .In places where our stay was short, some would take us by the hand and with tears in their eyes bid us God's speed. Elder Brown led two into the waters of baptism, at the Petty John creek in the Arkansas; these were the only two we baptised while together. . . .On our journey we passed two boats that had sunk, we also saw the dead and wounded carried from the third, caused by the bursting of her pipes, and arrived in Kirtland, Nov. 25. I have been absent from this place two years and a half, in which time I have traveled between eight and nine thousand miles, principally in the south, and led 70 into the waters of baptism; and I feel to say, that wherever my lot may be cast, if I should live till my head blossoms with age, I shall remember the scenes of my spiritual youth, and the first fruits of my ministry; they are bound to me closer than the ties of consanguinity; yea, even by the ties of the blood of Christ: and while time may sever the ties of consanguinity, eternity cannot break the ties of celestial love that disembogues from the fount of eternal life.

W. WOODRUFF.
—December 1836, pages 431-432.

Kirtland, Dec. 30, 1836.

Pres. O. Cowdery:

Sir,—I left Kirtland on the 16th day of April last, and returned again last evening, (Dec. 29) having been absent a period of eight months and fourteen days. During this time I have been laboring entirely alone, in the western part of Pennsylvania.—But my heavenly Father has been with me, and given me power over much and heavy opposition; for I have often met with it, especially among the priests, that wear long faces. I have travelled about 1600 miles, back and forth; preached 220 sermons; obtained 20 subscribers for your interesting paper, and baptized 50 persons. I, thro' the grace of God, started one branch in Brush Valley township, Indiana county; one in Plumb Creek township, Armstrong county, and a third on the corners of Venango, Mercer and Butler counties. The work seems to be gaining ground fast wherever I have travelled; and I have often had calls for preaching 20 and 30 miles off, in every direction; and had about six to where I could fill one. I wish the Elders travelling east, would call and visit my brethren, and spread the word of life still more thoroughly through that country.

Yours in the bonds of the everlasting covenant.

ERASTUS SNOW.

—January 1837, page 440.

We have published entire, the letter of elder Orson Hyde, written from Liverpool, England. The reader will discover that it was designed as a private epistle to his wife, but, by consent we have published it for the information of the Saints here and elsewhere.

En.

Liverpool, July 18, 1837.

My Dear Wife:—

After a passage of 18 days, we have all safely arrived at this place. We sailed from New York on the 1st inst. I am truly happy to say to you, that a more pleasant and speedy passage from New York to this place has not been performed at this season of the year, in my opinion, for years. We were not becalmed ouce; neither had we any heavy storms; but a strong Southwardly and Westerly wind prevailed almost during the whole passage. The ship "Soath America" sailed from New York at the same time we did for this port; and there was a wager laid of ten thousand dollars by the owners of the two ships that each would arrive in Liverpool first: This day decided the contest: The two ships came sailing up the channel before a fair wind, under a full press of canvass: the "South America" about ten times her length astern of the Garrick, each ship carrying canvass enough to cover not much less than an acre of ground; and truly a more splendid sight is not often seen. Sometimes, during our passage, the ocean looked something like the hills and vallies round about Kirtland: and would roll out large whale once in a while. We saw four or five of them and other large fish without number. We were very civilly treated on board the ship. The officers and crew were very kind to us. I preached on board the ship on Sunday last to between two and three hundred hearers. I commenced by prayer, and never had greater liberty in calling on the Lord than on this occasion. I had but about forty minutes to speak and consequently could not investigate any subject to any very great extent. Yesterday the cabin passengers deputed one of their number to come to me to express their gratitude to me for the very excellent prayer which I made, saying, that there were gentlemen and ladies from three or four different nations; and were all unanimous in the opinion that the like they never heard before. . . .After the ship anchored at Liverpool there came a small boat along side and a number left the ship to go on shore, among whom were myself, Elder Kimball, Elder Goodson and Doct. Richards. As soon as the boat struck the dock, Elder Kimball and myself, (as if moved by one spirit) first leaped from the boat and gained the top of the quay. We then went and got a room for a few days; and then returned thanks to Almighty God for his great blessings towards us; and dedicated ourselves to the Most High, earnestly praying for you and for all our friends, that you may be prospered and preserved till we meet you all again. . . .We shall remain here for a few days until we can determine what course to pursue, and in what directions to travel. I feel highly gratified with the situation of things here and with the prospects before us. We all feel highly pleased with our situation and we are determined to raise the standard of truth in this country and we are confident that we can do it in the name of the Lord—I want to see you and the little babe very much; I have seen you a number of times in dreams, but when I awoke it was not a reality—May the Lord bless you and all that pertains to you; and when the voyages of life shall be over, may he bring us into that port of everlasting rest where storms and tempests will assail us no more, and where separation will not be known. . . .

am, as ever, your
affectionate husband.
ORSON HYDE.
—August 1837, pages 550-552.

REPORTS FROM LOCAL AND GENERAL CONFERENCES

The Saints in those days of instability and insecurity took advantage of every opportunity to draw together for mutual support and enlightenment. In addition to regular congregational meetings, conferences on a larger geographical scale were frequently called. These tended to be "elders' conferences," attended only by priesthood members. Here the business of the church was transacted. The kinds of concerns that comprised the "business of the church" can be seen in the following excerpts from conference reports.

In the November 1834 *Communications* column, Editor Cowdery gives a rationale for conferences:

> We have frequently expressed our opinion upon the utility and propriety of conferences. What can be more heart cheering to the weary laborer, after a long time spent in disseminating the principles of the gospel, than to sit down in social council with others alike weary, and commune with numbers whose bosoms glow with the same ardor for the salvation of the world, and who, with him, have to communicate the happy intelligence of numbers having been persuaded, thro' their instrumentality, that the sacred truths of heaven thus delivered, though perhaps in weakness, are of sufficient importance to awaken the mind to investigation? This is not all.
>
> By meeting frequently in conference, an acquaintance and familiarity is cultivated, which is so necessary for the promotion of the cause—Each elder is furnished with an account of the labors, and success of all; and is thus prepared, with authentic information, to carry the joyful intelligence to his respective congregation, where those whose duty requires their attendance on other matters, may be equally benefitted, and so the whole body of the saints of the Lord Jesus be refreshed with the news of the success of his cause.
>
> It may be thought superfluous in us, by our brethren, to add our earnest exhortation that meetings of this kind be conducted with solemnity, and in order; and it betrays a want of confidence in us, of their ability and wisdom; but, however we may appreciate their ability and experience, we feel that this subject cannot be too often set before them, and its importance spoken of.— Much, they will see depends upon their conduct on these occasions, in order to derive that peculiar benefit designed in the institution; and while they are thus toiling, we assure them that our heart is equally devoted, and our feeble petitions frequently put up, that we, with them, may be gathered with that assembly which will never close!
>
> November 1834, page 25.

Announcements concerning coming conferences appeared frequently in the *Messenger and Advocate*, usually following this form:

> Conference notices—A conference of the elders of the church of the Latter Day Saints, will be held at Freedom, Cattaraugus Co. N. Y. commencing, Friday, the 3rd day of April, 1835. Friday and Saturday will be occupied by the elders in transacting such business of the church as may be presented, and on Sunday the 5th, public preaching may be expected.
>
> Another conference will be held on Friday, the 5th of June, next, at Elder Winslow Farr's, in Charleston, Orleans, Co. Vt. Friday and Saturday will be occupied in church business, and the Sabbath following, instructions in the gospel will be given—Editor.
>
> —December 1834, page 41.

The minutes of the conference at Freedom, New York, were published in the April 1835 paper. Here are some excerpts from that report:

> *Freedom,* April 3, 1835.
> Brethren members of the Church of Latter Day Saints met in conference agreeably to previous appointment.
> 1st. Order being restored, brother Sidney Rigdon was called to the chair, and W. A. Cowdery was chosen Secretary.
> 2d. Opened conference by a few preliminary remarks from the chair, and a concert of prayer by the Elders present.
> 3d. Itinerant Elders gave a short relation of their travels and success in delivering the testimony of Jesus, the great head of the Church.
> 4th. Heard an address and instructions from the chair relative to the government, progress and prospects of the Church. . . .
> Saturday, April 4th, met agreeably to adjournment, and the conference was opened by prayer by the Chairman.
> Proceeded 1st. to business. Heard reports from the different churches represented.
> 2d. The church, in Westfield, Chautauque county, is not represented, but from a source of information entitled to our entire credence, we learn that the members are the same as represented at the last conference. And the church in Laoni in the same

county in point of numbers, is the same as at last conference, with the exception of one member removed. . . .

3d. After receiving the above reports, there was a call from the chair, on all Elders and Delegates present who had matters of difficulty to adjust in their respective churches, to present them for the consideration of this conference.

Whereupon, brother Reuben Hadlock, presented a charge against Chester L. Heath, an Elder in the Avon and Geneseo church for breach of covenant and not observing the word of wisdom.

4th. Moved by Elder J. Murdock, that C. L. Heath be expelled from the church. The motion was duly seconded. The evidence heard, and the question distinctly put and carried without a dissenting voice, that the said C. L. Heath be expelled.

5th. Moved and seconded that the Elders now present have their licences renewed and signed by the moderator and clerk of this conference.

6th. Resolved, That this conference adjourn sine die.

P. S. This character || on the margin is set opposite the returns of such churches or branches, as have not before been represented in any conference.

W. A. Cowdery, Sec'ary.
—April 1835, pages 101-102.

The following conference report is instructive in showing how the church was then dealing with "heresy."

On Saturday last we met the Elders of this branch of the church, and also those of the little branch at Laona, who were called upon by Elder Marsh, our presiding Elder, to represent to us the standing of these branches. The number of members in this branch was 75 in regular standing, in the branch at Laona, were 20. These two branches were rather low in spirits in consequence of some difficulties that were existing among them; which, however, we succeeded in settling. One travelling Elder had been guilty of teaching erroneous doctrine and perverting the word of God. Such, for instance, as the following. Christ said, the sun shall be darkened, and the moon turned to blood, and the stars fall from heaven, &c. He stated that the Jewish church was the sun, and when it was scattered the sun was darkened. The moon was the Gentile church, which would be cut off and then it should turn to blood, &c. &c. besides, something about the

135

Apocalyptic beast with seven heads and ten horns. He was shown his error and reproved sharply. He saw it and confessed his fault and made an humble acknowledgement and covenanted to be more careful, and we think he will be.

—May 1835, pages 115-116.

A conference in New York State was called upon to decide the case of a new member who was subject to receiving certain visions.

At Pillow-point, N. Y. Eleven branches of the church were represented, containing in all 109 members, who, with the others above, are said to be in good standing. The conference or council at this place, tried a brother "John Elmer (who had lately joined the church) for holding doctrines and views opposed to the principles of the church of the Latter Day Saints.—When called upon, he stated that he had had many visions and revelations, and he said that the Lord had revealed to him of a certainty that he would make his second appearance within fifteen years; also that the Spirit of God often came upon him and threw him down and caused him (as he expressed it) to disfigure himself, or die the death of the righteous, and also of the wicked, and then come to life again, in the presence of others in order to convince them that he was a man of God, and had great power. He also stated that in one of his visions the Lord Jesus appeared to him personally and laid his hand upon him, and sanctified him both soul and body; and that he was now immortal, or changed, so that he would never die. He stated many other curious notions and vagaries ascribing them all to the power of God, and that he never would deny them altho' the council and the whole church should decide against them. The council endeavored to show him that he was deceived by the adversary, but to no effect. He said he had rather be excluded from the church than to give up any of his views or say they were not of God: consequently the church lifted their hands against him."

—July 1835, page 153.

On August 17, 1834, a General Assembly was held at Kirtland in which the soon-to-be-published Book of Doctrine and Covenants was approved, as well as documents on marriage

136

and on "government and laws in general." These conference documents, which appeared in the August issue of *Messenger and Advocate*, have been retained as Doctrine and Covenants 108A, 111, and 112.

In January 1837 Joseph Smith presents a report of a conference held in the House of the Lord in Kirtland, on the preceding December 22.

> The authorities of the church being present; viz: the first Presidency, the High Council of Kirtland, the quorum of the Twelve, the Presidents of the Seventies, the President of the Elders and his counsellors, and many other official members, such as Priests, Teachers, Deacons, &c.:—The house was called to order, and the following motions were made, seconded, and carried by the unanimous voice of the Assembly.
>
> 1st. That it has been the case, that a very improper and unchristian-like course of conduct, by the Elders of this church, and the churches abroad, in sending their poor from among them, and moving to this place, without the necessary means of subsistence: whereas the church in this place being poor from the beginning, having had to pay an extortionary price for their lands, provisions, &c.; and having a serious burthen imposed upon them by comers and goers from most parts of the world, and in assisting the travelling Elders and their families, while they themselves have been laboring in the vineyard of the Lord, to preach the gospel; and also having suffered great loss in endeavoring to benefit Zion: it has become a serious matter, which ought well to be considered by us—
>
> Therefore, after deliberate discussion upon the subject, it was motioned, seconded and unanimously carried, that we have borne our part of this burthen, and that it becomes the duty, henceforth, of all the churches abroad, to provide for those who are objects of charity, that are not able to provide for themselves; and not send them from their midst, to burthen the church in this place, unless they come and prepare a place for them, and means for their support.
>
> 2nd. That there be a stop put to churches or families gathering or moving to this place, without their first coming or sending their wise men, to prepare a place for them, as our houses are all full, and our lands mostly occupied, except those houses and lands that do not belong to the church, which cannot be obtained without great sacrifice, especially when brethren with their families, are crowding in upon us, and are compelled to purchase at

any rate; and consequently are thrown into the hands of speculators, and extortioners, with which the Lord is not well pleased. Also, that the churches abroad do according to the revelation contained in the Book of Commandments, page 238, commencing at section 10, which is as follows:

"Now verily I say unto you, let all the churches gather together all their moneys; let these things be done in their time, be not in haste; and observe to have all these things prepared before you. And let honorable men be appointed, even wise men, and send them to purchase these lands; and every church in the eastern countries when they are built up, if they will hearken unto this counsel, they may buy lands and gather together upon them, and in this way they may establish Zion."

Pres't JOSEPH SMITH,
Chairman.
WARREN PARRISH, *Clerk.*
—January 1837, pages 443-444.

A "solemn assembly" was called for April 6, 1837, to celebrate the anniversary of the church's founding. Notice the extent of participation by priesthood quorums.

A short notice only was given that a solemn assembly would be called of the official members of this church on the 6th inst. for the purpose of washing, anointing, washing of feet, receiving instruction and the further organization of the ministry. We gave notice to a few churches by mail, and more would have been apprized had we been notified in due season to do so ourselves.

We proceed to give a synopsis of the proceedings. Meetings were held by the different quorums, on Monday, Tuesday and Wednesday evenings, to wash and anoin such of their respective members as had not been washed and anointed, that all might be prepared for the meeting on the sixth.

At an early hour on Thursday, the the sixth, the official members assembled in the house of the Lord, where the time, for the first two or three hours was spent by the different quorums in washing of feet, singing, praying and preparing to receive instruction from the Presidents of the church. The Presidents together with the Seventies and *their* presidents repaired to the west room in the attic story, where, for want of time the preceding evening, it became necessary to seal the anointing of those who had recently been anointed and not sealed. . . .

Joseph Smith jr. rose and spoke on the subject of the Priesthood. The Melchisedec High priesthood, he said was no other than the priesthood of the Son of God. There are certain ordinances which belong to the priesthood, and certain results flow from it. . . .He then closed at about 4 P. M. by uttering a prophesy saying this place must be built up, and would be built up, and that every brother that would take hold and help secure and discharge those contracts that had been made, should be rich.

President, Hyrum Smith then rose and addressed the audience. The main drift of his remarks alluded to the temporal affairs of the church. He censured those who counselled such brethren as moved to this place, when they were not authorized to give advice.

He also alluded in terms of disapprobation, to the practice of some individuals in getting money from brethren that come in, when it ought to be appropriated to the discharge of heavy debts that are now hanging over the heads of the church, or the payments of the land contracts which had been made for the benefit of the saints in this place. He closed his remarks by plain practical advice and exhortation, at 25 minutes before 5 P. M.

President Oliver Cowdery rose immediately and made a few brief and pertinent remarks relative to the preaching of the gospel and teaching the people. . . .

President Sidney Rigdon rose a little before five P. M. and said that the object of this mission & ministry, was the gathering together of the saints. The preaching of the gospel was the first thing. Nothing can effect the gathering of the saints but that. A place to gather them is also important and both are to be had in view, when we preach. . . .He exhorted to diligence, to faithfulness, and on these, promised deliverance; and thus closed his address at half past five P. M.

Bread and water were then distributed liberally among all the quorums, and it was truly a refreshing season to soul and body.— The meeting was then dismissed by a benediction.

Many brethren and sisters assembled in the evening for prayer and exhortation, and some few tarried nearly all night.

Thus ended our anniversary, and we hope and trust good was done. Important instructions were certainly given and enforced with an energy of expression and a clearness of thought and perception, not to be mistaken: and believing as we do, that a general good feeling pervaded the whole audience, we trust that it will be a time long to be remembered from important items of instructions being treasured up into good and honest hearts.

—April 1837, pages 486-489.

The Presidents of the Seventies, meeting in conference as a quorum, drew up some resolutions for general publication:

The Presidents of the Seventies met in council in the House of the Lord, on the 29th of April, 1837, and after opening the meeting by prayer, they proceeded to take into consideration some difficulties, either real or imaginary, existing among the Seventies; aud believing that every elder who is called to proclaim the gospel to the nations of the earth, should in all things conduct himself like a man of God, adopted, among others, the following resolutions:

1st.—That we will have no fellowship whatever with any Elder belonging to the quorums of the Seventies who is guilty of polygamy or any offence of the kind, and who does not in all things conform to the laws of the church contained in the Bible and in the Book of Doctrine and Covenants.

2d.—That we discard the practice of ball-playing, wrestling, jumping and all such low and degrading amusements, and above all the use of ardent spirits of any kind; and will have no fellowship with any member of our quorum who indulges himself in the practice of such things.

3d.—That these resolutions be signed by the chairman and clerk, publicly read on the next Sabbath for the approval of the Seventies, and published in the Messenger and Advocate.

DANIEL S. MILES, Chair.

Elias Smith, Clerk.

—May 1837, page 511.

REPORT OF EVENTS AT KIRTLAND

The development of a secular school at Kirtland under the auspices of church leaders was an unusual accomplishment that church members could look to with pride. The following announcement informs us of the curriculum:

140

Kirtland, Ohio, Feb. 27, 1833.

Having been requested by the Trusties of the "KIRTLAND SCHOOL," to give a small sketch of the number of students who have attended this institution, and of their progress in the different sciences, I cheerfully comply with the request, having been an instructor therein from its commencement, in Dec.—last.

The school has been conducted under the immediate care and inspection of

JOSEPH SMITH jr.
F. G. WILLIAMS,
SIDNEY RIGDON,
& O. COWDERY. } *Trustees*

When the school first commenced, we received into it both large and small, but in about three weeks the classes became so large, and the house so crowded, that it was thought advisable to dismiss all the small students, and continue those only who wished to study the sciences of penmanship, arithmetic, English grammar and geography. Before we dismissed the small scholars, there were in all about 130 who attended. Since that time there have been, upon an average, about 100, the most of whom have received lectures upon English grammar; and for the last 4 weeks about 70 have been studying geography one half day, and grammar and writing the other part.

T. Burdick's arithmetic, S. Kirkham's grammar and J. Olney's geography have been used, with N. Webster's dictionary, as standard.

Since the year 1827 I have taught school in five different States, and I have visited many schools in which I was not engaged, as teacher; but in none, I can say with certainty, have I seen students make more rapid progress, than in this. I expect myself to leave the institution, but yet, I have a great desire to see it flourish. I therefore most cheerfully recommend it to all those whose circumstances and situation will allow them to attend, as being a place where strict attention is paid to good morals as well as to the sciences.

W. E. M'LELLIN.

Notice.—The spring term of the "Kirtland School" will commence on the 20th of April next. Young gentlemen and ladies from a distance can obtain board, in respectable families for $1,00 to $1,25 per week.

The Trustees of this institution design introducing the higher branches of English literature, at as early a period as possible.

[Editor.]
—February 1835, page 80.

Two years later school work is still being carried on, now using facilities made available by the Kirtland Temple.

OUR VILLAGE.

Nothing can be more gratifying to the saints in this place and their friends and brethren abroad than to contemplate the scene now before them. Every Lords day our house of worship is filled to the overflowing with attentiv hearers, mostly communicants.

In the evening following the singers meet under the direction of Brother L. Carter and J. Crosby Jr. who give instructions in the principles of vocal music.

On monday evening the quorum of high priests meets in the west room of the attic story where they transact the buisiness of their particular quorum, speak, sing, pray, and so worship the God of heaven. On Tuesday evenings the Seventies, meet in the same room occupied by the high priests the preceding night. They then and there listen to the advice and instructions given them by their president, as well as speak, sing, pray and talk of the goodness and power of God.

On Wednesday evening the rooms are occupied by the quorum of Elders, where they receive instruction and advice from their venerable president and his able councellors.

On Thursday P. M. a prayer meeting is held in the lower part of the house where nny and all persons may assemble and pray and praise the Lord. This meeting, though free for all, is conducted more particularly by J. Smith senior, the patriarch of the church.

The members of the high council, and also "the twelve" meet but we believe not statedly in each week as do others, of the different quorums mentioned.

Dring the week a school is taught in the attic story of the house, denominated the "Kirtland High School" coning of about 135 or 40 students under the superintendence of H. M. Hawes Esq. professor of the Greek & Latin languages. The school is properly divided into three departments, (viz.) The classical, where the languages only are taught, the English department where mathematics, common Arithmetic, Geography, English grammar, writing and reading are taught, and the Juvenile department the first principles and rudiments of an education are taught. These two departments have each an instructor assigned them. The whole is under the supervision of Mr. Hawes as principal.

The school commenced in Nov. and on the first Wednesday in January the several classes passed a public examination in presence of the trustees of the School and the parents and guardians of the Scholars. We think the result of the examination, did honor to both teachers and scholars. Never did we witness greater progress in study in the same length of time and in so greart a number of scholars.

—January 1837, page 444.

The building of the Kirtland Temple was a remarkable undertaking, considering the size and resources of the church. The imagination of the whole church was stirred by this project. W. W. Phelps gives a progress report in the July 1835 issue of *Messenger and Advocate.*

"THE HOUSE OF GOD."

It will not be deemed improper for us to give the saints and friends of the everlasting gospel, a few words relative to the house of worship now erecting in Kirtland, Ohio. The first stone was laid on the twenty-third of July, 1833, when, without faith, yea precious faith in the promises of the Lord, the appearances of the church would have indicated any thing but a speedy completion. Let it be remembered that the unparalleled outrages of the mob of Jackson county, were committed about this time, and the church in its infancy, had to weep over this cruel tragedy as a sore affliction upon the children of Zion.

Trusting, however, in the God of Enoch, who succors the needy, and exalts the humble, a few commenced the work; and though other important matters rolled round, which, to many, would have seemed insurmountable, and calculated to retard the progress of the building, still, the walls and the timbers of the roof were finished, being raised late last fall: and the roof is now covered. . . .

The sum expended, thus far, towards its erection, may be computed at about *ten thousand dollars,* and the whole cost, when finished, will probably be from twenty to thirty thousand. Like many houses for public worship, this house has been, so far,

143

reared, and must be finished, by donations from the saints, and all that feel an interest in the salvation of the human family. As a sample of the liberality and faith of the saints at Kirtland, we have the pleasure of saying, that on Thursday the 18th of June last, $950 were subscribed for the work; and, that on Thursday the 25th of the same month, $6,232, were subscribed for the same glorious purpose, making *seven thousand one hundred and eighty two dollars.* So much for the laudable object of preparing a house where the incomings and the outgoings of the saints may be in the name of the Lord, as in old times.

—July 1835, pages 147-148.

A subsequent report soliciting donations appeared the following October.

THE HOUSE OF THE LORD.

We are glad to learn, that the building Committee have determined, if possible, to finish the house of the Lord this winter. The lower story is already in such a state of forwardness, as to induce us to say, that it can soon be completed for meetings. In order, however, to finish so large an house, in so short a time, it is necessary that the churches abroad, as Paul says in his vision, should *"come over into Macedonia, and help us"* with their substance, and prayers.

The Committee have instructed us to call upon the saints abroad, such as mean to assist, and such especially as have promised to subscribe, and assist in building the house, and say to them, *Now is the time to do good,* and fulfil your promises. Those who have subscribed are earnestly requested to pay the amount of their subscriptions as soon as they reasonably can. Thus the Committee may do unto others, as they wish others to do unto them.

Every one that wishes to spread the everlasting gospel; every one that wishes well to his fellow-beings; every one that wishes to have the elders instructed more perfectly in theory, doctrine and principle; and every one that wishes an house built where the Latter Day Saints can worship the Lord in spirit and in truth, have now an invitation to cast in their mites, for that purpose, and receive their reward hereafter, in that house not made with hands, eternal in the heavens.

P.

—October 1835, page 207.

144

In March of 1836 the edifice was completed. A seven-page accounting of the dedicatory services was given to the church through the *Messenger and Advocate.*

Kirtland, Ohio, March 27th, 1826.
Previous notice having been given, the Church of the Latter Day Saints met this day in the House of the Lord to dedicate it to him. The congregation began to assemble before 8 o'clock A.M. and thronged the doors until 9, when the Presidents of the church who assisted in seating the congregation, were reluctantly compelled to order the door-keepers to close the doors; every seat and aisle were crowded.—One thousand persons were now silently and solemnly waiting to hear the word of the Lord from the mouth of his servants in the sacred desk. President S. Rigdon began the services of the day, by reading the 96th and 24th Psalms. An excellent choir of singers, led by M. C. Davis sung the following Hymn:

TUNE—*Sterling.*

Ere long the vail will rend in twain,
The King descend with all his train :
The earth shall shake with awful fright,
And all creation feel his might. . . .

The speaker (S. Rigdon,) selected the 8th chapter of Matthew, the 18, 19 and 20th verses from which, he proposed to address the congregation, confining himself more closely to the 20th verse—He spoke two hours and a half in his usual, forcible and logical manner. At one time in the course of his remarks he was rather pathetic, than otherwise, which drew tears from many eyes. . . .
After closing his discourse he presented Joseph Smith jr. to the church as a Prophet and Seer. The Presidents of the church then all in their seats, acknowledged him as such by rising. The vote was unanimous in the affirmative.
The question was then put, and carried without a manifest dissenting sentiment to each of the different grades or quorums of church officers respectively and then to the congregation.—The following hymn was then sung:

TUNE—*Hosanna.*

Now let us rejoice in the day of salvation,
No longer as strangers on earth need we roam—
Good tidings are sounding to us and each nation,
And shortly the hour of redemption will come. . . .

145

Services closed for the forenoon.

Intermission was about 15 minutes during which none left their seats except a few females, who from having left their infants with their friends, were compelled to do so to take care of them. The P. M. services commenced by singing the following hymn:

TUNE—Adam-ondi-Ahman.

This earth was once a garden place,
With all her glories common;
And men did live a holy race,
And worship Jesus face to face,
In Adam-ondi-Ahman. . . .

President J. Smith jr. then rose, and after a few preliminary remarks, presented the several Presidents of the church, then present, to the several quorums respectively, and then to the church as being equal with himself, acknowledging them to be Prophets and Seers. The vote was unanimous in the affirmative in every instance.—Each of the different quorums was presented in its turn to all the rest, and then to the church, and received and acknowledged by all the rest, in the several stations without a manifet dissenting sentiment.

President J. Smith jr. then addressed the congregation in a manner calculated to instruct the understanding, rather than please the ear, and at or about the close of his remarks, he prophesied to all. that inasmuch as they would uphold these men in their several stations, alluding to the different quorums in the church, the Lord would bless them; yea, in the name of Christ, the blessings of Heaven shall be yours. . . .The following hymn was then sung:

TUNE—Dalston.

How pleased and blest was I,
To hear the people cry,
"Come, let us seek our God to-day!"
Yes, with a cheerful zeal,
We'll haste to Zion's hill,
And there our vows and honors pay. . . .

He then offered the dedication prayer, which was as follows:

THANKS be to thy name, O Lord God of Israel, who keepest covenant and shewest mercy unto thy servants, who walk uprightly before thee with all their hearts: thou who hast commanded thy servants to build an house to thy name in this place. (Kirtland.) And now thou beholdest, O Lord, that so thy servants have done, according to thy commandment. And now we ask thee, holy Father, in the name of Jesus Christ, the Son of thy bosom, in whose name alone salvation can be administered to the children of men: we ask thee, O Lord, to accept of this house, the workmanship of the hands of us, thy servants, which thou didst command us to build; for thou knowest that we have done this work through great tribulation: and out of our poverty we have given of our substance to build a house to thy name, that the Son of Man might have a place to manifest himself to his people. . . .

O hear, O hear, O hear us, O Lord, and answer these petitions, and accept the dedication of this house, unto thee, the work of our hands, which we have built unto thy name; and also this church to put upon it thy name. And help us by the power of thy Spirit, that we may mingle our voices with those bright shining seraphs, around thy throne with acclamations of praise, singing hosanna to God and the Lamb: and let these thine annointed ones be clothed with salvation, and thy saints shout aloud for joy. *AMEN and AMEN*

The choir then sung a hymn.

TUNE—Hosanna.

The Spirit of God like a fire is burning:
   The latter day glory begins to come forth;
The visions and blessings of old are returning:
   The angels are coming to visit the earth.
We'll sing & we'll shout with the armies of heaven:
   Hosanna, hosanna to God and the Lamb!
Let glory to them in the highest be given,
   Henceforth and forever: amen and amen! . . .

President Smith then asked the several quorums separately and then the congregation, if they accepted the prayer. The vote was, in every instance, unanimous in the affirmative.

The Eucharist was administered.—D. C. Smith blessed the bread and wine and they were distributed by several Elders present, to the church.

President J. Smith jr. then arose and bore record of his mission. D. C. Smith bore record of the truth of the work of the Lord in which we are engaged.

President O. Cowdery spoke and testified of the truth of the book of Mormon, and of the work of the Lord in these last days.

President F. G. Williams bore record that a Holy Angel of God, came and set between him and J. Smith sen. while the house was being dedicated.

147

President Hyrum Smith, (one of the building committee) made some appropriate remarks concerning the house, congratulating those who had endured so many toils and privations to erect it. That it was the Lord's house built by his commandment and he would bless them.

President S. Rigdon then made a few appropriate closing remarks; and a short prayer which was ended with loud acclamations of Hosanna! Hosanna! Hosanna to God and the Lamb, Amen. Amen and Amen! Three times. Elder B. Young, one of the Twelve, gave a short address in tongues; Elder D. W. Patten interpreted and gave a short exhortation in tongues himself; after which, President J. Smith jr. blessed the congregation in the name of the Lord, and at a little past four P. M. the whole exercise closed and the congregation dispersed.

We further add that we should do violence to our own feelings and injustice to the real merit of our brethren and friends who attended the meeting, were we here to withhold a meed of praise, which we think is their just due; not only for their quiet demeanor during the whole exercise, which lasted more than eight hours, but for their great liberality in contributing of their earthly substance for the relief of the building committee, who were yet somewhat involved. As this was to be a day of sacrifice, as well as of fasting,—There was a man placed at each door in the morning to receive the voluntary donations of those who entered. On counting the collection it amounted to nine hundred and sixty three dollars.

—March 1836, pages 274-281.

In the fall of 1835 the Kirtland area was buzzing with reports of new writings coming forth in connection with the sale of some Egyptian mummies to the young Prophet. These mummies and several papyrus manuscripts had come into the hands of the Smith family at a time when Joseph was wandering through the labyrinth of Hebrew grammar. Immediately he declared one manuscript to be the work of Abraham, and another to be the writings of Joseph of Egypt. The Prophet made a laborious but unsuccessful attempt to construct a manual of Egyptian grammar, a project that no scholar nor professor had apparently been able to do. Actually the secret of the mysterious hieroglyphs had already been

148

uncovered by Champollion with the aid of the Rosetta Stone, but the results of his efforts were not made available to the English-speaking world until 1837. Not to be daunted by his failure to produce a convincing Egyptian grammar text, Joseph sat down and dictated a "translation" of the scroll purported to be Abraham's story. Notice was taken of this project in the *Messenger and Advocate*, although it should be noted that no text claiming to be a translation of the scrolls was published until 1842.

> Upon the subject of the Egyptian records, or rather the writings of Abraham and Joseph, I may say a few words. This record is beautifully written on papyrus with black, and a small part, red ink or paint, in perfect preservation. The characters are such as you find upon the coffins of mummies, hieroglyphics, &c. with many characters or letters exactly like the present, (though probably not quite so square,) form of the Hebrew without points.
>
> These records were obtained from one of the catacombs in Egypt, near the place where once stood the renowned city of Thebes, by the celebrated French traveller Antonio Lebolo, in the year 1831. He procured license from Mehemet Ali, then Viceroy of Egypt, under the protection of Chevalier Drovetti, the French Consul, in the year 1828; employed 433 men four months and two days, (if I understood correctly, Egyptian or Turkish soldiers,) at from four to six cents per diem, each man; entered the catacomb June 7th, 1831, and obtained eleven Mummies. There were several hundred Mummies in the same catacomb: about one hundred embalmed after the first order, and deposited and placed in niches, and two or three hundred after the second and third order, and laid upon the floor or bottom of the grand cavity, the two last orders of embalmed were so decayed that they could not be removed, and only eleven of the first, found in the niches. On his way from Alexandria to Paris he put in at Trieste, and after ten days illness, expired. This was in the year 1832. Previous to his decease, he made a will of the whole to Mr. Michael H. Chandler, then in Philadelphia, Pa. his nephew, whom he supposed to have been in Ireland. Accordingly the whole were sent to Dublin, addressed according, and Mr. Chandler's friends ordered them sent to New York, where they were received at the custom house, in the winter or spring of 1833. In April of the same year Mr. Chandler paid the duties upon his Mummies, and

took possession of the same. Up to this time they had not been taken out of the coffins nor the coffins opened. On opening the coffins he discovered that in connection with two of the bodies, were something rolled up with the same kind of linnen, saturated with the same bitumen, which, when examined, proved to be two rolls of papyrus, previously mentioned. I may add that two or three other small pieces of papyrus, with astronomical calculations, epitaphs, &c. were found with others of the Mummies.

When Mr. Chandler discovered that there was something with the Mummies, he supposed, or hoped it might be some diamonds or other valuable metal, and was no little chagrined when he saw his disappointment. He was immediately told, while yet in the Custom House, that there was no man in that city, who could translate his roll; but was referred by the same gentleman, (a stranger,) to Mr. Joseph Smith, jr. who, continued he, possesses some kind of power or gifts by which he had previously translated similar characters. Bro. Smith was then unknown to Mr. Chandler, neither did he know that such a book or work as the record of the Nephites had been brought before the public. From New York he took his collection to Philadelphia, where he exhibited them for a compensation. . . .

While Mr. Chandler was in Philadelphia, he used every exertion to find some one who could give him the translation of his papyrus, but could not, satisfactorily, though from some few men of the first eminence, he obtained in a small degree, the translation of a few characters. Here he was referred to bro. Smith. From Philadelphia he visited Harrisburgh, and other places east of the mountains, and was frequently referred to bro. Smith for a translation of his Egyptian Relic.

It would be beyond my purposes to follow this gentleman in his different circuits to the time he visited this place the last of June, or first of July, at which time he presented bro. Smith with his papyrus. Till then neither myself nor brother Smith knew of such relics being in America. . . .

Being solicited by Mr. Chandler to give an opinion concerning his antiquities, or a translation of some of the characters, bro. S. gave him the interpretation of some few for his satisfaction. For your gratification I will here annex a certificate which I hold, from under the hand of Mr. Chandler, unsolicited, however, by any person in this place, which will show how far he believed bro. Smith able to unfold from these long obscured rolls the wonders contained therein:

"This is to make known to all who may be desirous, concerning the knowledge of Mr. Joseph Smith, jr. in deciphering the ancient Egyptian hieroglyphic characters, in my possession, which I have, in many eminent cities, shown to the most learned: And, from the information that I could even learn, or meet with, I find that of Mr. Joseph Smith, jr. to correspond in the most minute matters."

(signed)

"MICHAEL H. CHANDLER."

"Travelling with, and proprietor of Egyptian Mummies.". . .

The language in which this record is written is very comprehensive, and many of the hieroglyphics exceedingly striking. The evidence is apparent upon the face, that they were written by persons acquainted with the history of the creation, the fall of man, and more or less of the correct ideas of notions of the Deity. The representation of the god-head—three, yet in one, is curiously drawn to give simply, though impressively, the writers views of that exalted personage. . . .When the translation of these valuable documents will be completed, I am unable to say; neither can I give you a probable idea how large volumes they will make; but judging from their size, and the comprehensiveness of the language, one might reasonably expect to see a sufficient to develop much upon the mighty acts of the ancient men of God, and of his dealing with the children of men when they saw him face to face. Be there little or much, it must be an inestimable acquisition to our present scriptures, fulfilling, in a small degree, the word of the prophet: For the earth shall be full of the knowledge of the Lord as the waters cover the sea.

—December 1835, pages 234-237.

The slavery-abolitionist controversy was much discussed at Kirtland, as everywhere. The Prophet's hitherto vacillating position concerning the Negro question seems to have crystallized in favor of the Southern position. Here, in a general epistle, he states his opinions:

This place having recently been visited by a gentleman who advocated the principles or doctrines of those who are called abolitionists; if you deem the following reflections of any service, or think they will have a tendency to correct the opinions of the

151

southern public, relative to the views and sentiments I believe, as an individual, and am able to say, from personal knowledge, are the feelings of others, you are at liberty to give them publicity in the columns of the Advocate. . . .

I am aware, that many who profess to preach the gospel, complain against their brethren of the same faith, who reside in the south, and are ready to withdraw the hand of fellowship because they will not renounce the principle of slavery and raise their voice against every thing of the kind. This must be a tender point, and one which should call forth the candid reflection of all men, and especially before they advance in an opposition calculated to lay waste the fair States of the South, and set loose, upon the world a community of people who might peradventure, overrun our country and violate the most sacred principles of human society,—chastity and virtue.

No one will pretend to say, that the people of the free states are as capable of knowing the evils of slavery as those who hold them. If slavery is an evil, who, could we expect, would first learn it? Would the people of the free states, or would the slave states? . . .

And further, what benefit will it ever be to the slave for persons to run over the free states, and excite indignation against their masters in the minds of thousands and tons of thousands who understand nothing relative to their circumstances or conditions? I mean particularly those who have never travelled in the South, and scarcely seen a negro in all their life. How any community can ever be excited with the chatter of such persons—boys and others who are too indolent to obtain their living by honest industry, and are incapable of pursuing any occupation of a professional nature, is unaccountable to me. And when I see persons in the free states signing documents against slavery, it is no less, in my mind, than an array of influence, and a declaration of hostilities against the people of the South! What can divide our Union sooner, God only knows!

After having expressed myself so freely upon this subject, I do not doubt but those who have been forward in raising their voice against the South, will cry out against me as being uncharitable, unfeeling and unkind—wholly unacquainted with the gospel of Christ. It is my privilege then, to name certain passages from the bible, and examine the teachings of the ancients upon this matter, as the fact is uncontrovertible, that the first mention we have of slavery is found in the holy bible, pronounced by a man who was perfect in his generation and walked with God. And so far from that prediction's being averse from the mind of God it remains as

152

a lasting monument of the decree of Jehovah, to the shame and confusion of all who have cried out against the South, in consequence of their holding the sons of Ham in servitude!

> And he said cursed be Canaan; a servant of servants shall he be unto his brethren. And he said, Blessed be the Lord God of Shem: and Canaan shall be his servant.—God shall enlarge Japheth, and he shall dwell in the tents of Shem: and Canaan shall be his servant.—Gen, 8:25, 26, 27.

Trace the history of the world from this notable event down to this day, and you will find the fulfilment of this singular prophecy. What could have been the design of the Almighty in this wonderful occurrence is not for me to say: but I can say, that the curse is not yet taken off the sons of Canaan, neither will be until it is affected by as great power as caused it to come: and the people who interfere the least with the decrees and purposes of God in this matter, will come under the least condemnation before him; and those who are determined to pursue a course which shows an opposition and a feverish restlessness against the designs of the Lord, will learn, when perhaps it is too late for their own good, that God can do his own work without the aid of those who are not dictated by his counsel.

I must not pass over a notice of the history of Abraham, of whom so much is spoken in the scriptures. If we can credit the account, God conversed with him from time to time, and directed him in the way he should walk, saying, "I am the Almighty God: walk before me and be thou perfect." Paul says that the gospel was preached to this man. And it is further said, that he had sheep and oxen, men-servants and maid-servants, &c. From this I conclude, that if the principle had been an evil one, in the midst of the communications made to this holy man. he would have been instructed differently. And if he was instructed against holding men-servants and maid-servants, he never ceased to do it; consequently must have incurred the displeasure of the Lord and thereby lost his blessing—which was not the fact. . . .

Before closing this communication, I beg leave to drop a word to the travelling elders: You know, brethren, that great responsibility rests upon you, and that you are accountable to God for all you teach the world. In my opinion, you will do well to search the book of Covenants, in which you will see the belief of the church concerning masters and servants. All men are to be taught to repent; but we have no right to interfere with slaves contrary to the mind and will of their masters. In fact, it would be much better and more prudent, not to preach at all to slaves, until after their masters are converted; and then, teach the master to use

153

them with kindness, remembering that they are accountable to God, and that servants are bound to serve their masters, with singleness of heart, without murmuring. I do, most sincerely hope, that no one who is authorized from this church to preach the gospel, will so far depart from the scripture as to be found stirring up strife and sedition against our brethren of the South. Having spoken frankly and freely, I leave all in the hands of God, who will direct all things for his glory and the accomplishment of his work.

Praying that God may spare you to do much good in this life, I subscribe myself your brother in the Lord.

JOSEPH SMITH, jr.

—April 1836, pages 289-291.

In the same issue, support is given to Joseph's position by an editorial.

THE ABOLITIONISTS.

We particularly invite the attention of our readers to those communications upon the subject of Slavery. We have long looked upon this as a matter of deep moment, involving the dearest interests of a powerful, a wealthy, a free and happy republic. No one can appreciate more highly than ourself the freedom of speech, the liberty of conscience, and the liberty of the press.—Most sincerely do we believe ours to be one of the most happy forms of government ever established by men. But to see it distracted and rent to the center with local questions—questions which cannot be discussed without the sacrifice of human blood, calls forth the feelings and sympathy of every *Christian* heart.

There is no disposition in us to abridge the privilege of free discussion—far from this; but we wonder at the folly of men who push this important subject before communities, who are wholly unprepared to judge of its merits, or demerits, and call for public sentiment before the opposite side of the matter has been touched.

If those who run through the free states, exciting their indignation against our brothers of the South, feel so much sympathy and kindness towards the blacks, were to go to the southern states, where the alleged evil exists, and *warn* those who are guilty

154

of these enormous crimes, to repent and turn from their wickedness, or would purchase the slaves and then set them at liberty, we should have no objections to this provided they would place them upon some other continent than ours. Then we should begin to believe they were acting honestly; but till something of this is manifested, we shall think otherwise.

What benefit can the slave derive from the long harrangues and discussions held in the north? Certainly the people of the north have no legal right to interfere with the property of the south, neither have they a right to say they shall, or shall not, hold slaves. These states were admitted into the Union with the privilege of forming their own state governments; besides if they were now disposed, they are in no situation to let their slaves loose. If the evil is on them it was brought on them by the acts of their fathers, and endure it they must. But so long as they do not complain, why should we? If we dislike slavery we are free from it and are in no danger of being afflicted with it. If they are satisfied with it, it is their right as governments, and any interference with them on the subject, so as to endanger their lives, can have its origin from no other source than from such as seek the overthrow and dissolution of our government. . . .

We have travelled in the south, and have seen the condition of both master and servant; and without the least disposition to deprive others of their liberty of thinking, we unhesitatingly say that if ever the condition of the slave is bettered, under our present form of government, it must be by converting the master to the faith of the gospel and then teaching him to be kind to his slave. The idea of transportation is folly, the project of emancipation is destructive to our government, and the notion of amalgamation is develish!—And insensible to feeling must be the heart, and low indeed must be the mind, that would consent for a moment, to see his fair daughter, his sister, or perhaps, his bosom companion, in the embrace of a NEGRO!

We entreat our brethren of the Eastern, the free States, the Canadas, and all, wherever they may be found, not to be surprised or astonished at this step, which we have thus publicly taken: were they acquainted with the present condition of the slave, they would see that they could not be freed, and we enjoy our present, civil and social societies. And further, that this matter cannot be discussed without exciting the feelings of the black population, and cause them to rise, sooner or later, and lay waste and desolate many parts of the Southern country. . . .

Heretofore we have confined our comments to the principles of the gospel, the restoration of Israel, and matters connected with them, when ever attempting to write for the public eye; but owing to the great increase of the church, as it respects number, and the deep anxiety felt by our southern brethren on this subject, we have now simply stated our belief. It is a fact, and one which appeals to our heart with great force, that members of this church resident in the South, have long looked for something from this press, calculated to do away that bitter feeling existing against them, through unfounded jealoussy, on the subject of slavery. And we have asked the question, can they look to us and plead for assistance in vain; We answer No. They have our fellowship, they have our prayers, they have our best desires, and if we can give them influence by expressing our sentiments, and thereby enable them to be more beneficial and successful in proclaiming the gospel, we will not withhold.—And if our brethren of the free States differ from us, on these principles, we beseech them, in the name of Jesus Christ to withhold, and consider that every step they take to encourage that factious spirit so prevalent in our land, is not only closing up the way of the gospel in the mouths of the elders, but is, most certainly, endangering the life of every man who embraces it in the south.

We speak as an individual and as a man in this matter. Our strong feeling for liberty, and prejudice against the south, in consequence of education, at a former period, would have urged us, perhaps, to persue another course; but after examining this matter seriously, and looking at its principles from the scripture, as well as being some what prepared to judge from an actual experience in the south, we again repeat, that the condition of the slave cannot be bettered other than by converting the master to the faith of the gospel.

It was an inhuman thing to tear a people of another color from their friends and homes, and bring them to a strange land, and cause them to endure the toils of servitude; and that which was done by a few ship's loads by our fathers, has now involved us, their children, in trouble and difficulty; but, I am more inclined to take the garment upon my shoulders and walk backward, and cover their folly, than expose them further to shame, or laugh at their conduct. . . .

In this matter we consider we have spoken in behalf of the slave, as well as the slave holder. It has not been a thing of hasty conclusion; but deliberately and carefully examined, and we are sensible, if their are any who believe the gospel as we, and differ from us in point of national government, and would take the pains to inform themselves, not only by searching the holy scriptures, but by visiting the south, they would soon commend us for the course we have now taken.

Those who feel disposed, may easily ascertain the feelings of this church, as published in the book of doctrine and covenants; and from that, and what has already been said, those who are laboring in the south, will be able to set the matter in a fair light, and we trust, escape persecution and death: which we hope God will order, for his Son's sake.

—April 1836, pages 299-301.

The biggest disaster to hit Kirtland during this relatively calm period began auspiciously when some of the church leaders determined to organize a bank at Kirtland for the benefit of the membership. Oliver Cowdery was commissioned to journey to Philadelphia to order plates for the printing of the bank notes, while Orson Hyde was sent to the state capital to apply for an act of incorporation. Oliver succeeded in his mission but Orson did not. Since the plates had already been procured, the problem was resolved by organizing an anti-bank instead of a bank, with this anti-banking agency fulfilling the same functions as a bank. On the notes, a simple "anti" before banking was sufficient to fulfill the letter of the law. In the January 1837 paper, sixteen "Articles of Agreement" of the Kirtland Safety Society Anti-Banking Company were published, followed by this note from Joseph Smith:

In connexion with the above Articles of Agreement of the Kirtland Safety Society, I beg leave to make a few remarks to all those who are preparing themselves, and appointing their wise men, for the purpose of building up Zion and her Stakes. It is wisdom and according to the mind of the Holy Spirit, that you should call at Kirtland, and receive counsel and instruction upon those principles that are necessary to further the great work of the Lord, and to establish the children of the Kingdom, according to the oracles of God, as they are had among us. And further, we invite the brethren from abroad, to call on us, and take stock in our Safety Society. And we would remind them also of the sayings of the prophet Isaiah, contained in the 60th chapter, and

157

more particularly the 9th and 17th verses, which are as follows:
"Surely the isles shall wait for me, and the ships of Tarshish first,
and to bring thy sons from far, their silver and their gold (not
their bank notes) with them, unto the name of the Lord, thy
God, and to the holy one of Israel, because he hath glorified thee.

For brass I will bring gold, and for iron I will bring silver, and
wood brass and for stones iron: I will also make thy officers
peace, and thine exactors righteousness." Also 62 ch. 1st vrs.
"For Zion's sake will I not hold my peace, and for Jerusalem's
sake I will not rest, until the righteousness thereof go forth as
brightness, and the salvation thereof as a lamp that burneth.

J. SMITH jr.

—January 1837, page 443.

The Kirtland Safety Society had entered the chaotic banking system of Ohio in November of 1836, and after only a
month began to decline. No one in Kirtland was aware that
the nation was on the verge of a financial crash, the famous
"Panic of 1837." The Kirtland notes, as all other paper
money, depreciated in value rapidly. By February they were
worth twelve and one half cents on the dollar. Saints who
had trusted the officials' statements that the Kirtland Safety
Society would be a blessing to the nation as well as to the
church were distressed to see the anti-banking society fold up
in the same manner as many banks in the same region. Editor
W. A. Cowdery's explanation of the anti-bank's failure took
up seven of the paper's sixteen pages in July. Never before
had so much space been devoted to a controversial issue.
Obviously confidence in the church's leadership had been
shaken and a response of some kind needed to be made. In
the excerpts following, the identity of the "one man" who
usurps "absolute and despotic" control is an open question.
While the author was probably not referring to the Prophet,
many readers took it that way, and the Prophet's relationships with several prominent persons in the community were
strained severely.

It is a well known and established fact, that in the latter part
of the year 1836 a bank, or monied institution, was established in

158

this place denominated the "Kirtland Safety Society Bank." Plates were engraved in Philadelphia, paper struck, and the bank commenced discounting in the early part of the present year. It was considered a kind of joint stock association, and that the private property of the stockholders was holden in proportion to the amount of their subscription, for the redemption of the paper issued by the *bank.* No charter was obtained for the institution, which operated as one cause to limit the circulation of the bills, destroy public confidence in them, and stimulate the holders of them to return them again to the bank and demand the specie for them. Other banks which had been at the expense of procuring charters, refused the bills of this bank in payment of any debts due their respective institutions. This stand taken by other banks operated as might be reasonably supposed, to destroy the currency of these bills with men of business who had deal with the banks already chartered and established by law. . . .

The great scarcity of money operated upon community to make every one anxious to have the new bills in circulation. There were two classes of people and both appeared equally anxious, but they were actuated by diamatrically opposite motives. The one part were anxious to pay their debts, supply themselves with food, and build up the place: the other being enemies, had our ruin in view, and were willing to receive the bills, come and demand the specie on them, and when the notes become due that were given for bills at the bank, avail themselves of that clause of the statute which we have quoted to avoid payment, still the officers of the bank continued to redeem, their paper when presented. . . .

These causes, we are bound to believe, operated to induce the officers of the bank to let out larger sums than their better judgements dictated, which almost invariably fell into, or passed through the hands of those who sought our ruin. Our enemies foresaw, and every man might foresee without the gift of prophecy, the down fall of the institution, as plainly as Belshazzar saw the hand that wrote his doom on the wall of his palace. The bills, as might be expected, were at this time rather rising in the estimation of unprejudiced men abroad, having assurances when they received them that they were good, and should be made good to the holders. Hundreds who were enemies, either came or sent their agents and demanded specie till the officers thought best to refuse payment. This fact was soon rumored abroad as upon the wings of the wind; some returned their bills with curses, and some with entreaties for their redemption according to the character, temper and disposition of the holders. . . .Money we all know is power, and he who posesses most of it, has the most men in his power. If we give all our privileges to one man, we virtually give him our money and our liberties, and make him a monarch, absolute and despotic, and ourselves abject slaves or fawning sycophants. If we grant privileges and monopolies to a few, they always continue to undermine the fundamental principles of freedom, and sooner or later, convert, the purest and most liberal form of Government into the rankest aristocracy. These we conceive, are matters of history, matters of fact that cannot be controverted. Well may it be said, if we thus barter away our liberties, we are unworthy of them. . . .

From a review of what we have written we remark.

1st Relative to the paper, purporting to be bank bills issued in this place, we say there is much of it in circulation, but not much in this place. It has been bought up here and elsewhere, sometimes at one rate of discount and sometimes at another, and carried to a distance: we have frequent rumors from different places respecting its currency; in some places reports say it is good and current as other bank paper, but here and in other places it is not. We are aware that the currency of any paper circulating as money, depends on one simple fact, to make it so.—The public mind must be impressed with the belief that it can be converted into the precious metals, to the same amount that is stamped on the bill or bills; so long as the current of public opinion goes to establish that point, just so long and so far, any paper will be current and no farther. If there are but five dollars in the vault of the bank that issued the paper, while the public mind is satisfied that it is perfectly solvent and good, the currency would be no better were the same vault the depository of half a million. . . .

2 Respecting the mangement of our banking institution, much has been said, and various opinions and conjectures offered by friends and foes. We are not bankers, bank stock holders, or financiers. We believe that banking or financiering is as much a regular science, trade or business, as those of law, physic or divinity, and that a man may be an eminent civilian, and know nothing of consequence of the principles of medicine. He may be a celebrated divine, and be no mechanic no financier, and be as liable to fail in the management of a bank as he would in constructing a balloon or the mechanism of a watch if he had never seen either.

We are not prepared in our feelings to censure any man, we wish to extend that charity to others, which under similar circumstances we should claim at their hands. . . .

3 Relative to currency generally, we have few remarks to make. We all know that the paper circulation, is unsound, fluctuating and precarious.—We believe that, from present appearances it will be more so, and that our brethren as prudent men, should not exchange real estate or any other property for it, other than according to their currency, in market, and then only so far as is to be laid out and expanded for immediate use and present benefit. Although bank bills, nominally may pass for the price stamped upon them, still it is a notorious fact, that they have in reality fallen in value, and that brokers and bankers will pay a premium on gold and silver above its marked or estimated value, while the best of paper is below it. We have made these remarks because we have considered all monied institutions at the present time unsound and precarious.

4 Relative to manopolies generally we are unfriendly to them, any farther than their privileges tend to foster a spirit of improvement, in labor saving, in the facilities of procuring means of subsistence for a greater number of inhabitants, and are identified with the best interests of the people. But to those monopolies or companies with exclusive privileges of making money and oppressing the people, and that too, with a fictitious foundation, we are opposed as they are generally conducted, *toto celo.*

—July 1837, pages 535-543.

Our last mention of this unfortunate affair in the *Messenger and Advocate* is a warning from Joseph Smith to beware of bogus bills.

CAUTION.

To the brethren and friends of the church of Latter Day Saints, I am disposed to say a word relative to the bills of the Kirtland Safety Society Bank. I hereby warn them to beware of speculators, renegadoes and gamblers, who are duping the unsuspecting and the unwary, by palming upon them, those bills, which are of no worth, here. I discountenance and disapprove of any and all such practices. I know them to be detrimental to the best interests of society, as well as to the principles of religion.

JOSEPH SMITH Jun,

—August 1837, page 560.

HYMNS AND POEMS

The developing hymnody of the church was enhanced by
the publication of the Restoration movement's first hymn-
book, a compilation of ninety hymns selected by Emma
Smith and W. W. Phelps. Even with such a publication, new
hymns and poems continued to appear in the *Messenger and
Advocate.* Of the twenty-six hymns found in the three volumes, ten are preserved in Mormon hymnody while four are
still found in *The Hymnal* of the Reorganized Church (Nos.
35, 260, 283, 442).

Some of the movement's folklore was becoming institu-
tionalized into doctrinal form. The following hymn crystal-
lizes some of the notions current in the church of that day
concerning a place called Adam-ondi-Ahman, where Adam
was said to have gathered his posterity to bless them three
years before his death. In May 1838 the exact locale was
designated to be Spring Hill, Daviess County, Missouri.

Adam-ondi-Ahman.
By W. W. Phelps.

This world was once a garden place,
   With all her glories common;
And men did live a holy race,
And worship Jesus face to face,
   In Adam-ondi-Ahman.

We read that Enoch walk'd with God,
   Above the power of Mammon:
While Zion spread herself abroad,
And saints and angels sung aloud
   In Adam-ondi-Ahman.

Her land was good and greatly blest,
   Beyond old Israel's Canaan;
Her fame was known from east to west;
Her peace was great, and pure the rest—
   Of Adam-ondi-Ahman.

> Hosanna to such days to come—
> The Savior's second comin'—
> When all the world in glorious bloom,
> Affords the saints a holy home
> Like Adam-ondi-Ahman.

—June 1835, page 144.

A rather utopian view of Zion is disclosed in the hymn entitled "Home." The Saints' expectation of final success and ultimate triumph is caught up in this little poem.

HOME.

> How sweet is the mem'ry of all that we love,
> The saints who have laid up their treasures above,
> And have waited in faith for the Savior to come,
> With a fulness of glory to crown them his own
> At home, blessed home—
> Where the weary can rest, and the wicked ne'er come:
>
> How sweet is the prospect when saints shall be blest,
> And Zion extend from the east to the west;
> And heaven shall echo 'tis done, it is done!
> And parents and children, united as one,
> Praise God face to face,
> As clear as the moon, and as fair as the sun.

—September 1835, p. 192.

The sentiments of many members concerning the Prophet, which in some cases approached a worshipful reverence, are expressed in the following hymn penned by W. W. Phelps:

> Now we'll sing with one accord,
> For a prophet of the Lord,
> Bringing forth his precious word,
>   Cheers the saints as anciently.
>
> When the world in darkness lay,
> Lo, he sought the better way,
> And he heard the Savior say,
>   "Go and prune my vineyard, son!"

163

And an angel surely, then,
For a blessing unto men,
Brought the priesthood back again,
    In its ancient purity.

Even Joseph he inspires:
Yea, his heart he truly fires.
With the light that he desires
    For the work of righteousness.

And the book of Mormon true,
With its cov'nant ever new,
For the Gentile and the Jew,
    He translated sacredly.

The commandments to the church,
Which the saints will always search,
(Where the joys of heaven perch,)
    Came through him from Jesus Christ.

Precious are his years to come,
While the righteous gather home,
For the great Millenium,
    Where he'll rest in blessedness.

Prudent in this world of woes,
He will triumph o'er his foes,
While the realm of Zion grows
    Purer for eternity.

—October 1835, page 208.

The militant hymn of the Restoration movement, "The Spirit of God Like a Fire Is Burning," is well known to every Latter Day Saint. In addition to the three stanzas now appearing in *The Hymnal*, these additional stanzas appeared in the *Messenger and Advocate:*

We'll wash, and be wash'd, and with oil be anointed
    Withal not omitting the washing of feet:
For he that receiveth his PENNY appointed,
    Must surely be clean at the harvest of wheat.
We'll sing and we'll shout &c.

164

Old Israel that fled from the world for his freedom,
    Must come with the cloud and the pillar, amain:,
A Moses, and Aaron, and Joshua lead him,
    And feed him on manna from heaven again.
We'll sing and we'll shout &c.

How blessed the day when the lamb and the lion
    Shall lie down together without any ire;
And Ephraim be crown'd with his blessing in Zion,
    As Jesus descends with his chariots of fire!
We'll sing & we'll shout with His armies of heaven:
    Hosanna, hosanna to God and the Lamb!
Let glory to them in the highest be given,
    Henceforth and forever: amen and amen.

—January 1836, page 256.

The most ambitious poem is simply entitled "God." No author is credited. The concluding stanza raises a question as to whether or not the poet intended to suggest the doctrinal tenet that Godhood is within the grasp of man. This doctrine, which was to flower at Nauvoo, may here be represented in embryonic form.

GOD

O, THOU ETERNAL ONE! whose presence bright,
    All space doth occupy—all motions guide;
Unchanged through time's all devastating flight,
    Thou only God! There is no God beside.
Being above all beings! Mighty One!
    Whom none can comprehend, and none explore,
Who fillest existence with thyself alone;
    Embracing all—supporting—ruling o'er—
    Being whom we call God—and know no more!

In its sublime research, Philosophy
    May measure out the ocean deep—may count
The sands or the sun's rays—but God! for thee
    There is no weight nor measure; none can mount

Up to thy mysteries: Reason's brightest spark,
    Though kindled by thy light, in vain would try
To trace thy councils, infinite and dark;
    And thought is lost ere thought can soar so high,
    Even like past moments in eternity.

Thou from primeval elements, didst call
    First chaos, then existence—Lord on thee
Eternity had its foundation; all
    Sprung forth from thee; of light, joy, harmony,
Sole origin—all life, all beauty, thine.
    Thy word created all, and doth create;
Thy splendor fills all space with rays divine.
    Thou art, and wert, and shall be, glorious! great!
    Life giving, life sustaining Potentate.

Thy chains the unmeasured universe surround;
    Upheld by thee, by thee inspired with breath!
Thou the beginning with the end hast bound,
    And beautifully mingled life and death!
As sparks mount upward from the fiery blaze
    So suns are born—so worlds spring forth from thee!
And as the spangles in the sunny rays
    Shine round the silver snow, the pageantry
Of Heaven's bright army glitters in thy praise.

Yes, as a drop of water in the sea
    All this magnificence is lost in thee:
What are ten thousand worlds compar'd to thee?
    And what am I, then? Heaven's unnumber'd host,
Though multiplied by myriads, and arrayed
    In all the glory of sublimest thought,
Is but an atom in the balance weighed
    Against thy greatness—is a cypher brought
    Against infinity! What am I, then? Nought!

A million torches lighted by thy hand
    Wander unwearied through the blue abyss;
They own thy power; accomplish thy command,
    All gay with life, all eloquent with bliss:
What shall we call them? Piles of crystal light?
    A glorious company of golden streams?
Lamps of celestial ether burning bright?
    Suns lighting systems with their joyous beams?
But thou to these art as the noon to night.

Nought!—but the effluance of thy light divine,
    Pervading worlds, hath reached my bosom too;
Yes, in my spirit doth thy spirit shine
    As shines the sun-beam in a drop of dew.
Nought!—but I live, and on hope's pinions fly,
    Eager toward thy presence; for in thee
I live, and breathe, and dwell; aspiring high;
    Even to the throne of thy Divinity.
    I am, O God, and surely thou must be!

Thou art directing, guiding all. Thou art!
    Direct my understanding then to thee;
Control my spirit, guide my wandering heart;
Though but an atom 'midst immensity,
Still I am something, fashioned by thy hand!
    I hold a middle rank, 'twixt heaven and earth,
On the last verge of being stand,
    Close to the realm where Angels have their birth,
Just on the boundary of the spirit land!

The chain of being is complete in me;
    In me is matter's last gradations lost,
And the next step is spirit—Deity!
    I can command the lightning, and am dust,
A monarch, and a slave, a worm, a God!
    Whence came I here, and how? so marvellously
Constructed and conceived unknown! This clod
    Lives surely through some higher energy,
    For from itself alone it could not be.

—June 1837, page 528.

RESPONDING TO NOTICE FROM THE OUTSIDE WORLD

The editors of the *Messenger and Advocate* delighted in publishing favorable reports on Latter Day Saintism from those outside the fold. Such reports, however were few and far between. Here is one such item:

The following is taken from the Brookville (Ia.) Enquirer; and we copy it into the Advocate to show our friends the different feeling with which the elders of this church are received. All we have to say *now* on the extract, is that the Editor *could* not have been a sectarian—We judge him to be a Republican, and a gentleman.

[Editor]

"The Latter day Saints, or Mormons.

On last Saturday evening, for the first time, in this place, a gentleman, and minister belonging to this new sect, preached in the court house, to a very respectable audience; and discoursed briefly on the various subjects connected with his creed; explained his faith and gave a brief history of the book of Mormon—united it with the Holy Bible, &c.

By request, he tarried over Sabbath, and at 2 o'clock again opened public worship by an able address to the Throne of the Most High. He spoke for about an hour and a half to a very large audience, during which time he explained many important passages of the prophecies contained in the Old & New Testaments, and applied them according to their *literal* meaning. He was not lame in the attempt, and in a succinct and lucid manner imparted his belief to the audience.

He believes the book of Mormon to be a series of revelations, and other matters appertaining to the Ephraimites, Lamanites, &c. whom he believes to have been the original setters of this continent; and that an ancient Prophet caused the plates from which the book of Mormon was translated to be buried nearly two thousand years ago, in what is now called Ontario county; New York. He is also of the belief that Joseph Smith was cited to the plates by an angel from Heaven, and endowed with the gift to translate the engraving upon them into the known language of the country.

This book, he is of opinion, is an event intended to prepare for the great work, the second appearance of Christ, when he shall stand on the Mount of Oliver, attended by Abraham and all the Saints, to reign on the Earth for the space of a thousand years.

After he had closed his discourse, on Sabbath afternoon, he remarked that if "no one had any thing to say, the meeting would be considered as closed." Rev. Daniel St. John, a clergyman of the universal order, ascended the pulpit and in his usual eloquent strain held forth for a considerable time; taking exceptions to some of the positions of the preceeding speaker—more particularly as regarded his belief as to the second appearance of Christ, and his doctrine of future rewards and punishments. An interesting debate of about three hours ensued in which each had four hearings, and at the request of the audience, a division of the house was called for on the merits of the argument, and carried in favor of the Latter Day Saint by an overwhelming vote.

Though in some things he characterised the fanatic; yet, in the main, his doctrines were sound and his positions tenable. We would do injustic to the gentleman were we to omit stating, that in all the discourses of the like character, that we have ever heard it has never fallen to our lot to hear so much harmony in the arrangement of quotations from the sacred book. No passage could be refered to that would in the least produce discord in his argumants. The whole of his discourses were delivered in a very clear and concise manner, rendering it obvious that he was thoroughly acquainted with the course he believed he was called upon to pusue, in obedience to his Master's will.

If a man may be called eloquent who transfers his own views and feelings into the breasts of others—if a knowledge of the subject, and to speak without fear— are a part of the more elevated rules of eeloquence we have no hesitancy in saying ORSON PRATT was eloquent; and truly verified the language of Boileau: "What we clearly conceive, we can clearly express."

—February 1835, page 77.

Much anti-Restoration criticism was noted, but always in conjunction with an appropriate response from the editor or from one of the church leaders. In the following article, Oliver Cowdery replies to some criticism that appeared in the *New York Mercury*:

SLANDEROUS.

The following slanderous slip is cut from the New-York Mercury, of June, 25:

"An Angel Caught. .—The Magazine and Advocate says, that while the Mormon Prophet, Jo. Smith, was in Ohio, engaged in proselyting the people to the faith of the "Golden Bible," he sought to give additional solemnity to the baptismal rite, by affirming that on each occasion an angel would appear on the opposite side of the stream, and there remain till the conclusion of the ceremony. The rite was administered in the evening in Grand River, near Painesville, not by the Prophet in person, but by his disciples. In agreement with the prediction of the Prophet on each occasion a figure in white was seen on the opposite bank,

and the faith of the faithful was thereby greatly increased. Suspicions, as to the incorporeal nature of the reputed angel at length induced a company of young men (unbelievers of course) to examine the quality of the ghost, and having secreted themselves, they awaited its arrival. Their expectations were soon realized, by its appearance in its customary position, and rushing from their lair, they succeeded in forcing it into the stream, and although its efforts at escape were powerful, they succeeded in bearing it in triumph to the opposite side of the stream, when who should this supposed inhabitant of the upper world be but the Mormon Prophet himself!–*Rochester Rep.*"

There are, in our day, many kinds of craft; some have but a small, while others have a large support. Some have many advocates while others have few; but among them all, one would suppose that the great Babylon, spoken of in the Apocalypse, might be found—that notable city, which is to fall in one hour, while the inhabitants of the earth lament and mourn.

I do not suppose that the Messenger and Advocate will fall into the hands of but a few, if any, of those who severally read this ridiculous falsehood in the "Magazine and Advocate," which appears was the first to give it publicity; neither the patrons of the "Rochester Republican," (which I did believe possessed too much patriotism and liberality to give any attention to such a tale without proof,) and the "Mercury" which eagerly follows; but that a few thousand, among the many, may know that it adds another to the numerous catalogue, framed by designing men, and put in circulation by them and their dupes, and that it is noticed enough to be contradicted.

It may be distinctly understood that Joseph Smith, jr. the translator of the book of Mormon, has since the winter of 1831, resided in the State of Ohio, and for the most part of the time, within nine miles of Painesville; and had any occurrence of the kind ever transpired, it would have been proclaimed, through this region, upon the house tops;—and further, that he never baptized any one, neither were he present when an individual was baptized, into this church, near Painesville. It carries the stamp of its author upon the face of it.

Every well-wisher of his fellow-men will say at once, that such reports are only put forth with a design to calumniate the innocent and abuse the public, by forestalling their opinion before a man can be heard, or his character and principles known. Are the editors of either of those papers acquainted with the character of Joseph Smith, jr? Whether they are or are not, I venture to

say, that it is as good in the sight of either God or man as theirs.
Did they ever see him? Were they present on the occasion of
which they have mentioned? Or have they seen a person who says
he was? I venture to say, again, that if they are acquainted with
the one who reported the lie, he is among that class who think
scandal no harm, nor falsehoods upon the innocent, a crime; and
if they have seen the man who says he were present when such an
occurrence transpired, or ever heard Mr. Smith make or give such
a promise to any one, they have given publicity to the falsehood
of an individual who was ready to laugh them in their face for the
credulity, and blush at their folly.—C.

—July 1835, pages 148-149.

An exchange between Olion Barr and Sidney Rigdon was
followed with much interest. This was an age in which debate
was engaged in with relish. Notice in the following excerpts
how Sidney Rigdon's attitude changes during the course of
the interchange.

*The following communications have been handed to us for
publication, we have given them entire. Truth can loose nothing
by investigation, and error cannot gain any thing.*

Dear Brother:
It was with much pleasure that I read yours of the 16th August, and shall now, with equal pleasure, examine some of its
most important features.
1. You say "the plan of salvation was devised in Heaven." I say
so too; II. You say "that that plan was on the principle of revela
tions, miracles," &c. And that plan you say *"I utterly deny,"* I
presume you think so, but you are mistaken.
Now my Brother, I say to you, that that plan of salvation
which was devised in heaven, would always have remained in
heaven had it not been made known to men by *revelation.*—There
was no other way they could learn it, Human wisdom could never
have sought it out, and the book of nature could never have
taught it.
The design of revelation was, then, 1. To make known the
being of God, 2. To make known his will, and 3. To make known
the consequence of doing, or not doing his will. Two queries now
arise. 1. How was this revelation made to men? 2. How can we
know that it is a revelation from God? . . .

171

1. Did not *Jesus Christ,* and his *Apostles* deliver the Gospel, and the *whole* Gospel to the world? 2. And did they not receive it by *revelation* from God? 3. Were not the miracles they wrought, expressly to *convince the world,* that they were divinely authorised teachers, and that what they taught was from God? 4. And were not the miracles which they wrought, abundantly sufficient to confirm the fact that, God spoke by them? 1. If they delivered the *whole Gospel.* What more is there to be revealed—Or what reasons have we to expect more revelations? 2. And if no *New revelation* is to be made, Why should miracles be continued? Now my Brother I am candid in these queries, and that you may know where I am, I say to you, that I answer the first four queries all in the affirmation, and in reference to the last two, I say, I have no reason to expect any more revelation, consequently no more miracles. These are my honest convictions, after much prayerful investigation of the subject. . . .

Now my Brother, I wish you and some of the wisest of your Mormon teachers to make out my errors, and teach me a better way if you can. I wish you, and them also, to give a candid answer to my queries. Come now, do not shun a fair investigation, truth will suffer nothing by it. You think I am in error,— That I am not in the kingdom of God,—And that I must come into that new work in order to be saved. Now Brother, if I am wrong I am worth righting, and I am willing to be righted. If I am not safe, I am worth saving, and willing to be saved. And I think that you are deceived, and many others, and I want a chance to show you wherein.—And I am willing to spend some time, and some paper and ink to do it, whether I succeed, or not. And on my part I say, if you, or any of your people can, and will answer my honest objections to your theory, I shall be a Mormon.

I am as ever, Your
Affectionate Brother,
OLION BARR.

E. Barr.
Conneaut, Sept. 22nd, 1835.

Kirtland, November 15, 1835.

Elder O. Barr,

Dear Sir:—A letter written by you to your brother of this place, was put into my hands by him some time since, with a request that I should answer it. A press of business prevented me of doing it until now.

I can say that it is with a degree of pleasure, that I avail myself of the opportunity of forming an acquaintance with a stranger,

172

by investigating an item of our holy religion, believing that there is nothing in this world, which could profit us more, than a fair and candid investigation of the subject of revealed religion: being myself a firm believer in revelation.

Before I proceed to answer your four principle queries, I will notice some things said in the preceeding part of your letter. You say, "The design of revelation, was, then, 1st To make known the being of God." To this I must object, and my reasons for so doing are the following. Revelations from God were at all times the result of the faith of those who received them; for without faith it is impossible to please him." [God] Now if revelations were the result of the *faith* of those who received them, this faith could not exist, without the persons having it, had personally an idea of the being of God. "For how can they believe on him of whom they have not head" is an apostilic maxim, founded both in reason and revelation. This being the fact, no revelation could come only through those who previously had the idea of the being of God. . . .

While I am on the subject of revelations, and by way of reply to your obbervations on that subject,—Let me observe, that though there were men chosen of God through whom he gave revelations to the world, yet it does not follow of necessity, that those for whose use the revelations were given, had no other way of testing their truth, but the veracity of those through whom they came. This would to all intents be staying ourselves on man, and making flesh our arm; which is strictly forbidden in the word of the Lord.

I conceive Sir, that the heavens have always been accessible to the saints of God, and that God who gave revelations would also give testimony to the truth of them by his spirit, to those who sought it in sincerity and truth. So that the saints at no preriod of the world, were indebted to the veracity of inspired men alone for their firm reliance on revelations. . . .

I wish you to understand distinctly that I believe as much as you can believe, that Christ and his apostles preached the gospel, and the *whole* gospel; but I also believe that it was a very different thing from what is now preached for gospel in the world. Let me invite your attention to some of the differences between the gospel of Christ and what is now proclaimed in the world.

The first difference then I shall mention is that of the priesthood. That gospel had a priesthood attached to it, which had the power of getting revelations, and obtaining visions, as well as the ministering of angels. They had power to administer in the name of the Lord Jesus to the sick, and in his name to rebuke diseases of all kinds, they had also power to give the Holy Spirit by the laying on of the hands, they obtained revelations, not only for their own direction in the world; but for that of the churches also that they raised up. So that they were truly ministers of Christ sent forth to minister in his name to all who would believe, and by means of this ministry, and power, they could build up the kingdom of Christ among men, and establish his cause in the world. The gospel that men preach in these days have no such ministry or priesthood: the priesthood of modern times has no such power or authority. No revelations; no ministring of angels; no heavenly visions; no ministering of the Holy Spirit by the laying on of the hands, and yet claim to be the ministers of Christ acting under the same commission, and the same authority as they did. Surely the disparity is too great not to be seen by the least discerning. . . .

The second grand difference is the different effects which is produced by the two. The gospel preached by the Savior and his apostles produced the most marvelous effects, the persons who were administered to by the pristhood of that gospel, found themselves in possession of something very different from the rest of mankind. They too could lay hands on the sick and they would recover, they could take up serpents and they could not hurt them, they could drink any deadly thing and yet be unhurt. They also had the power of getting revelations, of seeing visions, of prophesying enjoying the ministering of angels as well as many other marvelous things, which are no where found among those who embrace the gospel of Modern times; but enjoyed by all those who received the gospel administered by the apostles. . . .

If I should ask by what power did the former day saints heal the sick, cast out devils, raise the dead, take up serpents, drink deadly things and yet not be hurt, work miracles, speak with tongues, interpret tongues, prophesy, dream dreams, see visions, &c. &c.—The answer would be, that it was by the power of the gospel by which they did such things, as administered by the Savior and his apostles. And this is what is proposed in the gospel as proclaimed by the former day saints, and if those who received it did not enjoy these blessings, they did not receive the blessings proposed to them in the gospel.

This then, is what I contend for; that the gospel as proclaimed by the Savior and his apostles, and as written in the new testament has disappeared with the ministry thereof, and this is the reason why revelation has ceased, and the power of the Holy Spirit known no more. If the gospel of the new testament was

174

proclaimed, all the effects of it would follow those who received it,—So that the same order of things would be on the earth now as was then.

You ask "If they revealed the whole gospel, what reason have we to expect any more revelation."

Let me ask a question in connection with this "If the world has departed from the gospel revealed by the Savior and his apostles so as to loose both its ministry and its effects? How will the God of heaven restore it to them again, but by revealing unto them that they are wrong, and showing to them and that by revelation too wherein they are wrong, that they may repent and turn to him and obtain forgiveness.—Or can you show me when it was, that a generation of people had apostatized from the truth, and ever turned back to it again without revelation being given unto them?

When you answer these questions I will answer yours.

Now Sir, having noticed every thing in your letter which I consider of importance I submit it to your inspection, desiring that you would reply as fully as the case requires hoping that this communication will be received in as good feelings as it was written.

In consideration of high respect, I subscribe myself your friend and well wisher,

SIDNEY RIGDON.

—February 1836, pages 257-263.

Mr. Sidney Rigdon,

Sir, yours of Dec. 1835 was duly received, and has been candidly, and I think impartially examined, and as the subject of religion is one of infinit importance, so it demands our most serious and prayerfull consideration. To err on some *minor* points, is but the fruits of our imperfect judgments, but to be mistaken in some of the *cardinal* points of religion, may involve us in a dilemma awful in its nature, & eternal in its consequences, Hence, to know God's will, demands our most serious enquiry, and to do it, calls for the most diligent application of all our powers—

While I acknowledge the kind spirit in which you have been pleased to notice my letter to my brother Ebenezer, I indulge the fond hope, that in the same spirit of christian kindness, you will answer two or three more of my interrogatories, founded on some remarks in your letter, remarks, which to me are new, and containing ideas of vast importance,—Ideas, on which, I have not

175

been in the habit of reflecting, yet, ideas which I wish not to *receive,* or *reject,* without candidly examining. My queries, Sir, were originated by your remark "that the Gospel as proclaimed by the Savior and his Apostles, and as written in the new testament *has disappeared.*" You will therefore confer a signal favor on me, and satisfy my inquiring mind, by giving a deffinite answer to the following interogatories. 1. What is the Gospel? Is what is now written in the New Testament the Gospel? Is it the whole Gospel? 2. Where is the Gospel? 3. Have the Mormons got the Gospel? Have they got the whole Gospel?

Dear Sir, as those queries engross my whole thoughts on this interesting topic, I hope you will indulge me with an explicit answer to each, when I pledge myself to notice candidly, your whole communication.

Hoping that this correspondence may result in God's glory, and our best interest. I subscribe myself,

Yours in Christian kindness,

S. Rigdon   O. BARR.

Kirtland, March, 1836.

Mr. O. Barr,

Sir:—Yours of February has come to hand. by which you request me to answer a number of questions; this is something which I did not expect, as I intended in mine to you to be so explicit as to have rendered your interrogatories unnecessary, particularly, on the points on which you have required information, in this, it appears by yours, I have failed.

You ask me, "What is the gospel?" In answering this question I think I will render it unnecessary to give a formal answer to the rest of your queries, as I shall answer them all by answering this one.

I answer then in the language of the New Testament Romans 1:16, "The gospel is the power of God unto salvation, to all that believe:" or in other words, it is God's scheme of saving men, and this scheme is made known in the New Testament, which scheme of things (or gospel) consists in putting men in possession of the power of God; for it is God's *power* to save men, and how is it God's power, unto salvation? . . .

The whole matter then comes to this, that the gospel as set forth in the New Testament, is an order of things through which men were made partakers of the power of God while in the flesh, and that by one man administering to another by the authority of God in the name of Jesus Christ, this is what is called the gospel in the New Testament. It was enjoyed by the ministery of Apos-

176

tles, Prophets, Evangelists &c. and through the ministry of these
men the power of God was received; they administered to the
believers by the laying on of the hands, and the power of God
attended, and thus men in days of old received the power of God
unto salvation, and it was because of this, that the gospel is called
the power of God unto salvation.

You ask if we have the gospel, and where is the gospel?

I answer that the power of administering in the name of the
Lord Jesus to men through which they were made partakers of the
power of God, was never enjoyed by any of the human family
but by the revelation of Jesus Christ as Paul got it, if we have got
the gospel that is the way we have got it, and this power we
profess to have, and we obtained it by the ministering of Holy
Messengers.

Thus I have answered your queries in as few words as possible
in order to cut the work short in righteousness.

I shall await your reply to my whole communication, hoping I
shall not have to wait long.

Believe me, Yours in
the best of feelings,
S. RIGDON.

—March 1836, pages 273-274.

President Rigdon:

Dear Sir, As the investigation in which you are now participating first commenced with my brother Eebuezer, I consider it
proper to state to you the origin of this controversy; that you
may see the nature and design of the remarks, and hence the
better understand them. What gave rise to my remarks on revelation and miracles, was, my brother charged me of "utterly denying that plan of salvation founded on revelation, miracles," &c.
To convince him of his mistake, I affirmed to be a believer in
both, and attempted to show him the design of both revelation
and miracles. . . .

I have attentively examined your communication, and as I do
not wish to multiply words, I have endeavored to mark only the
prominent features of difference; and shall now, caudidly examine them.

The principal points of difference are, 1. The design of revelation. 2. The design of miracles. 3. In reference to what the gospel
is. And 4. Relation to the necessity of revelation and miracles at
the present day. . . .

177

You say, "this then, is what I contend for, that the gospel as preached by the Savior and his apostles, and as written in the new testament has disappeared"

This question will be determined by ascertaining what the gospel is.

I have asked you, "is that which is now written in the New Testament the gospel." You say the gospel is the power of God. Well, what is the power of God? You say it is "God's scheme of saving men." What then is God's scheme of saving men? You say "it is putting men into possession of the power of God." Now look at it. The gospel is the power! The power is the scheme!! and the scheme is the putting men into possession of the power!!! This is like the boy's answer to his father, when he asked him, where is the chain, he said the chain is with the plow. Where is the plow? He said, it is with the drag. Now when the father can find out where the drag is, he can find where the chain is also: So with me, when I can learn the last, I shall know the first.

But sir, leaving your vague and indefinite answer; in reviewing your whole communication, I conclude that what you call the gospel is that power by which the sick are healed—miracles wrought &c. And that this power to work miracles—confer the Holy Spirit, speak with tongues &c. has disappeared, I agree with you. But sir, I hope to show you that that power is one thing, and the gospel another.

The gospel then, is the glad tidings of a Savior, and of salvation to all nations. This is the gospel which was "preached before unto Abraham, saying in thee shall all nations be blessed,"...

One of two conclusions sir, you must come to. You must say that what is written in the New Testament is not the gospel, or the whole gospel; or you must say that your visions, revelations and prophecies are no part of the gospel. If the whole gospel was revealed by Christ and his apostles—and that gospel is written in the New Testament, then sir, no after revelation can be any part of the gospel; and if you, or I, or an "angel from heaven, preach any other gospel," than that the primitive saints received, Paul says, "let him be accursed" If you preach what Christ and the apostles preached, you preach the gospel; but if you preach any thing they did not, you do not preach the gospel, or you preach "another gospel." And if you preach only what they did. you reveal nothing, you only proclaim what was before revealed....

While I thus plead that we have the gospel, I admit that the sects, (not excepting your own) have departed from its order. You ask, "if the world has departed from the gospel, how is it to be restored but by revelation?" I answer, the gospel does not need to be restored to the world. Let the world return back to the gospel, and its order, and all will be well.

I will now conclude this letter, by requesting you to reflect what further light you can on this subject.

And subscribe myself
Yours in Christian kindness,
OLIVER BARR.

President S. Rigdon,
   Kirtland,
Conneaut, May 24th, 1836.
P. S. As you have published our correspondence thus far, I shall expect you will publish this also, and entire.

O. B.

Kirtland, June, 1836.

Mr. O. Barr:

Sir—I have received your last, and I think that it will not be strange to you, that I should be surprised at receiving such a production from your pen.

When a gentleman, gratuitously, gives a challenge to a whole society, and any one of them sees proper to accept it, and replies to him in a respectful manner, it will surely be expected that he will be treated with common courtesy. This, sir, was my expectation; but you must know if it were, that in reading your letter I must have been greatly disappointed; for surely you know, that so far from its being respectful, it is scurrilous. Your plow and drag story, savors of any thing but christian propriety and decorum; but perhaps you designed it to be as the shade in the picture, to make the other parts of your letter appear more brilliant. If this were the case, I think, you acted wisely; for it would certainly require the very dregs of vulgarity to have that effect upon your letter. . . .

And seeing you have declared that you are among the number of unbelievers. I warn you in the name of Jesus Christ, and by virtue of the Holy Priesthood confered on me by the revelation of Jesus Christ, to repent of your sins, and be baptized for the remission of them, and receive the gift of the Holy Spirit by laying on of the hands of those who are ordained in these last days unto that power, or you shall be damned; for your great ignorance of the things of God, clearly manifests that you are in the gall of bitterness, and bonds of iniquity, and an entire stranger to the gospel of Christ: having a form of Godliness but denying the power thereof, from such my master commands me to turn away, as I do from you; believing that if I were to indulge you in

179

writing any more to be published in the papers in this place, I should offend the readers thereof. Seeing that the least discerning cannot help but see, that you are capable of any violation of the rules of investigation and of the most unwarrantable affrontery; and that the fear of God is not before your eyes, for if it were, you would not put at defiance all scripture, all reason, all language, all common sense; for surely your letter is shocking to all.

Before you ever present yourself again as a braggadocio challenging with a high hand, people to investigate with you the subject of religion, I would seriously recommend to you to get some Yankee school master to give you some lessons on english grammar, that you may know that them apostles is not quite according to the rules of grammar, and also get some country girl to give you a few lessons on logic, so that you may be enabled to tell the difference, between a man's first ideas and his knowledge.

By way of conclusion I say sir that I feel myself insulted by being brought into contact with such a man and the correspondence between you and I closes. Farewell.

SIDNEY RIGDON.
—June 1836, pages 321-329.

OFFICIAL ANNOUNCEMENTS

The *Messenger and Advocate* was an important instrument in enforcing disciplinary action as, for example, in this short notice concerning the silencing of a minister.

> Bro. Cowdry,
> Sir:
> From satisfactory evidence received from Connecticut concerning the conduct of elder Gladden Bishop, we say that he is suspended as a preacher of the gospel until such times as an investigation can be had before the traveling elders from Kirtland at some one of the conferences noticed in the preceding Number of the Advocate. We are not fond of having the church of the Latter Day Saints represented by men whose conduct and teaching will not stand the test of the most rigid investigation.
> O. HYDE.
> W. E. M'LELIN. *Clerks of conference.*
> *Kirtland, Ohio, April 27, 1835.*

—April 1835, page 103.

Happier circumstances are evident when the ban of silence is lifted, or the litigant in a church court case is acquitted.

Extracts of Conference Minutes.
Council met in Kirtland, Sept 28; and took into consideration the case of Elder G. Bishop, who had previously been suspended by the travelling council, for interpreting some passages of Scripture in an improper manner; and also for persisting in said erroneous opinions, &c. He made a humble confession and asked the forgiveness of the councils and the church; and promised to do better for the future.—He was forgiven, restored and received in fellowship.*

*The points on which Elder Bishop was suspended, were not points on the gospel, as we know of; but of some other mysterious passages: for instance one respecting the two witnesses: Rev. chap. XI. He stated that J. Smith, jr. and O. Cowdery were the two persons alluded to, &c. which is incorrect.

Also, Elder P. H. Young, who had been disfellowshiped by the High Council, for alledged improper conduct, perrsonally appeared before said council; and the charge not being sustained, he was honorably acquitted, and restored to his former standing and fellowship.

WARREN PARRISH, *Clerk.*
—September 1835, page 186.

A plea for brevity is promulgated in this notice:

☞ To save any improper feelings among the servants of the Lord, we have to say, that want of space and time, have caused us to abridge & condense the letters which come in from the travelling elders, &c. And we take this opportunity of suggesting the propriety of *brevity*: short letters, containing matters of fact, are what we want, and what the saints need to build them up in righteousness. To worship God in spirit and truth, can be done without much speaking; and facts may be told in few words.

—July 1835, page 155.

The Prophet faced the problem of having to pay the postage on mail sent to him. This is how he responded:

To the Editor of the Messenger and Advocate:
Dear Brother—I wish to inform my friends and all others, abroad, that whenever they wish to address me thro' the Post Office, they will be kind enough to pay the postage on the same.

My friends will excuse me in this matter, as I am willing to pay postage on letters to hear from *them;* but am unwilling to pay for insults and menaces,—consequently, must refuse *all,* unpaid.

Yours in the gospel,
JOSEPH SMITH, jr.
Kirtland, Dec. 5, 1835.

—December 1835, page 240.

Another related problem is how to get patrons to pay their bills. Sometimes a huffy reminder appears:

SEE TO IT.

☞ All persons indebted for the Messenger and Advocate, are requested to make PAYMENT.

—October 1835, page 203.

On occasion an announcement is inserted to squelch a rumor. In some cases we are left to conjecture what that rumor might have been.

To the inhabitants of Milton and Palmyra, Portage county Ohio:

Having learned from a respectable source that rumors were afloat and had gained some credence in your towns, that were derogatory to the characters of Joseph Smith Jr. and the family of Sidney Rigdon We therefore deemed it our duty to say in defence of injured innocence, that we have the best of reasons for saying that the reports to which we have alluded, are without any foundation in truth. Since our acquaintance with J. Smith Jr. there has been the strongest ties of friendship existing between himself and S. Rigdon. And we hazard nothing in saying, were those reports true that must have originated in your vicinity, the bonds of friendship would have been severed forever between them. We are fully sensible, and are willing, as far as the character of J.—— Smith Jr. is concerned, (his enemies themselves in this place being judges) to pronounce the whole a sheer fabrication.

Relative to the family of Sidney Rigdon, we have to say, that it is large, consisting mostly of females, young innocent, un-

suspecting, without reproach and for ought we know, above
suspicion.—Ed.

—September 1837, page 566.

MISCELLANEOUS MATERIALS

While selections from previously published materials were
at a minimum, a few made their way into the pages of the
Messenger and Advocate, most notably two chapters from
"Fox's history of the Martyrs," a whole section of Thomas
Dick's *Philosophy of a Future State* (apparently very influential in shaping the metaphysics of some of the church
leaders), and a passage from "Milner's Church history" describing the heresies faced by the Christians of the second
and third centuries.

A series of eight essays on ancient history appears in the
Messenger and Advocate, apparently authored by W. A.
Cowdery. A great amount of research is evident, as the
author discusses the civilizations of ancient Egypt, Phoenicia,
and Greece.

Only two issues, June and July of 1837, carry a summary
of "news of the day." A survey of nations is attempted:

> Accounts from foreign prints announce the death of Wm.IV
> the King of England: and give particulars of the splendid funeral
> arrangements.— Arrangements are making for the new Govern-
> ment under the reigning Queen. . . .
>
> Our relations with foreign powers, remain unchanged since our
> last, we believe they are all of a friendly nature. Mexico has
> manifested some little uneasiness in consequence of the part some
> of our citizens have taken in behalf of Texas, which Mexico con-
> siders in the light of revolted subjects. We believe humanly speak-
> ing, we have nothing to fear from Mexico, but we hope and trust
> our Government will be as ready and as willing to mete out
> justice to Mexico as to England France or Russia. Texas appears
> confident she shall maintain her Independence, and is prepared
> and preparing to resist any and every aggression of her rights.
>
> Our domestic concerns do not essentially differ from what
> they were one month since. trouble and distress are the topics of
> conversation among politicians, merchants, mechanics and
> demagogues; money, banks and bankruptcies are reiterated by

183

some, while others contend there is no distress other than that caused by overtrading. Our travels and observations warrent us in saying that crops are very good almost universally through our own country. The public prints for the most part go to establish the same fact.

Crimes misdemeanors and casualities, continue to occupy a space in all public journals.

Transgression is prevalent, sin abounds, time rolls on, with its accustomed velocity, the world is in commotion, and every circumstance, with every evidence to our senses, show that the adversay of all righteousness is not yet bound.

—July 1837, pages 534-535.

SUMMARY OF THE NEWS OF THE DAY.

Relative to our intercourse with the eastern nations, it is on an amicable footing and of a friendly, reciprocal nature. Our government is envied by despots, loved by the friends of liberty, and its citizens and its flag respected in almost every clime.

The great pressure in the money market has been felt in England as well as in America, but the latest advices, bring accounts more favorable to returning prosperity.

Bread stuffs are every where high, throughout our whole country. The season has been cool, wet, and consequently backward, and the prospect of the husbandman, gloomy and foreboding; but present prospects here, and recent accounts from abroad, are far more cheering than they were but a few short weeks since. We now hope for a good harvest and good crops. Fruit trees are heavily laden as far as we have travelled or learned by others.

The Indians in and about our extreme southern borders, continue at intervals a kind of cowardly, predatory warfare, upon the sparse population of that country, rather than open, manly hostilities.

Mexico, our southern neighbor, by no means acknowledges the independence of Texas, but considers her inhabitants as rebellious subjects.

Spain is divided against herself and is exhausting her blood and treasure in her own destruction.

Portugal has long been wasting her own resources to pamper her princes, or gratify the different competitors for the crown, till she hardly holds a respectable rank among nations.

Russia is powerful in men and means, holds the balance of power in Europe, and at home in her high northern latitude and severe climate may defy the combined attack of all her neighbors.

184

Poor Poland has lost her rank among the nations and become extinct, to gratify the ambition of Nicholas, the Autocrat of Russia.

China is nearly in *statu quo,* while the Turkish or Mohamedan power is rather on the wane.

Of Africa we can say but little, only that it was once the home of the black man. Liberia is situated on its coast and is famous for the colony of emancipated negroes established there, by the munificence of citizens of our own government.

But to return again to our own continent, our own country, the land that gave us birth—we look around and see men reckless of consequences abuse one another, to gratify prejudice, envy or party rancor, and we blush at their folly; we then reflect that we have a government of laws, with balances and checks—and the acts of all are subjects of free discussion.

—June 1837, page 527.

One of the paper's saddest functions was to call attention to deaths that had occurred within the ranks of the church fellowship. The fact that so many young women of child-bearing age were listed reminds us of how far the medical science of obstetrics has advanced since that time. Some of the obituaries tell of the demise of persons "ripe with age," while others more sadly inform the membership of deaths involving more tragic circumstances. Here are some typical examples.

—Clay co. Mo. the 27th of November last, *Christain Whitmer,* one of the first elders of the church of Latter Day Saints, aged about 38 years. He died of severe affliction upon one of his legs, which he bore for a long time with great patience. He has gone home to his Creator rejoicing in the new and everlasting covenant. "Blessed are the dead that die in the Lord."

—December 1835, page 240.

Died in this town, on Monday Oct. 24th 1836, after a short illness, Hazen M. Sweat aged two years & fourteen days, and on Saturday the 30th following, Benjamin W. Sweat aged five years six months and six days. These were the only children of Benjamin and Ede Sweat, who had then but recently arrived in this place.

—January 1837, page 447.

185

DIED—In this town, on the 9th inst. Elizabeth Ann, daughter of Oliver and Elizabeth Ann Cowdery, aged five months and twenty-five days.

—In Brownhelm, Ohio, on the 3d inst. Francis Weedon, who had been a member of the church of Latter Day Saints about five years. He appeared sensible that the time of his departure was at hand, and manifested a willingness to go. . . .   [Com.

DROWNED, in Wolf creek, in the town of Copley, Medina county, Ohio, Corydon, son of David Taylor, aged five years.[Com.

—May 1837, p. 512.

Died, at Independence, Cuyahoga Co. Ohio August 9th 1836, sister Chloe Rudd aged 78 years and 8 months. She had been a member of the church of Latter Day Saints, more than three years. She has "gone down to the grave in a good old age like a shock of corn fully ripe."

—September 1836, page 382.

Died in this place on the evening of the 19th inst. elder Seth, Johnson, aged 30 years. Elder J. was a young man of promising talents, and of strict religious principles; ever manifesting, by his acts, the warm affection of a heart devoted to the cause of God, and to that most dear to him of all things, the religion of the Lord Jesus; but his Master has accepted his work and taken him home, where he can receive that reward promised to the pure in heart.

Though dust returns to dust, and his spirit has fled to Christ, we drop this as a tribute to his worth—*HE WAS A SAINT.*—*[Editor]*

—*February 1835, page 74.*

In this town on Friday, the 16th inst. Samuel Carvel, infant son of elder S. Rigdon, aged two weeks and four days. . . .

In Benson, Vt. on the 26th Dec. last, Caroline, late consort of elder *Harlow Redfield,* age 30 years.

She was among the first who embraced the fulness of the gospel in that country, and has ever maintained a steady, circumspect and virtuous walk. She bore with becoming fortitude, her last illness, and only longed for the anxious hour when her spirit should take its welcome exit to be with Jesus.—*Editor.*

—January 1835, page 63.

DIED—In this place, on the 15th inst. Naomi Harmon, daughter of Oliver and Sarah Harmon; aged 11 years, 11 months and 12 days. She was a member of the church of the Latter Day Saints, and died in the triumph of faith, often saying to her parents, and to her brothers and sisters, not to weep for her; or in other words, not to feel bad, for she said that it was better for her to go than to stay! for she knew that she should be happy, she wanted to go and be with Christ and her brothers that had died and gone before her.

—June 1836, page 329.

Died at Shoal Creek Mo. on the 23 of August last Roxana, consort of A. C. Lyon formerly a resident of Willoughby, Cuyahoga, Co. O. Sister Lyon was far on the declivity of life and has left the partner of her youthful days, a family of children and a circle of friends to deplore her loss. Surely the destroyer executes his office reckless of consequences.

—January 1837, pages 447-448.

Birth announcements were never printed, but toward the closing days of the paper's existence wedding announcements were being inserted with increasing frequency. Here is an example of a "Hymenial":

Hymenial.

Married in this town on the 13th inst. by F. G. Williams Esq. Elder Jonathan H. Holmes to Miss Marietta Carter, Elder Willford Woodruff to Miss Phebe W. Carter, and Elder George W. Robinson to Miss Athalia Rigdon all of this town.

Should the propriety of our elders entering into matrimonial contracts be questioned, we just say in the language of Paul, "have we not power to lead about a sister, a wife as well as other apostles, and as the brethren of the Lord & Cephas?"

—April 1837, page 496.

187

With the arrival of the paralyzing financial crisis of 1837, many subscribers fell behind in remitting their subscription fees. Finally, it was determined that the *Messenger and Advocate* would have to cease by reason of insolvency. Out of 1,500 subscribers, 1,000 were not paying their bill. Immediately plans were formulated for a new magazine, to be entitled the *Elders' Journal*, to replace the *Messenger and Advocate*, picking up the paying customers of the earlier paper but discarding the "dead weight" of its subscription list. The prospectus for the new journal was published in the August 1837 *Messenger and Advocate*, and reprinted verbatim in the following (and last) issue.

In later years, many Saints in retrospect looked back upon these days at Kirtland with nostalgia, as a brief respite from the turmoil that plagued the church during its early formative years. After the death of the Prophet, when Sidney Rigdon went to Pittsburgh, alienated from the Twelve and intending to maintain himself as guardian over the remnants of the church that likewise rejected the apostles' leadership, he recovered this old name, *Messenger and Advocate*, for his own periodical, perhaps hoping that those who knew the peace and prosperity of these "golden days" at Kirtland would more readily rally to his banner.

The House of the Lord, Kirtland, Ohio

Chapter 5

ELDERS' JOURNAL

With Joseph Smith, Jr., as editor, Sidney Rigdon as assistant editor, and Don Carlos Smith (brother of the Prophet) in charge of correspondence and business matters, the *Elders' Journal of the Church of Latter Day Saints* was officially launched in the fall of 1837 at Kirtland. Intended to be a monthly publication, this periodical, the same size and price as its predecessor, was issued only four times. Burdened with delinquent subscribers from the *Messenger and Advocate* list, witnessing a revolt within the church ranks and agitation from without, and experiencing a 150-mile change of locale were a few of the difficulties with which the producers of the *Elders' Journal* had to cope.

The church leaders had envisioned the *Journal* as an effective means of communication among the elders in which several aims could be achieved: to inform the public about the work and progress of the church, to be an instrument for making known "our own history," and to be a reporter of and commentator upon world news. Only the first objective was realized.

After the second issue (November 1837), the printing office was destroyed by fire, and publication ceased for a period of seven months. By that time, Joseph Smith had relocated to Far West, Missouri. Also, a new name for the church had come into being. And so in July 1838, the *Elders' Journal of the Church of Jesus Christ of Latter Day Saints* was published, again with the Prophet listed as editor.

The last issue of this publication came forth one month later. By that time the numerous details involved in getting out a periodical were becoming too great a burden in light of the threat of mob action. Far West, once considered by the

Saints as, "an oasis in the desert called Missouri," was becoming the scene of increasing confusion and instability. Finally, all of the anti-Mormon forces were unleashed when Governor Boggs issued his infamous "extermination order." When General Lucas' militia, six thousand strong, surrounded Far West, demanding the surrender of the community's leaders to stand trial for treason and the relinquishing of all property and firearms, the *Elders' Journal* press and type were hastily buried. The Saints could ill afford the loss of another press on top of all their other woes. At a later time, this equipment was dug up and transported to Nauvoo where it was employed in turning out the *Times and Seasons*.

Since only four numbers of the *Elders' Journal* need to be considered, we will look at some of their contents by number rather than by topic.

ELDERS' JOURNAL
OF THE CHURCH OF LATTER DAY SAINTS

Vol. I. No. 1.]   KIRTLAND, OHIO, OCTOBER, 1837.   [Whole No. 1.

The bulk of the first issue was taken up with four missionary reports and a letter exchange between a "Mormon" preacher and a "Campbellite" minister.

Heber Kimball writes from faraway Britain concerning the work of evangelism in that nation.

> *Preston, Lancashire, Eng. Sept.* 2 1837
>
> My Dear Companion,
>
> I take this opportunity to write a few lines to you, to let you know I am in the land of the living. I am a pilgrim on the earth, and a stranger in a strange land far from my home, and among those that seek my life because I preach the truth and those things that will save their lives in the day of tribulation. On the 18 of July we landed in Liverpool in the forenoon. I had peculiar feelings when we landed, the Spirit of God burned in my breast; and at the same time I felt to covenant before God, to live a new life, and to pray that the Lord would help me to do the same. We remained there three days, resting our bodies; on saturday the 22

we took coach for Preston, the distance 31 miles, we arrived there at four in the afternoon. . . .Eight days after we arrived at Preston, nine presented themselves for baptism, and I was appointed to baptise, on sunday morning, and Br. Russel was appointed to preach in the market place at half past two in the afternoon; this was concluded upon on saturday evening, and we retired to bed as usual.—A singular circumstance occurred before morning, which I will quote from Br. Hydes journal, as he wrote it down, he commences as follows, "Elder Russel was much troubled with evil spirits and came into the room where Elder Kimball and myself were sleeping, and desired us to lay our hands on him, and rebuke the evil spirit: I arose upon the bed, and Br. Kimball got upon the floor and I sat upon the bed; we laid our hands on him, and brother Kimball rebuked and prayed for him but just before he had finished his prayer, his voice faltered, and his mouth was shut, and he began to tremble and real to and fro, and fell on the floor like a dead man, and uttered a deep groan, I immediately seized him by the shoulder, and lifted him up, being satisfied that the devils were exceding angry because we attempted to cast them out of Br. Russel, and they made a powerful attempt upon Elder Kimball as if to dispatch him at once, they struck him senseless and he fell to the floor; Br. Russel and myself then laid our hands on Elder Kimball, and rebuked the evil spirits, in the name of Jesus Christ; and immediately he recovered his strength in part, so as to get up; the sweat began to roll from him most powerfully, and he was almost as wet as if he had been taken out of the water, we could very sensibly hear the evil spirits rage and foam out their shame. Br. Kimball was quite weak for a day or two after: it seems that the devils are determined to destroy us, and prevent the truth from being declared in England.". . .

You stated in your letter that some of the twelve were coming to England next spring, and you say they are calculating to bring their wifes with them; this I have no objections to, but if they come they had better bring money to support themselves; I think they had better take up with Br. Joseph's advice, and leave their wifes at home, for if they bring them here, they will repent the day they do it, I do not wish to bring my wife to this place to suffer, if they could see the misery that I do they would not think of such a thing, the Savior says, "he that is not willing to leave father and mother, and wife and children, brothers and sisters, houses and lands for my sake and the gospel, are not worthy of me." We have had our own hired house, since we have been here, and bought our own provisions; we do not eat but one meal at home, for the brethren invite us to eat dinner and supper with them.

Br. Russel and Snider that went North, we have not had the particulars from. We have preached in the streets the most of the time, until our lungs are injured much, we have large congregations to hear, and the houses are very small in this place.

We have had the Cock-pit to preach in, two Sundays once a day, and next sunday we have the privilege of preaching in it twice: it will hold six or seven hundred people. . . .I felt much gratified with the news you wrote in your kind letter; I had many sorrowful hours thinking of the things in Kirtland: it has been my prayer ever since I left, that a reconciliation should take place. I feel contented about you I know the Lord will take care of you, and preserve you till I come home; and feed you, and clothe you, and the children. And he will take care of me; give me your prayers, and you shall have mine: be faithful my dear companion, our labours will soon be over, when we shall meet to part no more forever. I am glad you have sister Fielding with you, I hope she will stay with you till I come home. Tell William and Hellen and Heber to be good children, and pray for me, my love to all enquiring friends; write when you receive this, and let this sheet be an example for you, this to my dearest friend.

HEBER KIMBALL.

—pages 4-7.

The first issue carries the news of the passing of Jerusha T. Smith, wife of Hyrum Smith, Joseph's brother.

Died, in this place on the 13th Inst. after an illness of about ten days, Mrs. Jerusha T. Smith, the wife of Hyrum Smith. She has left five small children together with numerous relatives to mourn her loss, a loss which is severely felt by all.

Our Sister was beloved and highly esteemed by every lover of truth and virtue; but she has been taken from us in an untimely, or rather an unexpected hour, as her companion was from home perhaps near one thousand miles at the time of her decease, and was deprived of the privilege of witnessing her exit from a world of sorrow and perplexity, to the paradise of God.

But, Alas! she is gone home! yes, (using her own language to one of her tender offsprings when on her dying bed,) *Tell your father when he comes that the Lord has taken your mother home, and left you for him to take care of.*

192

She had her senses until the last, and fell asleep, leaving this assurance behind as a reward for leaving all that was dear for the sake of a risen Savior, and enduring in faith on his name to the end, that she should have a part in the first resurrection, and come forth and inherit the mansion that is prepared for the faithful, and receive the welcome plaudit "Come ye blest of my Father inherit that kingdom prepared for you from before the foundation of he world."

—Page 16.

In an editorial in the second issue, Joseph Smith, in setting forth a point of editorial policy, attacks the earlier efforts of W. A. Cowdery, probably in reference to his treatment of the failure of the Kirtland Safety Society.

We would say to the patrons of the Journal, that we calculate to pursue a different course from that of our predecessor in the editorial department.—We will endeavor not to scandalize our own citizens, especially when there is no foundation in truth for so doing; we consider that when a man scandalizes his neighbor, it follows of course that he designs to cover his own iniquity: we consider him who puts his foot upon the neck of his benefactor, an object of pitty rather than revenge, for in so doing he not only shows the contraction of his own mind but the wickedness of his heart also.

—Page 27.

The Prophet continues by describing a trip to Far West, undertaken for the purpose of establishing stakes for the gathering.

Be it known unto the Saints scattered abroad greeting:
That myself together with my beloved brother Sidney Rigdon, having been appointed by a general conference of elders held in Kirtland in the house of the Lord on the 18th of Sept. for the purpose of establishing places of gathering for the Saints &c. we therefore would inform our readers that we started from Kirtland in company with V. Knight and Wm. Smith on the 27th of Sept. last, for the purpose of visiting the Far West, and also to discover situations suitable for the location of the Saints who are gathering

193

for a refuge and safety, in the day of the wrath of God which is
soon to burst upon the head of this generation, according to the
testimony of the prophets; who speak expressly concerning the
last days: We had a prosperous and a speedy journey; we held one
meeting in Norton township Ohio, and three in Doublin, Ia. one
between Doublin and Tere Haute, Ia. two in Tere Haute, one in
Palmyra, Mo. 2 in Huntsville, one in Carlton; all of which were
tended with good success and generally allayed the prejudice and
feeling of the people, as we judge from the treatment we received,
being kindly and hospitably entertained. On our arrival at the city
of Far West, we found the church of Latter Day Saints in that
place in as prosperous a condition as we could have expected, and
as we believe enjoying a goodly portion of the Spirit of God, to
the joy and satisfaction of our hearts.

The High council was immediately called and many difficulties
adjusted, and the object of our mission was laid before them,
after which the subject of the propriety of the Saints, gathering
to the city Far West, was taken into consideration, after a lengthy
discussion upon the subject, it was voted, that the work of the
gathering to that place be continued, and that there is a plenty of
provisions in the upper counties for the support of that place, and
also the emigration of the Saints; also voted that other Stakes be
appointed in the regions round about, therefore a committee was
appointed to locate the same; consisting of Oliver Cowdery,
David Whitmer, John Corril, and Lyman Wight; who started on
their mission before we left. . . .We would also say to the Saints,
that we were much pleased with the location of the Far West, and
also the society of that place; and we purpose of locating our
families in that place as soon as our circumstances will admit.

—Pages 27, 28.

**The minutes of a general assembly held at Far West reveal
a rift in the leadership ranks of the church in that place.**

Far West, Mo. Nov. 7, 1837.

At a general assembly of the church of Latter Day Saints,
assembled at Far West, to take into consideration and transact the
business of said church, Elder Thomas B. Marsh was chosen
Moderator, and Oliver Cowdery appointed Clerk.

After singing, the Moderator addressed the throne of grace in
prayer; after which pres't. Sidney Rigdon explained the object of
the meeting, giving a relation of the recent re organization of the

194

church in Kirtland—the minutes of said meeting were read by the Moderator, who also nominated Joseph Smith jr. the first pres't. of the whole church, to preside over the same. All were requested (males and females to vote—who was unanimously chosen. He then made a few remarks, accepting the appointment, requesting the prayers of the church in his behalf.

President Smith then nominated pres't. Sidney Rigdon to be one of his Counselors—who was unanimously chosen.

He then nominated pres't. Frederick G. Williams to be his next Counselor, who was objected to by Elder Lyman Wight, in a few remarks, refering to a certain letter, written to this place by the said F. G. Williams: also Elder Marsh objected to pres't. Williams. Elder James Emmet also object to pres't Williams. . . .

President S. Rigdon then nominated pres't. Hyram Smith to take pres't. Williams' place. He then called for a vote in favor of pres't. Williams, who was rejected. He then called for a vote in favor of pres't. Hyram Smith, which was carried unanimous.

Some few remarks were made by pres'ts. David Whitmer and S. Rigdon.

David Whitmer was nominated as the President of this branch of the church, and was objected to by Elder Marsh. Bishop Partrage said he should vote for pres't. Whitmer Elder Wm. E. McLellin made a few remarks. Elder George M. Hinkel made remarks in favor of pres't. Whitmer—also Elder King Follet.

Elder Caleb Baldwin spake against pres't Whitmer—also Elder Seymore Brunson.

Elder Elisha H. Groves spake in favor of pres't. Whitmer. Further remarks from Elder McLellin by request of pres't. Whitmer who made satisfaction for him. Remarks from pres't. Joseph Smith jr. who called for an expression which was carried by almost a unanimous vote in favor of pres't. Whitmer.

President Joseph Smith jr. then nominated John Whitmer for an assistant president, who was objected, and Elder Marsh spake in opposition to him and read a list of charges from a written document against him and pres't. Phelps. Pres't. John Whitmer then spake a few words by way of confession, and was followed by Elder Isaac Morley. The vote was called and carried unnimously. . . .

The congregation, after a few remarks from pres't. Rigdon, unanimousley voted not to support stores and shops, selling spirituous liquors, Tea, Coffee or Tobacco.

A vote was called on the subject of the pres'ts of the Seventies—and those who have recently been appointed to that office, were unaimously received.

The congregation then united with pres't. Rigdon, who, in the closing prayer, called upon the Lord to dedicate this land for the gathering of the Saints, and their inheritances.

THOMAS B. MARSH,
Moderator.
Attest. OLIVER COWDERY.
—Pages 29-30.

The lead article in this third issue describes the troubles that flared up at Kirtland and the subsequent removal of the church leadership to Far West.

Far West, May, 1838.

Notwithstanding all the efforts of the enemies to the truth, both from without and within, to the contrary, we are enabled to present this Journal, to the patrons, with the prospect of being able to continue it in time to come, without interruption.

Great have been the exertions of the opposers, to righteousness, to prevent us from sending abroad the doctrines of the church to the world: every effort has been used by the combined influence of all classes of enemies, and of all sects and parties of religion; and of those who are opposed to it, in all its forms to prevent it.

It is indeed somewhat unexpected to us, to be able to commence printing the Journal again so soon; but the general interest felt in it by the Saints in general, soon, in a degree, repaired the loss which was suffered in the burning of the press in Kirtland; and another establishment, by the exertions of the Saints in Far West, has been obtained, sufficiently large, to print the Journal; and soon will be greatly enlarged, so as to do all the printing necessary, for the whole church. . . .

In this place, the church is as pleasantly situated as could be expected, taking into consideration their circumstances, as the settlement here is but about eighteen months old, and the first settlers had been driven from their homes, and all their property destroyed, and had to come here without any thing.—But to their honor it may be said, that few people on earth have endured the same degree of persecution, with the same patience. . . .

An enconium too high, cannot be placed upon the heads of the enterprising and industrious habits of the people of this country. They are fast making for themselves, and their posterity after

196

them, as beautiful, interesting, and as profitable homes, as can be in any country.

In a very few years, and it will be said with propriety, "that the solitary place has become glad for them," and we can say, that the people will be as glad for it. . . .

The Saints here are at perfect peace with all the surrounding inhabitants, and persecution is not so much as once named among them: every man can attend to business without fear or excitement, or being molested in any wise. There are many of the inhabitants of this town, who own lands in the vicinity, and are at this time busily engaged in cultivating them. Hundreds of acres of corn have been planted already, in our immediate neighborhood; and hundreds of acres more are now being planted. (This is the fourth day of May.) . . .

Perhaps it might be thought by some necessary, that we should say something about the affairs of Kirtland.—The burning of the printing office here &c. But it is now, as in former days. In former days the destroyers of the Saints' property were of the baser sort of mankind, even so it is now. And as the Saints in former days considered a formal notice of them, beneath both their character and standing, so do the Saints in like manner now. Only say as they did; "That a gang of the baser sort, burned and wasted our property to the utmost of their power" regardless of law, justice, or humanity, and were upheld in their wickedness, by those who were like the high priest in Paul's day, who though, he sat to judge after the law, commanded Paul to be smitten contrary to law. So it was with our persecutors in the east: for notwithstanding they sat to judge after the law, yet, commanded they our property to be destroyed contrary to law.

And as Paul and Barnabas did at Iconium. So did we at Kirtland.—"When there was an assault made, both of the Gentiles, and also of the Jews, with their rulers, to use them despitefully, and to stone them. They were ware of it, and fled into Lystria and Derbe, cities of Lyconia, and unto the region that lieth round about. And there they preached the gospel."

So we did in like manner, taking them for our example. When there was an assault being made, of liars, thieves, and religionists, with their rulers all combined, we were ware of it, and fled to "Far West," and are here preaching the gospel whereunto we are called by the power of God. Let so much suffice for Kirtland.

We have the gratification of saying to the Elders abroad, that we hope to be able to furnish the Journal regularly, from hence forth, as long as it may be thought wisdom to continue it. And we hope on their part, they will use all their exertions to give it circulation.

The enemies have made so many attempts to destroy us, and always failed, that we now just laugh at them for fools, as the God of heaven said he would at their calamity.

—Pages 33, 34.

Further light on the Kirtland difficulties is given in a letter from Thomas B. Marsh to Wilford Woodruff in Britain.

Brother W. Woodruff,

Sir, your letter, of the 9th of March, directed to Bishop Partridge, Presidents Joseph Smith jr. Sidney Rigdon, Hyrum Smith, and the Saints in Zion, came safely to them, some days since. And on account of the press of business now on their hands, and the request of J. Smith Jr., I have taken it upon me to answer it.

You say, that you have heard of the deplorable state of things in Kirtland; and it gave me much joy to learn by your letter, that you received those things in their true light. Great has been the afflictions of the Saints in that place, particularly our beloved brethren Joseph Smith Jr. and Sidney Rigdon.

In the past summer, I journeyed from this place, in company with Wm. Smith and D. W. Patten, to Kirtland, for the purpose of meeting in Conference there, with the twelve. On our arrival, we soon learned the difficulties that then existed there: these, however, were all apparently settled, previous to my leaving Kirtland: And W. Parrish, who has since become an unbeliever in revealed religion, affected to repent and become satisfied with Br. Joseph and the church. Others also did the same:—But this settlement was not of long duration. Soon after this, President Hyrum Smith and myself, left Kirtland for the upper Missouri; and President Joseph Smith, President S. Rigdon, and Wm. Smith, soon followed us to Far West: and during their absence, it seems that Parrish, J. F. Boynton, Luke Johnson, Joseph Coe, and some others, united together for the overthrow of the church. President Smith, and his company, returned, on or about the 10th of December; soon after which this dissenting band, openly, and publicly, renounced the church of Christ, of Latter Day Saints, and claimed themselves to be the old standard; called themselves the church of Christ, excluded that of Saints, and set at naught Br. Joseph, and the whole church, denounced them as heretics. How blind and infatuated are the minds of men, when once turned from righteousness to wickedness. They did not understand, that by taking upon them the name of Latter Day Saints, did not do away that of the church of Christ. . . .

We have of late learned, that Parrish, and the most of this combination have openly renounced the book of Mormon, and become deists.

I will now leave Kirtland, and give you some account of the movement of things here, as they are and have been. . . .

Also, the church has had much sorrow during the past winter, on account of the unfaithfulness of Oliver Cowdery, David Whitmer, and Lyman E. Johnson, and in consequence of this, and their opposition to our beloved brother Joseph Smith jr. and the best interest of the church of Jesus Christ, and for persisting in the same, a number of charges have been substantiated against them, before the Council and Bishop of the church, and they have also been excluded from fellowship. "How has the gold become dim, the most fine gold changed!!!"

But I must drop this subtect for want of room. Suffice it to say, brethren Joseph Smith Jr. and Sidney Rigdon are now with us, the church now flourishes, and the Saints rejoice, and the internal enemies of the church, are *down.* You will see by the above prospectus, that your anxious desires for the Journal are about to be granted.

May the God of Abraham, Isaac, and Jacob, bless you, and keep you unto his coming and Kingdom. Amen.

My love to all the Saints in those regions.

Yours in the love of God,
THOMAS B. MARSH.

Wilford Woodruff.

P. S. Since Br. Joseph came to this place, we have been favored with a lengthy revelation, in which many important items are shown forth. First, that the church shall hereafter be called "the Church of Jesus Christ, of Latter Day Saints" Second, it says, "Let the City Far West be a holy and consecrated land unto me, and it shall be called most holy, for the ground upon which thou standests is holy:—Therefore, I command you to build an house unto me, for the gathering together of my Saints, that they may worship me." It also teaches, that the foundation or corner stone must be laid on the 4th day of July next, and that a commencement must be made in this following season, and in one year from the 26th of April last, the foundation must be again commenced, and from that time, to continue the work until it is finished. Thus we see that the Lord is more wise than men, for Phelps and Whitmer thought to commence it long before this, but it was not

the Lord's time, therefore, he overthrew it, and has appointed his
own time. The plan is yet to be shown to the first presidency; and
all the Saints, in all the world, are commanded to assist in building the house.

—Pages 36-38.

In the previous issue, the Prophet had listed twenty questions "which are daily and hourly asked by all classes of
people whilst we are traveling." he now answers them.

In obedience to our promise, we give the following answers to
questions, which were asked in the last number of the Journal.

Question 1st. Do you believe the bible?

Answer. If we do, we are the only people under heaven that
does. For there are none of the religious sects of the day that do.

Question 2nd. Wherein do you differ from other sects?

Answer. Because we believe the bible, and all other sects profess to believe their interpretations of the bible, and their creeds.

Question 3rd. Will every body be dammed but Mormons?

Answer. Yes, and a great portion of them unless they repent
and work righteousness.

Question 4th. How, and where did you obtain the book of
Mormon?

Answer. Moroni, the person who deposited the plates, from
whence the book of Mormon was translated, in a hill in Manchester, Ontario County New York, being dead, and raised again
therefrom, appeared unto me, and told me where they were and
gave me directions how to obtain them; I obtained them, and the
Urim and Thummim with them; by the means of which, I translated the plates; and thus came the book of Mormon.

Question 5th. Do you believe Joseph Smith Jr. to be a
prophet?

Answer. Yes, and every other man who has the testimony of
Jesus. "For the testimony of Jesus, is the spirit of prophecy."—
Rev. 49:10.

Question 6th. Do the Mormons believe in having all things
common?

Answer. No.

Question 7th. Do the Mormons believe in having more wives
than one.

Answer. No, not at the same time. But they believe, that if
their companion dies, they have a right to marry again. But we do

disapprove of the custom which has gained in the world, and has been practised among us, to our great mortification, of marrying in five or six weeks, or even in two or three months after the death of their companion.

We believe that due respect ought to be had, to the memory of the dead, and the feelings of both friends and children.

Question 8th. Can they raise the dead.

Answer. No, nor any other people that now lives or ever did live. But God can raise the dead through man, as an instrument.

Question 9th. What signs do Jo Smith give of his divine mission.

Answer. The signs which God is pleased to let him give; according as his wisdom thinks best: in order that he may judge the world agreably to his own plan.

Question 10. Was not Jo Smith a money digger.

Answer. Yes, but it was never a very proffitable job to him, as he only got fourteen dollars a month for it.

Question 11th. Did not Jo Smith steal his wife.

Answer. Ask her; she was of age, she can answer for herself.

Question 12th. Do the people have to give up their money, when they join his church.

Answer. No other requirement than to bear their proportion of the expenses of the church, and support the poor.

Question 13th. Are the Mormons abolitionists.

Answer. No, unless delivering the people from priest-craft, and the priests from the prower of satan, should be considered such.—But we do not believe in setting the Negroes free.

Question 14th. Do they not stir up the Indians to war and to commit depredations.

Answer. No, and those who reported the story, knew it was false when they put it into circulation. These and similar reports, are pawned upon the people by the priests, and this is the reason why we ever thought of answering them.

Question 15th. Do the Mormons baptize in the name of Jo Smith.

Answer. No, but if they did, it would be as valid as the baptism administered by the sectarian priests.

Question 16th. If the Mormon doctrine is true what has become of all those who have died since the day of the apostles.

Answer. All those who have not had an opportunity of hearing the gospel, and being administered to by an inspired man in the flesh, must have it hereafter, before they can be finally judged.

Question 17th. Does not Jo Smith profess to be Jesus Christ.

Answer. No, but he professes to be his brother, as all other saints have done, and now do.—Matthew, 12:49,50—And he stretched forth his hand toward his disciples and said, Behold my mother and my brethren: For whosoever shall do the will of my father which is in heaven, the same is my brother, and sister, and mother.

Question 18th. Is there anything in the Bible which lisences you to believe in revelation now a days.

Answer. Is there any thing that does not authorize us to believe so; if there is, we have, as yet, not been able to find it.

Question 19th. Is not the cannon of the Scriptures full.

Answer. If it is, there is a great defect in the book, or else it would have said so.

Question 20th. What are the fundamental principles of your religion.

Answer. The fundamental principles of our religion is the testimony of the apostles and prophets concerning Jesus Christ, "that he died, was buried, and rose again the third day, and ascended up into heaven;" and all other things are only appendages to these, which pertain to our religion.

But in connection with these, we believe in the gift of the Holy Ghost, the power of faith, the enjoyment of the spiritual gifts according to the will of God, the restoration of the house of Israel, and the final triumph of truth.

—Pages 42-44.

Under the title, "An Extract of a Revelation," the following document appears. While for some reason it was not published in the 1844 edition of the Doctrine and Covenants (which edition has formed the basis for most editions published by the Reorganized Church), it was admitted to the Utah LDS canon of scriptures in 1876 and is therefore now included in all LDS editions as Section 115.

AN EXTRACT OF REVELATION

Given, Far West, April 26th, A. D, 1838.

Verily thus saith the Lord unto you my servant Joseph Smith Jr., and also my servant Sidney Rigdon, and also my servant Hyrum Smith and your counsellors, who are, and who shall be hereafter appointed; and also unto my servant Edward Partridge and his Counsellors, and also unto my faithful servants who are of the High Council of my church in Zion (for thus it shall be called) and unto all the Elders and people of my church of Jesus Christ of Latter Day Saints scattered abroad in all the world; for thus shall my church be called in the last days. viz, The church of Jesus Christ of Latter Day Saints. Verily I say unto you all; arise and shine forth that thy light may be a standard for the nations, and that thy gathering together upon the land of Zion and upon her stakes may be for a defence and for a refuge from the storm and from wrath, when it shall be poured out without mixture upon the whole Earth. Let the City Far West be a holy, and a consecrated land unto me, and it shall be called most holy, for the ground upon which thou standest is holy. Therefore I command you to build an house unto me for the gathering together of my saints, that they may worship me, and let there be a beginning of this work, and a foundation, and a preparatory work for the foundation, in this following season, and let this beginning be made on the 4th day of July next, and from that time forth, let my people labor diligently to build an house unto my name; and in one year from this day, let them recommence laying the foundation of my house. Thus let them, from that time forth labor diligently until it shall be finished, from the corner stone thereof unto the top thereof; untill there shall not any thing remain that is not finished.

Verily I say unto you, let not my servant Joseph, neither my servant Sidney, neither my servant Hyrum, get in debt any more for the building an house unto my name.—But let my house be built unto my name according to the pattern which I will show unto them, and if my people build it not according to the pattern which I shall show unto their presidency; I will not accept it at their hands. But if my people do build it according to the pattern which I show unto their presidency, even my servant Joseph and his counsellors; then I will accept it at the hands of my people.

And again; Verily I say unto you, it is my will that the City Far West should be built up speedily by the gathering of my saints; and also that other places should be appointed for stakes in the regions round about as they shall be manifested unto my servant Joseph from time to time. For behold I will be with him, and I will sanctify him before the people; for unto him have I given the keys of this ministry, even so amen.

—Pages 52-53.

A brief editorial insert indicates that the highly volatile relationship of members and nonmembers in Missouri has

203

again become seriously strained. Hostilities have broken out once more.

In this paper, we give the procedings which were had on the fourth of July, at this place, in laying the corner stones of the temple, about to be built in this city.

The oration delivered on the occasion, is now published in pamphlet form: those of our friends wishing to have one, can get it, by calling on Ebenezer Robinson, by whom they were printed. We would reccommend to all the saints to get one, to be had in their families, as it contains an outline of the suffering and persecutions of the Church from its rise. As also the fixed determinations of the saints, in relation to the persecutors, who are, and have been, continually, not only threatening us with mobs, but actually have been putting their threats into execution; with which we are absolutely determined no longer to bear, come life or come death, for to be mobed any more without taking vengeance, we will not.

EDITOR.

—Page 54.

The celebration of the Fourth of July was combined with the laying of the cornerstone of the Far West temple.

CELEBRATION OF THE 4th OF JULY.

The order of the day for the 4th of July, as directed by the committee of arrangements.

The committee of arrangements, which had been previously chosen, to make arrangements for the celebration of the 4th of July, and laying the corner stones of the temple, reported the following which was strictly adhered to.

First that Presidents Joseph Smith Jr. be president of the day, Hyrum Smith vice president, and Sidney Rigdon orator.

Second that Reynalds Cahoon, be marshal of the day, and Col. George M. Hinkle and Major Jefferson Hunt, be assistant marshals.

Third that George W. Robinson act as Colonel for the day; Philo Dibble, as Lieut. Colonel; Seymour Brunson as Major, and Reed Peck as Adjutant.

Fourth that Jared Carter, Sampson Avard, and Cornelius P. Lott, act as Generals, before whom, the military band shall pass in review.

204

Fifth that the procession commence forming in the morning, at 10 o'clock A. M. in the following order.

First the Infanty in front.

Second the civil procession as follows:

1st the patriarchs of the Church.

2nd the President vice president and orator, of the day.

3rd the Twelve.

4th the Presidents of the stake with the high Council.

5th the Bishop and Council.

6th the architects

7th the ladies, and then the gentleman of the civil procession.

Then the Cavalry brought up the rear.

After the procession was formed, which was exceedingly large. The whole marched to the notes of a small band of music under the direction of Dimick Huntington, around the cellar which had been dug for the house. The ladies forming a circle immediately around the cellar, the gentleman, of the civil procession in a circle next to the ladies. The infantry in a circle next, and the cavalry outside.

After the whole procession was thus completely formed, prayer was made by the president of the day, and a tune played by the band, and then, proceeded to lay the corner stones, as follows.

1 The south east corner was laid, by the presidents of the stake, assisted by twelve men.

2 The south west corner, by the presidents of the Elders, assisted by twelve men,

3 The north west corner, by the bishop assisted by twelve men.

4 The north east corner, by the president of the teachers, assisted by twelve men.

After each stone was laid, the music played a tune.

When the ceremony of laying the stones was completed, the ladies were formed in a circle, immediately, around the stand, where the oration was to be delivered, and the whole procession formed around them, as previously at the cellar of the house. The gentleman visitors were invited to come to the stand.—After which the oration was delivered, at the close of which, there was a shout of hosanna. A song was then sung by Soloman Hancock, composed by Levi Hancock for the occasion.

The military band then marched from the stand, and the President, Vice President, an Orator of the day, attended with the visitors, marched to the south side of the public square, and the troops under the command of their officers chosen for the occasion, passed in review before them. After which the whole procession was dismissed.

The whole ceremony of the day, was performed without the least disorder or confusion, and the people, in the most perfect order, retired to their homes.

The Committee of arrangements, take this opportunity of tendering their thanks, to the whole multitude who was in attendance, for their good behavior on the occasion, and for the due respect which they paid to the solemnities of the scene.

—Page 60.

Ironically, one of the last notices to appear was an encouragement to gather to the Far West area.

To the Saints gathering into Zion:—

It is of importance that they should return their names to the recorders of the different stakes, in order that their names may be had in the general Church record.—Many have come and have settled at a distance without returning their names to the recorders of the stakes, in which they have settled. Thus rendering it very difficult for the general church record to be kept.

It is expected that all the saints coming up to this land, or gathering into Zion; will have their names recorded on the records of the respective stakes, where they may settle.

We further say to the saints gathering, that the rumors which have gone abroad of the scarcity of provisions in this part of the country, is absolutely *false*—there is a great abundance, and the present appearance for corn, was never surpassed in any part of the United States.

Therefore you need not fear, but gather yourselves together unto this land, for there is, and will be an abundance.

Done by order of the first presidency,

GEO. W. ROBINSON, Scribe.

—Page 62.

But already the beginning of the end of the Far West settlement had come. Within a short time, this final haven for the Saints in Missouri—the colony with such promise—would be deserted, with Illinois becoming the temporary resting place for the Saints in their pilgrimage toward their Zion.

206

Chapter 6

TIMES AND SEASONS

In the midsummer of 1839 a prospectus for a new church periodical was published at Commerce, Illinois. The press that was to be used had been exhumed from its hiding place at Far West and brought to the tiny village on the east bank of the Mississippi River. Just as the old name of the settlement, Commerce, soon gave way to a new name, Nauvoo (of Hebrew derivation, meaning "beautiful plantation"), so the name *Elders' Journal* was abandoned in favor of a term that was probably borrowed from Acts 1:17, the *Times and Seasons.* Ebenezer Robinson and Don Carlos Smith, the first editors, announced their intention to provide the Saints with "all general information respecting the church; as also, a history of the unparalleled persecution . . . received in Missouri by order of the Executive of that State." The editors also intended not to admit anything "calculated to engender strife or turmoil" or anything that would "interfere with political matters."

The prospectus was distributed in July. Not until four months later was the first issue ready. The delay was related to the fact that malaria had been contracted by the two editors. While they were bedfast, the paper they had procured for the first issue mildewed and spoiled, since the press had been set up in the damp basement of an old warehouse—a dismal place with no floor and no light.

By November of 1839, however, the obstacles were being rapidly overcome. The Saints were eager to subscribe to the new periodical in order to keep up with the news of the church. Nonmembers in the area were anxious to receive the *Times and Seasons* in order to find out more about the new immigrants to Hancock County. Because of this enthusiastic subscriber response, a printing house was built from the proceeds of advanced subscriptions. Editor Robinson and his wife, also ill from malaria fever, were carried into the upper rooms of the printing office on their beds. A printer was hired and Ebenezer Robinson directed the printing of the first number of *Times and Seasons* from his sickbed.

For nearly six years the *Times and Seasons* was published regularly; the first twelve numbers were issued monthly, followed by a change to a twice-monthly schedule. Each issue contained sixteen large octavo pages.

By the end of the second volume, *Times and Seasons* was circulating in every state and territory of the nation as well as in Canada and Europe. Agents for the paper were found in more than half the states, although comparatively little of their correspondence found its way into print. The early success of the paper was marred by personal tragedy, however. Editor Don Carlos Smith, brother of the prophet, died in August 1841 from the lingering, debilitating effects of long hours of overtime spent in the midst of unsatisfactory working conditions.

The first issue of *Times and Seasons* carried an "Address" setting forth the objectives for the new periodical. The purpose of the paper was to lay before the reader, "in plainness, the great plan of salvation" and to "treat freely upon the gathering of Israel, which is to take place in these last days." A further purpose, and one that was more systematically pursued, was to "give a detailed history of the persecution and suffering, which the members of the Church of Jesus Christ of Latter Day Saints, has had to endure in Missouri, and elsewhere, for their religion." Eleven articles on this subject gained considerable sympathy in Illinois for the Latter Day Saint people. Relations between the Missourians and the Illinois settlers were already strained over the issue of slavery, with the Missourians claiming that the people of Quincy, Illinois, in particular were notorious for helping slaves from across the river escape into Canada.

Times and Seasons served several important functions in a time of great enthusiasm and burgeoning prosperity for the Saints. The paper, for one thing, kept alive the Saints' complaints against the Missourians. As long as the issue of "bleeding Zion" was held up before the church members, there was hope in the minds of the Saints for redress, for reclamation of the Missouri property, and for reinstatement in the "center place" of Zion. Often, therefore, the editors took occasion to air the issues involved.

Turnover in editors was fairly frequent, with R. B. Thompson, Joseph Smith, Jr., and John Taylor alternating duties with Ebenezer Robinson and, until his untimely death, Don Carlos Smith. Each new editor or team of editors would have his own editorial concerns and his own favorite set of issues to air.

In March of 1842 Joseph Smith's private journal was introduced to the paper's reading public. Extracts from that journal continued through February of 1846, making available to the church a fairly comprehensive history of the church as seen through the eyes of the prophet, covering the period from the Restoration's beginning until the summer of 1834.

While the *Times and Seasons* first attempted to avoid reference to political issues, this policy was doomed to failure in the developing church. Joseph Smith, Jr., in this period was allowing his life to take shape around several tasks or roles; he was at once a city planner, a realtor, a politician, a soldier, an innkeeper and storekeeper, an editor, and a Mason, as well as a prophet. It was natural that the *Times and Seasons* should come to reflect a wide variety of concerns, mirroring the multidimensional approach to life that Joseph and many other church leaders were taking. Thus we find an increasing emphasis on political matters. Early in 1842 we find Joseph Smith recommending to the Saints specific candidates for the governorship and lieutenant-governorship of Illinois. The paper later reported regularly on city government proceedings, municipal court actions, and Nauvoo Legion orders and court-martials. By early 1844 Joseph Smith was addressing his fellow countrymen concerning his stand on national and international political issues through the pages of the *Times and Seasons*, eventuating in his declared candidacy for the Presidency of the United States. Sidney Rigdon, who at that time was living in Pittsburgh, Pennsylvania, was selected to be Joseph's running mate after it was determined that James Arlington Bennett, Joseph's first choice, was ineligible because of being foreign born.

Certain topics continually recur in the *Times and Seasons*, reflecting, no doubt, the interests of the reading public as well as the personal concerns of the editors. Essays on the Jews and the hope for their return to Palestine and news reports of earthquakes, tidal waves, and other natural and man-made disasters were commonplace. Attention was also given from time to time to Indian affairs in the nation. An abundance of mission reports were included, with the same themes repeated over and over again—positive response among a community's citizenry to Latter Day Saint missionary activities, negative reaction and sometimes persecution by religious leaders, continuing growth in the branches with the membership remaining faithful in spite of the opposition against them and the sacrifice required of them. The British Mission work was well reported, especially during those periods in which members of the Council of Twelve were supervising the work. Long, newsy letters were printed in *Times and Seasons* to allow the whole church to sense the exhilaration that the missionaries were feeling in the face of such remarkable success in proselyting. A newspaper set up to serve the Saints in Britain, the *Millennial Star*, began publication in 1840 and provided material for reprint in *Times and Seasons*. Another source of material were the reports on "Mormonism" given in other newspapers of the day. The increased confidence of the Saints was evidenced by the fact that grossly exaggerated accounts or misinterpretations of Latter Day Saint doctrine and practices could now be reprinted in the Latter Day Saint press without lengthy comment or retort. Only on occasion did the editor feel constrained to lambast the offending party.

In order to present excerpts from the material found in six volumes of the *Times and Seasons*, we will organize it under three general time settings:

1. *Early Nauvoo* from the beginning of the paper in November 1839, until the disaffection of one of the most influential men in the town and church, John C. Bennett.

2. *Middle Nauvoo* from mid-1842 until the martyrdom of Joseph and Hyrum Smith.

3. *Late Nauvoo* from the tragic aftermath of the murder until the last issue in February 1846.

EARLY NAUVOO

A BACKWARD LOOK

Since the previous communication with the church at large had ended so abruptly, it was deemed necessary to provide the membership with an explanation of what had transpired in the closing days of Far West. The article which undertook to provide this information was penned by the prophet and is entitled "Extract, From the Private Journal of Joseph Smith Jr."

> On the fourteenth day of March, in the year of our Lord one thousand eight hundred and thirty eight, I with my family, arrived in Far West, Caldwell county Missouri, after a journey of more than one thousand miles, in the winter season, and begin about eight weeks on our Journey; during which we suffered great affliction, and met with considerable persecution on the road. However, the prospect of meeting my friends in the west, and anticipating the pleasure of dwelling in peace, and enjoying the blessings thereof, buoyed me up under the difficulties and trials which I had then to endure. However, I had not been there long before I was given to understand that plots were laid, by wicked and designing men, for my destruction, who sought every opportunity to take my life; and that a company on the Grindstone forks of Grand river, in the county of Daviess, had offered

the sum of one thousand dollars for my scalp: persons of whom I had no knowledge whatever, and who, I suppose, were entire strangers to me; and in order to accomplish their wicked design, I was frequently waylaid &c.; consequently, my life was continually in jeopardy. . . .

In the latter part of September, A. D. 1838, I took a journey, in company with some others, to the lower part of the county of Caldwell, for the purpose of selecting a location for a Town. While on my journey, I was met by one of our brethren from Dewitt, in Carroll county, who stated that our people, who had settled in that place, were, and had been for some time, surrounded by a mob, who had threatened their lives, and had shot at them several times; and that he was on his way to Far West, to inform the brethren there, of the facts. I was surprised on receiving this intelligence, although there had, previous to this time, been some manifestations of mobs, but I had hoped that the good sense of the majority of the people, and their respect for the constitution, would have put down any spirit of persecution, which might have been manifested in that neighborhood. . . .

We thought it necessary to send immediately to the Governor, to inform him of the circumstances; hoping, from the Executive, to receive the protection which we needed, and which was guaranteed to us, in common with other citizens. Several Gentlemen of standing and respectability, who lived in the immediate vicinity, (who were not in any wise connected with the church of Latter Day Saints,) who had witnessed the proceedings of our enemies; came forward and made affidavits to the treatment we had received, and concerning our perilous situation; and offered their services to go and present the case to the Governor themselves. A messenger was accordingly despatched to his Excellency, who made known to him our situation. But instead of receiving any aid whatever, or even sympathy from his Excellency, we were told that "the quarrel was between the Mormons and the mob," and that "we might fight it out." . . .

We had now, no hopes whatever, of successfully resisting the mob, who kept constantly increasing: our provisions were entirely exhausted and we being wearied out, by continually standing on guard, and watching the movements of our enemies; who, during the time I was there, fired at us a great many times. Some of the brethren died, for want of the common necessaries of life, and perished from starvation; and for once in my life, I had the pain of beholding some of my fellow creatures fall victims to the spirit of persecution, which did then, and has since prevailed to

212

such an extent in Upper Missouri—men too, who were virtuous, and against whom, no legal process could for one moment, be sustained; but who, in consequence of their love to God—attachment to his cause—and their determination to keep the *faith,* were thus brought to an untimely grave.

Many houses, belonging to my brethren, were burned; their cattle diven away, and a great quantity of their property destroyed by the mob. Seeing no prospect of relief, the Governor having turned a deaf ear to our entreaties, the militia having mutinied, and the greater part of them ready to join the mob; the brethren came to the conclusion to leave that place, and seek a shelter elsewhere; they consequently took their departure, with about seventy waggons, with the remnant of the property they had been able to save from their matchless foes, and proceeded to Caldwell. During our journey, we were continually harrassed and threatened by the mob, who shot at us several times; whilst several of our brethren died from the fatigue and privations which they had to endure, and we had to inter them by the wayside, without a coffin, and under circumstances the most distressing.

On my arrival in Caldwell I was informed by General Doniphan of Clay county, that a company of mobbers eight hundred strong, were marching towards a settlement of our people's in Daviess county. He ordered out one of the officers to raise a force and march immediately to what he called Wight's town and defend our people from the attacks of the mob, until he should raise the militia in his, and the adjoining counties to put them down. . . .

On the retreat of the mob from Daviess, I returned to Caldwell, hoping to have some respite from our enemies, at least for a short time; but upon my arrival there, I was informed that a mob had commenced hostilities on the borders of that county, adjoining to Ray co. and that they had taken some of our brethren prisoners, burned some houses, and had committed depredations on the peaceable inhabitants. A company under the command of Capt. Patten, was ordered out by Lieutenant Col. Hinckle to go against them, and stop their depredations, and drive them out of the county. Upon the approach of our people, the mob fired upon them, and after discharging their pieces, fled with great precipitation, with the loss of one killed and several wounded. In the engagement Capt. Patten, (a man beloved by all who had the pleasure of his acquaintance,) was wounded and died shortly after. Two others were likewise killed and several wounded. Great excitement now prevailed, and mobs were heard of in every direction who seemed determined on our destruction. They burned the houses in the country and took off all the cattle they could find. They destroyed cornfields, took many prisoners, and threatened death to all the Mormons. On the 28th of Oct. a large company of armed soldiery were seen approaching Far West, They came up near to the town and then drew back about a mile and encamped for the night. We were informed that they were Militia, ordered out by the Govornor for the purpose of stopping our proceedings; it having been represented to his excellency, by wicked and designing men from Daviess, that we were the aggressors, and had committed outrages in Daviess &c. They had not yet got the Governors orders of *extermination,* which I believe did not arrive until the next day. On the following morning, a flag was sent, which was met by several of our people, and it was hoped that matters would be satisfactorily arranged after the officers had heard a true statement of all the circumstances. Towards evening, I was waited upon by Colonel Hinckle, who stated that the officers of the Militia desired to have an interview with me, and some others, hoping that the difficulties might be settled without having occasion to carry into effect the exterminating orders, which they had received from the Governor. I immediately complied with the request, and in company with elders Rigdon and Pratt, Colonel Wight, and Geo. W. Robinson, went into the camp of the militia. But judge of my surprise, when instead of being treated with that respect which is due from one citizen to another, we were taken as prisoners of war, and were treated with the utmost contempt. The officers would not converse with us, and the soldiers, almost to a man, insulted us as much as they felt disposed, breathing out threats against me and my companions. . . .

I was then taken back to the camp and then I with the rest of my brethren. viz: Sidney Rigdon, Hyram Smith, Parley P. Pratt, Lyman Wight, Amasa Lyman, and George W. Robinson, were removed to Independence, Jackson county. They did not make known what their intention or designs were in taking us there; but knowing that some of our most bitter enemies resided in that county, we came to the conclusion that their design was to shoot us, which from the testimony of others, I do think was a correct conclusion. While there, we were under the care of General Lucas and Wilson, we had to find our own board, and had to sleep on the floor with nothing but a mantle for our covering, and a stick of wood for our pillow. After remaining there a few days, we were ordered by General Clark to return; we were accordingly taken back as far as Richmond, and there we were thrust into

214

prison and our feet bound with fetters. . . .We were then removed to Liberty jail in Clay county, and there kept in close confinement in that place for more than four months. while there, we petitioned Judge Turnham for a writ of habeas corpus, but on account of the prejudice of the jailor all communication was cut off; at length however, we succeeded in getting a petition conveyed to him, but for fourteen days we received no answer. We likewise petitioned the other Judges but with no success. After the expiration of fourteen days Judge Turnham ordered us to appear before him, we went and took a number of witnesses, which caused us considerable expense and trouble; but he altogether refused to hear any of our witnesses. The lawyers which we had employed refused to act; being afraid of the people. This being the case, we of course could not succeed, and were consequently remanded back to our prison house.—We were sometimes visited by our friends whose kindness and attention, I shall ever remember with feelings of lively gratitude, but frequently we were not suffered to have that privilege. Our vituals were of the coarsest kind, and served up in a manner which was disgusting. We continued in this situation, bearing up under the injuries and cruelties we suffered as well as we could, until we were removed to Daviess county, where we were taken in order to be tried for the crimes with which we had been charged. The grand jury (who were mostly intoxicated,) indibted us for treason etc. etc.—. . .

I was in their hands as a prisoner about six months, but notwithstanding their determination to destroy me, with the rest of my brethren who were with me; and although at three different times (as I was informed) we were sentenced to be shot, without the least shadow of law, (as we were not military men,) and had the time, and place apointed for that purpose; yet, through the mercy of God, in answer to the prayers of the saints, I have been preserved, and delivered out of their hands, and can again enjoy the society of my friends and brethren, whom I love; and to whom I feel united in bonds that are stronger than death: and in a state where I believe the laws are respected, and whose citizens, are humane and charitable.

During the time I was in the hands of my enemies; I must say, that although I felt great anxiety, respecting my family and friends, who were so inhumanly treated and abused; and who had to mourn the loss of their husbands and children, who had been slain; and after having been robbed of nearly all that they possessed be driven from their homes, and forced to wander as strangers in a strange country, in order, that they might save themselves and their little ones, from the destructions they were

JOSEPH REBUKING THE GUARDS
At Richmond Jail, Ray Co., Missouri.

"In one of those tedious nights we had lain as if in sleep until the hour of midnight had passed. I had listened until I had become so disgusted, shocked, horrified, and so filled with the spirit of indignant justice, that I could scarcely refrain from rising upon my feet and rebuking the guards: but said nothing to Joseph or anyone else, although I lay next to him and knew he was awake. On a sudden he rose to his feet, and spoke in a voice of thunder, or as the roaring of a lion, uttering, as near as I can remember, the following words:

" *'SILENCE, ye fiends of the infernal pit. In the name of Jesus Christ, I rebuke you and command you to be still. I will not live another minute and hear such language. Cease such talk, or you or I die this INSTANT!'*

"He ceased to speak. He stood erect in terrible majesty. Chained, and without a weapon: calm, unruffled and dignified as an angel, he looked upon the quailing guards, whose weapons were lowered or dropped to the ground, whose knees smote together, and who, shrinking into a corner or crouching at his feet, begged his pardon, remaining quiet until a change of guards.

"I have seen the ministers of justice clothed in magisterial robes and criminals arraigned before them, while life was suspended upon a thread, in the courts of England: I have witnessed a Congress in solemn assembly to give laws to nations: have tried to conceive of kings, of royal courts of thrones and crowns and emperors assembled to decide the fate of kingdoms: but *Dignity* and *Majesty* have I seen but *once, as it stood in chains, at midnight, in a dungeon, in an obscure village of Missouri.*"—Autobiography of Parley P. Pratt, page 229.

216

A HISTORY OF THE PERSECUTION, OF THE CHURCH OF JESUS CHRIST, OF LATTER DAY SAINTS IN MISSOURI.

CONTINUED.

It was before said that the Governor had long sought an opportunity to destroy us, and drive us from the state; he now had all things arranged according to his liking, an army of several thousand men were now arayed against a few, innocent, unofending citizens who had always been strict to obey the laws of the country; and several thousand more were on their march to Far West, and all this according to the orders of the Governor: the following is the exterminating order under which this mob militia were acting.

Head Quarters of the Militia,
City of Jefferson,
Oct. 27th 1838.

Sir,

Since the order of the morning to you, directing you to come with four hundred mounted men, to be raised within your Division, I have received, by Amos Rees, Esq., and Wiley C. Williams, Esq., one of my aids, information of the most appalling character, which changes entirely the face of things, and places the Mormons in the attitude of an avowed defiance of the Laws, and of having made war upon the people of this State. Your orders are therefore, to hasten your operations and endeavor to reach Richmond in Ray county, with all possible speed.—The Mormons must be treated as enemies and must be exterminated, or driven from the State, if necessary for the public peace.

county and there to unite with Gen. Doniphan of Clay—who has been ordered with five hundred men, to proceed to the same point for the purpose of intercepting the retreat of the Mormons to the north. They have been directed to communicate with you by express. You can also communicate with them if you find it necessary. Instead therefore, of proceeding as at first directed to re-instate the citizens of Daviess in their houses, you will proceed immediately to Richmond and, there operate against the Mormons.—Brigadier General Parks of Ray, has been ordered to have four hundred of his Brigide in readiness to join you at Richmond. The whole force will be placed under your command.

(Sined) L. W. BOGGS,
Govenor and Commander-in-Chief

We would here observe that the large army, or rather mob, just before they reached Far West, took a man prisoner by the name of Carey who was a stranger in the country; and one of their number, coolly and deliberately beat out his brains with the breech of his gun. He was then thrown into a wagon and taken with them to their encumpment. His family were not allowed to see him, or even permitted to administer to his wants, in the hour of death; he was given up to his family a few minutes before he expired.—This was known by all the officers, but was considered, probally, an act of *bravery.*

An aged man by the name of Tanner was taken about the same time and regardless of grey hairs, that were evident maks of hardship in the service of his country, he was struck over the head with the breech of a gun, and his skull laid bare: but to return. We here quote from S. Rigdon's Appeal to threatened with in Missouri: yet, as far as I was concerned, I felt perfectly calm, and resigned to the will of my heavenly Father. I knew my innocency, as well as that of the saints; and that we had done nothing to deserve such treatment from the hands of our oppressors consequently, I could look to that God, who has the hearts of all men in his hands, and who had saved me frequently from the gates of death, for deliverance: . . . thank God, we have been delivered; and although, some of our beloved brethren, have had to seal their testimony with their blood; and have died martyrs to the cause of truth; yet,

Short, though bitter was their pain:
Everlasting is their joy. . . .

It would have been some consolation, if the authorities of the State had been innocent in this affair, but they are involved in the guilt thereof; and the blood of innoceuce, even of *children,* cry for vengeance upon them. I ask the citizens of this vast republic, whether such a state of things is to be suffered to pass unnoticed, and the hearts of widows, orphans and patriots, to be broken, and their wrongs left without redress? No! I invoke the genius of our constitution, I appeal to the patriotism of Americans, to stop this unlawful and unholy proceedure; and pray that God may defend this nation from the dreadful effects of such outrages. Is there not virtue in the body politic? Will not the people rise up in their majesty, and with that promptitude and zeal, which is so characteristic of them, discountenance such proceedings, by bringing the offenders to that purnishment which they so richly deserve; and save the nation from that disgrace and ultimate ruin, which otherwise must inevitably fall upon it?

—Vol. I, pages 2-9,
November 1839.

While incarcerated with several companions in the jail at Liberty, Missouri, Joseph Smith wrote several letters. Two of them, sent over the signatures of five prisoners and addressed "to Bishop Partridge and to the Church of Jesus Christ of Latter Day Saints, in Quincy Illinois, and to those scattered abroad, throughout all the regions round about" were deemed to be of sufficient importance to warrant their publication one year after the event. Here are selected extracts from this correspondence.

Your humble servant Joseph Smith jr. prisoner for Christs' sake, and the saints, taken and held by the power of mobocracy under the exterminating reign of his excellency Governor Lilburn W. Boggs, in company with his fellow prisoners and beloved brethren, Caleb Baldwin, Lyman Wight, Hyrum Smith, and Alexander McRae, send unto you greeting: May the grace of God the Father, and the Lord and Saviour Jesus Christ, rest upon you all, and abide with you for ever; and may faith, virtue, knowledge, temperance, patience, godliness, brotherly-kindness and charity dwell in you and abound, so that you may not be barren or unfruitful.

We know, that the greater part of you are acquainted with the wrongs, high toned injustice and cruelty which is practised upon us; we have been taken prisoners, charged falsely with all kind of crimes and thrown into a prison enclosed with strong walls, and are surrounded with a strong guard who are as endefategable in watching us, as their master is in laying snares for the people of God. Therefore under these circumstances, dearly beloved brethren, we are the more ready to claim your fellowship and love. Our situation is calculated to awaken our minds to a sacred remembrance of your affection, and kindness; and we think that your situation will have the same effect; therefore, we believe, that nothing can separate us from the love of God, and our fellowship one with another; and that every species of wickedness and cruelty practised upon us, will only tend to bind our hearts and seal them together in love. . . .

Dearly beloved brethren, we realize that perilous times have come, as have been testified of in ancient days, and we may look with certainty and the most perfect assurance, for the rolling in of all those things which have been spoken of by all the holy prophets: lift up your eyes to the bright luminary of day, and you can say, soon thou shalt veil thy blushing face, for at the behest of Him who said, "let there be light, and their was light," thou shalt withdraw thy shining. Thou moon, thou dimmer light, and luminary of night, shalt turn to blood. We see that the prophecies concerning the last days are fulfilling, and the time shall soon come when the "Son of man shall descend in the clouds of heaven, in power and great glory.". . . .

From the information we received, the public mind has been for some time turning in our favor, and the majority is now friendly, and the lawyers can no longer browbeat us by saying, that this or that is a matter of public opinion, for public opinion is not willing to brook all their proceedings, but are beginning to look with feelings of indignation upon our oppressors.—We think that truth, honor, virtue, and innocence will eventually come out triumphant.

We should have taken out a writ of habeas corpus, and escaped the mob in a summary way, but unfortunately for us, the timber of the wall being very hard, our auger handles gave out which hindred us longer than we expected, we applied to a friend for assistance, and a very slight uncautious act gave rise to suspicion, and before we could fully succeed, our plan was discovered. We should have made our escape, and succeeded admirably well, had it not been for a little imprudence, or over anxiety on the part of our friend.

The Sheriff and Jailor did not blame us for our attempt; it was a fine breach, and cost the county a round sum; public opinion says, we ought to have been permitted to have made our escape, but then the disgrace would have been on us, but now it must come on the State. We know that there cannot be any charge sustained against us, and that the conduct of the mob—the murders at Hawn's mill—the exterminating order of Govenor Boggs, and the one sided, rascally proceedings of the Legislature, has damned the state of Missouri to all eternity. . . .

God has said, he would have a tried people, and that he would purify them as gold is purified; now, we think he has chosen his own crucible to try us, and if we should be so happy as to endure and keep the faith it will be a sign to this generation, sufficient to leave them without excuse; and that it will be a trial of our faith equal to that of Abraham or any of the ancients, and that they will not have much cause to boast over us, in the persecutions and trials they endured. After passing through so much suffering and sorow, we trust that before long a ram may be caught in the thicket, so that the sons and daughters of abraham may be re-lieved from their fears and anxiety, and that their faces may once more be lighted up with joy and salvation, and be enabled to hold out unto everlasting life. Now concerning the places for the loca-tion of the saints, we would say that we cannot council you in this thing as well as if we were with you; and as to the things written to you before, we did not consider them binding; we would ad-vise, that while we remain in prison and in bondage, that the affairs of the church be conducted by a general conference of the most faithful and respectable of the authorities of the church, and that the proceedings of the same be forwarded to your humble servants, and if there be any corrections by the word of the Lord they shall be freely transmitted, and we will cheerfully approve of all things which are acceptable to God. . . .

Ignorance, bigotry, and superstition are frequently in the way of the prosperity of this church, and are like the torrent of rain rushing down from the mountains, which floods the clear stream with mire and dirt, but when the storm is over and the rain has ceased the mire and dirt are washed away, and the stream again is pure and clear as the fountain, so shall the church appear when ignorance, superstition and bigotry are washed away. What power can stay the heavens, as well might man stretch forth his puny arm to stop the mighty Missouri river in its course, as to hinder the Almighty from pouring down knowledge from heaven upon the hearts of the Latter day saints: what is the Governor with his murderous party, but willows on the shore to stop the waters in their progress? As well might we argue that water is not water, because the mountain torrent sends down mire and riles the crystal stream; or that fire is not fire because it can be quenchable, as to say that our cause is down because renegadoes, liars, priests and murderers, who are alike tenacious of their crafts and creeds have poured down upon us a flood of dirt and mire from their strong holds. No, they may rage, with all the powers of hell and pour forth their wrath, indignation and cruelty like the burning lava of mount Vesuvius, yet, shall Mormonism stand. Truth is Mormonism, and God is its author, by Him we received our birth, by Him we were called to a dispensation of his gospel, in the beginning of the fulness of times, it was by him we received the book of Mormon, by him we remain unto this day and shall continue to remain if it be to his glory; we are determined to endure tribulation as good soldiers, unto the end: when you read this, you will learn, that prison walls, iron doors, screaching hinges, guards and jailors have not destroyed our confidence, but we say, and that from experience, that they are calculated in their very nature to make the soul of an honest man, feel stronger than the powers of hell.

—Volume I, pages 99-103,

May 1840.

We would suggest the propriety of the brethren settling in such places where they may find safety, which may be found between Kirtland and Far West, it will be necessary to do so for the present, until God shall open out a more effectual door.—Again we would suggest to the brethren, that there be no organization of large bodies upon common stock principles until the Lord shall signify it in a proper manner; as it opens such a field for the avaricious, the indolent, and the corrupt hearted, to prey upon the virtuous, the industrious, and the honest. We have reason to believe that many things were introduced among the saints, before God had signified the time, and notwithstanding the principles and the plans may have been good, yet aspiring men, who had the form of godliness but not the substance, by their aspiring notions brought trouble, both upon themselves and the saints at large: However the time is coming, when God will signify many things, which are expected for the well being of the saints. . . .

We say that God is true, that the constitution of the United States is true, that the bible is true, the book of Mormon is true, that Christ is true, that the ministering of angels is true; and "we know we have a house not made with hands, eternal in the heavens, whose builder and maker is God," and consolation which our oppressors cannot feel, when fortune or fate may lay its hand on them as it has on us. We ask; what is man? Remember brethren that time and chance happeneth to all men.

We subscribe ourselves your sincer friends and brethren, in the bonds of the everlasting gospel, and prisoners of Jesus Christ.

JOSEPH SMITH Jr.,
HYRUM SMITH,
LYMAN WIGHT,
CALEB BALDWIN,
ALEXANDER Mc RAE.

—Volume I, pages 132-134,

July 1840.

THE CITY OF NAUVOO

Church members all over the country were interested in developments at Nauvoo. Whether or not they had ever visited Nauvoo, this was still their city, the place where all their hopes for the kingdom were focused. Progress reports concerning the growth of the city were eagerly read. In "A Proclamation To the Saints Scattered Abroad," the First Presidency provided the following information:

Beloved Brethren:—
The relationship which we sustain to the Church of Jesus Christ of Latter Day Saints, renders it necessary that we should

make known from time to time, the circumstances, situation, and
prospects of the church, and give such instructions as may be
necessary for the well being of the Saints, and for the promotion
of those objects, calculated to further their present and everlasting happiness. . . .

The name of our city (Nauvoo,) is of Hebrew origin, and signifies a beautiful situation, or place, carrying with it, also, the
idea of *rest;* and is truly descriptive of this most delightful situation. It is situated on the eastern bank of the Mississippi river, at
the head of the Des Moines Rapids, in Hancock County; bounded
on the east by an extensive prairie of surpassing beauty, and on
the north, west, and south, by the Mississippi. This place has been
objected to by some, on account of the sickness which has prevailed in the summer months, but it is the opinion of Doctor
Bennett, a physician of great experience and medical knowledge,
that Hancock Co., and all the eastern and southern portions of
the City of Nauvoo, are as healthy as any other portions of the
western country, (or the world, to acclimated citizens,) whilst the
northwestern portion of the city has experienced much affliction
from ague and fever, which, however, he thinks can be easily
remedied by draining the sloughs on the adjacent island in the
Mississippi.

The population of our city is increasing with unparralled rapidity, numbering more than three thousand inhabitants. Every
facility is afforded in the city and adjacent country, in Hancock
County, for the successful prosecution of the mechanical arts,
and the pleasing pursuits of agriculture. The waters of the Mississippi can be successfully used for manufactoring purposes, to an
almost unlimited extent. . . .

The Temple of the Lord is in progress of erection here, where
the Saints will come to worship the God of their fathers, according to the order of his house, and the powers of the holy priesthood, and will be so constructed as to enable all the functions of
the priesthood to be duly exercised, and where instructions from
the Most High will be received, and from this place go forth to
distant lands.

Let us then concentrate all our powers, under the provisions of
our *magna charta* granted by the Illinois Legislature, at the "City
of Nauvoo," and surrounding country, and strive to emulate the
actions of the ancient covenant fathers, and patriarchs, in those
things, which are of such vast importance to this and every succeeding generation.

The "Nauvoo Legion," embraces all our military power, and
will enable us to perform our military duty by ourselves, and thus

afford us the power, and privilege, of avoiding one of the most fruitful sources of strife, oppression, and collision with the world. It will enable us to show our attachment to the state and nation as a people, whenever the public service requires our aid—thus proving ourselves obedient to the paramount laws of the land, and ready at all times to sustain and execute them.

The "University of the City of Nauvoo," will enable us to teach our children wisdom—to instruct them in all knowledge, and learning, in the Arts, Sciences and Learned Professions. We hope to make this institution one of the great lights of the world, and by and through it, to diffuse that kind of knowledge which will be of practical utility, and for the public good, and also for private and individual happiness. . . .

In order to erect the Temple of the Lord, great exertions will be required on the part of the Saints, so that they may build a house which shall be accepted of by the Almighty, and in which his power and glory shall be manifested. Therefore let those who can, freely make a sacrifice of their time, their talents, and their property, for the prosperity of the kingdom, and for the love they have to the cause of truth, bid adieu to their homes and pleasant places of abode, and unite with us in the great work of the last days, and share in the tribulation, that they may ultimately share in the glory and triumph.

We wish it, likewise, to be distinctly understood that we claim no privilege but what we feel cheerfully disposed to share with our fellow citizens of every denomination, and every sentiment of religion; and therefore say, that, so far from being restricted to our own faith, let all those who desire to locate themselves in this place or the vicinity, come, and we will hail them as citizens and friends, and shall feel it not only a duty, but a privilege, to reciprocate the kindness we have received from the benevolent and kind hearted citizens of the State of Illinois.

JOSEPH SMITH,
SIDNEY RIGDON,
HYRUM SMITH,
Presidents of the Church.

Nauvoo, January 15, 1841.

—Volume 2, pages 273-277,

January 15, 1841.

The charter of the city of Nauvoo, granted by the Illinois legislature in December 1840, is printed in its entirety in this same issue. This extremely liberal document gave Nauvoo the status of a relatively independent city-state.

In the *Times and Seasons* dated April 15, 1841, an interesting account of some community festivities is presented under the caption, "Celebration of the aniversary of the church—Military parade—Prest. Rigdon's address—Laying the corner stones of the Temple."

> At an early hour, on the 6th Inst. the several companies constituting the Nauvoo Legion, with two volunteer companies from Iowa T. making sixteen companies in all, assembled at their several places of rendezvous, and were conducted in due order to the ground assigned for general review. The appearance, order, and movements of the Legion, were chaste, grand, and imposing; and reflect great credit upon the taste, skill, and tact of the men comprising said Legion, especially the chief officer of the day, Maj. General Bennett. We doubt whether the like can be presented in any city in the western country.
>
> At half past 7 o'clock, A. M., the fire of artillery announced the arrival of Brigadier Generals Law, and Smith, at the front of their respective Cohorts; and at 8 o'clock Major General Bennett was conducted to his post under the discharge of cannon, and took command of the Legion.
>
> At half past 9 o'clock A. M. Lieutenant General Smith with his guard, staff and field officers, arrived at the ground, and were presented with a beautiful silk national flag, by the Ladies of Nauvoo, which was respectfully received and hailed by the firing of cannon, and borne off by Colonel Robinson, the Cornet, to the appropriate position in the line; after which, the Lieutenant General with his suit passed the lines in review. At 12 M. the procession arrived upon the Temple ground, inclosing the same in a hollow square, with Lieutenant General Smith, Major General Bennett, Brigadier Generals Law and Smith, their respective staffs, guard, field officers, distinguished visiters, choir, band, &c. in the center, and the ladies and gentlemen citizens surrounding in the interior. The superior officers, to gether with the banner, architects, principal speaker &c. were duly conducted to the stand at the principal corner stone, and the religious services were commenced by singing from page 65 of the new hymn book.
>
> Pres't. Sidney Rigdon then addressed the assembly. We regret that the address cannot be given to our readers entire instead of a very imperfect outline. He remarked,

"That the circumstances under which he addressed the people were of no ordinary character, but of peculiar and indescribable interest—that it was the third occasion of a similar nature, wherein he had been called upon to address the people, and to assist in laying the corner stones of houses to be erected in honor of the God of the Saints—various scenes had transpired since the first was laid—he, with some who were with him on that occasion, had waded through scenes, that no other people had ever been, not cursed, but blessed with—had seen the blood of the innocent flow, and heard the groans of those dying for the witness of Jesus—in all those scenes of tribulation, his confidence, his courage, and his joy had been increasing instead of diminishing—now the scene had changed; persecution had in a measure subsided; peace and safety, friendship and joy, crowned their assembling; and their endeavors to serve God were respected and viewed with interest—that the Saints had assembled, not to violate law and trample upon equity and good social order; not to devastate and destroy; but to lift up the standard of liberty and law, to stand in defence of civil and religious rights, to protect the innocent, to save mankind, and to obey the will and mandate of the Lord of glory; to call up to remembrance the once crucified, but now exalted and glorified Savior—to say that he is again revealed, that he speaks from the heavens, that he reigns; in honor of him to tell the world that he lives, and speaks, and reigns, and dictates—that not every people can build a house to him, but those only whom he himself directs—that the present military display is not to usurp; but to command as they are commanded and directed; to honor, not the world, but him that is alive and reigns. . . .

The speaker then gave out a hymn, page 205, and closed by prayer.—When we consider the feeble health of the speaker, worn down, as he has been, by a long, and arduous, and ever hazardous service of the gospel truth, the unpropitious circumstances in which he was called to speak, in the open air, and to almost an innumerable multitude, there being probably not less than ten thousand persons present, we are constrained to say he acquitted himself honorably, and in a manner which, the almost breathless attention of the multitudes hanging upon the words that flowed from his lips, as he was borne on by the inspiration of his theme, fully manifested, was deeply interesting and satisfactory.

The architects then, by the direction of the First Presidency, lowered the first (S. E. corner) stone to its place, and Pres't. Joseph Smith pronounced the benediction as follows, "This principal corner stone, in representation of the First Presidency, is now duly laid in honor of the great God; and may it there remain

226

until the whole fabric is completed; and may the same be accomplished speedily; that the Saints may have a place to worship God, and the Son of Man have where to lay his head." Pres't. Sidney Rigdon then pronounced the following, "May the persons employed in the erection of this house be preserved from all harm while engaged in its construction, till the whole is completed; in the name of the Father, and of the Son, and of the Holy Ghost; even so *Amen.*" Adjourned for one hour.

Assembled according to adjournment and proceeded to lay the remaining corner stones, according to previous order.

The second (S. W. corner) stone, by the direction of the Pres't. of the High Priesthood, with his Council, and Pres't. Marks, was lowered to its place, when the Pres't. of the High Priesthood pronounced the following: "The second corner stone, of the Temple now building by the church of Jesus Christ of Latter Day Saints, in honor to the great God, is duly laid, and may the same unanimity, that has been manifested on this occasion, continue, till the whole is completed; that peace may rest upon it to the laying of the top stone therof, and the turning of the key thereof; that the Saints may participate in the blessings of Israel's God within its walls, and the glory of God rest upon the same; *Amen.*"

The third (N. W. corner) stone, superintended by the High Council, as representative of the Twelve, (they being in Europe,) was then lowered to its place, with the benediction of Elias Higbee as follows: "The third corner stone, in representation of the Twelve, is now duly laid; and as they are, in some measure the support of the church, so may this stone be a firm support to the corner, that the whole may be completed as before purposed, and according to the order of the Priesthood."

The fourth (N. E. corner) stone, superintened by the Bishops, was then lowered to its place, and Bishop Whitney pronounced the following, "The fourth and last corner stone, expressive of the Lesser Priesthood, is now duly laid; and may the blessings before pronounced, with all others desirable, rest upon the same forever; *Amen.*

The services were then declared closed, and the military, retired to the parade ground and were dismissed with the approbation and thanks of the commanding officers.

The military band under the command of Capt. Duzett, made a conspicuous and dignified appearance, and performed their part honorably. Their soul stiring strains, met harmoniously the rising emotions that swelled each bosom, and stimulated us onward to the arduous, but pleasing and honorable duties of the day.

The choir also, under the direction of B. S. Wilber, deserve commendation.

What added greatly to the happiness we experienced on this interesting occasion, is the fact, that we heard no obscene or profane language; neither saw we any one intoxicated. Can the same be said of a similar assemblage in any other city in the Union? Thank God, that the intoxicating beverage, that bane of humanity in these last days, that—what shall we call it? *devil?* is becoming a stranger in Nauvoo.

In conclusion we will say, we never witnessed a more imposing spectacle than was presented on this occasion, and during the session of conference. Such an almost countless multitude of people, moving in harmony, in friendship, in dignity, told with a voice not easily misunderstood, that they were a people of intelligence and virtue, and order; in short, that they were *saints;* and that the God of love, purity, and light was their God, their examplar, and director; and that they were blessed and happy.

—Volume 2, pages 375-377,

April 15, 1841.

The importance of Nauvoo as the spiritual and temporal center of church activities is underscored by this notice disorganizing all stakes except those in the vicinity of Nauvoo.

TO THE SAINTS ABROAD.

The First Presidency of the Church of Jesus Christ of Latter Day Saints, anxious to promote the prosperity of said church, feel it their duty to call upon the saints who reside out of this county, to make preparations to come in, without delay. This is important, and should be attended to by all who feel an interest in the prosperity of this the corner stone of Zion. Here the Temple must be raised, the University be built, and other edifices erected which are necessary for the great work of the last days; and which can only be done by a concentration of energy, and enterprise. Let it therefore be understood, that all the stakes excepting those in this county, and in Lee county, Iowa, are discontinued, and the saints instructed to settle in this county as soon as circumstances will permit.

JOSEPH SMITH.

City of Nauvoo, Hancock co., Ill.,
May 24th 1841.

—Volume 2, page 434.

June 1, 1841.

228

A report of discrimination of Latter Day Saints against
religious minorities in Nauvoo provoked this heated response:

From the N. Y. Evangelist.

"It is stated in the Banner and Pioneer that a law has been
passed by the authorities of Nauvoo, "with a heavy fine annexed,
as a penalty for speaking against the Mormon doctrine." Such a
measure, in this land of freedom of speech, must be suicidal to
any dogma or any set of opinions."

We pronounce the above, a *base* falsehood, notwithstanding it
came from our good Baptist friends. Comment is useless in this
case, as there is no argument sufficiently powerful to induce our
religious enemies to tell the truth concerning us, when a lie will
answer their ends better. Here follows the law, and the only law,
on that subject: *An Ordinance in relation to religious societies.*

Sec. 1. Be it ordained by the City Council of the City of
Nauvoo, That the Catholics, Presbyterians, Methodists, Baptists,
Latter Day Saints, Quakers, Episcopalians, Universalists, Uni-
tarians, Mohammedans, and all other religious sects and denominations, whatever, shall have free toleration, and equal privileges,
in this city, and should any person be guilty of ridiculing, abus-
ing, or otherwise depreciating another, in consequence of his religion, or of disturbing, or interrupting, any religious meeting,
within the limits of this city, he shall on conviction thereof before the Mayor, or Municipal Court, be considered a disturber of
the public peace, and fined in any sum not exceeding five hundred dollars, or imprisoned not exceeding six months, or both, at
the discretion of said Mayor, or Court.

Sec. 2. It is hereby made the duty of all municipal officers to
notice, and report to the Mayor, any breach or violation of this or
any other ordinance of this City that may come within their
knowledge, or of which they may be advised; and any officer
aforesaid is hereby fully authorized to arrest all such violators of
rule, law, and order, either with, or without, process.

Sec. 3. This ordinance to take effect and be in force, from and
after its passage. Passed, March, 1st, A. D. 1841.

JOHN C. BENNETT, Mayor.

James Sloan, Recorder.

—Volume 2, page 558,
October 1, 1841.

The development of a university at Nauvoo excited the
interest of all persons in the Nauvoo area, church members

and nonmembers alike. For a frontier town to have a civic university would be a "feather in their caps," attracting national attention. Church and community leaders later became distracted with other projects in a way that allowed the original plans for the university to languish. We can see in the December 15, 1841, *Times and Seasons* that the university leadership was to be provided by church leaders, some of whom had questionable academic credentials.

UNIVERSITY OF THE CITY OF
NAUVOO.
Board of Regents.

Chancellor—John C. Bennett.
Registrar—William Law.
Regents—Joseph Smith, Sidney Rigdon, Hyrum Smith, Wm. Marks, S. H. Smith, Daniel H. Wells, N. K. Whitney, Charles C. Rich, John T. Barnett, Wilson Law, John P. Green, Vinson Knight, Isaac Galland, Elias Higbee, Robert D. Foster, James Adams, Samuel Bennett, Ebenezer Robinson, John Snider, George Miller, Zenos M. Knight, John Taylor, and H. C. Kimball.

Faculty,

President—

Professors.

Mathematics and English Literature—Orson Pratt.
Languages—Orson Spencer.
Rhetoric and Belles Letters—Church History—Sidney Rigdon.
School Wardens for Common Schools.

First Ward.

WARDENS—John P. Green, N. K. Whitney, A. Morrison.

Second Ward.

WARDENS—Charles C. Rich, Wilson Law, Elias Higbee.

Third Ward.

WARDENS—Daniel H. Wells, R. D. Foster, S. Winchester.

Fourth Ward.

WARDENS—Vinson Knight, William Law, Ebenezer Robinson.
It will be seen that some of the Chairs of the university are yet vacant; the department of Mathematics and English Literature, however, is in successful operation under the supervision of Professor Pratt; and the department of Languages will be opened in a few days under the direction of Professor Spencer. The Chairs which have been filled are occupied by some of the most able men the nation affords in their respective departments.

230

Professor Pratt is a self-made man, and has had to encounter great difficulties in the acquisition of an education; but he has surmounted them all. As a teacher of Mathematics and English Literature, he is equaled by few, and surpassed by none this side of the great waters; as the proficiency of the matriculates of the university now under his care abundantly testifies.

Professor Spencer is a graduate of Union College, N. Y., in the Arts; and of the Baptist Literary and Theological Seminary, N. Y., in Divinity. He is a ripe scholar, and well fitted for the department to which he has been elected by the Regency.

Professor Rigdon is too well known to require any commendatory article to introduce him to public consideration, and popular favor. He has long been regarded, by both enemies and friends, as an accomplished Belles Letters scholar, and eloquent orator,—deeply learned in that department of collegiate education which has been assigned to him in the university.

The opportunity which thus presents itself to the citizens of this city, and the surrounding country, for acquiring a thorough and useful education, should not be neglected. While this city is lengthening her cords, and strengthening her stakes, and exhibiting such a spectacle of bustle and enterprise as was never before witnessed, it is to be hoped that mental culture will not be passed over as a little thing. Knowledge is power—a finished education always gives an influence in cultivated society, which neither wealth nor station can impart or control: let those, then, who desire to be useful in their day, come forward at once, and matriculate in some department of the university, that mind may grapple with mind in seeking after hidden treasures.

—Volume 3, pages 630-631,

December 15, 1841.

Nauvoo, like any community, had its share of social problems. Some of the Saints who migrated to the city came empty-handed and therefore taxed severely the resources of the community. No one found life on the frontier very prosperous and comfortable, with the possible exception of the land speculators. As a result of the increasing array of social problems facing the community, the women of Nauvoo were mobilized under the leadership of Emma Smith to help provide for the needs of the town. The following notice appeared in the April 1, 1842, issue:

LADIES' RELIEF SOCIETY.

A society has lately been formed by the ladies of Nauvoo for the relief of the poor, the destitute, the widow and the orphan; and for the exercise of all benevolent purposes. The society is known by the name of the "Ladies' Relief society of the City of Nauvoo;" and was organized on Thursday the 24th of March A. D. 1842.

The society is duly organized with a Presidentess or Chairwoman, and two Councillors, chosen by herself; a Treasurer and Secretary. Mrs. Emma Smith takes the Presidential chair, Mrs. Elizabeth Ann Whitney, and Mrs. Sarah M. Cleveland are her Councillors; Miss Elvira Cole is Treasuress, and our well known and talented poetess, Miss Eliza R. Snow Secretary.

There was a very numerous attendance at the organization of the society and also at their subsequent meetings of some of our most inteligent, humane, philanthrophic, and respectable ladies; and we are well assured from a knowledge of those pure principles of benevolence that flow spontaneously from their humane, and philanthrophic bosoms, that with the resources they will have at command they will fly to the relief of the stranger, they will pour in oil and wine to the wounded heart of the distressed; they will dry up the tear of the orphan, and make the widow's heart to rejoice.

Our Ladies have always been signalized for their acts of benevolence and kindness; but the cruel usage that they have received from the barbarians of Missouri, has hitherto prevented their extending the hand of charity in a conspicuous manner; yet in the midst of their persecutions, when the bread has been torn from their helpless offsprings by their cruel oppressors, they have always been ready to open their doors to the weary traveller, to divide their scanty pittance with the hungry; and from their robbed and impoverished wardrobes, to divide with the more needy and destitute; and now that they are living in a more genial soil, and among a less barbarous people, and possess facilities that they have not heretofore enjoyed, we feel convinced that with their concentrated efforts the condition of the sufferring poor, of the stranger and the fatherless will be ameliorated.

We had the privelege of being present at their organization, and were much pleased with their *modus operandi,* and the good order that prevailed; they are strictly parliamentary in their proceedings; and we believe that they will make pretty good democrats.—ED.

—Volume 3, page 743.

April 1, 1842.

Worship life in the city of Nauvoo, during fair weather at least, often consisted of open air mass meetings in which sermons were delivered by the church authorities. The following account of such a service describes a combination baptismal, confirmation, and funeral observance.

SABBATH SCENE IN NAUVOO;
March 20th 1842.

A large assembly of Saints gathered together at the place of meeting at an early hour, to hear a discourse delivered by President Joseph Smith, upon the subject of Baptism. A child of Mr. Windsor P. Lyons being deseased, the body of which lay before the assembly, called forth many remarks from the speaker upon the subject of death and the resurrection, which were in the highest degree interesting and edifying, as were also his remarks upon the subject of baptism.

The following is a brief synopsis of some of the items delivered by the speaker.

President Smith read the 14th chap. of Rev. and said,

"We have again the warning voice sounded in our midst which shows the uncertainty of human life; and in my leisure moments I have meditated upon the subject, and asked the question, Why it is that infants, innocent children are taken away from us? especially those that seem to be the most intelligent and interesting? and the strongest reasons that present themselves to my mind are these;—This world is a very wicked world; and it is a proverb that the 'world grows weaker and wiser' if it is the case, the world grows more wicked and corrupt. In the early ages of the world, a righteous man and a man of God, and of intelligence, had a better chance to do good, to be believed and received, than at the present day; but in these days such a man is much opposed and persecuted by most of the inhabitants of the earth; and he has much sorrow to pass through here, the Lord takes many away even in infancy that they may escape the envy of man, and the sorrows and evils of this present world; they were too pure, too lovely, to live on earth; therefore if rightly considered instead of mourning we have reason to rejoice as they are delivered from evil, and we shall soon have them again. . . .

All children are redeemed by the blood of Jesus Christ, and the moment that children leave this world they are taken to the bosom of Abraham. The only difference between the old and young dying, is, one lives longer in heaven, and eternal light and

233

glory than the other, and is freed a little sooner from this miserable wicked world.—Notwithstanding all this glory, we for a moment lose sight of it, and mourn the loss; but we do not mourn as those without hope.

"My intention was, to have spoken upon the subject of baptism, but having a case of death before us I thought proper to refer to that subject. I will now however say a few words upon baptism, as I intended. God has made certain decrees which are fixed, and immovable, for instance; God set the sun, the moon, and the stars in the heavens; and gave them their laws, conditions, and bounds which they cannot pass, except by his commandments; they all move in perfect harmony in their sphere, and order, and are as lights, wonders, and signs unto us. The sea also has its bounds which it cannot pass. God has set many signs on the earth, as well as in the heavens, for instance; the oak of the forest, the fruit of the tree, the herb of the field; all bear a sign that seed hath been planted there; for it is a decree of the Lord that every tree, plant, and herb, bearing seed, should bring forth of its kind, and cannot come forth after any other law, or principle. Upon the same principle do I contend that baptism is a sign ordained of God, for the believer in Christ to take upon himself in order to enter into the kingdom of God, "for except ye are born of water, and of the spirit ye cannot enter into the kingdom of God," saith the Saviour. . . .

"As concerning the resurrection I will merely say that all men will come from the grave as they lie down, whether old or young, there will not be 'added unto their stature one cubit;' neither taken from it; all will be raised by the power of God, having spirit in their bodies, and not blood. Children will be enthroned in the presence of God, and the Lamb; with bodies of the same stature that they had on earth; having been redeemed by the blood of the Lamb, they will there enjoy the fulness of that light glory, and intelligence which is prepared in the Celestial kingdom: 'Blessed are the dead who die in the Lord; for they rest from their labors and their works do follow them.'

The speaker before closing called upon the assembly before him, to humble themselves in faith before God, and in mighty prayer and fasting to call upon the name of the Lord, until the elements were purified over our heads, and the earth sanctified under our feet; that the inhabitants of this city may escape the power of disease and pestilence, and the destroyer that rideth upon the face of the earth; and that the Holy Spirit of God may rest upon this vast multitude. At the close of the meeting President Smith informed the congregation that he should attend to

234

the ordinance of Baptism in the river near his house, at 2 o'clock;
and at the appointed hour the bank of the Mississippi was lined
with a multitude of people, and President Joseph Smith went
forth into the river and baptized with his own hands 30 persons,
for the remission of their sins; and what added joy to the scene
was, that the first person baptized was Mr. L. D. Wasson, a
nephew of Mrs. Emma Smith; the first of her kindred that have
embraced the fulness of the Gospel. At the close of this interesting scene the administrator lifted up his hands towards heaven,
and implored the blessing of God to rest upon the people; and
truly the spirit of God did rest upon the multitude, to the joy and
consolation of our hearts. After baptism the congregation again
repaired to the grove, near the temple, to attend to the ordinance
of confirmation; and, notwithstanding, President Smith had
spoken in the open air to the people, and stood in the water and
baptized about 80 persons, about 50 of those baptized received
their confirmation under his hands, in the after part of the day.
While this was progressing great numbers were being baptized in
the font.

Those who wish for further information concerning the scenes
of the Sabbath in Nauvoo, or any other day in the week would do
well to "come and see."   W. WOODRUFF.

—Volume 3, pages 751-753,

April 15, 1842.

CONFERENCE REPORTS

The first general conference held at Nauvoo convened on
October 5, 1839. This assembly provided for the organization
of a stake in the city of Nauvoo and a branch of the church
across the river in Iowa. A variety of other matters were also
considered.

Proceedings of the general Conference, held at Commerce,
Hancock County, Illinois, on Saturday the 5th day of October,
1839.

The meeting was opened by prayer, by President Joseph Smith
Jr. after which he was appointed president and James Sloan,
Clerk of the Conference, by the unanimous voice of the meeting.

The President then spoke at some length upon the situation of
the Church, the difficulties they had had to contend with, and

the manner in which they had been led to this place; and wished
to know the views of the brethren, whether they wished to appoint this a stake or not, stating that he believed it to be a good
place and suited for the saints.

It was then unanimously agreed upon, that it should be appointed a stake and a place of gathering for the saints. The following officers were then appointed viz:

William Marks to be President.

Bishop Whitney, to be bishop of Middle Ward.

Bishop Patridge, to be bishop of Upper Ward.

Bishop Knight to be bishop of Lower Ward.

George W. Harris,	Thomas Grover
Samuel Bent,	Newel Knight,
Henry G. Sherwood,	Charles C. Rich,
David Fulmer,	David Dort,
Alpheus Cutler,	Seymour Brunson,
Wm. Huntington,	Lewis D. Wilson,

to be high Council; who being respectfully
called upon, accepted af their appointment.

It was then voted, that a branch of the Church be established
on the other side of the river, in Iowa Territory; over which Elder
John Smith was appointed President:

Alanson Ripley, Bishop, and

Asahel Smith,	David Pettegrew,
John M. Burke,	Elijah Fordham,
A. Owen Smoot,	Edward Fisher,
Richard Howard,	Elias Smith,
Williard Snow,	John Patton,
Erastus Snow,	Stephen Chase,

Were elected high council. . . .

John Gaylord, was admitted into the church upon his confession.

Abel Casto was confirmed by the laying on of hands.

The meeting then adjourned until Sunday morning after which
six were baptized by Joseph Smith Jr.

Sunday morning October the 6th.

The Conference met pursuant of adjournment at 8 o'clock,
A.M.

When.

Samuel Williams,	Reuben Foot,
Orlando D. Hovey,	Junis Rappleyee,
Sheffield Daniels,	Albert Miner,
David B. Smith,	Ebe'r Richardson,
Pleasant Ewell,	William Helm,

Were appointed Elders of the church and were ordained under the hands of Reynolds Cahoon. Seymour Brunson, Samuel Bent and Alpheus Cutler.

After some remarks from the President respecting observing order an- decorum during conference, Elder Lyman Wight, spoke as to the duties od Priests, Teachers, tc.

President J. Smith, Jr. then spoke as to appointing a Patriarch and other matters connected with the well being of the church. Having now got through the business matters, the President proceeded to give instructions to the Elders respecting preaching the gospel, and pressed upon them the necessity of getting the spirit, so that they might preach with the Holy Ghost sent down from heaven, to be careful in speaking on those subjects which are not clearly pointed out in the word of God, which lead to speculation and strife. . . .

Elder Lyman Whight spoke on the subject of the resurrection, and other important subjects. When he offered the following resolution, which passed unanimously:

Resolved, That a new edition of Hymn Books be printed immediately, and that the one published by D. W. Rogers, be utterly discarded by the church.

Elder Ezra Hayes was then put upon trial for teaching doctrine injurious to the church, and for falsehoods; which having been proved against him his license was withdrawn and he required to give satisfaction to those whom he had offended.

Charges having been prefered against Brother Rogers, it was agreed that the case be handed over to the high council.

Asahel Perry made application to be received into fellowship, and was voted into his former standing.

After having referred the business not gone into, to the high council; the president then returned thanks to the conference for their good attention and liberality; and having blessed them in the name of the Lord, the conference was dismissed.

The next conference was appointed to be held on the 6th day of April next.

—Volume 1, pages 30-31,
December 1839.

The fall conference of 1840 is noteworthy in that a new doctrine was formally propounded from the pulpit—baptism for the dead. Most of the other business of the conference was perfunctory in nature or of an informative character, such as the report concerning the resolution concerning Temple construction.

> *Minutes of the general*
> *conference of the church of Jesus Christ of*
> *Latter Day Saints, held in Nauvoo, Hancock*
> *County, Illinois Oct., 3rd* 1840.
> The conference was opened by prayer by President W. Marks.
> Joseph Smith jr. was then unanimously called to the chair, and R. B. Thompson, chosen clerk. . . .
> The president then spoke of the necessity of building a "House of the Lord" in this place.
> Whereupon it was resolved, that the saints build a house for the worship of God, and that Reynolds Cahoon, Elias Higbee, and Alpheus Cutler, be appointed a committee to build the same.
> On motion Resolved, that a commencement be made ten days from this date, and that every tenth day be appropriated for the building of said house. . . .
> President Joseph Smith jr. then arose and delivered a discourse on the subject of baptism for the dead, which was listened to with considerable interest, by the vast multitude assembled. . . .
> Elder Lyman Wight addressed the conference on the subject of baptism for the dead and other subjects of interest to the church.
> The president then made some observations, and pronounced his benediction on the assembly.
>
> —Volume I, pages 185-187,
> October 1840.

Minutes of branch conferences or business meetings were often forwarded to the *Times and Seasons* for publication, particularly when they involved conference actions that had far-ranging effects that affected members' relationships to the whole church, such as the "cutting off" of members for neurotic or "unchristian" behavior. The following report, though somewhat embarrassing to the church, is an example of such a published local report.

> At a Conference meeting, of the branch of the church of Jesus Christ of Latter Day Saints in the city of New York, held at the

house of Elder G. J. Adams agreeably to previous appointment, on the evening of December 4th, 1840. Elder Orson Hyde was unanimously chosen Chairman of the meeting, and Elder L. R. Foster, Clerk.

The meeting was opened by singing, "Guide us O, thou great Jehovah," &c. and by the President addressing the throne of grace.

The President then read from Rev. 2nd chap. 12th verse, and onward; after a few preliminary remarks the President proceded to give his reasons for believing that the spirit which had been manifested among us, since the coming of Elder Sidney Roberts, was not from the Lord.

The items objected to are, having a revelation that a certain brother must give him a suit of clothes, and a gold watch, the best that could be had; also, saluting the sisters with what he calls a holy kiss, taking them on his lap, and putting his arms around them, &c.

After concluding, the President invited Elder G. W. Harris to speak on the subject, he declined, but afterwards did speak.

The accused, Sidney Roberts, answered for himself, he spoke at some length, and attempted to justify himself concerning these things; after remarks by several brethren, the President proposed that if he would confess his transgressions, he might retain his membership, but that his license must be demanded. He arose and stated that he knew the revelations which he had spoken were from God, and that he had no confession to make, whereupon the Conference cut him off from the church, and demanded his license, which he refused to give up.

—Volume 2, pages 306-307,
February 1, 1841.

Conferences in Nauvoo were held out of doors, usually in April and in October. In case of inclement weather, the conference would not meet as scheduled. This was hard on travelers from distant places and also on their hosts, but it was unavoidable since no building in Nauvoo could accommodate the crowds.

Matters of a personal or even delicate nature were often laid before the conference assembly. For example, a special conference was held in April 1842 to consider the charge that

239

John E. Page had willfully disobeyed the Lord by failing to accompany Orson Hyde on his mission to the Holy Land.

Special Conference of the Church of Jesus Christ of Latter-Day Saints, met according to appointment in the City of Nauvoo, April 6, 1842.

The day being wet, the First Presidency did not attend, and Elder Page addressed those present upon the subject of the charges against him, and said he would be happy to have an opportunity of laying his statement before the Conference, at a convenient time. . . .

April 7. Conference met, Pres't. Joseph Smith had the several quorums put in order, and seated: he then made some very appropriate remarks concerning the duties of the church, the necessity of unity of purpose in regard to the building of the houses, and the blessings connected with doing the will of God; and the inconsistency folly and danger of murmuring against the dispensations of Jehovah.

He said that the principal object of the meeting was to bring the case of Elder Page before them, and that another object was to choose young men, and ordain them, and send them out to preach, that they may have an opportunity of proving themselves and of enduring the tarring and feathering and such things as those of us who have gone before them, have had to endure.

Elder Page having arrived, was called upon, and addressed the congregation in relation to the nonperformance of his mission to Jerusalem: he said that when he started with Elder Hyde, joy filled their hearts, and they were aware of the responsibility of their mission. Elder Hyde's vision was that he should be in Jerusalem alone, E. P. considered Elder Hyde to be his father and guide in the mission, and felt it his duty to submit to Elder Hyde's opinion in all things; no elders ever were more in concert on a mission than they were while together; they made a covenant in Quincy to stand by each other while on the mission; that if they were insulted, or imposed upon they would stand by each other even unto death, and not separate unless to go a few miles to preach a sermon; that all monies should go into one purse, and it did so. Elder Hyde in Indiana first said he would go to visit Br. Knight, and that Elder Page should stay and preach, he assented, and he went and returned to Indianapolis. . . .

Elder Page returned to Dayton, and Milton, and sold books, with the intention of following Elder Hyde as soon as practicable; but he stayed a day or two too long, and the river closed by the frost, from one to two weeks earlier than usual; Elder Hyde told him that it was possible they might be from one to two years before they would leave America, as it would take upwards of $1000 each to take them to Jerusalem and back, that it would be slow gleaning in England, and assigned this as a reason for not immediately following Elder Hyde, thinking that he would be sure of seeing him in the spring.

Elder Page accused himself of not using better economy in proceeding on his journey; there came out a piece in the paper stating the displeasure of the Lord respecting Elder Hyde and Elder Page, he sat down and wrote a piece to put in the paper acknowledging the justice of the charge, but wisdom prevented its being published, preached about Washington &c., gathered funds for the mission, in Westchester and in Philadelphia. Elder Hyde raised funds on behalf of the mission, by applauding Elder Page's talents, wisdom &c., but they were disappointed in him when they saw him, he raised funds for the mission, the most liberal was in Philadelphia; he intended to sail on the 25th of July, but the brethren said that if he would remain two weeks they would raise funds for him, they found that it would take longer and he decided to stay a month, he then received a command through a letter from Pres't. H. Smith to an official character in Philadelphia, requesting him to return; he wrote to ascertain the reason but did not get an answer, he was then called in by Pres't. J. Smith, and Elder B. Young. Elder Hyde would often renew the covenant between them to never part with each other in that mission. Elder Page had no blame to attach to Elder Hyde; he supposed that he had done right; but if he had been in his place he would have tarried for him until the spring.

The reports of his having apostatized &c. returned even from this place to New York. Many reproved him for leaving Cincinnati for Dayton.

Pres't. J. Smith then arose and stated that it was wrong to make the covenant referred to by him; that it created a lack of confidence for two men to covenant to reveal all acts of secrecy or otherwise to each other—and Elder Page showed a little grannyism. He said that no two men when they agreed to go together ought to separate, that the prophets of old would not and quoted the circumstances of Elijah and Elisha III Kings 2 chap. when about to go to Gilgal, also when about to go to Jericho, and to Jordan, that Elisha could not get clear of Elijah, that he clung to his garment until he was taken to heaven and that Elder Page should have stuck by Elder Hyde, and he might have gone to Jerusalem, that there is nothing very bad in it, but by the experience let us profit; again, the Lord made use of Elder Page as a scape-goat to procure funds for Elder Hyde.

When Elder Hyde returns we will reconsider the matter, and perhaps send them back to Jerusalem, we will fellowship Elder Page until Elder Hyde comes, and we will then weld them together and make them one. A vote was then put, and carried that we hold Elder Page in full fellowship.

Voted, that Elder Page be sent to Pittsburgh. Sung a hymn—Adjourned for one hour and a half, at one o'clock.

—Volume 3, pages 761-762,

April 15, 1842.

DOCTRINAL EXPOSITION

An address by Judge Higbee and Parley P. Pratt to the citizens of the city of Washington was printed in the March 1840 *Times and Seasons*. This was an attempt to give a succinct statement of what Latter Day Saints believe. Here are some excerpts:

The "Latter-Day Saints" believe in the true and living God, and in Jesus Christ, the son of God, who was crucified, according to the Scriptures, and who rose from the dead the third day, and is now seated at the right hand of God as a mediater.

We also believe in the Holy Scriptures of the prophets and apostles, as being profitable for doctrine, reproof, correction, and instruction in righteousness, and that all mysticism or private interpretation of them ought to be done away. The Scriptures should be taught, understood, and practised in their most plain, simple, easy, and literal sense, acording to the common laws and usage of the language in which they stand—according to the legitimate meaning of words and sentences precisly the same as if found in any other book.

Words are but signs of ideas; and if the Deity would communicate ideas to mankind by words, he must of necessity do it according to the laws of the language; otherwise the communication would be unintelligible or indefinite, and therefore unprofitable.—The prophetical and doctrinal writings contained in the Bible are mostly adapted to the capacities of the simple and unlearned—to the common sense of the people. They are designed

242

to be understood and practised; without which no one can profit by them.

The gospel dispensation revealed and established one Lord, one faith, one baptism, one Holy Spirit; in short one system of religion, one church, or assembly of worshippers united in their doctrine and built upon the *truth*; and all bearing the general name of Saints. God is not the author of jarring and discordant systems. His Kingdom is not divided against itself; and for this reason we have no confidence in the sects, parties, systems, doctrines, creeds, commandments, traditions, precepts, and teachings of modern times, so far as they are at variance with each other, and contrary to the Scriptures of truth. We have, therefore, withdrawn from all these systems of error and delusion, and have endeavored to restore the ancient doctrine and faith which was once delivered to the saints, and to build society upon the truth, in its purity and fullness, hoping thereby to enjoy the peculiar gifts and blessing which were so abundantly bestowed upon the church in ancient times.

In saying this we do not call in question the morality, the sincerity, or the spiritual enjoyment of individuals belonging to any religious system. On the contrary, we feel assured that there are many sincere and zealous persons in every denomination. It is the Principles we reject, not men. It is the System that we wish to see established in purity, that those who are builded upon it may be pure also. It is the fountain that should be pure, and then the stream is easily kept so.

But if any persons prefer their own doctrines to those which we consider to be true, and we cannot by reason and argument convince them of the correctness of ours, we wish them to have the privilege of enjoying their religious rights unmolested. We have no disposition to persecute them.

We hold it as the duty of all men to believe the gospel to repent of their sins, and to be immersed in water in the name of Jesus Christ for remission of sins. And we hold that all who do this in a proper manner, and under proper authority, are legally entitled to the remission of sins, and to the gift of the Holy Ghost, according to the Scriptures.—Now faith and repentance go before baptism as a necessary qualification; and, therefore, infant baptism is of no use. All penitent believers should be baptized with the faith and expectation of receiving remission of sins and the gift of the Holy Ghost, as much so as Naaman the Assyrian washed seven times in Jordan with the expectation of being healed of his leprosy; or as much so as the Israelites sounded the trumpets around the walls of Jericho with the expectation of their being thrown down; for the same God who attached a promise to the performance in these cases, has attached a promise to the conditions of the gospel (See Acts, chapter 2.)

The "Latter-day Saints," after immersion, lay on hands, in the name of Jesus, for the gift of the Holy Ghost according to the ancient pattern. They are then considered saints, or members of the Church of Christ, in full fellowship and communion. They are then taught to obserrve all things which are required or commanded by Christ and his apostles—such as meeting together often to sing, to pray, to exhort, to testify, to prophesy, to speak with tongues, to interpret, to relate their visions, revelations, and in short, to edify and perfect each other, by a free exercise of all the gifts of God as set in order among the ancient churches. We also teach them to walk in all the ordinances of God blameless: such as the partaking of bread and wine, in remembrance of his broken body and shed blood, on the first day of the week; and also, to send for the elders of the church, when any of them are sick, that they may pray for them, and lay their hands on them in the name of Jesus, or anoint them with oil in the name of the Lord, that they may be healed, according to the Scriptures. We also teach them to abstain from all immorality: such as injustice, pride, vanity, dishonesty, evil-speaking, falsehood, hatred, envy, avarice, intemperance, adultery, fornication, lasciviousness, and to practise all the virtues; such as love to God and good will to man, brotherly kindness, charity, temperance, and industry. He that has two coats let him impart to him that has none, and he that has food let him do likewise; but he that will not work neither shall he eat. In short, we teach them to do all the good in their power—to visit the widow and the fatherless in their affliction, and to keep themselves unspotted from the world.

As to the fufillment of prophecy, we believe in the great restoration of Israel, and the rebuilding of Jerusalem, in Palestine, and that, when that time comes, the Saviour will come in the clouds of Heaven, and all the saints with him; that the dead in Christ will rise to meet him; and that he will destroy the wicked by the brightness of his coming, and bring the whole earth under his own dominion and put it into the possession of the saints; when there will be a reign of universal peace for one thousand years; after which comes the resurrection of the wicked and the last judgment.

As to the signs of the times, we believe that the gathering of Israel and the second advent of Messiah, with all the great events connected therewith, are near at hand. That it is time for the saints to gather together and prepare for the same. But we dis-

claim all fellowship with the predictions of the Rev. Mr. Miller,
Rev. Joseph Wolff, and others—such as, that the Lord will come
in 1840, 1841, 1843, 1847, and so on. We do not believe that he
will come until the Jews gather to Palestine and rebuild their city.

—Volume 1, pages 68-69,

March 1840.

The doctrine of baptism for the dead was mentioned in the
October 1840 *Times and Seasons* in the conference minutes
already cited, but no explanation of what was meant by this
doctrine was given. In the minutes of the conference held the
following April, we read,

Prest. Rigdon delivered a discourse to the conference on the
subject of "Baptism for the dead" which was set forth in a manner new and interesting, and with an eloquence peculiar to the
speaker, which was listened to with intense interest by the assembly.

Gen. Bennett made some very appropriate observations in con-
tinuation of the subject.

Pres't. Smith likewise followed on the same subject, threw
considerable light on the doctrine which had been investigated.

But the reader had to wait until the next issue to receive
some of the reasoning that had produced this doctrine. The
oblique reference to this practice as recorded in I Corinthians—"Why are they then baptized for the dead"—was apparently the basis, or at least the starting point, for the development of this doctrine. An article authored by G. H.
(possibly George Hills) brought this topic to the fore and
opened it up for discussion.

A knowledge of the state and condition of the dead has been
anxiously desired and sought after, by almost every nation and
people in all ages of the world. This knowledge was once, by
revelation, unfolded and understood; but like other truths of
divine teaching, through neglect, contempt, and the malicious
operations of the prince of darkness was shrouded, and lost, and
mankind were left to mourn in dispair over the ashes of their
departed friends and associates. . . .

Salvation for the living and the dead was proclaimed, "through the redemption that is in Christ Jesus," faith in him established as a condition, and baptism with water, as a seal and pledge of the latter, and the effusion of the Holy Spirit, as an earnest of the promised and desired inheritance. No wonder the multitudes "*gladly* received the word, and were baptized;" when, by simply trusting in the Son of God and going down into the laver of regeneration, in obedience to his command, they could come forth filled with hope and joy; and by the laying on of the hands of his duly commissioned and authorized servants, receive the fulness of his spirit; to lead them into all truth; to show them things to come; to take of the things of the Father and convey them unto them; to assure them that death was deprived of his sting, and the grave robbed of its victims; and to point them to a state of existence free from woes and ills, and glorious in all its associations and enjoyments. Such was the gospel. And as such it was proclaimed, by Christ and his apostles, to the living and to the *dead*; for we learn from Peter, that Christ went spiritually, "and preached to the spirits in prison; which sometime were disobedient, when once the long-suffering of God waited in the days of Noah, while the ark was a preparing, wherein few (that is eight) souls were saved by water. The like figure whereunto baptism doth now also save us (not the putting away the filth of the flesh, but the answer of a good conscience towards God,) by the resurrection of Jesus Christ; who is gone into heaven, and is on the right hand of God; angels, and authorities, and powers, being made subject unto him" 1. Peter III. 19-22.

Speaking of the wicked Gentiles, he says [IV. 5, 6,] "who shall give account to Him that is ready to judge the quick and the dead. For for this cause was the gospel preached also to them that are dead, that they might be judged according to men in the flesh, but live according to God in the spirit."—We see by the above, and by other scriptures, what is the gospel method of saving mankind—faith in him, and obedience to his commands by submission to the ordinance of baptism, administered by those duly authorized and commissioned. How the living, who hear the gospel and have the means of obedience within their reach, stand affected, is plain and not easily misunderstood; "He that believeth and is baptized shall be saved, but he that believeth not and and is not baptized shall be damned.

Here we leave the living and inquire for the dead. How are they affected by the gospel? We have seen that the gospel has been, and we infer *is still,* preached to the dead—that is, to dis-

246

embodied spirits. St. Peter has informed us why the gospel is preached to the dead; "that they might be judged according to men in the flesh."—Men in the flesh are judged according as they believe and obey the gospel, or disbelieve and reject it. Inasmuch then as the gospel is preached to the dead, they have a capacity and agency, to believe and in some way obey it, or the contrary. It is easy to imagine how the departed spirit may be made to see, to understand, to comprehend, and to embrace truths which were not manifested to, nor embraced by that spirit while incarnated; but how that spirit could render acceptable obedience, is the subject of our present inquiry. . . .

But we have not so learned of Christ. He offers pardon, peace, holiness, and eternal life to the quick and the dead—the living on condition of faith and baptism for remission of sins; the departed on the same condition of faith in person, and baptism by a living kinsman in his behalf. It may be asked, will this baptism by proxy necessarily save the dead? we answer no: neither will the same necessarily save the living. But this, with the other requisites will save both the living and the dead. and God will raise them up to glorify him together

—Volume 2, pages 397-399,

May 1, 1841.

At first members were baptized in the Mississippi River for dead relatives and acquaintances and later, as temple construction permitted, in a large font supported on the backs of twelve wooden oxen in the temple basement. In time the ordinance of baptism for the dead would suggest the need for other ordinances performed on behalf of the deceased. Thus the temple came to be seen not only as a place where the living could congregate to worship God but also as a place where the dead could have sacramental works done for them.

A clever way of presenting Latter Day Saint beliefs was to put questions and comments into the mouths of two fictional characters, as is done in this "Dialogue on Mormonism."

Between Mr. Mathews & Mr. Roberts.
Mr. M. Good morning Mr. R. Did you go to hear the Mormon preach last evening?

Mr. R. No, indeed I did not, I think it below my notice to listen to those babblers.

Mr. M. Why Mr. R., do you call them babblers and think so meanly of them? I'm sure I heard nothing objectionable in the discourse last evening.

Mr. R. Why! have you not heard the reports which are in circulation respecting them?

Mr. M. Yes, I have heard a great many stories about this people, but some of them were so extravagant and carried their own refutation on the face of them, that I thought I would hear both sides of the question.

Mr. R. Well, for my part, I am astonished that any respectable person should give ear to them. Such imposters should be discarded.

Mr. M. Probably, you may have been mis-informed, and have heard reports which have no foundation in truth. I think if you were properly informed on the subject, you would not feel so inimical to them. You know what the scriptures say "Prove all things and hold fast that which is good," and you know that public opinion is not always a proper standard for us to judge by, if it were so, our Savior would not have been crucified by the Jews, nor would the apostles have had to flee from one city to another, and be brought before magistrates and rulers.

Mr. R. Well, well Mr. M., that is good reasoning enough; but the idea of walking on the water, their pretensions of raising the dead, and other extravagant notions, are so absurd and ridiculous that I wonder any men of common sense should join them.

Mr. M. I have heard such stories, but when I talk with them on the subject, I find that they make no such pretensions, but speak very rationally, and I assure you they argue very logically on the scriptures.

Mr. R. Why! do you mean to say, that they believe any thing of our bible? Dont you know that they have discarded our scriptures and have got a bible of their own?

Mr. M. Why sir, the preacher last evening confined himself exclusively to the scriptures of the old and new testament, and proved the doctrines he advanced from the same. I, afterwards, had some conversation with him, and made some enquiries respecting the Mormon bible as it is termed, and he very freely and candidly answered my enquires, and said that the "Book of Mormon," was a record of the aborigines of this continent, which had been preserved on plates, and handed down from generation to generation until, on account of the wickedness of the people, they were hid up; and that Joseph Smith was informed by a heavenly messenger where those plates were—was instructed to obtain, and power was given him to translate them. I have not yet had time to examine the book, but I shall certainly read it, and then afterwards, I shall judge; but they certainly beleive our bible Mr. R.

Mr. R. Really Mr. M., this is strange news. Why how can people get up such wonderful stories? There must be some foundation for them. Again, you know that the Rev. Mr. H. and other very worthy ministers, who are eminent for their piety and learning, speak hard things against them, and warn their people against receiving them into their houses, and not to countenance such renegadoes.

Mr. M. I am aware that this is the fact, and I am sorry that the preachers should have no better weapons to use than to publish the reports which they have done. If Mormonism is a deception why do they not argue the subject like men and christians? If the doctrines they teach are so monstrous, why do not the ministers of the different denominations, expose them and prove them so from the scripture? Such a course would be far more honorable than retailing slanderous reports.

Mr. R. But do the Mormons wish to have their religion investigated? Do they not assume a high dictatorial bearing, and refuse to answer any questions; but say, that if reason and scripture come in contact with their doctrines, they do not care, but assert, that they know that there doctrines are true?

Mr. M. Such have been the reports; but when the preacher had got through his discourse last evening, he said, that inasmuch as there were many reports in circulation respecting their church, and the doctrines they advanced, he would give an opportunity for any one to ask any questions on the subject, and, if any one had any objections to urge against the doctrines he had advanced, they were at liberty to do so.

Mr. R. Did any one make any objections?

Mr. M. No sir. The doctrines he advanced were elucidated with so much clearness, and proof upon every point he advanced was so abundant, that I saw no possibility of making any. Some questions were asked respecting the book of Mormon which were answered very satisfactory, and then the meeting separated. I remained some time longer and coversed with him on the various subjects he had advanced and found him very communicative indeed, and seemed to take considerable pleasure in giving information respecting their faith and doctrine. I wish you had been there Mr. M. I think you would have a better opinion of these people if you could once hear them preach.

Mr. R. I probably might, but I do not think I should. I can never have a great opinion of any people who will condemn the whole world, and say "The temple of the Lord are we, and heathens all beside."—No, Mr. M. they cannot catch old birds with chaff. I should be sorry to indulge in predjudice against any sect; neither would I persecute any man for his religious opinions. But, really Mr. M., this Mormon doctrine is monstrous.

Mr. M. I have ever considered you a liberal minded person, and I really do think, that if you were to hear them preach once, you would think differently of them to what you do now; or, if you were to converse with them on the subject. I invited the preacher to come and spend the afternoon at my house, to converse with him more fully on these subjects; I should be very much pleased indeed, if you and Mrs. R., could make it convenient to come over, and chat with us awhile. I believe you will find the preacher a gentleman, very affable; and probably we may both hear some thing that may tend to our benefit.

Mr. R. I am obliged to you for your kind invitation and good feelings, probably I shall comply with your request; I shall go home and see if it will be convenient for Mrs. R. to accompany me.—However there is one privilege I wish to have, and that is, if I find the preacher garbling the scriptures, or advancing any erroneous notions, I want to expose him fully and treat him as he may deserve.

Mr. M. I am not afraid of your over-stepping the bounds of a gentleman.—Good morning Mr. R.

Mr. R. Good morning.

—Volume 2, pages 456-457,

July 1, 1841.

A similar dialogical presentation of doctrinal considerations appeared in the Feb. 15, 1842 issue. The difference is that the dialogue here is based upon an actual encounter between two real persons.

From Elder John Taylor's Journal, Liverpool, May 5, 1838, being a dialogue between Elder Taylor, and the Rev. John James, a celebrated "Church of England" Minister, in Liverpool, England.

"I was baptizing on the North Shore, when a Church of England minister, by the name of James, entered into conversation with some of the brethren while I was baptizing; after I got through I went to the company, when he addressed me rather uncourteously, saying:—

Mr. James.—This is Mr. Taylor, I suppose?

Mr. Taylor.—Yes sir, I answered.

J. I am told that you can answer me any question, and give a reason of the hope that is within you.

T. If sir, it is asked in meekness and humility.

J. Oh, that is the condition, is it sir?

T. I suppose, sir, that it will remain discretionary with me.

J. What need have we of any further revelation?

T. Because we have transgressed the laws, changed the ordinances, corrupted the gospel, and lost the priesthood.

J. Did not our Savior say that the gates of hell should not prevail against his church.

T. If, sir, it was built upon the rock spoken of.

J. Christ is that rock; and he said he would build his church upon that, and the gates of hell should not prevail against it.

T. It will be necessary, sir, to examine the context:—our Savior asks, "whom say men that I the son of man am?" The disciples answer, some say Moses, some Elias, and some that John the Babtist is risen from the dead. But whom say ye that I am? was asked by the Savior.—Peter answered, "thou art Christ, the son of the living God." How did you know it Peter? Flesh and blood hath not revealed this unto thee, but my father who is in heaven. It is evident that Peter had demonstrative evidence, from the revelations of God, that Jesus was the Messiah; and our Savior says, "Thou art Peter; and on this rock will I build my church, and the gates, &c." Now, although Christ might be said to be the chief corner stone, the rock, they, they, (the people) did not know him: some thought that he was one person, and some another; none, however, had positive evidence but Peter, and he obtained his knowledge through revelation, and if they could not know him they did not build upon him; they could not be his church; and that promise could not apply to them; and wherever, and whenever the church is built upon that rock, and have the revelation of heaven for their guide, as Peter had, the gates of hell cannot prevail against it. But Paul, in writing to the Romans, says, "The Jews were broken off because of unbelief; and thou standest by faith, be not highminded but fear; for if God spared not the natural branches, take heed lest he also spare not thee." He moreover tells them that if they do not continue in faith, they shall be cut off. Why were the Jews cut off? Because they killed the prophets, and stoned those that were sent unto them. And

what did the Gentiles do with their prophets and apostles? They
killed them, as the Jews did, and according to Paul's testimony
must be cut off. Besides, Daniel speaks of a certain power that
was to "make war with the Saints, and prevail against them, until
the ancient of days come."

J. That shews that there must be saints!

T. Daniel further says that he should "think to change times,
and seasons, and they should be given into his hand." &c. and if
that power, being hostile to God, prevails against them, and they
are given into his hand, what becomes of the church?

J. I will prove sir, that there has been a priesthood of apostolic
succession, and a pure church, from the Savior's day until the
present.

T. If you will, sir, and that church has pure, scriptural ordinances, I will give up my preaching, depart from this church, and
join myself to that standard.

J. I refer you, sir, to Mosheim's and Milner's Church history,
who shew that thing clearly.

T. I must have demononstration, sir, show me the church.

J. We ought to have confidence in the testimony of good,
accredited historians.

T. But you say, sir, that it not only did exist, but does exist,
consequently it is not only a matter of history, but a matter that
can be now demonstrated, if such a church is now in being.

J. The Church of England, ordains as you do.

T. But they sprinkle infants, sir, and that is unscriptural.

J. Peter says, "The promise is unto you, and to your children."

T. But it does not say to your *infants;* a man may have a child
thirty years old and he is as much his child as though he were an
infant; and you cannot point me out one single instance in scripture of an infant's being baptized.

J. Do not misunderstand me, sir, I do not find fault with your
baptism.

T. But I should with yours, sir, if you were pointing out a true
church, which you said that you could prove, had been in existence, and still existed.

J. We do it, either by dipping, pouring, or sprinkling.

T. This is singular indeed, sir, you believe that a man, is sent of
God, to teach, and does not know which ordinance to administer
in; but must leave it to those that he is teaching to decide upon
the matter: Peter did not do so.

J. The Baptists baptize by immersion.

T. But do they lay on hands, for the gift of the Holy Ghost?

J. I do not know.

T. They baptize, and you lay on hands: they have got one limb of the body and you another but none of you have the whole body.

J. I can, (beginning at our Savior,) trace an unbroken chain of apostolic succession until the present.

T. I suppose, sir, through the medium of the Roman Catholic Church.

J. Yes, sir.

T. You say that the Church of Rome is fallen; that she is the mother of harlots: if so, sir, how can she impart authority.

J. Just the same as she can the scriptures.

T. "Can an impure fountain, send forth pure streams? Our Savior said not.

J. Oh, it makes no difference.

T. Then, sir, if she had power to "bind on earth, and to bind in heaven," she also professed the power, (according to the scriptures) to "*loose on earth, and to loose in heaven,*" and you know, that she cut off, and excommunicated, the Church of England, and all Protestant Reformers, and that would place you, sir, according to your creed, in a curious situation.

J. Do you believe in your heart, sir, that she had power to confer this?*

T. If she had not there is no priesthood; and if she had she took it away from you, sir, and from all Protestants; consequently you have no priesthood or authority in either case:—You say that she is apostate, the mother of harlots; and she says that you are heretics; so I leave the matter between you, and both of your testimonies shall decide the case.

J. I can trace regular succession of authority, independent of the Church of Rome, in two different ways; one through the Waldenses, and Albigenses, and the other through the Welsh church.

T. As it regards the first of those, sir, I want to know where it is?

J. There may be some of them in the valleys of Piedmont; and if, at the time of the reformation, some of them went from this country to America, they might be there.

T. *And if, and if,* and *may be* is no demonstration, sir, there *may not be* any in the valleys of Piedmont, *and if* at the time of the reformation some having authority went to America there

---

*Why he should ask this question I do not know; except he did not believe himself, what he said, he could prove, as the statement was of his own propounding.

would be no priesthood there, and consequently no priesthood in existence that you can prove. And as it regards the other churches you know sir that the whole of the Church of England was under the dominion of the Pope in Henry the eighth's time, and all submitted to his authority.

J. There was always a few that protested against it.

T. The Church of England is not that few; nor the Church of Scotland; nor are the Methodists, Presbyterians, or Baptists; nor any body that you can point me out in England; and all the Episcopal form of Church Government in the United States, came either directly from the Church of Rome, through the Church of England or indirectly from the Church of England, through the Methodists, and is consequently all a figment.

J. And you belong to a church only ten years old, ten years old, ten years old.

T. These, sir, are my reasons for believing my former statements—That we had transgressed the laws, changed the ordinances, corrupted the Gospel, and lost the Priesthood, and your potent arguments have not convinced me to the contrary, especially your last ten years old one.

—Volume 3, pages 693-695,

February 15, 1842.

Many of the Saints remembered the stir caused a few years previous by the Smith family's acquisition of some Egyptian papyri, which the prophet identified as containing writings of Abraham and Joseph of Egypt. The subject was revived at Nauvoo when the March 1842 issues carried facsimiles of drawings from "The Book of Abraham" and a "translation" of the text. Nowhere is the claim made that the material is to be considered "inspired," but we may be sure that many of the church members, with a relatively unsophisticated notion of the nature and origin of scripture, would have construed the writings to be of divine origin. The apparent polytheistic assumptions of the Book of Abraham would later give support to those at Nauvoo who were developing a pluralistic metaphysics which involved the existence of multiple deities.

254

No. 1.

EXPLANATION OF THE ABOVE CUT.

Fig. 1. The Angel of the Lord. 2. Abraham fastened upon an altar. 3. The idolatrous priest of Elkenah attempting to offer up Abraham as a sacrifice. 4. The altar for sacrifice by the idolatrous priests, standing before the gods of Elkenah, Libnah, Mahmackrah, Korash, and Pharaoh. 5. The idolatrous god of Elkenah. 6. The idolatrous god of Libnah. 7. The idolatrous god of Mahmackrah. 8. The idolatrous god of Korash. 9. The idolatrous god of Pharaoh. 10. Abraham in Egypt. 11. Designed to represent the pillars of heaven, as understood by the Egyptians. 12. Raukeeyang, signifying expanse, or the firmament over our heads; but in this case, in relation to this subject, the Egyptians meant it to signify Shaumau, to be high, or the heavens, answering to the Hebrew word, Shaumahyeem.

A TRANSLATION

Of some ancient Records that have fallen into our hands, from the Catecombs of Egypt, purporting to be the writings of Abraham, while he was in Egypt, called the BOOK OF ABRAHAM, written by his own hand, upon papyrus.

The Book of Abraham.

In the land of the Chaldeans, at the residence of my father, I, Abraham, saw that it was needful for me to obtain another place of residence, and finding there was greater happiness and peace and rest for me, I sought for the blessings of the fathers and the right whereunto I should be ordained to administer the same; having been myself a follower of righteousness, desiring also to be one who possessed a great knowledge, and to be a greater follower of righteousness, and to possess a greater knowledge, and to be a father of many nations, a prince of peace; and desiring to receive instructions, and to keep the commandments of God, I became a rightful heir, a high priest, holding the right belonging to the fathers, it was conferred upon me from the fathers; it came down from the fathers, from the beginning of time, yea, even from the beginning, or before the foundations of the earth, to the present time, even the right of the first born, on the first man, who is Adam, or first father, through the fathers, unto me.

2. I sought for mine appointment unto the Priesthood according to the appointment of God unto the fathers, concerning the seed. My fathers having turned from their righteousness, and from the holy commandments which the Lord their God had given unto them, unto the worshipping of the Gods of the heathens, utterly refused to hearken to my voice; for their hearts were set to do evil, and were wholly turned to the God of Elkenah, and the God of Libnah, and the God of Mahmackrah, and the God of Korash, and the God of Pharaoh, King of Egypt; therefore they turned their hearts to the sacrifice of the heathen in offering up their children unto their dumb idols, and hearkened not unto my voice but endeavored to take away my life by the hand of the priest of Elkeuah; the priest of Elkenah was also the priest of Pharaoh.

3. Now, at this time it was the custom of the priest of Pharaoh, the King of Egypt to offer up upon the altar which was built in the land of Chaldea, for the offering unto these strange Gods, both men, women and children. And it come to pass that the priest made an offering unto the God of Pharaoh, and also unto the God of Shagreel, even after the manner of the Egyptians. Now the God of Shagreel was the Sun. Ever, the thank-

offering of a child did the priest of Pharaoh offer upon the altar, which stood by the hill called Potiphar's Hill, at the head of the plain of Olishem. Now, this priest had offered upon this altar three virgins at one time, who were the daughters of Onitah, one of the Royal descent, directly from the loins of Ham. These virgins were offered up because of their virtue; they would not bow down to worship Gods of wood or of stone, therefore they were killed upon this altar, and it was done after the manner of the Egyptians.

4. And it come to pass that the priests laid violence upon me, that they might slay me, also, as they did those virgins, upon this altar; and that you might have a knowledge of this altar, I will refer you to the representation at the commencement of this record. It was made after the form of a bedstead, such as was had among the Chaldeans, and it stood before the gods of Elkenah, Libnah, Mahmackrah, Korash, & also a God like unto that of Pharaoh King of Egypt. That you may have an understanding of these Gods, I have given you the fashion of them in the figures, at the beginning, which manner of the figures is called by the Chaldeans Rahlcenos, which signifies Hyeroglyphics.

5. And as they lifted up their hands upon me, that they might offer me up, and take away my life, behold, I lifted up my voice unto the Lord my God; and the Lord hearkened and heard, and he filled me with a vision of the Almighty, and the angel of his presence stood by me, and immediately unloosed my bands, and his voice was unto me. Abram! Abram! behold, my name is JEHOVAH, and I have heard thee, and have come down to deliver thee, and to take thee away from thy fathers house, and from all thy kin-folks, into a strange land, which thou knowest not of, and this because they have turned their hearts away from me, to worship the God of Elkenah, and the God of Libnah, & the God of Mahmackrah, & the God of Korash, and the God of Pharaoh King of Egypt; therefore I have come down to visit them, and to destroy him who hath lifted up his hand against thee, Abram, my son, to take away thy life: Behold I will lead thee by my hand, and I will take thee, to put upon thee my name, even the priesthood of thy father: and my power shall be over thee; as it was with Noah so shall it be with thee; that through thy ministry my name shall be known in the earth forever, for I am thy God.

6. Behold, Potiphar's Hill was in the land of Ur, of Chaldea; and the Lord broke down the altar of Elkenah, and of the Gods of the land, and utterly destroyed them, and smote the priest that he died; and there was great mourning in Chaldea, and also in the

court of Pharaoh, which Pharaoh signifies King by royal blood.—
Now this King of Egypt was a descendant from the loins of Ham,
and was a partaker of the blood of the Canaanites by birth. From
this descent sprung all the Egyptians, and thus the blood of the
Canaanites was preserved in the land.

7. The land of Egypt being first discovered by a woman, who
was the daughter of Ham, and the daughter of Egyptus, which, in
the Chaldea, signifies Egypt, which signifies, that which is forbidden. When this woman discovered the land it was under water,
who afterwards settled her sons in it: And thus, from Ham,
sprang that race which preserved the curse in the land. Now the
first government of Egypt was established by Pharaoh, the eldest
son of Egyptus, the daughter of Ham, and it was after the manner
of the government of Ham, which was Patriarchal. Pharaoh, being
a righteous man, established his kingdom and judged his people
wisely and justly all his days, seeking earnestly to imitate that
order established by the fathers in the first generations, in the
days of the first Patriarchal reign, even in the reign of Adam, and
also Noah, his father, who blessed him with the blessings of the
earth, and with the blessings of wisdom, but cursed him as pertaining to the priesthood. . . .

16. And I, Abraham, had the Urim and Thummim, which the
Lord my God had given unto me, in Ur of the Chaldees; and I saw
the stars also that they were very great, and that one of them was
nearest unto the throne of God; and there were many great ones,
which were near unto it; and the Lord said unto me, these are the
governing ones; and the name of the great one is Kolob, because
it is near unto me: for I am the Lord thy God, I have set this one
to govern all those which belong to the same order of that upon
which thou standest. And the Lord said unto me, by the Urim
and Thummim, that Kolob was after the manner of the Lord,
according to its times and seasons in the Revolutions thereof, that
one revolution was a day unto the Lord, after his manner of
reckoning, it being one thousand years according to the time
appointed unto that whereon thou standest; this is the reckoning
of the Lord's time, according to the reckoning of Kolob.

17. And the Lord said unto me, the planet, which is the lesser
light, lesser than that which is to rule the day, even the night, is
above, or greater than that upon which thou standest, in point of
reckoning, for it moveth in order more slow: this is in order,
because it standeth above the earth upon which thou standest,
therefore, the reckoning of its time is not so many as to its
number of days, and of months, and of years. And the Lord said
unto me, now, Abraham, these two facts exist, behold thine eyes

258

seeth it; it is given unto thee to know the times of reckoning, and the set times, yea the set time of the earth upon which thou standest, and the set time of the greater light, which is set to rule the day, and the set time of the lesser light, which is set to rule the night.

18. Now the set time of the lesser light, is a longer time as to its reckoning, than the reckoning of the time of the earth upon which thou standest; and where these two facts exist, there shall be another fact above them, that is, there shall be another planet whose reckoning of time shall be longer still; and thus there shall be the reckoning of the time of one planet above another, until thou come nigh unto Kolob, which Kolob, is after the reckoning of the Lord's time; which, Kolob, is set nigh unto the throne of God, to govern all those planets which belong to the same order of that upon which thou standest. And it is given unto thee, to know the set time of all the stars, that are set to give light, until thou come near unto the throne of God.

19. Thus I, Abraham, talked with the Lord, face to face, as one man talketh with another; and he told me of the works which his hands had made; and he said unto me, my son, my son, and his hand was stretched out, behold I will shew you all these. And he put his hand upon mine eyes, and I saw those things, which his hands had made, which were many; and they multiplied before mine eyes, and I could not see the end thereof: and he said unto me this is Shinehah, (which is the sun.) And he said unto me, Kokob, which is star. And he said unto me, Olea, which is the moon. And he said unto me, Kokaubeam, which signifies stars, or all the great lights, which were in the firmament of heaven. And it was in the night time when the Lord spake these words unto me, I will multiply thee, and thy seed after thee, like unto these; and if thou canst count the number of sands so shall be the number of thy seeds.

20. And the Lord said unto me, Abraham, I shew these things unto thee, before ye go into Egypt, that ye may declare all these words. If two things exist, and there be one above the other, there shall be greater things above them; therefore, Kolob is the greatest of all the Kokaubeam that thou hast seen, because it is nearest unto me: now if there be two things, one above the other, and the Moon be above the earth, then it may be that a planet, or a star may exist above it, and there is nothing that the Lord thy God shall take in his heart to do, but what he will do it: Howbeit that he made the greater star, as, also, if there be two spirits, and one shall be more intelligent than the other, yet these two spirits, notwithstanding one is more intelligent than the other, yet they

have no beginning, they existed before; they shall have no end, they shall exist after, for they are Gnolaum, or Eternal.

21. And the Lord said unto me, these two facts do exist, that there are two spirits, one being more intelligent than the other, there shall be another more intelligent than they: I am the Lord thy God, I am more intelligent than they all. The Lord thy God sent his angel to deliver thee from the hands of the Priest of Elkenah. I dwell in the midst of them all; I, now, therefore, have come down unto thee, to deliver unto thee the works which my hands have made, wherein my wisdom excelleth them all, for I rule in the heavens above, and in the earth beneath, in all wisdom and prudence, over all the intelligencies thine eyes have seen from the beginning; I came down in the beginning in the midst of all the intelligencies thou hast seen.

22. Now the Lord had shewn unto me, Abraham, the intelligences that were organized before the world was; and among all these there were many of the noble and great ones, and God saw these souls that they were good, and he stood in the midst of them, and he said, these, I will make my rulers; for he stood among those that were spirits, and he saw that they were good; and he said unto me, Abraham, thou art one of them, thou wast chosen before thou wast born. And there stood one among them that was like unto God, and he said unto those, who were with him, we will go down, for there is space there, and we will take of these materials, and we will make an Earth whereon these may dwell; and we will prove them herewith, to see if they will do all things whatsoever the Lord their God shall command them; and they, who keep their first estate, shall be added upon; and they, who keep not their first estate, shall not have glory in the same kingdom, with those who keep their first estate; and they, who keep their second estate, shall have glory added upon their heads forever and ever.

23. And the Lord said, who shall I send? And one answered like unto the Son of Man, here am I, send me. And another answered and said, here am I, send me. And the Lord said, I will send the first. And the second was angry, and kept not his first estate, and, at that day, many followed after him. And then the Lord said, let us go down; and they went down at the beginning, and they organized and formed, (that is, the Gods,) the heavens and the earth. And the earth, after it was formed, was empty and desolate; because they had not formed anything but the earth: and darkness reigned upon the face of the deep, and the spirit of the Gods was brooding upon the faces of the water.

24. And they said, the Gods, let there be light, and there was light. And they, the Gods, comprehended the light, for it was bright; and they divided the light, or caused it to be divided from the darkness, and the Gods called the light day, and the darkness they called night. And it came to pass that from the evening until morning, they called night; and from the morning until the evening, they called day; and this was the first, or the beginning of that which they called day and night.

—Volume 3, pages 703-705, 719-720,

March 1, 1842.

The famous "epitome of faith" which has been a doctrinal touchstone for several generations of Latter Day Saints appeared first in the "Wentworth Letter" published in *Times and Seasons* on March 1, 1842. Here is an excerpt from that document.

Persecution has not stopped the progress of truth, but has only added fuel to the flame, it has spread with increasing rapidity, proud of the cause which they have espoused and conscious of their innocence and of the truth of their system amidst calumny and reproach have the elders of this church gone forth, and planted the gospel in almost every state in the Union; it has penetrated our cities, it has spread over our villages, and has caused thousands of our intelligent, noble, and patriotic citizens to obey its divine mandates, and be governed by its sacred truths. It has also spread into England, Ireland, Scotland and Wales: in the year of 1830 where a few of our missionaries were sent over five thousand joined the standard of truth, there are numbers now joining in every land.

Our missionaries are going forth to different nations, and in Germany, Palestine, New Holland, the East Indies, and other places, the standard of truth has been created: no unhallowed hand can stop the work from progressing, persecutions may rage, mobs may combine, armies may assemble, calumny may defame, but the truth of God will go forth boldly, nobly, and independent till it has penetrated every continent, visited every clime, swept every country, and sounded in every ear, till the purposes of God shall be accomplished and the great Jehovah shall say the work is done.

We believe in God the Eternal Father, and in his son Jesus Christ, and in the Holy Ghost.

261

We believe that men will be punished for their own sins and not for Adam's transgression.

We believe that through the atonement of Christ all mankind may be saved by obedience to the laws and ordinances of the Gospel.

We believe that these ordinances are 1st, Faith in the Lord Jesus Christ; 2d, Repentance; 3d, Baptism by immersion for the remission of sins; 4th, Laying on of hands for the gift of the Holy Ghost.

We believe that a man must be called of God by "prophesy, and by laying on of hands" by those who are in authority to preach the gospel and administer in the ordinances thereof.

We believe in the same organization that existed in the primitive church, viz: apostles, prophets, pastors, teachers, evangelists &c.

We believe in the gift of tongues, prophesy, revelation, visions, healing, interpretation of tongues &c.

We believe the bible to be the word of God as far as it is translated correctly; we also believe the Book of Mormon to be the word of God.

We believe all that God has revealed, all that he does now reveal, and we believe that he will yet reveal many great and important things pertaining to the kingdom of God.

We believe in the literal gathering of Israel and in the restoration of the Ten Tribes. That Zion will be built upon this continent. That Christ will reign personally upon the earth, and that the earth will be renewed and receive its paradasaic glory.

We claim the privilege of worshipping Almight God according to the dictates of our conscience, and allow all men the same privilege let them worship how, where, or what they may.

We believe in being subject to kings, presidents, rulers, and magistrates, in obeying, honoring and sustaining the law.

We believe in being honest, true, chaste, benevolent, virtuous, and in doing good to *all men*; indeed we may say that we follow the admonition of Paul "we believe all things we hope all things," we have endured many things and hope to be able to endure all things. If there is anything virtuous, lovely, or of good report or praise worthy we seek after these things. Respectfully &c.

JOSEPH SMITH.

—Volume 3, pages 709-710,
March 1, 1842.

262

POEMS AND HYMNS

About 120 poems were published in the six volumes of *Times and Seasons*, giving the budding young poets as well as the more established ones a stage from which they could address the whole membership. The poet laureate of the Nauvoo years was Eliza R. Snow. At least forty-nine poems were penned by her, probably more since seventeen poems do not identify the author and some of these are undoubtedly the work of Miss Snow. As chief poetess for the Nauvoo settlement, she chronicled the major events in the history of the community, as can be seen merely by skimming over the titles of her known works:

The Slaughter on Shoal Creek, Caldwell County Missouri

The Word of Wisdom

Elegy on the death of the dearly beloved, and much lamented father in Israel, Joseph Smith Sen., a Patriarch in the church of Latter Day Saints; who died at Nauvoo, Sept. 14th, 1840.

Song of the Exiled Saints

Columbia—My Country

Though Outward Trials Throng Your Way

Awake! Ye Saints of God, Awake!

The Invocation

When I Espous'd the Cause of Truth

On the Death of President Harrison

Replication

To Mrs. Emma Smith, on the arrest of her husband

The Nauvoo Legion

Psalm

The Temple of God

To the Memory of Alice Olney

Lines, Written on the Death of Gen. Don Carlos Smith

The Funeral of Brig. General Smith

The Assassination of Gen'ls. Joseph Smith and Hyrum Smith,
First Presidents of the Church of Latter Day Saints; Who Were
Massacred by a Mob, in Carthage, Hancock County, Ill, on the
27th June, 1844

To Elder John Taylor

A Song for the Latter Day Saints

Lines written on the birth of the infant son of Mrs. Emma, widow
of the late General Joseph Smith

To President Brigham Young

The Venerable Lucy Smith

My Father in Heaven

Four stanzas of Miss Snow's "Awake! Ye Saints of God,
Awake!" have survived in our hymnody as No. 307 in *The
Hymnal*. Here are the three other stanzas of the seven-stanza
poem:

> Tho' Zion's foes have counsel'd deep,
> Altho' they bind with fetters strong—
> The God of Jacob does not sleep,
> His vengeance will not slumber long.
>
> With constant faith and fervent prayer
> With deep humility of soul—
> With steadfast mind and heart prepare,
> To see th'eternal purpose roll.
>
> For God in judgment will come near;
> His mighty arm he will make bare:
> For Zion's sake he will appear—
> Then O ye Saints! awake! prepare!

—February 1, 1841, page 309.

The Saints' feelings of esteem for the Nauvoo Legion are
captured by Miss Snow in her tribute to the militia.

THE NAUVOO LEGION.

The firm heart of the Sage and the Patriot is warm'd
By the grand "Nauvoo Legion:" The "Legion" is form'd
To oppose vile oppression, and nobly to stand
In defence of the honor, and laws of the land.
Base, illegal proscribers may tremble—'tis right
That the lawless aggressor should shrink with affright,
From a band that's united fell mobbers to chase,
And protect our lov'd country from utter disgrace.

Fair Columbia! rejoice! look away to the West,
To thy own Illinois, where the saints have found rest:
See a phoenix come forth from the graves of the just,
Whom Missouri's oppressors laid low in the dust:
See a phoenix—a "Legion"—a warm hearted band,
Who, unmov'd, to thy basis of freedom will stand.

When the day of vexation rolls fearfully on—
When thy children turn traitors—when safety is gone—
When peace in thy borders, no longer is found—
When the fierce battles rage, and the war-trumpets sound;
Here, here are thy warriors—a true hearted band,
To their country's best int'rest forever will stand;
For *then* to thy standard, the "Legion" will be
A strong bulwark of Freedom—of pure Liberty.

Here's the silver-hair'd vet'ran, who suffer'd to gain
That Freedom he now volunteers to maintain:
The brave, gallant young soldier—the patriot is here
With his sword and his buckler, his helmet and spear;
And the horseman whose steed proudly steps to the sound
Of the soul-stirring music that's moving around;
And here, too, is the orphan, whose spirit grows brave
At the mention of "Boggs," and his own father's grave;
Yes, and bold hearted Chieftains as ever drew breath,
Who are fearless of danger—regardless of death;
Who've decreed in the name of the Ruler on high
That the Laws *shall be honor'd*—that treason *shall die.*

Should they need re-enforcements, those rights to secure,
Which our forefathers purchas'd; and Freedom ensure.
There is still in reserve a strong Cohort above;
    "Lo! the chariots of Israel and horsemen thereof."
City of Nauvoo, June 2nd, 1841.

> —Volume 2, page 467,
>
> July 1, 1841.

That the rearing of the temple at Nauvoo is seen as preparation for the second coming of the Lord is not left in doubt by Miss Snow's poetic treatment of the place of the temple in the divine scheme of things.

THE TEMPLE OF GOD.
By Miss Eliza R. Snow.

"Behold! I will send my messenger, and he shall prepare the way before me: and the Lord, whom ye seek, shall suddenly come to his temple, even the messenger of the covenant whom ye delight in! behold, he shall come, saith the Lord of Hosts. But who may abide the day of His coming! and who shall stand when he appeareth? for he is like a refiner's fire, and like fuller's soap! And he shall sit as a refiner and purifier of silver; and he shall purify the sons of Levi, and purge them as gold and silver, that they may offer unto the Lord, an offering in righteousness. Then shall the offerings of Judah and Jerusalem be pleasent unto the Lord, as in the days of old, and as in former years." Malachi iii. 1, 2, 3, 4.

Lo, The Savior is coming, the prophets declare—
The times are fulfilling; O Zion, prepare!
The Savior is coming: but where shall he come?
Will he find in the palace of princes, a home?
No! O no, in his temple he'll surely attend;
But O where, is the "temple," where Christ
        shall descend?

Since the ancient apostles and christians are dead
The heavens have been scal'd—they are brass o'er the head
Of a world of professors, presuming to claim
A belief in the gospel of Jesus' blest name;
Who profess to believe it, yet boldly deny
Its most prominent feature, the gifts from on high.
And deny that the word of the Lord should come forth.

The Nauvoo Temple as drawn by W. Murphy

As it anciently did, to the saints upon earth!
Then, to whom shall Jehovah his purpose declare?
And by whom shall the people be taught to prepare
For the coming of Jesus—a "temple" to build,
That the ancient predictions may all be fulfil'd?

When a Moses of old, was appointed to rear
A place, where the glory of God should appear;
He receiv'd from the hand of the high King of Kings,
A true model—a pattern of heavenly things.
The eternal Jehovah will not condescend,
His pure wisdom, with human inventions to blend;
And a temple—a house, to the name of the Lord,
Must be built, by commandment, and form'd of his word,
Or he will not accept it, nor angels come down
In the light of His presence, the service to crown,
O! then who, upon earth, uninstructed, will dare
Build a house to the Lord! But the scriptures declare
That Messiah is coming—the time's drawing nigh!
Hark! a scheme is divulg'd—'twas concerted on high;
With divine revelation the saints have been bles't—
Every doubt has subsided—the mind is at rest.

The great God, has establish'd, in mercy and grace
The "strange work," that precedes the concluding of days—
The pure gospel of Jesus again is restor'd;
By its power, thro' the prophet, the word of the Lord
Is again coming forth; and intelligence rolls
From the upper eternity, cheering our souls.
"Build a house to my name," the Eternal has said
To a people, by truths holy principles led:
"Build a house to my name, where my saints may be blest;
Where my glory and pow'r shall in majesty res"
When its splendor will gladden the heaven y choir,
And high Gabriel's own hand shall awaken the lyre.

Oh, ye saints, be admonish'd by Time's rolling car;
It is rapidly onward! Hear, ye from afar!
Come, and bring in your treasures—your wealth from abroad:
Come. and build up the city and Temple of God:
A stupendous foundation already is laid,
And the work is progressing—withhold not your aid.
When you gather to Zion, come, not "looking back"—

Let your hearts not be faint—let your hands not be slack,
For great honor, and glory, and grace, and renown,
Shall appear on their heads, whom the Savior will crown;
And the Savior is coming. the prophets declare,
The times are fulfilling—to Zion repair:
Let us "watch and be sober"—the period is near"
When the Lord in his temple, will surely appear.

—Volume 2, pages 493-494,

August 2, 1841.

A glimpse into the grief of the community on the death of Don Carlos Smith comes with Miss Snow's description of his funeral. Notice the important role that the Nauvoo Legion assumes in the town's farewell to one who was at the same time editor of the *Times and Seasons* and brigadier general of the militia.

It was a Sabbath day.—The morning came,
But came not with the usual joyousness
With which the consecrated day was wont,
In Nauvoo City, ever and anon,
To usher its broad radiance on a train
Of humble, cheerful worshipers. Nature
Seem'd conscious of the mournful knell
That broke upon the sadden'd heart of man!

The sun arose, muffled with clouds that hid
His own bright beams, and in effusions soft
And gentle, as the soothing feeling tones
Of sorrow, dropt a sympathetic tear.
At length the clouds dispers'd—the sun pour'd forth
His glorious rays in brilliant majesty;
And I beheld upon the beautious plain
That fronts the noble Mississippi's wave,
A might host—a pow'rful warrior band
Whose rich escutcheons glitter'd in the sun.

I heard the sound of martial music, but
It came with solemn, slow and mournful air,
Unlike the bold, and thrilling notes that call

The restless warrior to the battle field!
There was no clash of arms—no din of war—
The sword was sheath'd, and every martial brow
Was mellow'd into sadness! Mounted high
Upon a fiery steed, a Chieftain sat
And issued the command: and then, anon,
In double file—in open columns form'd,
With Cheiftains in the front—then horse and foot,
In solemn order, mov'd across the wide
Extended plain, the Nauvoo Legion. 'Twas
A splendid sight—a sight that would have charm'd
The eye of each beholder; but alas!
That grand display, was the last honors paid
To the departed!

                In the Legion's rear,
Still length'ning out the vast procession; walk'd
A crow'd of citizens of every rank—
Of either sex; and last of all closed in
A long and glitt'ring train of carriages.

I gaz'd upon the grand procession, till
It disappear'd amid the dwellings which
Stand thickly cluster'd near the river's edge.
I listen'd—all was still—the music notes
No longer sounded on the pensive breeze,
But hark! the notes awaken'd, and I saw
The mighty host returning with the same
Slow, melancholy tread! A horse was borne
Along with solemn, yet bold martial pomp,
That plainly signiffed, (sic) a mighty one,
One of no ordinary rank, had fallen!

Near to the summit of an eminence
Rising in bold relief, to dignify,
The beauty of the verdant plain beneath;
In Nature's temple, with no other wall,
Than the horizon; and no other arch,
Than the broad canopy of heaven; shaded
With clust'ring boughs, whose foliage waves around;
Is rais'd an altar to the living God.
There the procession march'd—it halted there;
And in the front of weeping relatives,

The herse of him was placed, who *there,* in life
Had been a fervent, constant worshipper!

His arms and armor, on his coffin lay
And other swords than his, lay crossing there.
His brother officers, who form'd with him,
The noblest Military Staff, our fair
Columbia has to boast, were seated by
In shining armor clad; but ah! they seem'd
Divested of the martial haughtiness—
That warlike pride that fires the warrior's eye—
It lay concel'd beneath the brow of grief.

The invocation and the sacred chant,
Open'd the solemn service of the day;
And then the man of God arose. In tones
Of truth's impassion'd eloquence, he spoke
Of the late sad occurence, which had touch'd
The hearts of all; and universally
Was calling forth, a "fellowship of grief"
Each soldier, mourn'd a general—each saint,
A brother—and each citizen, a friend!
But when he come to paint the glories of
The world to come; wrapt in the visions of
Eternal Truth; e'en grief itself, bow'd down,
And the vast multitude, for once, forgot
To weep. And then he sweetly dwelt upon
The character of the deceas'd, without
A stain—his christian life, that seem'd without
A blemish—and his military course,
A path of honor. Tho' he had not stood
Before the cannon's mouth—altho' he ne'er
Had been in battle', front amid the rage
Of war, and clash of arms; and altho' now,
H'd fall'n according to the common course
Of Providence, and had not perrish'd by
The sword; he was no less a patriot—
He lov'd his country—he'd prepar'd himself,
By stepping high, in military rank,
To do her service at her earliest call.
And then the chaplain spoke of him, in the
Retir'd relations of domestic life.
There sat his aged, widow'd mother, whom

He'd honor'd with most filial sanctity—
To whom, he'd been a constant solace in
Those scenes of persecution and distress.
Which she had suffer'd for the gospel's sake.
While, as a brother, he had ever prov'd,
Firm as Giberalter's rock—true unto death.
And then he come still nearer home, and touch'd
The finest fibre of the human heart;
And spoke of her, the lonely widow, of
The noble fallen chieftain—the bereft
Companion of his bosom, whom he'd lov'd
Gith faithful tenderness. Ah! who can now,
Enter the halo of her feelings—sothe her grief
For him who only could reciprocate
Her bosom's sympathies? He too, had been
A loving and indulgent father to
Her lonely, weeping babes—left fatherless!
To soothe the bleeding heart, the speaker then
Spoke of the blest reunion, that awaits
The faithful worshippers of the Most High.

Thus clos'd the man of God.—The service done;
Again the great procession form'd, and once
Again, the bearers took the silent pall
And bore it onward to the "narrow house!"

Then came the parting scenery that clos'd
The service of the living to the dead.

Whether the olive branch the cypress bough
Or myrtle wreath, it matters not, 'twas given
As the last token of profound respect—
Emblem of friendship—of eternal life:
The Legion, one by one, deposited
Within the grave, a green unwither'd bough;
And passing onward left the trophied urn!
A voice was heard slowly pronouncing, "Earth
To earth—Ashes to ashes—Dust to dust,
Return this body to its mother earth;
While on the coffin fell the parted clod
Beside the grave, the Legion's *playing band,*
Awoke Melodia's sweetest strain. A chord
Was touch'd that echoed music to the springs
Of life, and fell as soft upon the ear,

As if seraphic harpers had come down
To charm the sleeper in his lowly rest.

The music ceas'd—Another chaplains voice
With heavenly eloquence pour'd forth in pray'r
To the Eternal God, responding pass'd
From heart to heart of the vast multitude—
The mourning concourse in the burial grove.
And there, beneath Time's monument the oak;
Whose umptage wav'd luxrious to the breeze,
They left the shrouded buried corpse of one,
Belov'd in life and *honor'd in his death*;
Waiting the trump of God, to call it forth
To hail its own bright spirit from the skies!

City of Nauvoo. August 13th 1841.

—Volume 2, pages 532-533,
September 1, 1841.

Next to Miss Snow, William W. Phelps was the most pro-
lific poet, with at least fourteen of his poems appearing in
Times and Seasons, most of them in the later years of the
paper's existence. Brother Phelps, one-time editor of the *Evening and the Morning Star*, had become disaffected from the
church leadership at Far West and was consequently cut off
from the church. In the February 1, 1841, *Times and Seasons*, however, a notice of his reinstatement is given, along
with a lengthy letter of apology from Brother Phelps himself.

W. Waterman Phelps, the son of the poet, authored a
couple of articles for the *Times and Seasons*, but we may
assume that poems credited to W. W. Phelps or W. W. P. are
the work of the elder Phelps. His poetic contributions to the
church's literature resumed more than a year after his reinstatement with the publication of his poem, "The Temple of
God at Nauvoo."

Ye servants that so many prophets foretold,
Should labor for Zion and not for the gold,
Go into the field ere the sun dries the dew,
And reap for the kingdom of God at Nauvoo.

Go carry glad tidings, that all may attend,
While God is unfolding "the time of the end;"
And say to all nations, whatever you do,
Come, build up the Temple of God at Nauvoo.

Go say to the Islands that wait for his law,
Prepare for that glory the prophets once saw,
And bring on your gold and your precious things, too,
As tithes for the Temple of God at Nauvoo.

Go say to the great men, who boast of a name;
To kings and their nobles, all born unto fame,
Come, bring on your treasures, antiquities, too,
And honor the Temple of God at Nauvoo.

Proclaim the acceptable year of the Lord,
For now we have prophets to bring forth his word,
And reveal to the church what the world never knew,
By faith in the Temple of God at Nauvoo.

To spirits in prison the gospel is sent,
For on such a mission the Savior once went;
And we are baptiz'd for the dead—surely, too,
In the font at the Temple of God at Nauvoo.

Up; watch! for the strange work of God has begun,
And new things are opening, now, under the sun:
And knowledge on knowledge will burst to our view,
From Seers in the Temple of God at Nauvoo.

—Volume 3, page 830,

June 15, 1842.

Four poems were authored by one who signed himself "A Converted Jew." Almost certainly this was Alex Neibaur, a surgeon dentist who supplemented his income in Nauvoo by giving private lessons in German and Hebrew. One of his poems is still used as a hymn by the Church of Jesus Christ of Latter-day Saints.

Come, thou glorious day of promise,
Come and spread thy cheerful ray,

When the scattered sheep of Israel
Shall no longer go astray
    When hosannas
With united voice they cry.

Lord, how long wilt thou be angry?
Shall thy wrath forever burn?
Rise, redeem thy ancient people,
Their transgressions from them turn;
    King of Israel
Come and set thy people free.

Oh, that soon thou would'st to Jacob
Thine enliv'ning spirit send;
Of their unbelief and misery
Make, O Lord! a speedy end
    Lord Messiah!
Prince of peace, o'er Israel reign.

—Volume 3, page 668,

January 15, 1842.

Another poem still used in the hymnody of that church is on the subject of baptism for the dead and is authored by Joel H. Johnson. After quoting I Corinthians 15:29, the poem proceeds as follows:

The glorious gospel light has shone
    In this the latter day.
With such intelligence that none
    From truth need turn away.

For 'mong things which have been sealed,
    And from the world kept hid;
The Lord has to his saints revealed,
    As anciently he did.

And thro' the Priesthood now restored,
    Has e'en prepar'd the way,
Through which the dead may hear his word,
    And all its truths obey.

As Christ to spirits went to preach,
    Who were in prison aid;
So many saints have gone to teach
    The gospel to the dead.

And we for them can be baptized,
    Yes for our friends most dear!
That they can with the just be rais'd,
    When Gabria s' trump they hear.

That they may come with Christ again,
    When he to earth descends;
A thousand years with him to reign,
    And with their earthly friends.

Now, O! ye saints, rejoice to day,
    That you can saviors be
For all your dead who will obey
    The gospel and be free.

Then let us rise without restraint,
    And act for those we love;
For they are giving their consent,
    And wait for us to move.

—Volume 2, page 565,

October 1, 1841.

It has often been maintained that poetry is the language of deep feelings and the best vehicle for conveying profound emotions. This is substantiated by an anonymous poem appended to the obituary column in the September 1840 issue. This short, simple poem not only causes us to feel something of the anguish of those who must lay to rest the remains of a two-year-old daughter but also shares with us something of the hope and comfort felt by those who trusted in God for the final victory over death.

—In this place, on the 2nd day of August last, Tabitha Talle, consort of Lewis Talle, aged 35 years.

—On the 17 of July in Lee county lawn Territory Sarah Emma
Woodruff aged 2 years and 3 days.

> Thus the iron hand of death,
> Laid heavy on, and stopped the breath,
> Of one who lived but to beguile,
> Our lonely moments, with a smile.
> Beloved she lived, beloved she died,
> Her fathers joy and mothers pride—
> Beloved by all who did her see,
> Yea, and more beloved by me.
> There was no bell for to toll,
> But many a briny tear did fall—
> With anxious looks our hearts did tell,
> Little Sarah, dear, farewell!
> Ye, little Sarah, lovely one, [come—
> Sleep on, sleep on, till Christ shall
> Then thou wilt rise, shake off thy dust,
> And be numbered with the just.

—Volume 1, page 176,

September 1840.

Another poem occasioned by the death of a loved one is
"The Infant's Grave" by P. H. Young. The images in the
poem are rather confused, so that it is difficult to pinpoint
exactly what caused the child's death. This makes for an
interesting puzzle, the final solution of which may forever
escape the present-day readers of this poem. This tragedy
may date back to the Far West period of church history, in
which case "those who caused her heart to bleed" could
possibly refer to the Missourians who drove the Latter Day
Saints from their homes in northern Missouri. The child may
have died from overexposure on the journey to the safety of
Illinois, but this is strictly conjecture.

"Myself and wife buried our first-born on the banks of Grand
River, in the deep solitude of the western forest."

P. H. YOUNG.

THE INFANT'S GRAVE.

We laid him low by the moon's dim light,
And his dirge was the murmuring billow;
The prairie grass was his winding sheet,
And a cold moss stone his pillow:
'Twas a mournful sight for eye to see
The mother's grief, who bore him,
As she left her first-born, there to sleep
With the tall grass waving o er him.

He was born the hope of his father's heart,
But he died in a gloomy hour:—
And the joy of the mother was swept away
In that frail, but lovely flower;
And he lays there still in his prairie bed
'Neath the oak where his father laid him,
And the Indians say, the "Prairie Bird"
Chants the mourner's requiem o'er him.

And were they *men,* that mother drove
Forth from her peaceful home,
To bury her child in the forest wild
And leave him to sleep alone?
Oh no! for if they had but known
The pangs of a childless bride,
They had mingled their blood together there
And buried her by his side.

Yet weep not now, though his ashes rest
From his kindred far away;
The mother will meet her long lost child
Where all tears are wiped away;
Then those who caused her heart to bleed
Will hear the Judge proclaim,
Depart from me, ye wretched ones
To everlasting flames.

—Volume 3, page 622,

December 1, 1841

THE TWELVE AND THE BRITISH MISSION

The first issue of *Times and Seasons* carried an epistle addressed "To the elders of the church of Jesus Christ of Latter Day Saints, to the churches scattered abroad, and to all the saints." After counseling faithfulness in the midst of persecution, the apostles turned their attention to instructing the elders in their duties, particularly as they engaged in mis-

279

sionary work. Announcement was then made of the intention
of the Twelve to go to England to continue the work of
evangelization in that nation.

We are glad, dear brethren, to see that spirit of enterprise and
perseverance, which is manifested by you in regard to preaching
the gospel; and rejoice to know that neither bonds nor imprisonment, banishment nor exile, poverty or contempt, nor all the
combined powers of earth and hell, hinder you from delivering
your testimony to the world; and publishing those glad tidings
which has been revealed from heaven, by the ministering of
angels, by the gift of the holy Ghost, and by the power of God,
for the salvation of the world in these last days. And we would
say to you, that the hearts of the twelve are with you, and they,
with you, are determined to fulfil their mission, to clear their
garments of the blood of this generation, to introduce the gospel
to foreign nations, and to make known to the world those great
things which God has developed; they are now on the eve of their
departure for England, and will start in a few days, they feel to
pray for you, and to solicit an interest in your prayers, and in the
prayers of the church, that God, may sustain them in their arduous undertaking; grant them success in their mission, deliver them
from the powers of darkness, the stratagems of wicked men, and
all the combined powers of earth and hell. And if you, unitedly
seek after unity of purpose and design, if you are men of humility, and of faithfulness, of integrity and persevereance, if you
submit yourselves to the teachings of heaven, and are guided by
the Spirit of God, if you at all times seek the glory of God, and
the salvation of men, and lay your honor prostrate in the dust, if
need be, and are willing to fulfil the purposes of God in all things;
the power of the priesthood will rest upon you, and you will
become mighty in testimony: the widow, and the orphan will be
made glad, and the poor among men rejoice in the holy one of
Israel. Princes will listen to the things that you proclaim, and the
nobles of the earth will attend with deference to your words;
Queens will rejoice in the glad tidings of salvation, and King's
bow to the sceptre of Immanuel; light will burst forth as the
morning, and intelligence spread itself as the rays of the sun; the
cringing sycophant will be ashamed, and the traitor fle from your
presence; superstition, will hide its hoary head, and infidelity be
ashamed. And amid the clamour of men, the din of war, the rage
of pestilence, the commotion of nations, the overthrow of kingdoms, and the dissolution of Empires, truth will stalk forth with

280

gigantic strides, and lay hold of the honest in heart among all nations: Zion shall blosom as a rose, and the nations flock to her standard and the kingdoms of this world shall soon become the kingdoms of our God and of his Christ, and he shall reign for ever and ever, Amen.

BRIGHAM YOUNG,
HEBER C. KIMBALL,
JOHN E. PAGE.
WILFORD WOODRUFF
JOHN TAYLOR,
GEORGE A. SMITH.

—Volume 1, pages 14, 15,

November 1839.

A communication from the traveling apostles was written from New York City as the Twelve waited for their boat to leave.

New York. Feb. 19th, 1840.

Brigham Young, H. C. Kimball, Orson Pratt, and P. P. Pratt, to the church of Jesus Christ of Latter Day Saints in Commerce, Ill. and to the Saints in general, Greeting.

Dear brethren, after so long a time we have met in New York and are about to sail for England. We have bespoke our passage on the old ship Garrick, which carried ont Elder Kimball, and others three years since. we sail on Tuesday the 25 inst.

Bro. George Smith was here also, and is gone to Pensylvania on a short mission and will probably be here to go with us. Bro. Hadlock is here, and is also going; Elders Taylor, Woodruff, Turley, and Clark have already gone over to Eng. Most of us have had a very long and tedious journey, and have suffered much from sickness &c. and some are not yet wholly free from the lingering chills and fever, more particularly elder Smith. In journeying through the several states we found many brethren, friends and churches, and many elders who were laboring to advantage; the work is rolling on.— Indeed there were many elders whom we had never heard of before, that were preaching and baptizing, and ordaining other elders, who were still rolling the work of truth, wide and more wide; and thus it spreads. . . .

When we reflect upon the mountains of embarrassment which

281

have intervened, to prevent the Twelve from accomplishing their present mission, and consider that most of them have persevered, through mobs, murderers, robbers, thieves; and through storms of persecution, poverty, sickness and death, and at last find themselves upon the sea shore, in health and peace and plenty; ready to set sail, it is a matter of joy and consolation to us and fills our hearts with gratitude to that god who commanded us to cross the mighty deep for Christ's sake and the gospel's. We consider that there is no instance on record where men have been called to so great an undertaking, under the same circumstances of poverty, sickness and distress; both ourselves, families, and brethren; but yet through the mercy of God, we think the mission will be accomplished, and will stand on record, for the wondering gaze of succeeding ages, and to God and the Lamb be all the praise and glory. . . .

Elder P. P. Pratt has just returned from Washington city, after warning them faithfully. Whether he will be able to go with us to Eng. at this time is uncertain; he could have done it had he not been called to Washington just as he was getting ready to cross the ocean. But it is a good thing that he went to Washington, for by so doing we can go from America feeling our duty to this Government for the present more fully done.

We must now close by saying, may the the God of Israel bless and preserve the saints in America, and deliver them from their great tribulation, may he go before us and be with us and enable us to return to this land with our hundreds of thousands of souls saved in the kingdom of God.

—Volume 1, pages 70-71,

March 1840.

Two months later the apostles were in England, sending to America very encouraging reports of how substantial the evangelistic gains in Britain had been. In the following letters, we are given the minutes of the Twelve's special sessions and also minutes of a "general Conference" held at Preston.

After a long and tedious journey of 28 days on the water we landed in Liverpool: Eld's. H. C. Kimball, P. P. Pratt, O. Pratt, G. A. Smith, R. Hadlock, and myself were in company; we rejoiced in the Lord, and when we cast our minds upon the saints in that country, we could by faith participate in their joys; realizing they

were met in conference, it being the 6th day of April. We soon
found a room that we could have to ourselves, which made our
solemn assembly glorious: we blest each other and prepared for
our labor. The next day we found Elder Taylor in the city; there
had been about 30 baptized. On Wednesday went to Preston, met
with the church on Sunday, bore testimony of the things the
Lord is doing in these last days. President Joseph Fielding gave
out an appointment for a conference, for the church on Wednesday the 15th.

At a council of the Twelve, held in Preston, Lancashire, England, on the 14th of April, 1840, it being the 9th day of the 1st
month, of the 11th year, of the rise of the church of Jesus Christ.
Elders Brigham Young, Heber C. Kimball, P. P. Pratt, Orson Pratt,
Wilford Woodruff, John Taylor, & George A. Smith being present.

Elder Brigham Young was called to preside, and Elder John
Taylor chosen secretary: the council was opened by prayer by
Elder B. Young. Elder Willard Richards was ordained to the office
of an apostle, and received into the quorum of the Twelve by a
unanimous voice, according to previous revelation: Elder Brigham
Young was unanimously chosen as the standing president of the
Twelve.

Resolved, that he who acts as the secretary of the quorum,
shall prepare the minutes of the conferences of the quorum, and
deposit them in the hands of the president for keeping.

Moved by Elder Kimball, and seconded by Elder Richards,
that twenty of the Seventies be sent for, and that it be left
discretionary with the president of the Twelve, to send for more
if he think proper: conference adjourned, was closed by prayer
by Elder Kimball.

At a general Conference of the church of Jesus Christ of Latter
Day Saints, held in the Temperance Hall, Preston, Lancashire,
England, on the 15th of April, 1840.

President Joseph Fielding called upon Elder Kimball to preside, and Elder Wm. Clayton chosen clerk, it being the 10th day
of the first month, of the 11th year of the rise of the church; the
meeting was opened by singing and prayer by Elder Kimball.

Elder Kimball then called upon the elders to represent the
different branches of the church. . . .Moved and sec'd. that the
publishing of the Hymn book, shall be done by the direction of
the Twelve. carried. Moved and sec'd. that a monthly periodcal
shall be published under the direction & superintendance of the
Twelve; for the benefit and information of the church, as soon as
a sufficient number of subscribers shall be obtained, carried.

Moved and sec'd. that brother John Blazard of Sambsbury, be ordained to the office of a priest, carried. Moved and sec'd. that bro. James Corbridge of Thornly, be ordained to the office of a Priest, carried.

Elder Kimball then laid before the conference, the importance and propriety of ordaining a Patriarch, to bestow Patriarchal blessings on the fatherless, &c. referred to the Twelve, whose business it is to select one and ordain him according to the directions of the Spirit. . . .

The council met pursuant to adjournment, April 16th, 1840. The number of the Quorum the same as on the 14th. Moved by elder Young, sec'd. by elder Taylor, that elder P. P. Pratt be chosen as the Editor of the monthly periodical for the Church. Moved by elder Kimball, sec'd. by P. P. Pratt, that a committe of three be appointed to make a selection of Hymns. Moved by elder Orson Pratt and sec'd. by elder Wilford Woodruff, that elders Brigham Young, P. P. Pratt, and John Taylor form the committe for that purpose.—Moved by elder Willard Richards sec'd. by elder G. A. Smith, that the name of the paper, or periodical be the "Latter Day Saints Millenial Star."

—Volume 1, pages 119-121,

June 1840.

The kind of success in proselyting being enjoyed by the missionaries and membership in Britain was demonstrated by some statistics which appeared in the December 15, 1840, *Times and Seasons.* "Official members" of the conference would be similar to today's "conference delegates" in their relationship to the "general Conferences" mentioned in the report.

Elders Kimball and G. A. Smith continued their labors in the city until the first of October at which time we met together again in Staffordshire and enjoyed each others company while journeying together to Manchester, at which place, the quorum of the traveling council, with many elders and Saints had the privilege of once more sitting in a general Conference together on the 6th of October, in the Carpenter's Hall in Manchester at which place we heard represented,

3626 Saints and 383 official members.
At the July Conference there was
2513 Saints and 256 official members,
Making an increase in three months, of
1113 Saints and 127 official members

besides over 200 Saints including many elders, priests, teachers and deacons who have emigrated to America which would make over 1300 additions to the churches in Europe during the last three months, and over 2000 since our Conference held in Preston on the 15th of April, which representation at that time was, 1671 Saints and 132 official members.

—Volume 2, page 252,

December 15, 1840.

Not all of the communication is from Britain to America. Joseph Smith on occasion penned "epistles to the elders in England." The *Times and Seasons* would sometimes publish extracts from these epistles. In the following one, the prophet commends the Twelve for their "good labors" and relays some news about conditions in Nauvoo.

To the travelling high council and elders of the church of Jesus Christ, of Latter Day Saints in Great Britain.

Beloved Brethren,

May grace, mercy and peace rest upon you, from God the Father and the Lord Jesus Christ:—

Having several communications lying before me from my brethren the Twelve, some of which have ere this merited a reply, but from the multiplicity of business which necessarily engages my attention, I have delayed communicating to you to the present time. Be assured beloved brethren, that I am no disinterested observer of the things which are transpiring on the face of the whole earth; and amidst the general movements which are in progress, none is of more importance than the glorious work in which you are now engaged, consequently I feel some anxiety on your account, that you may, by your virtue, faith, diligence and charity commend yourselves to one another, to the church of Christ, and to your Father which is in heaven, by whose grace you have been called to so holy a calling, and be enabled to perform the great and responsible duties which rest upon you. And I can assure you that from the information I have received, I feel satisfied that you have not been remiss in your duty; but that your dilgence and faithfulness have been such as must secure you the smiles of that God whose servants you are, and also the good will of the Saints throughout the world. . . .

Being requested to give my advice respecting the propriety of your returning in the spring, I will do so, willingly. I have reflected upon the subject some time, and am of the opinion that it would be wisdom in you to make preparations to leave the scene of your labors in the spring. Having carried the testimony to that land, and numbers having received it; consequently the leaven can now spread without your being obliged to stay—another thing, there has been some whisperings of the spirit that there will be some agitations, some excitements and some trouble in the land in which you are now laboring. I would therefore say in the mean time, be diligent, organize the churches and let every one stand in his proper place, so that those who cannot come with you in the spring, may not be left as sheep without a shepherd.

I would likewise observe, that inasmuch as this place has been appointed for the gathering of the Saints, it is necessary that, it should be attended to in the order that the Lord intends it should—to this end I would say, that as there are great numbers of the Saints in England who are extremely poor and not accustomed to the farming business, who must have certain preparations made for them before they can support themselves in this country, therefore, to prevent confusion and disappointment when they arrive here, let those men who are accustomed to making machinery, and those who can command a capital, though it be small, come here as soon as convenient, and put up machinery and make such other preparations as may be necessary, so that when the poor come in they may have employment to come to. This place has advantages for manufacturing and commercial purposes, which, but very few can boast of; and by establishing cotton factories, founderies, potteries, &c. &c., would be the means of bringing in wealth and raising it to a very important elevation. I need not occupy more space on this subject, as its reasonableness must be obvious to every mind. . . .

If Elder P. P. Pratt should wish to remain in England some time longer than the rest of the Twelve, he will feel himself at liberty to do so, as his family are with him, consequently his circumstances are somewhat different from the rest; and likewise it is necessary that some one should remain, who is conversant

286

with the rules and regulations of the church, and continue the
paper which is published; consequently, taking all these things
into consideration, I would not press it upon Bro. Pratt to return
in the spring.

I am happy to inform you that we are prospering in this place,
and that the Saints are more healthy than formerly: and from the
decrease of sickness this season, when compared with the last, I
am led to the conclusion that this must eventually become a
healthy place.

There are, at present, about 3,000 inhabitants in Nauvoo, and
numbers are flocking in daily. Several stakes have been set off in
different parts of the country, which are in prospering circumstances. Provisions are much ower than when you left—Flour is
worth about $4 per barrel. Corn and potatoes about 25 cents per
bushel, and other things in proportion. There has been a very
plentiful harvest throughout the Union.

You will observe by the Times and Seasons that we are about
building a Temple. for the worship of our God, in this place:
preparations are now making; every tenth day is devoted by the
brethren for quarrying rock. &c. We have secured one of the most
lovely situations for it that there is in this region of country; it is
expected to be considerably larger than the one in Kirtland, and
on a more magnificent scale, and which will undoubtedly attract
the attention of the great men of the earth.

We have a bill before the Legislature, for the incorporation of
the city of Nauvoo, and for the establishing of a Seminary of
learning and other purposes, which I expect will pass in a short
time.

You will also have received intelligence of the death of my
father, which event although painful to the family and to the
church generally, yet the scaling testimony of the truth of the
work of the Lord, was indeed satisfactory. Brother Hyrum succeeds him as Patriarch of the church, according to his last directions and benedictions. . . .

The work in which we are unitedly engaged is one of no ordinary kind the enemies we have to contend against are subtle and
well skilled in maneuvering it behooves us to be on the alert to
concentrate our energies, and that the best feelings should exist in
our midst, and then by the help of the Almighty, we shall go on
from victory to victory, and from conquest to conquest, our evil
passions will be subdued, our prejudices depart, we shall find no
room in our bosoms for hatred, vice will hide its deformed head,
and we shall stand approved in the sight of heaven and be ac-

knowledged the sons of God. Let us realize that we are not to live
to ourselves but to God, by so doing the greatest blessings will
rest upon us both in time and in eternity.

JOSEPH SMITH.

—Volume 2, pages 258-261,

January 1, 1841.

The following summer those of the apostles who had been
laboring in Britain, with the exception of Parley P. Pratt,
returned home. The following report to the church recounts
their daring exploits and urges the eldership of the church to
sacrifice in similar ways for the sake of the church's growth
and further outreach.

THE TWELVE.

All of the quorum of the Twelve who were expected here this
season, with the exception of Elder Woodruff, have arrived.

We have listened to the accounts which they give of their
success and the prosperity of the work of the Lord in Great
Britain, with great pleasure. They certainly have been the instru-
ments, in the hands of God, of accomplishing much, and must
have the satisfaction of knowing that they have done their duty.

Perhaps no men ever undertook such an important mission
under such peculiarly distressing forbidding, and unpropitious
circumstances.—Most of them when they left this place, nearly
two years ago, were worn down with sickness and disease, or were
taken sick on the road.—Several of their families were also afflicted and needed their aid and support. But knowing that they
had been called by the God of Heaven to preach the gospel to
other nations, they confered not with flesh and blood; but
obedient to the heavenly mandate, *without purse or scrip,* commenced a journey of five thousand miles, entirely dependant on
the providence of that God who had called them to such a holy
calling. . . .

Under the instrumentality of the Twelve and their fellow
laborers, large and flourishing churches have been built up in
various parts of England, Scotland, Ireland, and the Isle of Man;
and when they left, the work was progressing with rapid strides.

We cannot too strongly urge upon the Elders of Israel, to

imitate the example which these servants of God have set them, and, whenever they shall be called to proclaim the gospel to the enlightened European, or the dark and benighted African, they will manifest the same zeal and laudable enterprise, trusting in the arm of the Lord for assistance and support, and undoubtedly, the same blessings will crown their labors and their toil.

We are aware that it is something contrary to the feelings of most men, to undertake such a journey without purse or scrip, entirely dependant on the arm of Jehovah. However it has been done, and those that have gone forth trusting in the name of the Lord, have found his promise true, and have not been suffered to lack any good thing. Let not the faithful laborers be discouraged, but let them gird up their loins, and ever be prepared to move in the direction their Heavenly Father would have them go, and labor with all their mights, for a great work remains to be accomplished, and the laborers are but few. If the Lord's people be a willing people in the day of his powers, then every obstacle can be overcome, every difficulty can be surmounted, and the work will roll forth with power and great glory. Israel shall be hunted up from the rocks and corners where they have been hid from the gaze of the world, many shall run to and fro and knowledge shall be increased.

—Volume 2, pages 487-488,

August 2, 1841.

The Saints in Britain were instructed to leave their homeland as soon as circumstances permitted in order to come to Nauvoo to build up the stakes of Zion in that place. An apostolic epistle, intended for publication in the *Millennial Star*, was shared with the readership of the *Times and Seasons*.

AN EPISTLE OF THE TWELVE.

To the saints scattered abroad in England, Scotland, Ireland, Wales, the Isle of Man and the eastern continent, Greeting;

Beloved Brethren:— We rejoice and thank our Heavenly Father daily in your behalf, that we hear of your faithfulness and diligence in the great work unto which you have been called by the Holy Spirit, through the voice of the servants of the Most High, who have been and are now amongst you, for the purpose of instructing you in those principles, which are calculated to prepare the children of men for the renovation of the earth and the restitution of all things spoken by the prophets.

Several months have passed away, since we bid adieu to our brethren and sisters on the islands of the sea, and passed over the great deep to our homes, our kindred, the bosom of the church and the stakes of Zion; but neither time nor distance can efface from our memories the many expressions of kindness which we have heard from your lips and experienced from your hands, which have so often ministered to our necessities, while we were wandering in your midst, like our master, having no place to lay our heads only as furnished by your liberality and benevolence; and it is a subject of no small consolation to us that we have this testimony of so many of your that you are the disciples of the Lord Jesus; and we give you our warmest thanks, and our blessing that you have not only ministered to us, but that you continue to minister to our brethren, who are still laboring amongst you, for which, an hundred fold shall be returned into your bosoms. . . .

Since our arrival in this place there has been one special and one general conference of the church, and the twelve have been called to tarry at home for a season, and stand in their lot next to the first Presidency and assist in councilling the brethren and in the settling of emigrants &c., and the first great object before us, and the saints generally, is to help forward the completion of the Temple and the Nauvoo House; buildings which are now in progress according to the revelations, and which must be completed to secure the salvation of the church in the last days, for God requires of his saints to build him a house wherein his servants may be instructed, and endued with power from on high, to prepare them to go forth among the nations. and proclaim the fullness of the gospel for the last time, and bind up the law and seal up the testimony, leaving this generation without excuse, and the earth prepared for the judgments, which will follow. In this house all the ordinances will be made manifest, and many things will be shown forth. which have been hid from generation to generation.

The set time to favor the stakes of Zion is at hand, & soon the Kings and the Queens, the princes and the nobles, the rich and the honorable of the earth, will come up hither to visit the Temple of our God and to enquire concerning his strange work; and as Kings are to become nursing fathers, and Queens nursing mothers in the habitations of the righteous, it is right to render honor to whom honor is due; & therefore expedient that such, as well as the saints, should have a comfortable house for boarding and lodging when they come hither, and it is according to the revelations that such a house should be built. . . .

He that believeth shall not make haste, but let all the saints who desire to keep the commandments of heaven and work righteousness, come to the place of gathering as soon as circumstances will permit. It is by united efforts that great things are accomplished, and while the saints are scattered to the four winds, they cannot be united in action, if they are in spirit; they cannot all build at one city, or lift at one stone of the great Temple, tho' their hearts may all desire the same thing. We would not *press* the subject of the *gathering* upon you, for we know your hearts, and your means; and so far as means fail, let patience have its perfect work in your souls, for in due time you shall be delivered if you faint not.

We are not altogether ignorant of the increase of difficulty among the laboring classes in England, since our departure, through the stoppage of factories and similar occurrences, and we would council those who have, to impart unto those, who have not, and cannot obtain: remembering that he who giveth unto the poor lendeth unto the Lord, and he shall receive in return four fold. . . .

If you are prepared for all these things; if you choose rather to suffer afflictions with the people of God than to enjoy the pleasures of sin, for a little moment, come up hither; *Come direct to New Orleans, and up the Mississipi river,* for the expense is so much less, and the convenience of water navigation is so much greater than it is by Montreal, New York or Philadelphia, that it is wisdom for the saints to make *New Orleans* their *general established port,* and be *sure* to start at *such times* that they *may arrive here during the cold months,* for the change from the cold climate of England, to this place, in the hot season, is too great for the health of emigrants, till there is more faith in the church.

In this region of country there are thousands and millions of acres of beautiful prairie, unoccupied, which can be procured on reasonable terms, and we will hail the time with joy when these unoccupied lands shall be turned into fruitful fields, and the hands of those who are now idle for want of employ, shall be engaged in the cultivation of the soil. When the brethren arrive they will do well to call on some of the twelve, inasmuch as they desire council, for by so doing, they may escape the influence of designing men, who have crept in unawares, and would willingly subvert the truth, by conniving to their own advantage, if they have the opportunity.

The church has commenced a new city 20 miles below this, and 1 mile below Warsaw called, *Warren,* where many city lots, and farms in the vicinity, can be had on reasonable terms; and it will be wisdom for many of the brethren to stop at that place, for the opportunity for erecting temporary buildings will be greater than at this place, also the chance for providing food, will be superior, to those who wish to labor for it. . . .

Brethren pray for us, and the First Presidency, the leader of the people, even Joseph, that his life and health may be precious in the sight of heaven, till he has finished the work which he has commenced; and for all the elders of Israel, that every man may be faithful in his calling, the whole household of faith, and all subjects of prayer.

Brethren farewell. May the blessings of heaven and earth be multiplied unto you, in spirit and in body, in basket and in store, in the field and in the shop, on the land and on the sea, in the house and by the way, and in all situations and circumstances, until you shall stand on Mount Zion, and enter the celestial city, in the name of Jesus Christ. Amen.

BRIGHHM YOUNG,
HEBER C. KIMBALL,
ORSON PRATT,
WILLIAM SMITH,
LYMAN WIGHT,
WILLFORD WOODRUFF,
JOHN TAYLOR,
GEO. A. SMITH,
WILLARD RICHARDS.

Nauvoo, Hancock co., Ill. Nov. 15, 1841.

—Volume 3, pages 600-603,
November 15, 1841.

THE MISSION TO THE HOLY LAND

One of the conference appointments that most captured the imagination of the church in the early 1840's was the calling of Orson Hyde to journey abroad to consult with Jewish leaders and officials concerning the "ripeness of the times" for the return of the Jews to their ancestral home in Palestine. Joseph Smith provided a report and explanation of the conference action in the April 1840 *Times and Seasons.*

292

To all people unto whom these presents shall come.—Greeting.

Be it known that we the constituted authorities of the Church of Jesus Christ of Latter Day Saints, assembled in conference, at Nauvoo, Hancock county and State of Illinois, on this, sixth day of April, in the year of our Lord, one thousand, eight hundred and forty, considering an important event at hand, an event involving the interest and fate of the Gentile nations throughout the world. From the signs of the times, and from declarations contained in the oracles of God, we are forced to come to this conclusion.

The Jewish nation have been scattered abroad among the Gentiles for a long period; and in our estimation, the time of the commencement of their return to the Holy land, has already arrived.

As this scattered and persecuted people are set among the Gentiles as a sign unto them of the second coming of the Mesiah; and also, of the overthrow of the present kingdom's and Governments of the earth, by the potency of his Almighty arm in scattering famine and pestilence like the frosts and snows of winter, and sending the sword, with nation against nation to bathe it in each others blood: It is highly important, in our opinion, that the present views and movements of the Jewish people be sought after, and laid before the American people for their consideration, their prophet and their learning; and feeling it to be our duty to employ the most efficient means in our power to save the chilren of men from the "abomination that maketh desolate."—We have, by the counsel of the Holy Spirit, appointed Elder Orson Hyde, the bearer of these presents, a faithful and worthy minister of Jesus Christ, to be our agent and representative in foreign lands, to visit the cities of London, Amsterdam, Constantinople and Jerusalem; and also other places that he may deem expedient, and converse with the priests, rulers and Elders of the Jews, and obtain from them all the information possible, and communicate the same to some principal paper for publication, that it may have a general circulation throughout the United States.

As Mr. Hyde has willingly and cheerfully accepted the appointment to become our servant, and the servant of the public in distant and foreign countries for Christs' sake, we do confidently recommend him to all religious and christian people, and to gentlemen and ladies, making no profession, as a worthy member of society, possessing much zeal to promote the happiness of mankind, fully believing that they will be forward to render him all the pecuniary aid he needs, to accomplish this laborious and hazardous mission for the general good of the human family.

Ministers of every denomination, upon whom Mr. H. shall call, are requested to hold up his hands and aid him by their influence, with an assurance that such as do this, shall have the prayers and blessings of a poor and an afflicted people whose blood has flowed to test the depths of their sincerity, and to crimson the face of freedoms soil with MARTYR'S BLOOD.

Mr. Hyde is instructed by this conference to transmit to this country nothing but simple facts for publication, entirely disconnected with any peculiar views of theology, leaving each class to make their own comments and draw their own inferences.

Given under our hands, at the time and place before mentioned.

JOSEPH SMITH, jr. Ch'r.

Robert B. Thompson, Clerk.

Bro's Smith and Robinson, will discover, by the conference minutes, that our worthy brother, Elder John E. Page, was duly appoicted by said conference to accompany me in this mission; and to receive the same credentials as my own.

Yours sincerely,
ORSON HYDE.

—Volume 1, pages 86-87,
April 1840.

In the January 15, 1841, issue, a terse public reprimand appeared in the form of the following notice:

Elders Orson Hyde and John E. Page are informed that the Lord is not well pleased with them in consequence of delaying their mission, (Elder John E. Page in particular,) and they are requested by the First Presidency to hasten their journey towards their destination.—Page 287.

That spring Orson Hyde, unaccompanied, left for Europe. In a series of letters written during the next year, he chronicles his trip through Europe to the Holy Land. For Elder Hyde, the climax of his journey came as he stood upon the Mount of Olives and, in a dedicatory prayer, consecrated the land for the return of the Jews and the rebuilding of the temple at Jerusalem. The following excerpts are from a letter written in Alexandria, Egypt, for publication in the *Millennial Star*. The *Times and Seasons* printed this letter on April 1, 1842.

294

Alexandria, Nov. 22, 1841.

Dear Brother Pratt,

A few minutes now offer for me to write, and I improve them in writing to you.

I have only time to say that I have seen Jerusalem precisely according to the vision which I had. I saw no one with me in the vision; and although Elder Page was appointed to accompany me there, yet I found myself there alone.

The Lord knows that I have had a hard time, and suffered much, but I have great reason to thank him that I enjoy good health at present, and have a prospect before me of soon going to a civilized country, where I shall see no more turbans or camels. The heat is most oppressive, and has been all through Syria. . . .

On Sunday morning, October 24, a good while before day, I arose from sleep, and went out of the city as soon as the gates were opened, crossed the brook Cedron, and went upon the Mount of Olives, and there, in solemn silence, with pen, ink, and paper, just as I saw in the vision, offered up the following prayer to him who lives for ever and ever:—

"O Thou! who art from everlasting to everlasting, eternally and unchangeably the same, even the God who rules in the heavens above, and controlls the destinies of men on the earth, wilt Thou not condescend, through thine infinite goodness and royal favour, to listen to the prayer of thy servant which he this day offers up unto thee in the name of thy holy child Jesus, upon this land where the Sun of Righteousness sat in blood, and thine *Anointed One* expired.

"Be pleased, O Lord to forgive all the follies, weaknesses, vanities, and sins of thy servant, and strengthen him to resist all future temptations. Give him prudence and discernment that he may avoid the evil, and a heart to choose the good; give him fortitude to bear up under trying and adverse circumstances, and grace to endure all things for thy name's sake, until the end shall come, when all the saints shall rest in peace.

"Now, O Lord! thy servant has been obedient to the heavenly vision which thou gavest him in his native land; and under the shadow of thine outstretched arm, he has safely arrived in this place to dedicate and consecrate this land unto Thee, for the gathering together of Judah's scattered remnants, according to the predictions of the holy prophets—for the building up of Jerusalem again after it has been trodden down by the Gentiles so long, and for rearing a temple in honour of thy name. . . ."

On the top of Mount Olives I erected a pile of stones as

295

a witness according to the ancient custom. On what was anciently
called Mount Zion, where the Temple stood, I erected another,
and used the rod according to the prediction upon my head.

I have found many Jews who listened with intense interest.
The idea of the Jews being restored to Palestine is gaining ground
in Europe almost every day. . . .

I am now about to go on board a fine ship for Triste, and from
thence I intend to proceed to Regensburgh, and there publish our
faith in the German language.—There are those who are ready and
willing to assist me.

I send you this letter by Capt. Withers, an English gentleman,
who goes direct to England on board the Oriental steamer. He has
come with me from Jerusalem. If I had money sufficient I should
be almost tempted to take passage on board of her to England,
but this I cannot do.

On receipt of this, I wish you to write to me immediately, and
direct to Regensburgh, on the Danube, Beyern, or Bavaria. If you
know any thing of my family, tell me.

My best respects to yourself and family, to brothers Adams
and Snow, and to all the saints in England.

May grace, mercy, and peace, from God our Father, and from
the Lord Jesus Christ, rest upon you all from this time, henceforth, and forever.   Amen.

Your brother in Christ,
ORSON HYDE.

—Volume 3, pages 739-742,
April 1, 1842.

ANNOUNCEMENTS

In terms of human interest, some of the short announcements published in the *Times and Seasons* are priceless. The
ones selected for review here include such divergent items as
information on thievery in the Nauvoo community, advertise-
ments for patent medicines, and reasons for disfellowshiping
members from the church. Emotions evoked among the
Saints by these announcements ranged from a gloating satisfaction that Governor Boggs of Missouri had "fallen from
grace" politically to a sympathetic sorrow for the parents
who lost their daughter during a steamer trip.

By the High Council at Nauvoo, it is ordered to be published in the Times & Seasons, that they disfellowship any and all persons, who shall ferry, or carry over the river, persons or freight, to the injure of the ferry, from Commerce or Nauvoo, to Montrose. Or who shall, knowingly, suffer or allow any animals, (subject to their controll,) to destroy any crops, fruits or plants, to the injury of the owner thereof.

Also, that whereas, in times past, the house of Joseph Smith Jr. has been much thronged with crowds of visitors, to the great inconvenience of his family. It is by this Council thought advisable, that in future, he be exempt from the burthen and inconvenience thereof.

H. G. SHERWOOD, Scribe.

—Volume 1, page 127,

June 1840.

TO THE AFFLICTED.

Just received and for Sale by Robinson and Smith, the following Medicines.

GRIDLEY's

SALT RHEUM. OINTMENT.

A Safe, Certain, and Final Cure for Salt Rheum, Tetter, Michigan or Prairie Itch, Illinois Mange, Soald Head, Scrofula, Ringworm, Obstinate Old Sores, of long standing, and almost all Cutaneous Diseases.

More than twelve thousand Bottles of this Ointment have been sold in the State of New York, within the last three years.

N. B. The money refunded in all cases of failure in the cure of the above named diseases (scrofula excepted,) provided the directions for use have been faithfully followed.—Price 75 cents. This Ointment is also kept constantly on hand for retail by the following Druggists, viz:

C. G. SHANE and Co., Cincinnati;
STICKLAND, GAYLORD and Co., Cleveland.
A. H. BROWN and Co., Mount Vernon;
ROBERT LEWIS, Chillicothe.

ROBINSON and SMITH have also for sale,

BLISS' PURGATIVE

Billious Pills.

297

These Pills are an effectual remedy for all disorders arising from a deranged state of the stomach and bowels—as, Indigestion or Dyspepsia, Cholic, Constipation, and especially for all billious affections, incident to warm climates or an unhealthy atmosphere.—When taken at the commencement or forming stage of fever, so as thoroughly to evacuate the bowels, they will, nine cases in ten, cut short the disease. Price 25 cents per box.

—Volume 2, page 208,

November 1, 1840.

LOOK OUT FOR THIEVES!!

This place has been infested of late with a gang of *thieves,* insomuch that property of almost all kinds, has been unsafe unless secured with bolts and bars; cattle and hogs have been made a free booty. The community are awake to ferret them out, and have already made some inroads among them; the measures that are taking, have created a general *alarm* among the midnight *pilagers,* and they are making *tracks* as fast as possible. As it is very possible that some may escape *justice,* and palm themselves upon an unsuspecting community, we give this notice as a timely warning, that all may be on the look out. We sincerely hope that all those who escape justice here, will soon be overtaken in their wickedness—ALTON is a suitable place for all such characters.

Volume 2, page 204,

November 1, 1840.

A GOOD CHANCE.

All those living adjacent to Nauvoo, who desire the accommodation, can have the privilege of suiting themselves, as wood flour, meal, pork, lard, butter and cheese will be received in payment for the "Times and Seasons." Printers, like all other men, live by *eating;* and in cold weather, *fire is very useful*—now do not let them suffer.

—Volume 2, page 240,

December 15, 1840.

Painful and awful Death!!!

Died, (politically,) at the City of Jefferson, of MORMON MANIA, on the 17th of Nov., the notorious Lilburn W. Boggs, in the fourth year of his reign. DIED Lilburn as a fool dieth, yea he gathered up his feet and slept with his fathers; and all the people rejoiced exceedingly. Thus has passed from the political arena one of the proudest, most cruel, and feeble despots, that ever swayed a princely sceptre—his life, despised; his death, unlamented.—(COMMUNICATED.)

—Volume 2, page 271,

January 1, 1841.

Hyrum Smith who some time since received the appointment of Patriarch in the church in place of Joseph Smith, Sen., deceased, has recently, by revelation, been appointed a Prophet and Revelator.

William Law has recently, by revelation, been appointed one of the first Presidency, in place of Hyrum Smith, appointed as above.

—Volume 2, page 310,

February 1, 1841.

INFORMATION WANTED.

As the Steam Boat General Pratt, was on her way from New Orleans to St. Louis, on the 15th of Nov. last, while about half way on her passage Mary, the eldest daughter of William and Mary Butterworth of Macclesfield, Eng. 11 years of age, accidentally fell over board, and although the captain of the boat instantly returned some distance and used every exertion to recover the body, nothing has yet been heard of it. If any one has found the body, and will give information thereof and the place of its deposite, they will greatly oblige, and soothe the feelings of the afflicted parents by giving notice to the Editor of the Times and Seasons.

Editors on the Mississippi will please copy.

—Volume 3, page 654,

January 1, 1842.

REPRINTS FROM OTHER SOURCES

The *Times and Seasons* editors delighted in reprinting articles from other periodicals if those articles were friendly in spirit to what was happening at Nauvoo. Such articles might be generally favorable in their assessment of church beliefs and practices while at the same time reflecting certain misconceptions about the Latter Day Saints. On the other hand, there were also articles intent upon exposing the church and defaming the church leaders. When this latter type of reprint was used, there would often, though not always, be an indignant response from the *Times and Seasons* editor, trying to "set the record straight." The excerpts below are typical of the different kinds of attention being given to the Nauvoo settlement and the Latter Day Saint faith by the secular press of the day.

> The following article we cut from the St. Louis Evening Gazette of Nov. 5. We agree perfectly with the writer, especially where he says, *"we believe they might as well worship us, as Joe. Smith or Sidney Rigdon;"* far be it from us to be man worshipers, we believe in *only one* Living and True God. . . .
>
> . *"Times and Seasons."*—We have received from "Nauvoo," a monthly paper under this title. It is of Mormon origin and advocates the Mormon cause. The Mormons, Shakers and a few other select bands of people seem to be the only honest and disinterested body of men now extant.
>
> We see the Mormons have eleven agents in England. Indeed there can be no doubt that their numbers are rapidly increasing. If they respect the laws and walk orderly, as we have no doubt they always intended to do, they can protect themselves. They will be too strong for any marauders in their viciny who want to pillage their lands and goods; and by now and then arming themselves, in self-defence, with the "sword of the flesh," any consequences which may follow their efforts at resisting the violence of their persecutors, will be looked upon in the same light that similar acts of self-defence in other men are regarded. In tact they can place themselves in an attitude, which will command respect, and awe away the profligate scoundrels, who have been heretofore making them their prey.

300

Let them obey the laws. If they do this, they should demand—not toleration—there is no such thing as toleration in this country—they should demand their *rights.* Every man, under our free Constitution, has a *right* to worship God as he pleases. Every man has a right to believe what he pleases. The laws of Missouri did not protect them in the enjoyment of these rights, and they were overpowered—crushed by the weight of popular fanaticism and official tyranny.

If the laws of Illinois will not protect them, they ought to protect themselves. They as men ought to know—what in truth their faith teaches—that there are ten thousand things worse than death. Submission to enormous wrong—consigning their lands to robbery and pillage—banishment from their homes fire sides and alters—are each and all worse than death.

The Mormons have had in us a true and steady friend from the beginning. We believe that they are laboring under a monstrous delusion. We believe they might as well worship us as Joe Smith or Sidney Rigdon. Their whole system of faith is, we believe, in its inception a gross imposture. But what of that? So long, as in the language of that true son of Freedom—Thomas Jefferson of glorious and immortal memory—They neither break my leg nor pick my pocket; so long as they do not molest me in my belief or meddle with me in my conduct—I care not what they believe. I may have my opinion that certain systems of belief have a better effect upon society than certain other systems. And I may try by persuasion and argument to make others believe as I do. But I can and will take no measures to force my belief upon them.

Let then the Mormons rest, and if they can let them flourish. Let them rest, at least, from the scandalous persecutions, which they underwent in this State—persecutions which disgrace and damn all those who were participators in or accessaries to it.

—Volume 2, pages 218-219,

November 15, 1840.

We gave in our last, a copy of an article from the St. Louis Daily Gazette for two reasons—to show that there are some who are willing to speak freely, and treat such high toned injustice in a manner it so richly deserves, also, as a strong testimony in our favor, coming from the very State in which those outrages were perpetrated. In this No. we give an extract from an article published in the Western Messenger, printed at Cincinnati Ohio, which we commend to the perusal of our readers, as it defends nobly the cause of the injured, and pleads strongly for insulted justice.

From the Western Messenger.
OUTRAGES OF MISSOURI MOBS
ON MORMONS.

Reader! Let not the word *Mormon* repel you! Think not that you have no interest in the cruelties perpetrated on this poor people! Read, we pray you, the history of this persecuted community; examine the detailed facts of these attrocities; reflect upon the hallowed principles and usages trampled under foot by ruffians; bring before your mind the violations of all law human and divine, of all right, natural and civil, of all ties of society and humanity, of all duties of justice, honor, honesty, and mercy, committed by so called freemen and Christians—and then speak out, speak out for prostrate law, for liberty disgraced, for outraged man, for heaven insulted;

"Loud as a summer thunderbolt shall waken A People's voice."

We speak strongly, for we feel strongly; and we wish to attract attention to a tragedy of almost unequalled horror, which has been unblushingly enacted in a state of this Union. Its history should be trumpeted abroad until the indignant rebuke of the whole land compels the authors, abettors and tolerators of these wrongs, to make the small return now in their power, for their aggravated injustice. Life cannot be restored to the murdered, nor health to the broken down in body and soul, nor peace to the bereaved; but the spoils on which robbers are now fattening, can be repaid; the loss of the destitute can be made up; the captive can be freed, and, until by legislative acts she makes redress— *Missouri is disgraced!*

It seems like some horrid dream, that these enormities, which Nicholas would have shrunk from inflicting on the Poles, have been deliberately committed in an age of peace, in a land of laws and freedom, upon our own brethren. Is it actually true, that citizens, peacable, industrious, temperate, orderly citizens, have been driven from their property, their houses burned, the furniture broken and scattered, their crops laid waste, their stores plundered, their cattle killed, their horses stolen, their clothes stripped from them, and themselves expelled under threats of instant death? Is it true that men have been tarred and feathered, whipt till they were raw from head to foot, till their bowels gushed out, that their skulls have been knocked in, and brains scattered with musket-buts, that they have been shot down while crying for quarter, shot down unarmed and defenceless like hogs in a pen? Is it true that sick women have been driven from burning houses at midnight on the snowy prairies, where they have given birth to children on the frozen ground, that they have forded rivers with helpless infants in their arms, fleeing from heartless pursuers, that they have been insulted when their natural protectors were hid from the murderers, that they have been violated by the guards appointed for their defence? And were the guilty instigators and executioners of these massacres, arsons and rapes, really men of standlng, ministers of the gospel, judges, senators, military officers, and the Governor of the state? Were not the evidence on which the narrative of each one of these cruelties rests *incontrovertible,* no one could conceive that such fiend-like acts had actually been wrought by beings in human shape. Would, that, for the honor of our nature, they could be discredited. Our statement is strictly, *unexaggeratedly* true. It is only *too meagre, too feeble. . . .*

Now Let every one on reading this tale of horror, speak out fully, fearlessly. Had the Mormons been pirates, blood-stained, had they been Indians, girdled with scalps, they would have deserved better treatment. Let the unsupported accusations brought against them be true, and yet the conduct of their plunderers and murderers was utterly without a palliation or excuse. Before the face of heaven, and in the sight of men, such acts are devilish.

What, in a word, were the causes of the madness of these mobs? The Mormons were deluded, obstinate, zealous, exclusive in their faith. They used the vague, prophetic denunciations of an enthusiastic sect. They retaliated the reproaches heaped upon them by religious opponents. This, we believe, was the great exciting cause. Their first persecutions were attacks on their opinions, and ridicule of their absurdity.

Again, there were suspicions against the sincerity of their leading men.—They were thought to be speculators on the credulity of the ignorant. Blind prejudice multiplied evil suspicions, enmity misconstrued natural acts, slander swelled trifles into monstrous wrongs, idle curiosity, greedy of alarm, and eager to gossip, circulated rumors. Now add that they were a larger and growing community, allied together both by necessity and choice, and *withal prosperous,* and we have an explanation of the fear, jealousy, envy and hatred felt against them; *an explanation, but no justification.* The same elements were active and fierce in these Missouri outrages, which have kindled the faggot, and bared the sword, and opened the dungeon in all times. These elements were bigotry, ignorance, panic. And when we talk of living in an age of enlightenment liberty, and law, let us recollect with shame the burning of the convent at Charlestown, the absurd humbug of

Maria Monk, and the countless wrongs which other mobs, for as slight pretexts, have wrought in almost every State in the Union. The blaze of these other disgraceful proceedings, is lost, however, in the hot glare of this infernal outbreak.

—Volume 2, pages 235-238,

December 1, 1840.

From the Upper Mississippian.
LETTERS ABOUT THE WEST.
Number Three.
Nauvoo—Mormon Religion

Nauvoo City. This place is in the north western part of Hancock county, Illinois, and was formely known by the name of Commerce, but has recently received a city charter by the name of *Nauvoo,* the name given by the Mormons. The town is situated upon a slightly inclined plain, or piece of ground, of from one to two miles in extent, projecting westward into the Mississippi, somewhat in the shape of a man's arm, half bent; presenting a fine appearance for some miles above and below the town. Since the Mormons, or *"Latter Day Saints,"* (as they call themselves) were so wantonly driven from their homes and estates in Missouri, by an *armed mob,* under the excited authorities of that State, these persecuted people have settled in this town, and the adjacent country upen both sides of the Mississippi—and added from 75 to 100 buildings, mostly neat and painted, spread over a large extent of ground, and covering the plain and the bluffs in the rear.—These numerous new, bright looking buildings, scattered about amongst the trees and shrubbery which abound here, present, in warm weather, a delightful appearance. Under the shade of some beautiful shrubbery near the river's brink, seats are erected for the accommodation of the society, at their religious meetings. The spot selected is favorable to a calm and serene temper, and a devotional frame of mind.

Nauvoo is said to have a population of about 3000 inhabitants some 300 buildings, several small traders, Tavern keepers, Phisicians, and various kinds of mechanics and laborers: and some water craft, among which is a small steam-boat called Nauvoo. The landing, soil and timber about the town, are favorable to its future growth but being at the *head,* instead of the foot of the Rapids, its location is not so advantageous for trade as that of *Warsaw* or *Keokuck,* mentioned in my last letter. Besides this, there being considerable low lands upon the Islands in its vicinity, their decomposing vegetable matter is supposed to send forth delaterious exhaltat ons prejudicial to the health of the town. However, Nauvoo has a fine country in its rear, and if to many drones and rogues do not creep in among these generally quiet, industrious and economical people, we may expect to see a very considerable city built up here—particularly as many of this sect in Europe, are now known to be about removing to this country—and indeed some two hundred have already arrived at Nauvoo, and the vicinity. Mr. Smith is reported to have said that it is destined to be the largest city in the world! It is some 18 miles above Warsaw, and 6 or 8 below Fort Madison.

Religion of the Mormons. In the course of two land journeis between Stephenson and Quincy, I stopped over night at Nauvoo, rode one day in company with a Mormon preacher, and two days with one of the most respectable private members of the society. I also saw, in Stephenson, the celebrated Joseph Smith, but had no opportunity to converse with him respecting the peculiar tenets of their religion. Mr. Smith (commonly called *"Joe. Smith,"*) is a stout, muscular, course looking man, of about 32 or 33 years of age, and six feet high—and is said to be a man of good natural talents, but of inferlor education—and that, as a scholar and logician, Mr. Rigdon is much his superior. Dr. Bennett, one of their preachers, and with whom I rode as above, appeared to be a man of considerable reading and general intelligence—to possess a christian temper, and pretty correct ideas of personal piety. He was courteous and gentlemanly in his deportment, though somewhat *selfish, exclussve and bigoted* in notions about other sects and creeds. I, however, derived considerable information, and consequent satisfaction from conversing with him upon the subject of this strange religion. I may not be able in this brief and hasty newspapei sketch, to do full and exact justice to their creed as represented by this and the other gentleman, but I will *aim* to do so.

I understood from them as follows, vix:—That their society did not recognize *Mormon,* as a Prophet or Teacher sent from God to the *"Latter Day Saints"*—that they did not discard the Bible as used by other christian sects—that the book, commonly called *"the Mormon Bible,"* was considered by them as an additional revelation from heaven, made by God himself, to Joseph Smith, when 17 years of age, and under deep and prayerful concern of mind about his spiritual condition—that it relates principally to the history of the house of Ephraim and their descendants, which these people say was lost, or omitted, in the compliation of the generally accredited christian Bible. That the Almighty spoke orally, and disclosed to Smith, in a vision, where to

305

find the long buried *"Brass Plates,"* containing some unknown hieroglyphics, the further and hitherto undiscovered history of this branch of the Jewish nation—which history foretells, as they say, the character, condition and duty, of the *"Latter Day Saints,"* or Mormons—and the persecutions which they have endured in Missouri and elswhare, on account of their religion. They hold that the Lord made a verbal, personal communication to Smith, an uneducated and ignorant youth of 17, and instructed him to emyloy persons to translate the history contained in these few strange characters, engraven upon these brass plates, and that the Almighty stood by, and by a miraculous exercise of infinite power and wisdom, told Smith the meaning of the letters and characters upon the plates, and directed him to communicate it to the ignorant and uninspired translators, to be by them penned down for publication. And also that at a certain stage of the proceeding, the Almighty directed Smith to cease the work of translation, and again to bury the plates until mankind should become more virtuous, and better qualified for the reception of a further and complete revelation of the whole matter, at which time the Lord would again appear upon earth, and direct Smith how to proceed upon this momentuous subject!!!

The object and plan of these letters will not admit of pursuing this matter further, or commenting upon the monstrous delusion that could take possession of so many apparently sensible and intelligent people— or upon the success with which an uneducated man, like Smith, has impressed belief in this extraordinary imposition, which fact induces the belief that he is a man of very considerable talents. But I really believe that these people, after all, are generally quite conscientious in this matter—are more to be pitied than despised, and *"more sinned against than sinning."*

When putting the preceding article in type we intended to have made some corrections, but time will not admit in this number; we will make them in a future No. The writer, no doubt, intended to give a fair statement, and in the main, did; but respecting our faith, (on some points,) the book of Mormon, &c., he is widely from the mark.—Ed.

—Volume 2, pages 322-324,

February 15, 1841.

FALSEHOODS REFUTED.
For the Times & Seasons.

E. Robinson, Esq.:—
The following article from the pen of the sapient, Editor of

the Warsaw Signal is worthy of preservation for the number of palpable falsehoods it contains—

"DIFFICULTY AT MONTROSE.

We understand that on Monday last at Montrose, there was a military training at which the Mormons and citizens united indiscriminately. After the troops were paraded Joe Smith and Gen. Bennett came over from Nauvoo and attempted to inspect them. Upon this Mr. Kilbourn invited the citizens to withdraw from the ranks—which was accordingly done. The Mormons then insulted them, causing much excitement, and at the time our informant left a row was anticipated.

Now what right, we ask, has Joe Smith to go into Iowa Territory, and attempt to order the citizens of that territory as a military officer? Is this not proof positive that he wishes to organize a military church? Else why should he take so much interest in the military improvement of his followers who live out of this State? We see in this thing the essential spirit of Mormonism, which is—treason to the Government. Joe Smith, in the government of his followers wishes to place his authority above that of the State. He is not content therefore that the laws of Iowa should regulate the parades of the saints; but he a citizen of Illinois must interfere his authority, and threaten violence because his authority is disregarded by those not members of his church."

1st. The military parade was not on Monday, (but on Tuesday the 14th,) and the Editor, in my opinion, did not so understand it.

2nd. Generals Smith and Bennett did not attempt to inspect the troops, and the Editor, in my opinion, did not so understand it.

3rd. The citizens did not leave the ranks on the invitation of Mr. Kilbourn and, in my opinion, the Editor was not so informed.

4th. The Mormons did not insult the other citizens, and there was no excitement, and the Editor was not, in my opinion, so informed.

5th. No row occurred, or was anticipated, between the Mormons and other citizens, neither was the Editor, in my opinion, so informed.

Generals Joseph Smith, John C. Bennett, and Hyrum Smith, and some other citizens of Nauvoo, attended the military parade, at Montrose, on the 14th, as visitors, on the special invitation of

General Swazey, and Colonel Fuller, of Iowa, the officers in command. Generals Joseph and Hyrum Smith attended attired in plain citizen's garb, as citizens, without the least military appearance about them Gen. Bennett, and some of his staff officers, it is true, appeared in the "splendid and brilliant uniform of the Nauvoo Legion," as the Editor of the Signal is pleased to term it. All passed off with perfect good feeling, and in a highly creditable manner; excepting a disturbance which the Messrs. Kilbourn's attempted to get up by the reading of the following proclamation, which I publish verbatim, et literatim, et punctuatim, from their pen; to wit:

Citizens of Iowa

The laws of Iowa do not require you to muster under or be *Reviewed* by

 Joe Smith or

 General Bennett

and should they have the impudence to attempt it, it is hoped that every person having a proper respect for himself will at once

 Leave the Ranks—

This, however, had no more effect than the noise of those two *dignitaries* usually produces. This is a plain statement of facts, and for their truth I appeal to Gen. Swazey, Col. Fuller, Lt. Col. Swazey, Maj's King and Billings, Capt's Davis, Swazey, Heffleman, or any other officers of the Montrose Regiment whose names I do not now recollect.

It is by this system of low vituperation, calumny, and detraction, that our enemies expect to abuse the public mind, and produce prejudice against us. The true secret of the case is, (and it may as well be told now as at any other time as the period is fast approaching when the trial will be had.)—the Editor of the Signal wishes to have Hancock County divided, and Warsaw made a county seat—to this the Mormons are generally opposed; and for this opposition, and to accomplish the aforesaid object, an Anti-Mormon party has been organized with the determination of accomplishing it, or driving us from the State—but this I trust, will not be effected, as we are a law abiding people, and under it and the broad folds of the Constitutions of our State and Nation we take refuge.

Yours, &c.

W. WATERMAN PHELPS.

—Volume 2, pages 562, 563,

October 1, 1841.

From the (Columbus,) Advocate.
NAUVOO AND THE MORMONS.

MR. EDITOR:—

Having recently had occasion to visit the city of Nauvoo, I cannot permit the opportunity to pass, without expressing the agreeable *disappointment* that awaited me there. I had supposed from what I had previously heard, that I should witness an impoverished, ignorant and bigoted population, completely priest ridden and tyranized over by Joseph Smith, the great prophet of these people. On the contrary, to my surprise, I saw a people apparently happy, prosperous and intelligent. Every man appeared to be employed in some business or occupation, I saw no idleness, no intemperance, no noise, no riot, all appeared to be contented; with no desire to trouble themselves, with any thing except their own affairs. With the religion of these people, I have nothing to do, if they can be satisfied with the doctrines of their *new Revelation,* they have a right to be so. The Constitution of the country guarantees to them the right of worshiping God according to the dictates of their own conscience, and if they can be *so easily* satisfied, why should we, who differ with them, complain. But I protest against the slanders and persecutions that are continually heaped on these people. I could see no disposition on their part to be otherwise than a peaceable and law-abiding people, and all they ask of the country is to permit them to live under the protection of the laws, and to be made amenable for their violations, they may have among them men of bad and desperate characters, and what community has not? but I am satisfied as a body the Mormon people will never be the agressors or violators of the law.

While at Nauvoo, I had a fine opportunity of seeing the people in a body.—There was a Masonic celebration, and the Grand Master of the State was present for the purpose of Publicly instaling the officers of a new Lodge. An immense number of persons assembled on the occasion, variously estimated from 5 to 10,000, and never in my life did I witness a better dressed or a more orderly and well behaved assemblage; not a drunken or disorderly person to be seen, and the display of taste and beauty among the females, could not well be surpassed any where.

During my stay of three days, I became well acquainted with their principal men, and more particularly with their Prophet, the celebrated "Old Jo Smith." I found them hospitable, polite, well informed and liberal. With Joseph Smith, the hospitality of whose house I kindly received, I was well pleased; of course on the subject of religion, we widely differed, but he appeared to be quite as willing to permit me to enjoy my right of opinion, as I think we all ought to be to let the Mormons enjoy theirs; but instead of the ignorant and tyranical upstart, judge my surprise at finding him a sensible intelligent, companionable and gentlemanly man. In frequent conversations with him, he gave me every information that I desired, and appeared to be only pleased at being able to do so. He appears to be much respected by all the people about him and has their entire confidence. He is a fine-looking man, about 36 years of age and has an interesting family.

The incorporated limits of Nauvoo, contains, it is said, about 7,000 persons; the buildings are generally small and much scattered. The Temple and Nauvoo House now building will probably, in beauty of design, extent and durability, excel any public buildings in the State, and will both be enclosed before winter. From all I saw and heard, I am led to believe that before many years the city of Nauvoo will be the largest and most beautiful city of the west, provided the Mormons are un-molested in the peacable enjoyment of their rights and privileges, and why they should be troubled while acting as good citizens, I cannot imagine; and I hope and trust that the people of Illinois have no disposition to disturb unoffending people who have no disposition but to live peaceably under the laws of the country and to worship God under their own vine and fig tree.

AN OBSERVER.

Adams co.. March 22, 1842.

—Volume 3, pages 749-750,

April 1, 1842.

ARTICLES BY JOHN C. BENNETT, ALIAS JOAB

In order to receive a town charter for Nauvoo, a petition had to be addressed to the Illinois legislature. Sometimes this process of petitioning the state government could be very time-consuming and costly. Someone with political expertise and a certain charm and suavity of manner was needed to guide the document through the labyrinth of governmental offices. The Saints found such a willing facilitator in the quartermaster general of the Illinois militia, John Cook Bennett. This aspiring young politician, then about thirty-five years old, had a long, impressive list of personal achievements. He had studied medicine in his youth and had served as a professor of "midwifery" at a college in Ohio. He had been a lay preacher for the Methodists before he separated from his wife and children.

Joseph Smith liked Bennett at first meeting, and perhaps felt somewhat obligated to him for his assistance in pushing the Nauvoo charter through the legislature in record time. Bennett was baptized into the church sometime in the summer of 1840. He immediately began a meteoric rise to prominence in the Nauvoo community and in the upper echelons of church leadership. Within a year he was "assistant president" of the church, acting in Sidney Rigdon's place as counselor during the latter's long and persistent illness, mayor of the city, chancellor of the University of Nauvoo, brigadier general of the Nauvoo Legion (second in command only to Joseph), and secretary of the Masonic lodge.

In the September 1840 issue of *Times and Seasons*, Bennett began a series of articles under the pen name of "Joab, General in Israel." Many nonmember readers, especially those across the river in Missouri, were disturbed to read what appeared to be ominous threats of violence against the enemies of the church.

Burglary! Treason!! ARSON!!!
MURDER!!!!

Lt. Col. Smith:—
I feel disposed to address you a few lines in relation to one of the darkest events that ever blackened the history of man in his most savage and barbarous state. The history of the Goths 'and Vandals,' the cruel Arabs, or the Savage Indians, does not contain a parallel—the heart sickens at the thought, and turns from the contemplation of it with loathing and disgust. In the year of our Lord 1838, it is generally known, (for it came heralded forth from the Grampion hills of the Saints of light, was written by a celestial messenger on the altar of God, and reflected on the heavenly canopy, that all the world might see,) L. W. Boggs,

Governor of Missouri, and Prince of midnight assassins and cowardly brigands, issued, in the face of high heaven, exterminating order (which was ratified by the Legislature,) against the Mormon people residing within his jurisdiction—directing his general officers, first to "drive them from the state;" second to "intercept their retreat;" and third to "exterminate them" with the weapons of war; but the Mormons threw their banners on the air, and under the proudest motto that ever blazed upon a warrior's shield—Sicut patribus sit Deus nobis; As God was with our fathers, so may he be with us—the great God of battles led his people victors, to this land of peace and plenty—the beloved Illinois—a state that has always shown one of the brightest Stars in the American Constellation—a precious glittering gem on the National Escutcheon, without spot or blemish—but no sooner had they began to build up Nauvoo a great city and resting place of the Saints scattered abroad, than does this same L. W. Boggs, not having the fear of God before his eyes, but being moved and instigated by his father, the devil, demand of his Excellency, Thomas Carlin, Governor of Illinois, that a portion of this people shall be given up to the brigand authorities of Missouri, or Western Egypt, to be inhumanly butchered! Look at the brutal, heathen, picture! Missouri wages war on the entire Mormon church— the church of Latter Day Saints—violates their women; shoots down, and scalps, their innocent, defenceless, children; confiscates their property, and throws it to the four winds of heaven—brings them from affluence to beggery in an hour; and orders them all exterminated, murdered, butchered, by an infuriated, savage, fiendish, diabolical, infernal, Missouri mob of ruthless brigands, or driven from the state—and declares them outlaws from the common family of man: and now, in the year of our Lord 1840, two years after, demands, this self-same people, whom she has wantonly outraged, violated, outlawed, prejudged, and condemned, for the slaughter, charging them with burglary, treason, arson, and murder, four of the foulest crimes in the black catalogue of hellish deeds: and all this in a land of boasted liberty—and simply because the Mormons wish, and are determined, to exercise one of our greatest and most dear and sacred constitutional rights—the liberty of conscience—the inestimable privilege of worshiping the God of heaven in the way that they believe to be pointed out! Should they be given up into the hands of wicked men and devils in order to enable them to celebrate a kind of Auto-da-fe, by burning them to the stake, or butchering them in the shambles, at Jefferson city, to satiate Missouri's inordinate thirst for blood? No. They will not be given up. Missouri has too long bathed her hands in crimson gore, and drank the blood of the innocent; she must now be checked in her wild and mad career—she has passed from the palmy state of her political glory to the sear and yellow leaf—the civilized world now turns from her with horror and ineffible contempt—and, should it become necessary, (which may God avert.) she must be met—Missouri must be met, not only by the Mormon people, but by the states—and all the friends of liberty and equal rights should gird on their armour, and sware by the everliving God that the sword shall not depart from the thigh, nor the buckler from the arm until the contest is ended. "And shall not God avenge his own elect, though he bear long with them? I tell you he will avenge them speedily," and that by the strong arm of military power. . . .

Missouri has hewn down the innocent and defenceless, it is true, but also is entirely destitute of military knowledge or prowess. The Poet truly describes her citizens when he says— "Their pow'r to hurt, each little creature feels, Bulls aim their horns, and asses lift their heels;" but the blood of the slain is crying from the ground for condign vengeance, and should she continue to pursue her present murderous policy, the day of righteous retribution and the avenging of blood will not be procrastinated—for her plains shall be bleached with the bones of the slain, and her rivers flow with blood, before another massacre will be suffered. More anon.

Yours, Respectfully,
JOAB,
General in Israel.

—Volume 1, pages 165-167,

September 1840.

Joab later turned to excoriating the thievery that had been plaguing Nauvoo. Some periodicals in the area were insinuating that the thefts, particularly those sustained by nonmembers in the city, were carried out under the auspices of church leadership. Bennett "waxes eloquent" in disavowing church sanction of any kind of crime.

ESCAPE THE FOWLER'S SNARE.

Nauvooans to the rescue! Your liberty is in danger! *Thieves* are in your midst! By day and by night are they prowling through your streets! Your property is in peril, and life, and limb, in jeopardy! Your love of justice, your personal honor, your attachment to your country, and your holy religion, all, all, loudly call upon you to assist in bringing the culprite to condign punishment. In the face of high heaven are they committing the most nefarious crimes, and the cause of Christianity is bleeding at every pore. Will, you, then, stand patient lookers on and see the fiends of hell, wolves in sheep's clothing not only perpetrating felonies themselves, but soliciting the just, the noble, and the good, to participate or become accessories—placing the bitter cup of iniquity to the lips of the Saints, desiring them to drink the dregs of pollution and crime; and, by fortuitous circumstances, or casual associations, dragging them down to the lowest depths of human degradation! Shall the just suffer with the unjust? Shall the righteous be punished with the wicked? Does the church tolerate crime? Does God approbate works of iniquity? No. God, angels, and all good men, must forever execrate such abominations. All should raise the voice and hand against such acts, and ferret out the perpetrators—the sore should be probed to the bottom—the church should be purged, and, like the lion of the forest, arise in her majesty and in her strength, and assert her honor, her purity, and her innocence, or everlasting infamy will rest upon us as a people. So long as we are pure we shall be honored, respected, loved, free from mobs and persecution here, but the moment we become impure, or countenance crime, or cherish the transgressor, "the Philistines will be upon us," we shall be like Samson shorn of his strength—*powerless* and *despised.* For our own sakes, then, for the sake of humanity, for the sake of the church and for God's sake, let us leave no stone unturned until the guilty are punished; and my heart's desire and prayer is that God may nerve our arms to the fight until iniquity shall hide its deformed head, and righteousness reign triumphant in the land. *God and Liberty!*

JOAB.
General in Israel.

—Volume 2, pages 221, 222,

November 15, 1840.

Another series of articles, this time under the byline of "Doctor J. C. Bennett, of Nauvoo," concerns the cultivation and the culinary use of the tomato plant. Then known to most Midwesterners as the "love apple," and commonly supposed to be poisonous when taken internally, the tomato, so Bennett claimed, could be eaten raw or cooked, with great benefit to one's health.

THE TOMATO.
BY DOCTOR J. C. BENNETT, OF NAUVOO.
ITS HISTORY.

On the history of the tomato, Dr. Reese, of the Cyclopedia, says, "It is a native of South America—a tender annual, cultivated in England ever since Gerarde's time, for the sake of its large, variously shaped scarlet or orange fruit, which many people esteem as a great luxury, etc. In the hotter parts of Europe, the tomato has more atidity and briskness of flavor, and is, therefore, more welcome in such climates. It has also the reputation of being stimulant, or aphrodisiacal." Mr. Thomas, in writing on the subject, says: "it is generally admitted that the tomato is indegenous to South America; but, under what circumstances it has been found there, I have not learned.

—Volume 2, page 267,

January 1, 1841.

ITS CULTURE.

The Editor of the Cincinnati Farmer and Mechanic, in his paper of July 30th. A. D. 1834, says: "Seeds that have fallen on the ground in autumn will vegetate in the spring, and the plants thus produced, when they have attained a suitable size, may be set out at *proper distances,* in a good wet soil, previously prepared. It will not be safe to rely on this method of obtaining plants. It is better to sow the seeds in seedbeds, about the first of April. For early plants, sow them in a hot-bed, sheltered with grass covers, about the first of March; and when the plants are two inches high, set them out, taking care to keep them covered when the weather is cool, particularly during cold nights. Some few plants might be left in the hot-bed, or potted and forced in a green house. As the tomato requires free access of air and sun to

315

ripen the fruit, shade should be avoided, and the plants tied up to
stakes.". . . Although the above opinions may be regarded as correct in most particulars, I must consider the writers in error in
some points. The tomato is a procumbent plant, and never intended therefore, by the God of Nature, to be trained up to any
thing; it should lie on the ground: and to this end large hills
should be raised at least eight feet apart, in a moderately wet soil,
and one plant placed in each hill.

—Volume 2, pages 238-239,

December 1, 1840.

Editorial support for these "strange ideas" about the love
apple was set forth in this brief reminder:

IMPORTANT.

Dr. Bennett is of the opinion that most of the bilious
affections to which our citzens are subjected during the hot season, can be prevented by the free use of the Tomato—we are of
the same opinion, and as health is essential to our happiness and
prosperity as a people, we would earnestly recommend its culture
to our fellow-citizens, and its general use for culinary purposes.
Do not neglect it.

—Volume 2, page 404,

May 1, 1841.

The inaugural address given by John C. Bennett when he
was sworn in as mayor of Nauvoo was so inspiring to the
townsfolk that it was printed in its entirety in the *Times and
Seasons*, from which these excerpts have come:

INAUGURAL ADDRESS.

City of Nauvoo, Illinois, Feb. 3rd, 1841.
Gentlemen of the City Council;

Aldermen and Councillors:—
Having been elected to the Mayoralty of this city by the unanimous suffrages of all parties and interests, I now enter upon
the duties devolving upon me as your Chief Magistrate under a

deep sense of the responsibilities of the station.—I trust that the confidence reposed in me, by my fellow citizens, has not been misplaced, and for the honor conferred they will accept my warmest sentiments of gratitude. By the munificence and wise legislation of noble, high-minded, and patriotic statesmen, and the grace of God, we have been blessed with one of the most liberal corporate acts ever granted by a legislative assembly. As the presiding officer of the law making department of the municipal government, it will be expected that I communicate to you, from time to time, by oral or written messages, for your deliberative consideration and action, such matters as may suggest themselves to me in relation to the public weal: and upon this occasion I beg leave to present the following as matters of paramount importance.

The 21st Sec. of the *addenda* to the 13th Sec. of the City Charter concedes to you plenary power "to tax, restrain, prohibit and suppress, tippling-houses, dram-shops," etc. etc., and I now recommend, in the strongest possible terms, that you take prompt, strong, and decisive measures to *"prohibit and suppress"* all such establishments. It is true you have the power "to tax," or *license and tolerate,* them, and thus add to the city finances; but I consider it much better to raise revenue by an *ad valorem* tax on the property of sober men, than by licensing dram shops, or taxing the signs of the inebriated worshippers at the shrine of Bacchus. The revels of bacchanalians in the houses of blasphemy and noise will always prove a disgrace to a moral people. *Public sentiment* will do *much* to suppress the vice of intemperance, and its concomitant evil results: but ample experience has incontrovertibly proven that it cannot do all—the law must be brought to the rescue, and an effective prohibitory ordinance enacted. This cannot be done at a better time than at the present. Let us *commence* correctly, and the great work of reform, at least so far as our peaceful city is concerned, can be summarily consummated. It would be difficult to calculate the vast amount of evil and crime that would be prevented, and the great good that would accrue to the public at large by fostering the cause of temperance; but suffice it to say that the one would be commensurate to the other.—No sales of spirituous liquors whatever, in a less quantity than a quart, except in cases of sickness on the recommendation of a physician or surgeon duly accredited by the Chancellor and Regents of the University, should be tolerated. The liberty of selling the intoxicating cup is a *false* liberty—it enslaves, degrades, destroys, and wretchedness and want are attendant on every step,—its touch, like that of the *poison Upas,* is

DEATH. Liberty to do good should be cheerfully and freely accorded to every man; but liberty to do evil, which is licentiousness, should be peremptorily prohibited. The public good imperiously demands it—and the cause of humanity pleads for help. The protecting aegis of the corporation should be thrown around every moral, and religious, institution of the day, which is in any way calculated to ennoble, or ameliorate the condition of the human family.

The immediate organization of the University, as contemplated in the 24th Sec. of the act incorporating our city, cannot be too forcibly impressed upon you at this time.—As all matters in relation to mental culture, and public instruction, from common schools up to the highest branches of a full collegiate course in the Arts, Sciences, and Learned Professions, will devolve upon the Chancellor and Regents of the University, they should be speedily elected, and instructed to perfect their plan, and enter upon its execution with as little delay as possible....

Our University should be a *"utilitarian* institution—and competent, industrious, teachers, and professors, should be immediately elected for the several departments. "Knowledge is power."—foster education and we are forever *free!* Nothing can be done which is more certainly calculated to perpetuate the free institutions of our common country, for which our progenitors "fought and bled, and died," than the general diffusion of useful knowledge amongst the people. Education should always be of a purely *practical* character, for such, and such alone, is calculated to perfect the happiness, and prosperity, of our fellow-citizens— ignorance, impudence, and false knowledge, are equally detestable,—shame and confusion follow in their train. As you now possess the power, afford the most ample facilities to the Regents to make their plan complete; and thus enable them to set a glorious example to the world at large. The most liberal policy should attend the organization of the University, and equal honors and privileges should be extended to all classes of the community....

As the Chief Magistrate of your city I am determined to execute all state laws, and city ordinances passed in pursuance to law, to the very letter, should it require the strong arm of military power to enable me to do so. As an officer I know no man; the peaceful unoffending citizen *shall* be protected in the full exercise of all his civil, political, and religious, rights, and the guilty vio-

later of law *shall be punished, without respect to persons.*
All of which is respectfully submitted.

JOHN C. BENNETT.

—Volume 2, pages 316-318,

February 15, 1841.

Many persons in the Restoration movement rejoiced that God had added to his church such a one who could charm governors and manipulate legislators with such ease. The political future of the church at Nauvoo looked bright indeed, with Brother Bennett counseling the prophet on all matters pertaining to the upbuilding of God's kingdom on the Mississippi River. To many Nauvooans the dream of "Zion in our time" seemed very close to realization. But then came the rude awakening.

MIDDLE NAUVOO

Rumormongers were as active in Nauvoo as in any other town. One of the first rumors concerning the mayor was that Mrs. Bennett had ample cause for leaving Mr. Bennett. The "cause" was other women, and many of them. Then the word got around that Mayor Bennett was not a "repentant sinner," as some who knew details of his background had supposed, but was instead actively attempting to involve some of the women of the town in his promiscuous affairs. The church leaders at first attempted to keep the lid on the impending scandal, but finally, in May of 1842, John C. Bennett was disfellowshiped. The high council excommunicated him on May 25. The following day, he appeared before them, weeping and pleading for another chance. The high council "forgave" him, but adopted a wait-and-see attitude. Their hesitancy to completely bury the past and let bygones be bygones proved well founded. Within a short time more evidence of Bennett's shady past and present came to light. The notice of his excommunication appeared in the June 15

Times and Seasons without any explanation of the charges leveled against him. This notice had been held in reserve since May 11. In the July 1 issue, details of Bennett's "unchristian conduct" were given in a fashion that completely discredited him in the eyes of the faithful Saints. Only a few excerpts are given here.

TO THE CHURCH OF JESUS CHRIST OF LATTER DAY SAINTS AND TO ALL THE HONORABLE PART OF COMMUNITY.

It becomes my duty to lay before the Church of Jesus Christ of Latter Day Saints, and the public generally, some important facts relative to the conduct and character of Dr. JOHN C. BENNETT, who has lately been expelled from the aforesaid church; that the honorable part of community may be aware of his proceedings, and be ready to treat him and regard him as he ought to be regarded, viz: as an imposter and base adulterer.

It is a matter of notoriety that said Dr. J. C. Bennett, became favorable to the doctrines taught by the elders of the church of Jesus Christ of Latter Day Saints, and located himself in the city of Nauvoo, about the month of August 1840, and soon after joined the church. Soon after it was known that he had become a member of said church, a communication was received at Nauvoo, from a person of respectable character, and residing in the vicinity where Bennett had lived. This letter cautioned us against him, setting forth that he was a very mean man, and had a wife, and two or three children in McConnelsville, Morgan county, Ohio; but knowing that it is no uncommon thing for good men to be evil spoken against, the above letter was kept quiet, but held in reserve.

He had not been long in Nauvoo before he began to keep company with a young lady, one of our citizens; and she being ignorant of his having a wife living, gave way to his addresses, and became confident, from his behavior towards her, that he intended to marry her; and this he gave her to understand he would do. I, seeing the folly of such an acquaintance, persuaded him to desist; and, on account of his continuing his course, finally threatened to expose him if he did not desist. This, to outward appearance, had the desired effect, and the acquaintance between them was broken off.

But, like one of the most abominable and depraved beings which could possibly exist, he only broke off his publicly wicked actions, to sink deeper into iniquity and hypocrisy. When he saw that I would not submit to any such conduct, he went to some of the females in the city, who knew nothing of him but as an honorable man, &c began to teach them that promiscous intercourse between the sexes, was a doctrine believed in by the Latter-Day Saints, and that there was no harm in it; but this failing, he had recourse to a more influential and desperately wicked course; and that was, to persuade them that myself and others of the authorities of the church not only sanctioned, but practiced the same wicked acts; and when asked why I publicly preached so much against it, said that it was because of the prejudice of the public, and that it would cause trouble in my own house. . . .

After I had done all in my power to persuade him to amend his conduct, and these facts were fully established, (not only by testimony, but by his own concessions,) he having acknowledged that they were true, and seeing no prospects of any satisfaction from his future life, the hand of fellowship was withdrawn from him as a member of the church, by the officers; but on account of his earnestly requesting that we would not publish him to the world, we concluded not to do so at that time, but would let the matter rest until we saw the effect of what we had already done.

It appears evident, that as soon as he perceived that he could no longer maintain his standing as a member of the church, nor his respectability as a citizen, he came to the conclusion to leave the place; which he has done; and that very abruptly; and had he done so quietly, and not attempted to deceive the people around him, his case would not have excited the indignation of the citizens, so much as his real conduct has done. In order to make his case look plausible, he has reported, "that he had withdrawn from the church because we were not worthy of his society;" thus instead of manifesting a spirit of repentance, he has to the last, proved himself to be unworthy the confidence or regard of any upright person, by lying, to deceive the innocent, and committing adultery in the most abominable and degraded manner.

—Volume 3, pages 839-841,

July 1, 1842.

When Bennett implicated the prophet in sharing his amatory style of life, various individuals and groups came forth to "rescue" Joseph's reputation by issuing affidavits denying Bennett's charges. Here are excerpts from the edi-

321

torial and affidavits found in the August 1 *Times and Seasons.*

JOHN C. BENNETT.

There has always been, in every age of the church those who have been opposed to the principles of virtue, who have loved the gain of this present world, followed the principles of unrighteousness, and have been the enemies of truth; hence Paul speaks of certain brethren who "coveted the wages of this present world;". . .

Daniel, in referring to the last days says, in speaking concerning the *"Holy Covenant,"* that many shall have indignation against it, and shall obtain information from those that *forsake* the Holy Covenant—and the *robbers* of thy people shall seek to exalt themselves, but they shall fall. This we have fully proven—we have seen them try to exalt themselves, and we have seen their fall. He goes on further to state, that "many shall cleave unto them by *flatteries."* Such was Dr. Avard, and John C. Bennett—with the latter we have to do at the present time, and in many of the foregoing statements and prophecies we shall see his character and conduct exemplified.—He professed the greatest fidelity, and eternal friendship, yet was he an adder in the path, and a viper in the bosom. He professed to be virtuous and chaste, yet did he pierce the heart of the innocent, introduce misery and infamy into families, reveled in voluptuousness and crime, and led the youth that he had influence over to tread in his unhallowed steps;—he professed to fear God, yet did he desecrate his name, and prostitute his authority to the most unhallowed and diabolical purposes; even to the seduction of the virtuous, and the defiling of his neighbor's bed. He professed indignation against Missouri saying, "my hand shall avenge the blood of the innocent;" yet now he calls upon Missouri to come out against the Saints, and he "will lead them on to glory and to victory."

It may be asked why it was that we would countenance him so long after being apprised of his iniquities, and why he was not dealt with long ago. To this we would answer, that he has been dealt with from time to time; when he would acknowledge his iniquity, ask and pray for forgiveness, beg that he might not be exposed, on account of his mother and other reasons, saying, he should be ruined and undone. He frequently wept like a child, and begged like a culprit for forgiveness, at the same time promising before God and angels to amend his life, if he could be forgiven. He was in this way borne with from time to time, until forbearance was no longer a virtue, and then the first Presidency, the Twelve, and the Bishops withdrew their fellowship from him, as published in the 16th number of this paper. The church afterwards publicly withdrew their fellowship from him, and his character was published in the 17th number of this paper; since that time he has published that the conduct of the Saints was bad—that Joseph Smith and many others were *adulterers, murderers,* &c.—that there was a secret band of men that would kill people, &c. called Danites—that he was in duress when he gave his affidavit, and testified that Joseph Smith was a virtuous man—that we believed in and practiced polygamy—that we believed in secret murders, and aimed to destroy the government, &c. &c. As he has made his statements very public, and industriously circulated them through the country, we shall content ourselves with answering his base falsehoods and misrepresentations, without giving publicity to them, as the public are generally acquainted with them already. E. D.

At a meeting of the citizens of the city of Nauvoo held in said city as the meeting ground, July 22d 1842.

Orson Spencer Esq. was called to the chair, and Gustavus Hills was appointed clerk.

The meeting was called to order by the chairman, who stated the object of the meeting to be to obtain an expression of the public mind in reference to the reports gone abroad, calumniating the character of Pres. Joseph Smith. Gen. Wilson Law then rose and presented the following resolution.

Resolved—That, having heard that John C. Bennett was circulating many base falsehoods respecting a number of the citizens of Nauvoo, and especially against our worthy and respected Mayor, Joseph Smith, we do hereby manifest to the world that so far as we are acquainted with Joseph Smith we know him to be a good, moral, virtuous, peaceable and patriotic man, and a firm supporter of law, justice and equal rights; that he at all times upholds and keeps inviolate the constitution of this State and of the United States.

A vote was then called and the resolution adopted by a large concourse of citizens, numbering somewhere about a thousand men. Two or three, voted in the negative. . . .

The "Ladies Relief Society," also drew up a petition signed by about one thousand Ladies speaking in the highest terms of the virtue, philanthrophy, and benevolence of Joseph Smith; begging that he might not be injured, and that they and their families might have the privilege of enjoying their peaceable rights. A petition was also drawn up by many citizens in, and near Nauvoo, who were not Mormons, setting forth the same things.

AFFIDAVIT OF THE CITY COUNCIL.

We the undersigned, members of the city council of the City of Nauvoo, testify that John C. Bennett was not under duress at the time that he testified before the city council May 19th 1842 concerning Joseph Smith's innocence, virtue, and pure teaching— his statements that he has lately made concerning this matter are false. . . .

AFFIDAVIT OF HYRUM SMITH.

On the seventeenth day of may, 1842, having been made acquainted with some of the conduct of John C. Bennett, which was given in testimony under oath before Alderman G. W. Harris, by several females, who testified that John C. Bennett endeavored to seduce them and accomplished his designs by saying it was right; that it was one of the mysteries of God, which was to be revealed when the people was strong enough in the faith to bear such mysteries—that it was perfectly right to have illicit inter-course with females, providing no one knew it but themselves, vehemently trying them from day to day, to yield to his passions, bringing witnesses of his own clan to testify that their was such revelations and such commandments, and that it was of God; also stating that he would be responsible for their sins, if their was any; and that he would give them medicine to produce abortions, providing they should become pregnant. . . .

On becoming acquainted with these facts, I was determined to prosecute him, and bring him to justice.—Some person knowing my determination, having informed him of it, he sent to me Wm. Law and Brigham Young, to request an interview with me and to see if their could not be a reconciliation made. I told them I thought there could not be, his crimes were so henious; but told them I was willing to see him; he immediately came to see me; he begged on me to forgive him, this once, and not prosecute him and expose him, he said he was guilty, and did acknowledge the crimes that were alleged against him; he seemed to be sorry that he had committed such acts, and wept much, and desired that it might not be made public, for it would ruin him forever; he wished me to wait; but I was determined to bring him to justice, and declined listening to his entreaties; he then wished me to wait until he could have an interview with the masonic fraternity; he also wanted an interview with Br. Joseph; he wished to know of me, if I would forgive him, and desist from my intentions, if he could obtain their forgiveness; and requested the privilege of an interview immediately. I granted him that privilege as I was acting

as master *pro. tem.* at that time; he also wishedan interview first
with Br. Joseph; at that time Brother Joseph was crossing the
yard from the house to the store, he immediately come to the
store and met Dr. Bennett on the way; he reached out his hand to
Br. Joseph and said, will you forgive me, weeping at the time; he
said Br. Joseph, I am guilty, I acknowledge it, and I beg of you
not to expose me, for it will ruin me; Joseph replied, Doctor!
why are you using my name to carry on your hellish wickedness?
Have I ever taught you that fornication and adultery was right, or
poligamy or any such practices? He said you never did. Did I ever
teach you any thing that was not virtuous—that was iniquitous,
either in public or private? He said you never did.

—Volume 3, pages 868-871,

August 1, 1842.

Bennett wrote a series of letters to the *Sangamo Journal* in
the state capital. These letters were later revised and published in book form as *The History of the Saints, or An
Exposé of Joe Smith and Mormonism.* Some of the charges
made against the prophet were so outlandish as to be in-
credible, but some allegations made by Bennett were generally believed by nonmembers to be a true picture of what was
going on both openly and in secret at Nauvoo. Ever afterward
in the public mind, Joseph's name was inseparably connected
with "plural wifism."

DOCTRINAL DEVELOPMENTS

It is difficult to perceive clearly the theological milieu at
Nauvoo during this period. Much of the doctrinal writings in
Times and Seasons continue the kinds of concerns and perspective evident in the earlier periodicals. For example, in
reply to a Baptist's view of the differences between the Baptists and the Latter Day Saints, the response takes the form
of delineating the differences between the Baptists and the
former-day Saints. Of course, the author was implying that
the Restoration movement is an exact duplicate of early

325

Christianity. This article was originally prepared for the *Millennial Star*.

From the "North Staffordshire Mercury."

DIFFERENCE BETWEEN THE BAPTISTS & LATTER-DAY SAINTS.

Sir,—In a late publication, you reported the case of some persons who were taken before T. B. Rose, Esq. for disturbing a congregation of "Latter-Day Saints," or believers in the "Book of Mormon." A teacher of that sect, on being asked by the magistrate wherein they differed from the Baptists, replied, "In the laying on of hands;" but declined making an honest confession of those peculiarities which separate them as widely from the Baptists, as from every other denomination of the christian church.— This was certainly prudent; but as the Baptists feel themselves dishonoured by such an alliance, they would be unjust to themselves were they to leave unanswered such a libel upon their denomination. The following very prominent marks of difference will enable your readers to judge for themselves.

I.—The Saints admit all persons indiscriminately to baptism, encouraging them to pass through that rite, with the promise that great spiritual improvement will follow. They baptize for remission of sins, without waiting for credible evidence of repentance for sin. But the Baptists admit none to that ordinance who do not exhibit this qualification in the most satisfactory manner; and if they found a candidate looking to the water of baptism as having virtue to cleanse him from sin, he would be put back until better instructed.

II.—After baptism the Saints kneel down, and their priest laying on his hands, professes to give them the Holy Ghost. If effects similar to those produced by the laying on of the Apostles' hands were seen to follow, scepticism must yield to the force of such evidence; but in their case no such effects are produced; the baptized sinner is a sinner still, though flattered and deluded with the epithet "Latter-day Saint." The Baptists regard such mummery with as much disgust as all Christians do.

III.—Having, as they suppose, the extraordinary gifts of the Spirit, the Saints consistently pretend to have the power of working wonders, and profess to heal the sick with Holy Oil; also to the power of prophecy. As most moral evils bring with them their own remedy, these lofty pretensions will ruin them in due time, by opening the eyes of the most deluded, as in the case of the countless sects of imposters who have appeared upon the stage before them. It need not be added, that the Baptists stand far removed from such conceits, and have no part in them.

IV.—Not satisfied with the Bible, as a complete revelation from God, the "Latter-day Saints" have adopted a romance written in America, as a fresh revelation, and have added a trashy volume of 600 pages to that Book, which we are forbidden to add to, or take from, under the most awful penalties! But even this is not enough for their impious presumption. They have published a monthly magazine, in which "new revelations" are served up fresh as they arrive, for the use of all who can swallow them.— The disgust with which the Baptists regard such a melancholy exhibition of human folly and wickedness, separates them to an impassable distance from such people.

V.—In order to carry on this order of things, the Latter-day Saints have appointed two Priesthoods. "The lesser, or Aaronic Priesthood, is to hold the keys of the Ministering of Angels, and to administer in outward ordinances." "The power and authority of the higher, or Melchisedeck Priesthood, is to hold the keys of all the Spiritual Blessings of the Church—to have the privilege of receiving the mysteries of the Kingdom of Heaven—to have the Heavens opened to them—to commune with the general assembly and Church of the Firstborn; and to enjoy the communion and presence of God the Father, and of Jesus the Mediator of the New Covenant." (See page 13.) So that in this wonderful priesthood, they have provided for an ample supply of new things in endless variety, and without end, from the hands of wretched men, who blasphemously aspire to a dignity which belongs alone to Him who is the only "Priest for ever after the order of Melchizedeck."

The fear of trespassing upon your valuable columns, Mr. Editor, prevents my enlarging upon these and very many other points of difference; but enough has been done to shew your readers, that no two sects can differ more widely from each other, than the Baptists and Latter-day Saints; and that to confound them in any way together is not only unjust to the former, but involves them in the disgrace of being partakers in a bold imposition, or a pitiable delusion, which they regard with equal abhorrence and disgust.

A Baptist.

Hanley, Feb. 16. 1841.

The foregoing article attempts to show the difference between the Baptists and Latter-Day Saints. We will now attempt to show the difference between the Baptists and Former-Day Saints.

1st.—The Former-Day Saints baptized *for remission of sins,* Acts ii. 38. The Baptists baptize those only who are supposed to have their sins forgiven before they are baptized.

2nd.—The Former-Day Saints admitted all persons indiscriminately to baptism, as soon as they professed faith and repentance, encouraging them to pass through that rite with the promise that great spiritual improvement would follow, Act ii. 38–41 inclusive. But if the Baptists found the penitent believer looking for remission of sins through that rite, they would be put back to "get religion" where they could find it.

3rd.—After baptism, the Former-Day Saints prayed for and laid hands on the disciples in the name of Jesus, and professed to give them the Holy Ghost, Acts viii. 17, also Acts xviv. 6. The Baptists say, "they regard such mummery with as much disgust as all Christians do."

4th.—Having, as they supposed the extraordinary gifts of the Spirit, the Former-day Saints consistently pretended to have the power of working wonders, and professed to heal the sick with Holy Oil. Jas. v. 14, 15. Also to the power of prophecy. First Corinthians from 12th to 14th chapter. It need not be added that, the Baptists stand far removed from "such conceits," and have no part in them; nor in any thing pertaining to the gifts and power of God: or to use the Apostle's own words, they have a form of Godliness, denying the power.

5th.—Not satisfied with the Bible as a complete revelation from God, the Former-day Saints have added a volume of several hundred pages (the New Testament,) to that book, which (according to Baptist logic) Moses forbid them to add to, or take from. Deut. iv. 2. But even this was not enough; but new revelations were served up almost daily, fresh as they arrived, for all those who could swallow them. "The disgust with which the Baptists regard such things, considering them but a melancholy exhibition of human folly and wickedness;" separates them to an impassable distance from the Former-day Saints: and how with all these differences the Baptists should ever have been thought by themselves, or any body else, to be the church of Christ, is difficult to imagine!

6th.—In order to carry on their strange work, or order of things, the Former-day Saints had two priesthoods. The Aaronic Priesthood administered in outward ordinances, as in the case of John the Baptist. The power and authority of the Higher, or Melchizideck Priesthood was to hold the *keys* of all the spiritual blessings of the Church, as Jesus said, "I give unto thee the *keys* of the kingdom of heaven—whatsoever thou shalt bind on earth shall be bound in heaven," &c. They were to have the privilege of knowing the mysteries of the kingdom of heaven. "To you it is given to know the mysteries of the kingdom,"—to have the heavens opened unto them—to commune with the general assembly and church of the firstborn; and to enjoy the communion and presence of God the Father, and of Jesus the mediator of the new covenant. Heb. xii. 22, 23, 24. So that in this wonderful Priesthood, they have provided for an ample supply of new things in endless variety, and without end, from those who are and were counted the off-scouring of all things; and who, as the baptists would insinuate, "did aspire to a dignity which they say "belongs only to him who is the only Priest for ever after the order of Melchizedeck."

The fear of trespassing upon the time and patience of our readers, prevents our enlarging upon these and many other points of difference; but enough has been said to shew that no two sects can possibly differ more widely from each other than do the Baptists and Former day-Saints,—and to amalgamate the two systems in any way is not only an act of injustice—but would involve the Baptists, who by the by are an honourable body, in the disgrace of that sect which was "every where spoken against." See Acts.

—Volume 3, pages 931-933,

October 1, 1842.

On occasion, an important doctrinal tenet would be clarified almost accidentally, it would seem. For example, in response to a caustic report from a clergyman who visited Nauvoo, Joseph Smith drops a remark about his notion of the Godhead.

A VISIT TO JOE SMITH.—We present the following extract from a letter received some days ago, from a clergyman now in Illinois:—*Exchange Paper.*

Nauvoo contains a population variously estimated at from five to ten thousand. Probably there are six or seven thousand people there. It is a beautiful location. The city is laid out in acre lots, each lot having a house, generally of one story: it extends from 3 to 4 miles along the river, and runs back about the same distance,

329

and this space is all built on. I called to see the prophet, and had a short but pleasant interview with him. I asked him about the *gold plates* which he professes to have dug up and translated into the Book of Mormon. He said: 'Those plates are not now in this country; they were exhibited to a few at first, for the sake of obtaining their testimony—no others have ever seen them, and they will never be exhibited again,' He next asked me—

'What is the fundamental doctrine of your faith?' 'The unity of God—one God in one person.' 'We don't agree with you. We believe in three Gods. There are three personages in Heaven—all equal in power and glory, but they are not one God.' I suppose, from what I heard, that Smith makes it a point not to agree with any one in regard to his religious opinions, and adapts himself to the person with whom he happens to be talking for the time being."

Tolerable fair:—Though the idea that Joseph Smith adapts his conversation to the company, is an error. Joseph Smith opposes vice and error, and supports his positions from revelation: no odds whether there be two, three, or "Gods many." The Father, and the Son are persons of Tabernacle; and the Holy Ghost a spirit, besides the sons of God: for the scriptures say: "Ye are Gods."

—Volume 3, page 926,

September 15, 1842.

One of the most revealing expositions of the prophet's views concerning the afterlife and the end of the age comes in a seventy-eight stanza poem penned by Joseph in response to a briefer poetic effort from W. W. Phelps. Here are selected stanzas from that poetic exchange.

FROM W. W. PHELPS TO JOSEPH SMITH:
THE PROPHET.

VADE MECUM, (TRANSLATED,) GO WITH ME.

Go with me, will you go to the saints that have died,—
To the next, better world, where the righteous reside;
Where the angels and spirits in harmony be
In the joys of a vast paradise? Go with me.

Go with me where the truth and the virtues prevail;
Where the union is one, and the years never fail;
Not a heart can conceive, nor a nat'ral eye see
What the Lord has prepar'd for the just. Go with me.

Go with me where there is no destruction or war;
Neither tyrants, or sland'rers, or nations ajar;
Where the system is perfect, and happiness free,
And the life is eternal with God. Go with me.

Go with me, will you go to the mansions above,
Where the bliss, and the knowledge, the light, and the love,
And the glory of God do eternally be?—
Death, the wages of sin, is not there. Go with me.
　　Nauvoo, January, 1843.

THE ANSWER.

To W. W. Phelps, Esq.
A Vision.

1. I will go, I will go, to the home of the Saints,
Where the virtue's the value, and life the reward;
But before I return to my former estate
I must fulfil the mission I had from the Lord.

2. Wherefore, hear, O ye heavens, and give ear O ye earth;
　　And rejoice ye inhabitants truly again;
For the Lord he is God, and his life never ends,
　　And besides him there ne'er was a Saviour of men.

3. His ways are a wonder; his wisdom is great;
　　The extent of his doings, there's none can unveil;
His purposes fail not; from age unto age
　　He still is the same, and his years never fail.

4. His throne is the heavens, his life time is all
　　Of eternity *now,* and eternity *then*;
His union is power, and none stays his hand,—
　　The Alpha, Omega, for ever: Amen.

5. For thus saith the Lord, in the spirit of truth,
    I am merciful, gracious, and good unto those
That fear me, and live for the life that's to come;
    My delight is to honor the saints with repose;
6. That serve me in righteousness true to the end;
    Eternal's their glory, and great their reward;
I'll surely reveal all my myst'ries to them,—
    The great hidden myst'ries in my kingdom stor'd—

7. From the council in Kolob, to time on the earth.
    And for ages to come unto them I will show
My pleasure & will, what my kingdom will do:
    Eternity's wonders they truly shall know.

8. Great things of the future I'll show unto them,
    Yea, things of the vast generations to rise;
For their wisdom and glory shall be very great,
    And their pure understanding extend to the skies:

    The sanctified pleasures when earth is renew'd,
What the eye hath not seen, nor the ear hath yet heard;
    Nor the heart of the natural man ever hath view'd.

11. I, Joseph, the prophet, in spirit beheld,
    And the eyes of the inner man truly did see
Eternity sketch'd in a vision from God.
    Of what was, and now is, and yet is to be.

12. Those things which the Father ordained of old.
    Before the world was, or a system had run,—
Through Jesus the Maker and Savior of all;
    The only begotten, (messiah) his son.

13. Of whom I bear record, as all prophets have,
    And the record I bear is the fulness,—yea even
The truth of the gospel of Jesus—*the Christ,*
    With whom I convers'd, in the vision of heav'n.

14. For while in the act of translating his word.
    Which the Lord in his grace had appointed to me,
I came to the gospel recorded by John,
    Chapter fifth and the twenty ninth verse, which you'll see.
    Which was given as follows:
"Speaking of the resurrection of the dead,—

"Concerning those who shall hear the voice of
"the son of man—
"And shall come forth:—
"They who have done good in the resurrection
"of the just.
"And they who have done evil in the resurrec-
"tion of the unjust."
15. I marvel'd at these resurrections, indeed!
    For it came unto me by the spirit direct:—
And while I did meditate what it all meant,
    The Lord touch'd the eyes of my own intellect:—

16. Hosanna forever! they open'd anon,
    And the glory of God shone around where I was;
And there was the Son, at the Father's right hand,
    In a fulness of glory, and holy applause.

17. I beheld round the throne, holy angels and hosts.
    And sanctified beings from worlds that have been,
In holiness worshipping God and the Lamb,
    Forever and ever, amen and amen!

18. And now after all of the proofs made of him,
    By witnesses truly, by whom he was known,
This is mine, last of all, that he lives; yea he lives!
    And sits at the right hand of God, on his throne.

19. And I heard a great voice, bearing record from heav'n,
    He's the Saviour, and only begotten of God—
By him, of him, and through him, the worlds were all made,
    Even all that career in the heavens so broad,

20. Whose inhabitants, too, from the first to the last,
    Are sav'd by the very same Saviour of ours;
And, of course, are begotten God's daughters and sons,
    By the very same truths, and the very same pow'rs.

23. And while I was yet in the spirit of truth,
    The commandment was write ye the vision all out;
For Satan, old serpent, the devil's for war,—
    And yet will encompass the saints round about.

24. And I saw, too, the suff'ring and mis'ry of those,
    (Overcome by the devil, in warfare and fight.)

In hell-fire, and vengeance, the doom of the damn'd;
  For the Lord said, the vision is further: so write.

25. For thus saith the Lord, now concerning all those
  Who know of my power and partake of the same;
And suffer themselves, that they be overcome
  By the power of Satan; despising my name:—

26. Defying my power, and denying the truth;—
  They are they—of the world, or of men, most forlorn,
The Sons of Perdition, of whom, ah! I say,
  'T were better for them had they never been born!

32. The myst'ry of Godliness truly is great;—
  The past, and the present, and what is to be;
And this is the gospel—glad tidings to all,
  Which the voice from the heavens bore record to me:

33. That he came to the world in the middle of time,
  To lay down his life for his friends and his foes,
And bear away sin as a mission of love;
  And sanctify earth for a blessed repose.

34. 'Tis decreed, that he'll save all the work of his hands,
  And sanctify them by his own precious blood;
And purify earth for the Sabbath of rest,
  By the agent of fire, as it was by the flood.

35. The Savior will save all his Father did give,
  Even all that he gave in the regions abroad.
Save the Sons of Perdition: They're lost; ever lost,
  And can never return to the presence of God.

39. And while I was pondering, the vision was closed;
  And the voice said to me, write the vision: for lo!
'Tis the end of the scene of the sufferings of those,
  Who remain filthy still in their anguish and woe.

40. And again I bear record of heavenly things,
  Where virtue's the value, above all that's pric'd—
Of the truth of the gospel concerning the just,
  That rise in the first resurrection of Christ.

41. Who receiv'd and believ'd, and repented likewise,
    And then were baptis'd, as a man always was,
Who ask'd and receiv'd a remission of sin,
    And honored the kingdom by keeping its laws.

48. Yea, the righteous shall dwell in the presence of God,
    And of Jesus, forever, from earth's second birth—
For when he comes down in the splendor of heav'n,
    All these he'll bring with him, to reign on the earth.

49. These are they that arise in their bodies of flesh,
    When the trump of the first resurrection shall sound;
These are they that come up to Mount Zion, in life,
    Where the blessings and gifts of the spirit abound.

50. These are they that have come to the heavenly place;
    To the numberless courses of angels above:
To the city of God; e'en the holiest of all,
    And the home of the blessed, the fountain of love:

51. To the church of old Enoch, and of the first born:
    And gen'ral assembly of ancient renown'd.
Whose names are all kept in the archives of heav'n,
    As chosen and faithful, and fit to be crown'd.

52. These are they that are perfect through Jesus' own blood,
    Whose bodies celestial are mention'd by Paul,
Where the sun is the typical glory thereof,
    And God, and his Christ, are the true judge of all.

53. Again I beheld the terrestrial world,
    In the order and glory of Jesus, go on;
'Twas not as the church of the first born of God,
    But shone in its place, as the moon to the sun.

54. Behold, these are they that have died without law;
    The heathen of ages that never had hope,
And those of the region and shadow of death,
    The spirits in prison, that light has brought up.

55. To spirits in prison the Savior once preach'd.
    And taught them the gospel, with powers afresh;
And then were the living baptiz'd for their dead,
    That they might be judg'd as if men in the flesh.

58. Again I beheld the telestial, as third,
    The lesser, or starry world, next in its place.
For the leaven must leaven three measures of meal,
    And every knee bow that is subject to grace.

59. These are they that receiv'd not the gospel of Christ,
    Or evidence, either, that he ever was;
As the stars are all diff'rent in glory and light.
    So differs the glory of these by the laws.

60. These are they that deny not the spirit of God,
    But are thrust down to hell, with the devil, for sins,
As hypocrites, liars, whoremongers, and thieves,
    And stay 'till the last resurrection begins.

68. The glory celestial is one like the sun;
    The glory terrestr'al is one like the moon;
The glory telestial is one like the stars,
    And all harmonize like the parts of a tune.

69. As the stars are all different in lustre and size,
    So the telestial region, is mingled in bliss;
From least unto greatest, and greatest to least,
    The reward is exactly as promis'd in this.

70. These are they that came out for Apollos and Paul;
    For Cephas and Jesus, in all kinds of hope;
For Enoch and Moses, and Peter, and John;
    For Luther and Calvin, and even the Pope.

71. For they never received the gospel of Christ,
    Nor the prophetic spirit that came from the Lord;
Nor the covenant neither, which Jacob once had;
    They went their own way, and they have their reward.

72. By the order of God, last of all, these are they,
    That will not be gather'd with saints here below.
To be caught up to Jesus, and meet in the cloud:—
    In darkness they worshipp'd; to darkness they go.

73. These are they that are sinful, the wicked at large,
    That glutted their passion by meanness or worth;

All liars, adulterers, sorc'rers, and proud;
    And suffer, as promis'd, God's wrath on the earth.

74. These are they that must suffer the vengeance of hell.
    'Till Christ shall have trodden all enemies down,
And perfected his work, in the fulness of times:
    And is crown'd on his throne with his glorious crown.

77. But the great things of God, which he show'd unto me,
    Unlawful to utter, I dare not declare;
They surpass all the wisdom and greatness of men,
    And only are seen, as has Paul, where they are.

78. I will go, I will go, while the secret of life,
    Is blooming in heaven, and blasting in hell;
Is leaving on earth, and a budding in space:—
    I will go, I will go, with you, brother, farewell.
                                    JOSEPH SMITH.
Nauvoo, Feb. 1843.

—Volume 4, pages 81-85,

February 1, 1842.

The poetic spirit continued to soar in the pages of the
Times and Seasons in the poem "God." How the majestic
images of the "only" "eternal" God propounded in this
poem fadge with some of the notions of the Godhead being
formulated at Nauvoo during this period of history is not
clear. While no author is listed, it is specified that the poem
was written expressly for the *Times and Seasons.*

GOD

O Thou Eternal One! whose presence bright
All space doth occupy—all motion guide;
    Unchanged thro' Time's all-devasting flight,
Thou only God! There is no God beside.
    Being above all being! Mighty One!
Whom none can comprehend, and none explore;
    Who fill'st existence with Thyself alone;
Embracing all—supporting—ruling o'er—
    Being whom we call God—and know no more!

in its sublime research, Philosophy
May measure out the Ocean deep—may count
Sole origin—all life, all beauty, Thine.
Thy word created all and doth create:
Thy splendor fills all space with rays divine.
Thou art and wert, and shalt be glorious! great!
Life-living, life-sustaining, Potentate.

Thy chains the unmeasured universe surround
Upheld by Thee, by Thee inspired with breath!
Thou the beginning, with the end hast bound,
And beautifully mingled Life and Death!
As sparks mount upward from the fiery blaze,
So suns are born, so worlds spring forth from Thee!
And as the spangles in the sunny rays
Shine round the silver snow, the pageantry
O! Heaven's bright army glitters in Thy praise;

A million torches lighted by Thy hand
Wander unwearied through the blue abyss;
They own thy power, accomplish thy command,
All gay with life, all eloquent with bliss;
What shall we call them? Piles of chrystal light?
A glorious companion of golden streams?
Lamps of celestial ether burning bright?
Suns, lighting systems with their joyous beams,
But Thou, to those, art as the noon to night.

Yes! as a drop of water in the Sea,
All this magnificence in Thee is lost:—
What are a thousand Worlds compared to Thee?
And what am I, when Heaven's unnumbered host,
Though multiplied by myriads, and arrayed
In all the glory of sublimest thought,
Is but an atom in the balance, weighed
Against Thy greatness—is a cypher brought
Against Infinity? What am I then? Nought!

Nought! but the effluence of Thy light divine,
Pervading worlds, hath reached my bosom too;
Yes, in my spirit doth Thy spirit shine,
As shines the sun-beam in a drop of dew,
Nought! but I live and on hope pinions' fly,
The sands, or the Sun's rays; but God! for Thee

There is no weight nor measure: none can mount
    Up to the mysteries. Reason's brightest spark,
Though kindled by Thy light, in vain would try
    To trace thy councils, infinite and dark;
And Thought is lost ere thought can soar so high,
    E'en like past moments in eternity.

    Thou, from primeval nothingness, didst call
First, Chaos, then Existence. Lord, on Thee
    Eternity had its foundation; all
Spring forth from Thee: of Light, Joy, Harmony,
Eager towards Thy presence; for in Thee
    I live, and breathe, and dwell; aspiring high,
Even to the throne of Thy Divinity,
I am, O God, and surely Thou must be!

    Thou art! directing, guiding all, Thou art!
Direct my understanding then to Thee;
    Control my spirit, guide my wandering heart;
Though but an atom midst immensity,
    Still I am Something fashioned by Thy hand!
I hold a middle rank, 'twixt Heaven and Earth,
    On the last verge of mortal being stand.
Close to the realm where angels have their birth,
Just on the boundary of the spirit land!

    The chain of being is complete in me;
In me is matter's last gradation lost,
    And the next step is Spirit—Deity!
I can command the light'ning, and am dust!
    A monarch, and a slave; a worm, a God!
Whence came I here, and how? so marvellously
    Constructed and conceived, unknown? This clod
Lives surely through some higher energy!
For from itself alone it could not be.

    Creator! Yes! Thy Wisdom and Thy Word
Created me! Thou source of Life and Good!
    Thou Spirit of my spirit, and my Lord!
Thy Light, Thy Love, in their bright plenitude
    Filled me with an immortal Soul, to spring
Over the abyss of Death, and bade it wear
    The garments of Eternal Day, and wing

Its heavenly flight beyond this little sphere,
Even in its source, to Thee, its Author, Thee.

O thought ineffable! O vision blest!
(Though worthless our conceptions all of Thee.)
Yet shall Thy shadowed image fill our breast,
And waft its homage to the Deity.
God! thus alone my lowly thoughts can soar;
Thus seek thy presence. Being wise and good!
Midst Thy vast works, admire, obey, adore;
And when the Tongue is eloquent no more,
The Soul shall speak in tears of gratitude.

—Volume 4, pages 366-367,

October 15, 1843.

EVENTS IN CHURCH AND COMMUNITY

The young people of Nauvoo were a source of great anxiety to their elders by reason of the frivolity and lack of responsibility that they often displayed. Some of the more serious-minded youth determined to change that situation and bridge the generation gap. With the Ladies' Relief Society providing a model for organization, some of the youth leadership in town, under the watchcare of Apostle Heber C. Kimball, banded together for the purposes of peer group association and social service. The first project of the group was the construction of a house for a disabled immigrant from England. The April 1, 1843, *Times and Seasons* carried "A Short Sketch of the Rise of the Young Gentlemen and Ladies' Relief Society of Nauvoo."

One evening in the latter part of January last, a few young people having assembled at the house of elder H. C. Kimball; the follies of youth, and the temptations to which they are exposed generally, but more especially in our city, became the topic of conversation. The company were lamenting the loose style of their morals—the frivolous manner in which they spent their

340

time—and their too frequent attendance at balls, parties, &c. &c., when elder Kimball proposed that an appointment should be given out expressly for the young ladies and gentlemen, and he would give them such instruction and advice as the spirit of the Lord might suggest to him; which, if followed, would doubtless lead to a reformation in the conduct of his young friends. This proposition was received with delight, and acted upon with alacrity. An appointment having been given out, a number of the young people assembled at the house of elder Billings, when elder Kimball addressed them for some time upon the duties of children to their parents, to society, and to their God; exhorting them to lay aside their vanity, lightmindedness, pride, and frivolity; and endeavor to show themselves worthy of the religion which they had embraced; advising them to shun evil company, (for by an individual's company is his character estimated,) and to be obedient to their parents, for this was the first commandment with promise.

This address was so well received by the assembled congregation, that it was voted, almost by acclamation, that a similar meeting should be held on the ensuing week. An appointment was accordingly circulated for the next Wednesday evening at Br. Farr's schoolroom, as elder Billings' house was too small to contain the assemblage.

On the appointed evening, the room was filled to overflowing. Elder Kimball addressed the crowded, but silent and attentive congregation, for the space of an hour; in that plain, simple, and affectionate manner, which goes directly to the heart, and which is so natural to the speaker. He first explained the duty which the youth owed to themselves, and the manner in which they might obtain honor and respect, viz: by applying their minds with determined perseverance to all the studies commonly deemed necessary to fit them for active life, and polish them for society; and not to be these, but also to the study of the Scriptures, by the book of Mormon, the book of Doctrine and Covenants, and the theological work of their most talented elders. By pursuing this course, said he, "you will be enabled to give a reason for the hope and the joy which exists within you—you will always be prepared to explain the doctrine in which you believe—you will ever be ready to prove and defend your religion—you will be well received in company, and will be esteemed by all wise and good men. . . ."

At the next meeting President Smith was present and addressed the young gentlemen and ladies for some time. He expressed his gratitude to elder Kimball in the strongest terms, for having commenced and carried on in so masterly a manner the good and glorious work he had undertaken. He said it would be the means of doing a great deal of good, and of benefitting his young friends more than they were aware of: that the gratitude of all good men, and of the young people whom he had so much benefitted, would follow him through life; and "when gray hairs should his temples adorn," he could look back with pleasure upon the winter of 1843, when he was engaged in promoting the cause of benevolence, and prepairing his young friends for the glorious career which awaited them.

He said that he stood before them with more embarrassment, than he would before kings, nobles, and great men of the earth, for he knew the crimes of which they were guilty, and knew precisely how to address them; but his young friends before whom he now stood were guilty of none of these crimes, and he hardly knew what to say. He said he had never in his life seen such a large company of young people assembled together, pay such strict attention, listen with such profound silence, and keep such good order, as the assembly now before him. He praised their good conduct, and taught them how to behave in all places, explained to them their duty, and advised them to organize themselves into a society for the relief of the poor. As a commencement to their benevolent efforts, he offered a petition from an English brother by the name of Modesley, who was lame, and who wished them to build him a house, that he might have a home among the saints: he had gathered together a few materials for this purpose, but was unable to use them; and, now, relying upon the active benevolence of the young people of Nauvoo, he sends in this petition that you may act upon it as you deem proper. He advised them to choose a committee to collect funds for this purpose, and perform this charitable work as soon as the weather became suitable.—He gave them much good advice, to guide their conduct through life and prepare them for a glorious eternity. He said he was very much pleased with the course elder Kimball had taken, and hoped he would continue his meetings and that the young people would follow his teachings. . . .

Pursuant to adjournment, the young men convened together on the 21st of March. The minutes of the last meeting were read and approved, and the same officers appointed to preside as on the former evening. The report of the committee was then called for, which was as follows:

Whereas, The young gentlemen and ladies, citizens of the city of Nauvoo, are desirous of aiding and ameliorating the condition of the poor and of carrying out the principles of charity and benevolence, as taught in the holy scriptures, therefore, be it

Resolved, That we form ourselves into a society to be styled the "Young Gentlemen and Ladies Relief Society of Nauvoo," and that we be governed by the following articles, to wit:

1st. There shall annually be elected by the society, on the last Tuesday in March, a president, vice president, treasurer and secretary.

2d. It shall be the duty of the president to preside over all meetings of the society. . . .

6th. There shall annually be chosen a committee of vigilance, consisting of five persons, whose duties it shall be to search out the poor of our city, and make known to the society the wants of those whom they, in their judgment, shall consider most deserving of our assistance.

7th. The society shall meet on the last Tuesday in each month, at 6 o'clock, P. M.

8th. A special meeting of the society can be called by a petition of twelve of the members, to the secretary, whose duty it shall be to give notice of the same, by posting up a written notice in at least, three of the most public places in the city, at least, three days previous to said meeting. . . .

This is in short, a history of the rise of this society, which bids fair to be one of the most useful and benevolent societies in the Union.—Throughout all of the meetings, the most profound silence and the best of order was kept continually. If the youth throughout our land would follow this good example and form themselves into such societies, there would be much less sin, iniquity, misery, and degradation among the young people than there is at the present day; there would not be as many suffering poor, neither would there be as much immorality among the people. But on the contrary, peace, good order, happiness, cheerfulness and plenty, would reign in the land, the Lord would look down from his holy habitation and smile upon us, and bless us all.

J. M. MONROE, Secretary.

—Volume 4, pages 154-157,

April 1, 1843.

Conferences continued to play a key role in the life of the church. Usually two conferences were held each year at Nauvoo, one in April and the other in October. In addition, other "general conferences" were held in various areas as well as the more common "branch conferences." The April 15, 1844, *Times and Seasons* listed forty-seven general conferences scheduled over a five-month period in the United States.

In April of 1843 a "Special Conference" was held at Nauvoo. How to speedily finance and construct the Nauvoo House, a boarding house for the constant stream of visitors and tourists, was one of the major concerns of the conference. The latter part of the conference dealt with claims that some church members were stealing with the blessing of the church leaders.

Thursday Morning, April 6, 1843.
11 o'clock, A. M.

A Special Conference of the Church of Jesus Christ of Latter Day Saints, was convened on the platform of the Temple. There were present, Hyrum Smith, Patriarch: Brigham Young, H. C. Kimball, Orson Pratt, Wilford Woodruff, John Taylor, Geo. A. Smith, and W. Richards, of the Quorum of the Twelve; and a very large assembly of the elders and saints.

Elder Brigham Young announced that President Joseph Smith was detained on business, but would be present soon. He called upon the choir to sing an Hymn. Elder Amasa Lyman opened by prayer, and another Hymn was sung. Elder Orson Pratt then read the 3d chapter of the 2d epistle of Peter, and spoke upon the subject of the resurrection. At ten minutes before 12 o'clock President Joseph Smith, Elder Sidney Rigdon, and Elder Orson Hyde arrived.

At 12 o'clock Elder Pratt gave way for the business of the Conference.

President Joseph Smith commenced by saying, We all ought to be thankful for the privilege we enjoy this day, of meeting so many of the Saints, and for the warmth and brightness of the heavens over our heads,—and it truly makes the countenances of this great multitude to look cheerly, and gladdens the hearts of all present.

He next stated the object of the meeting, which was,

First, to ascertain the standing of the first presidency, which he should do by presenting himself before the conference for trial.

Second, to take into consideration the expediency of sending out the Twelve, or some of them, or somebody else, amongst the branches of the church, to obtain stock to build the Nauvoo House, for the time has come to build it.

Third, the elders will have the privilege of appeals from the different conferences, to this, if any such cases exist. These, said the president, are the principle items of business which I have at present to lay before you. This is not a general, but an annual conference.

It is necessary that this conference give importance to the Nauvoo House. A prejudice exists against building the Nauvoo House, in favor of the Lord's House, and the conference are required to give stress to the building of the Nauvoo House. This is the most important matter for the time being, for there is no place in this city, where men of wealth, and character, and influence, from abroad, can go to repose themselves, and it is necessary we should have such a place. The church must build it or abide the result of not fulfilling the commandment.

President Joseph then asked the conference if they were satisfied with the First Presidency, so far as he was concerned, as an individual, to preside over the whole church; or would they have another? If, said he, I have done any thing that ought to injure my character, reputation, or standing; or have dishonored our religion by any means in the sight of men, or angels, or in the sight of men and women, I am sorry for it, and if you will forgive me, I will endeavor to do so no more. *I do not know that I have done anthing of the kind; but if I have, come forward and tell me of it.* If any one has any objection to me, I want you to come boldly and frankly, and tell of it; and if not, ever after hold your peace.

Motion was made and seconded that President Joseph Smith continue president of the whole church. After a few minutes silence, the motion was put by President Young, when one vast sea of hands was presented, and the motion was carried *unanimously.*

President Joseph returned his thanks to the assembly for the manifestation of their confidence, and said he would serve them according to the best ability God should give him.

The first presidency being disposed of, President Joseph said he did not know any thing against the Twelve if he did he would present them for trial. It is not right that all the burden of the Nauvoo House, should rest on a few individuals; and we will now consider the propriety of sending the Twelve to collect means for the Nauvoo House. There has been too great a solicitude, in individuals, for the building of the temple, to the exclusion of the

Nauvoo House. The agents have had too great latitude to practice fraud, by receiving donations and never making report. The church has suffered loss, and I am opposed to that system of collecting funds when any elder may receive moneys.

I am opposed to any man's handling the public funds of the church who is not duly authorzed.

I advise that some means be devised for transacting business on a sure foundation. The Twelve are the most suitable persons to perform this business; and I want the conference to devise some means to bind them as firm as the pillars of heaven, if possible. The Twelve were always honest, and it will do them no hurt to bind them. . . .

There have been complaints against the Temple Committee for appropriating church funds more freely for the benefit of their own children, than to others, who need assistance more than they do; and the parties may have till Saturday to prepare for trial.

It was then voted unanimously that the Twelve be appointed *a committee to collect funds to build the Nauvoo House, and receive moneys for the Temple,* with this proviso:

That the Twelve give bonds for the safe delivery of all funds, coming into their hands belonging to the Nauvoo House and Temple, to the Trustee in Trust, and that the payer, also, make immediate report to the Trustee in Trust, of all moneys paid by him to the Twelve; and that the instructions of President Joseph Smith, to the conference, be carried into execution.

Elder W. W. Phelps proposed that the Twelve sign triplicate receipts, for moneys received, for the benefit of the parties concerned.

Elder Brigham Young objected, and said he should never give receipts for cash, except such as he put into his own pocket, for his own use; for it was calculated to make trouble hereafter, and there were better methods of transacting the business; and more safe for the parties concerned; that he wished this speculation to stop, and would do all in his power to put it down: To which the Twelve responded, *amen.* Elder Young asked if any one knew any thing against any one of the Twelve, any dishonesty; if they did, he wanted it exposed; he said he knew of one who was not dishonest. He also referred to muzzling the ox that treadeth out the corn,&c.

President Joseph said, I will answer Brother Brigham. The Twelve need not spend all their time abroad, they can spend the time belonging to the Temple, for to collect funds; and the remainder of the time they may labor for their support; and they may call on the public to supply their wants. It is no more for the

Twelve to go abroad and earn their living in this way than it is for others. The idea of not muzzling the ox, is a good old Quaker song, but we will make the ox tread out the corn first and then feed him. I am bold to declare that I have never taken the first farthing of church funds for my own use, till I have first consulted the proper authorities. When there was no quorum of the Twelve or high priests for me to consult, I have asked the Temple Committee, who had no particular business with it, but I did it for the sake of peace. [Elder Cutler said it was so.] Let the conference stop all agents from collecting funds, except the Twelve.—When a man is sent to preach the first principles of the gospel, he should preach *that and let the rest alone.*

The choir sung a hymn, and elder O. Hyde prayed, and Twelve minutes before 2 o'clock P. M., conference adjourned for one hour. ______________________

3 o'clock, P. M.

Patriarch, Hyrum Smith, commenced by saying that he had some communications to make to the conference, on stealing, and he would do it while waiting for Joseph; and referred to the article in the last number of the 'Wasp.' Said he, I have had an interview with a man who formerly belonged to the church, and he revealed to me that there is a band of men, and some who pretend to be strong in the faith of the doctrine of the Latter Day Saints, but they are hypocrites, and some who do not belong to the church, who are bound together by secret oaths, and obligations and penalties, to keep the secret; and they hold that it is right to steal from any one who does not belong to the church provided they consecrate two-thirds of it to the building of the Temple. They are also making bogus money. . . .

President Joseph Smith said, I think it best to continue this subject. I want the elders to make honorable proclamation abroad concerning what the feelings of the first presidency is, for stealing has never been tolerated by them. I despise a thief above ground. He would betray me if he could get the opportunity. I would know that he would be a detriment to my cause, and if I were the biggest rogue in the world, he would steal my horse when I wanted to run away.

It has been said that some were afraid to disclose what they know of these secret combinations, consequently I issued a proclamation which you may read in the Wasp, No. 48, which the president read

—Volume 4, pages 180-184,

May 1, 1843.

347

Joseph Smith was in and out of jail many times in his short career. Throughout this whole period at Nauvoo, the threat of imprisonment for alleged crimes in Missouri was very real. In June of 1843 a crisis point was reached when the prophet was placed under arrest and ordered to stand trial. Three issues of the *Times and Seasons* were devoted to his arrest and subsequent trial. Hyrum Smith, Parley P. Pratt, George W. Pitkin, Lyman Wight, and Sidney Rigdon occupied the witness stand, testifying on behalf of the prophet. Here are portions of an article setting forth an account of the situation, followed by a poem by Eliza R. Snow on this subject:

MISSOURI *vs* JOSEPH SMITH.

It has fallen to our lot of late years to keep an account of any remarkable circumstance that might transpire, in, and about this, and the adjoining states; as well as of distant provinces and nations. Among the many robberies, earthquakes, volcanic eruptions, tornadoes, fires, mobs, wars, &c.&c., which we have had to record, there is one circumstance of annual occurrence, which it has always fallen to our lot to chronicle. We allude not to the yearly inundations of the Nile, nor the frequent eruptions of Vesuvius or Etna, but to the boiling over of Tophet, *alias* the annual overflow of the excressence of Missouri. . . .

Without entering here into the particulars of the bloody deeds, the high-handed oppression, the unconstitutional acts, the deadly and malicions hate, the numerous murders, and the wholesale robberies of that people; we will proceed to notice one of the late acts of Missouri, or of the Governor of that state towards us. We allude to the late arrest of Joseph Smith.

Some two yea s ago Mr. Smith was apprehended upon a writ issued by Gov. Carlin upon a requisition from the Governor of Missouri, charging Mr. Smith with murder, arson, treason, &c. &c. Mr. Smith obtained a writ of Habeas Corpus, which was made returnable at Monmouth; he appeared before Judge Douglas and was honorably acquitted. We thought then that the eyes of community would be opened, and that a stop would have forever been put to those unhallowed proceedings, but no! this could not be, she must still pursue her victim, and for want of some more plausible excuse, after that monster of iniquity Gov. Boggs, whose iniquitous exterminating order has rendered him notorious not only in this coun ry, but throughout Europe, had been shot at by some unknown ruffian, and his life jeopardized; it was

348

thought a good opportunity to commence an attack upon Joseph Smith, particularly as an election was near at hand in this State, and it was thought by some of our political demagogues that some political capital could be made of it; Joseph Smith must therefore be sacrificed at the shrine of the hellish despotism of Missouri, and that of political aspirants of this State. . . .

This case like the other was finally brought to an issue, and Mr. Smith after an immensity of trouble and expense was exculpated in Springfield, before Judge Pope of the United States Court for the District of Illinois. The persecution and injustice of Missouri, and the illegality of the case was then abundantly developed, and Judge Pope ordered the case to be inserted on the docket in a manner that Mr. Smith should no more be troubled in relation to that matter. [Governor Ford at that time manifested a friendly disposition, and seemed disposed to put a stop to that executive influence which had sought the destruction and overthrow of Mr. S.] Mr S. returned in peace to the bosom of his family, and was received with joyous acclamation by a numerous host of friends who felt to rejoice that innocence had triumphed over persecution, fanaticism, and despotism. . . .

Feeling perfectly secure, he set off with his family to Mr. Wassons', to visit his wife's sister, Mrs. Wasson and family, who resided about twelve miles from Dixon, Lee county, in this state. While he was there, a Mr. J. H. Reynolds, Sheriff of Jackson county, Missouri, (so he says) and Mr. Harman Wilson of Carthage, arrived at Dixon, professing to be Mormon preachers; from thence they proceeded to Mr. Wasson's, at whose house Mr. Smith was staying. They found Mr. Smith outside of the door, and accosted him in a very uncouth ungentlemanly manner, quite in keeping however, with the common practice of Missourians. The following is as near the conversation as we can gather. Reynolds and his coadjutor Wilson, both stepped up at a time to Mr. Smith with their pistols cocked, and without shewing any writ or serving any process, Mr. Reynolds with his pistol cocked at Mr. Smith's breast, cried out, "G—d d—n you if you stir I'll shoot—G—d d—n you—if you stir one inch I'll shoot you, G—d d—n you—be still or I'll shoot you by G—d." "What is the meaning of this?', interrogated Mr. Smith. "I'll show you the meaning by G—d, and if you stir one inch I'll shoot you, G—d d—n you." "I am not afraid of your shooting, answered Mr. Smith, I am not afraid to die." He then bared his breast, and said "shoot away, I have endured so much oppression I am weary of life and kill me if you please. I am a strong man however, and with my own natural weapons could soon level both of you; but if you have any legal process to serve, I am at all times subject to law and shall not offer resistance." "G—d d—n you if you say another word, we'll shoot you, by G—d." "Shoot away" answered Mr. Smith, "I am not afraid of your pistols." They then hurried him off to a carriage that they had, and without serving process, were for hurrying him off without letting him see, or bid farewell to his family or friends. Mr. Smith then said, "gentlemen if you have any legal process I wish to obtain a writ of Habeas Corbus." and was answered, "G—d d—n you, you sha'nt have one." Mr. Smith saw a friend of his passing and said these men are kidnapping me, and I wish a writ of habeas corpus to deliver myself out of their hands. This friend immediately proceeded to Dixon whence the Sheriff also proceeded full speed; on arriving at the house of Mr. McKennie, tavern keeper, Mr. Smith was thrust into a room and guarded there without being allowed to see anybody, and horses were ordered in five minutes. Mr. Smith then stated to Reynolds: "I wish to get counsel," and was answered "G—d d—n you, you sha'nt have counsel, one word more G—d d—n you, and I'll shoot you." "What is the use of this so often," said Mr. Smith, "I have often told you to shoot, and now tell you again to shoot away;" and seeing a person passing he said, I am falsly imprisoned here, and I want a lawyer. A lawyer came, and had the door banged in his face with the old threat of shooting if he came any nearer, another afterwards came and received the same treatment. Many of the citizens of Dixon by this time being apprised of his situation stepped forward, and gave the Sheriff to understand, that if that was their mode of doing business in Missouri, they had another way of doing it here, that they were a law-abiding people, and republicans, that Mr. Smith should have justice done him, and have the opportunity of a fair trial, but that if they persisted in their course, they had a very summary way of dealing with such people—and gave them to understand that Mr. Smith should not go without a fair and impartial trial. . . .

It was ascertained that the nearest tribunal authorised to hear and determine upon writs of habeas corpus, was at Nauvoo. On their arrival at Nauvoo, a writ of habeas corpus was sued out before, and made returnable to the Municipal court of the city of Nauvoo, directed to Mr. Reynolds, upon which said writ Mr. Reynolds did produce the body of said Smith before said court, objecting however, to the jurisdiction of said court. It was ascertained by the counsel for said Smith that the Municipal court had full and ample power to hear and determine upon writs of habeas corpus. Upon examination before said court he was discharged from said arrest upon the merits of said case, and upon the further ground of substantial defects in said writ so issued by the Governor of the State of Illinois. . . . It is impossible that the State of Missouri should do justice with her coffers groaning with the spoils of the oppressed and her hands yet reeking with the blood of the innocent. Shall she yet gorge her bloody maw with other victims? Shall Joseph Smith be given into her hands illegally? *Never!* No Never!! NO NEVER!!!

—Volume 4, pages 241-243,

July 1, 1843.

The Kidnapping of Gen. Joseph Smith,
On the 23d of June, by Reynolds, the Sheriff of Jackson County,
Mo. and Wilson, of Carthage, Hancock Co Ill.

BY MISS E. R. SNOW.

Like bloodhounds fiercely prowling,
   With pistols ready drawn—
With oaths like tempests howling,
   Those kidnappers came on.

He bared his breast before them,
   But as they hurried near,
A fearfulness came o'er them—
   It was the coward's fear.

Well might their dark souls wither
   When he their courage dared—
Their pity fled, O whither?
   When he his bosom bared?

"Death has to me no terrors,"
   He said, "I hate a life
So subject to the horrors
   Of your ungodly strife."

"What means your savage conduct?
   Have you a lawful writ?
To any legal process
   I cheerfully submit."

351

"Here," said these lawless ruffians,
    "Is our authority;"
And drew their pistols nearer
    In rude ferocity.

With more than savage wildness—
    Like hungry beasts of prey;
They bore, in all his mildness,
    The man of God away!

With brutish haste they tore him
    From her he loves so well,
And far away they bore him
    With scarce the word "farewell!"

Their hearts are seats where blindness
    O'er foul corruption reigns—
The milk of human kindness
    Flows not within their veins.

Their conduct was unworthy
    The meanest race of men;
'Twould better fit the tiger
    Emerging from its den!

Missouri! O, Missouri!
    You thus prolong your shame
By sending such as Reynolds
    Abroad to bear your name.

Could Jackson County furnish
    No tamer shrub than he?
Must legal office burnish
    Such wild barbarity?

Go search the rudest forests,
    The panther and the bear
As well would grace your suff'rage—
    As well deserve a share.

Then might the heartless Wilson,
    Thy shame, O Illinois!
Become confed'rate with them
    And teach them to destroy.

> So much ferocious nature
>   Should join the brutish clan,
> And not disgrace the features
>   That claim to be a man.
>
> But hear it, O Missouri!
>   Once more "the prophet's free"—
> Your ill-directed fury
>   Brings forth a "jubilee."

—Volume 4, page 288,

August 1, 1843.

If Joseph Smith was judged to be a base criminal by some persons, to others he seemed to be a man of presidential timber, worthy of being president not just of the church but of the nation as well. Thus it was a great shock to some, but no surprise to others, to find the prophet being discussed as a possible presidential candidate in the February 15, 1844, editorial, "Who Shall Be Our Next President?"

> This is an enquiry which to us as a people, is a matter of the most paramount importance, and requires our most serious, calm, and dispassionate reflection. Executive power when correctly wielded, is a great blessing to the people of this great commonwealth, and forms one of the firmest pillars of our confederation. It watches the interests of the whole community with a fatherly care; it wisely balances the other legislative powers, when overheated by party spirit, or sectional feeling; it watches with jealous care our interests and commerce with foreign nations, and gives tone and efficacy to legislative enactments. The President stands at the head of these United States, and is the mouth-piece of this vast republic. If he be a man of an enlightened mind, and a capacious soul—if he is a virtuous man, a statesman, a patriot, and a man of unflinching integrity; if he possess the same spirit that fired the souls of our venerable sires, who founded this great commonwealth, and wishes to promote the universal good of the whole republic, he may indeed be made a blessing to community. But if he prostrates his high and honorable calling, to base and unworthy purposes; if he makes use of the power which the people have placed in his hands for their interest, to gratify his

ambition, for the purpose of self-aggrandizement, or pecuniary interest; if he meanly panders with demagogues, loses sight of the interests of the nation, and sacrifices the union on the altar of sectional interests or party views, he renders himself unworthy of the dignified trust reposed in him, debases the nation in the eyes of the civilized world, and produces misery and confusion at home. 'When the wicked rule, the people mourn.'. . .

Under these circumstances the question again arises, who shall we support? GENERAL JOSEPH SMITH. A man of sterling worth and integrity and of enlarged views; a man who has raised himself from the humblest walks in life to stand at the head of a large, intelligent, respectable, and increasing society, that has spread not only in this land, but in distant nations; a man whose talents and genius, are of an exalted nature, and whose experience has rendered him every way adequate to the onerous duty. Honorable, fearless, and energetic; he would administer justice with an impartial hand, and magnify, and dignify the office of chief magistrate of this land; and we feel assured that there is not a man in the United States more competent for the task.

One great reason that we have for pursuing our present course is, that at every election we have been made a political target for the filthy demagogues in the country to shoot their loathsome arrows at. And every story has been put into requisition to blast our fame, from the old fabrication of "walk on the water" down to "the murder of ex-Governor Boggs." The journals have teemed with this filthy trash, and even men who ought to have more respect for themselves; men contending for the gubernatorial chair have made use of terms so degrading, so mean, so humiliating, that a billingsgate fisherwoman would have considered herself disgraced with. We refuse any longer to be thus bedaubed for either party; we tell all such to let their filth flow in its own legitimate channel, for we are sick of the loathsome smell.

Whatever may be the opinions of men in general, in regard to Mr. Smith, we know that he need only to be known, to be admired; and that it is the principles of honor, integrity, patriotism, and philanthropy, that has elevated him in the minds of his friends, and the same principles if seen and known would beget the esteem and confidence of all the patriotic and virtuous throughout the union.

Whatever therefore be the opinions of other men onr course is marked out, and our motto from henceforth will be GENERAL JOSEPH SMITH.

—Volume 5, pages 439-441,

February 15, 1844.

354

Did the prophet actually think that he had even the slightest chance in succeeding in his quest for the presidency of the United States? In all likelihood, no. More probably he intended to draw attention to the plight of the Saints and the unjust treatment they had received at the hands of the Missourians. He may have been using his declared candidacy as a shock tactic to convince his rapidly increasing supply of foes in Illinois that the Saints, once timid and weak, were now powerful, even to the point of sponsoring their leader for national office, and that they were thus capable of resisting any persecution that might now be directed toward them. Whatever Joseph's expectations, he gave himself to this new project as he did to everything else he ventured into—completely and without reserve. He instructed the elders who were out preaching the Latter Day Saint message to become campaign workers dedicated to getting the Latter Day Saint prophet elected to the highest office in the land. While the apostles, seventies, and elders fanned out into the eastern states to compaign for him, the prophet remained at Nauvoo to work on campaign speech and political policy statements. A nominating convention was held in May at which time a platform of "Jeffersonian democracy, free trade, sailors' rights, and the protection of person and property" was advanced. The following excerpts are from "Gen. Smith's Views on the Government and Policy of the U.S." published in the May 15, 1844, *Times and Seasons.* The position on slavery seems to be a shift from the earlier statements published in *Messenger and Advocate.*

> Born in a land of liberty, and breathing an air uncorrupted with the sirocco of barbarous climes, I ever feel a double anxiety for the happiness of all men, both in time and in eternity. My cogitations like Daniel's, have for a long time troubled me, when I viewed the condition of men throughout the world, and more especially in this boasted realm, where the Declaration of Independence "holds these truths to be self evident; that all men are created equal: that they are endowed by their Creator, with certain unalienable rights; that among these are life, liberty, and the pursuit of happiness," but at the same time, some two or

355

three millions of people are held as slaves for life, because the spirit in them is covered with a darker skin than ours; and hundreds of our own kindred for an infraction, or supposed infraction of some overwise statute, have to be incarcerated in dungeon glooms, or suffer the more moral penitentiary gravitation of mercy in a nut-shell, while the duellist, the debauchee, and the defaulter for millions, and other criminals, take the uppermost rooms at feasts, or, like the bird of passage find a more congenial clime by flight.

The wisdom, which ought to characterize the freest, wisest, and most noble nation of the nineteenth century, should, like the sun in his meridian splendor, warm every object beneath its rays: and the main efforts of her officers, who are nothing more or less than the servants of the people, ought to be directed to ameliorate the condition of all: black or white, bond or free; for the best of books says, "God hath made of one blood all nations of men, for to dwell on all the face of the earth.". . .

Petition your state legislature to pardon every convict in their several penitentiaries: blessing them as they go, and saying to them in the name of the Lord, *go thy way and sin no more.* Advise your legislators when they make laws for larceny, burglary or any felony, to make the penalty applicable to work upon the roads, public works, or any place where the culprit can be taught more wisdom and more virtue; and become more enlightened. Rigor and seclusion will never do as much to reform the propensities of man, as reason and friendship. Murder only can claim confinement or death. Let the penitentiaries be turned into seminaries of learning, where intelligence, like the angels of heaven, would banish such fragments of barbarism: Imprisonment for debt is a meaner practice than the savage tolerates with all his ferocity; "Amor vincit amnia." Love conquers all.

Petition also, ye goodly inhabitants of the slave states, your legislators to abolish slavery by the year 1850, or now, and save the abolitionist from reproach and ruin, infamy and shame. Pray Congress to pay every man a reasonable price for his slaves out of the surplus revenue arising from the sale of public lands, and from the deduction of pay from the members of Congress. Break off the shackles from the poor black man, and hire them to labor like other human beings; for "an hour of virtuous liberty on earth, is worth a whole eternity of bondage!" Abolish the practice in the army and navy of trying men by court martial for desertion; if a soldier or marine runs away, send him his wages, with this instruction, that *his country will never trust him again, he has forfeited his honor.* Make HONOR the standard with all men: be sure that good is rendered for evil in all cases: and the whole nation, like a kingdom of kings and priests, will rise up with righteousness: and be respected as wise and worthy on earth: and as just and holy for heaven; by Jehovah the author of perfection. More economy in the national and state governments; would make less taxes among the people: more equality through the cities, towns & country, would make less distinction among the people; and more honesty and familiarity in societies, would make less hypocrisy and flattery in all branches of community; and open, frank, candid, decorum to all men, in this boasted land of liberty, would beget esteem, confidence, union and love; and the neighbor from any state, or from any country, of whatever color, clime or tongue, could rejoice when he put his foot on the sacred soil of freedom, and exclaim: the very name of *"American,"* is fraught with *friendship!* Oh! then, create confidence! restore freedom!— break down slavery! banish imprisonment for debt, and be in love, fellowship and peace with all the world! remember that honesty is not subject to law: the law was made for transgressors: wherefore a Dutchman might exclaim: *Ein ehrlicker name ist besser als Reichthum,* (a good name is better than riches.)

For the accommodation of the people in every state and territory, let Congress shew their wisdom by granting a national bank, with branches in each state and territory, where the capital stock shall be held by the nation for the mother bank: and by the states and territories, for the branches: and whose officers and directors shall be elected yearly by the people with wages at the rate of two dollars per day for services: which several banks shall never issue any more bills than the amount of capital stock in her vaults and the interest. The nett gain of the mother bank shall be applied to the national revenue, and that of the branches to the states and territories' revenues. And the bills shall be par throughout the nation, which will mercifully cure that fatal disorder known in cities, as *brokerage;* and leave the people's money in their own pockets.

Give every man his constitutional freedom, and the president full power to send an army to suppress mobs; and the states authority to repeal and impugn that relic of folly, which makes it necessary for the governor of a state to make the demand of the president for troops, in cases of invasion or rebellion. The governor himself may be a mobber and, instead of being punished, as he should be for murder and treason, he may destroy the very lives, rights, and property he should protect. Like the good Samaritan, send every lawyer as soon as he repents and obeys the ordinances of heaven, to preach the gospel to the destitute, without purse or scrip, pouring in the oil and the wine: a learned priesthood is certainly more honorable than a *"hireling clergy"*.

As to the contiguous territories to the United States, wisdom would direct no tangling alliance: Oregon belongs to this government honorably, and when we have the red man's consent, let the union spread from the east to the west sea; and if Texas petitions Congress to be adopted among the sons of liberty, give her the the right hand of fellowship; and refuse not the same friendly grip to Canada and Mexico: and when the right arm of freemen is stretched out in the character of a navy, for the protection of rights, commerce and honor, let the iron eyes of power, watch from Maine to Mexico, and from California to Columbia; thus may union be strengthened, and foreign speculation prevented from opposing broadside to broadside.

Seventy years have done much for this goodly land; they have burst the chains of oppression and monarchy; and multiplied its inhabitants from two to twenty millions; with a proportionate share of knowledge: keen enough to circumnavigate the globe; draw the lightning from the clouds: and cope with all the crowned heads of the world. . . .

In the United States the people are the government; and their united voice is the only sovereign that should rule; the only power that should be obeyed; and the only gentlemen that should be honored; at home and abroad; on the land and on the sea: Wherefore, were I the president of the United States, by the voice of a virtuous people, I would honor the old paths of the venerated fathers of freedom: I would walk in the tracks of the illustrious patriots, who carried the ark of the government upon their shoulders with an eye single to the glory of the people and when that people petitioned to abolish slavery in the slave states, I would use all honorable means to have their prayers granted: and give liberty to the captive; by giving the southern gentleman a reasonable equivalent for his property, that the whole nation might be free indeed! When the people petitioned for a national bank, I would use my best endeavors to have their prayers answered, and establish one on national principles to save taxes, and make them the controllers of its ways and means; and when the people petitioned to possess the territory of Oregon or any other contiguous territory; I would lend the influence of a chief magistrate to grant so reasonable a request, that they might extend the mighty efforts and enterprise of a free people from the east to the west sea; and make the wilderness blossom as the rose; and when a neighboring realm petitioned to join the union of the

sons of liberty, my voice would be, *come:* yea come Texas: come
Mexico; come Canada; and come all the world—let us be brethren: let us be one great family; and let there be universal peace.
Abolish the cruel customs of prisons, (except certain cases,)
penitentiaries, and court-martials for desertion; and let reason and
friendship reign over the ruins of ignorance and barbarity; yea I
would, as the universal friend of man, open the prisons; open the
eyes; open the ears and open the hearts of all people, to behold
and enjoy freedom, unadulterated freedom: and God, who once
cleansed the violence of the earth with a flood; whose Son laid
down his life for the salvation of all his father gave him out of the
world; and who has promised that he will come and purify the
world again with fire in the last days, should be supplicated by
me for the good of all people.

    With the highest esteem,
        I am a friend of virtue
           and of the people,

                JOSEPH SMITH.

Nauvoo, Illinois, February 7, 1844.

                —Volume 5, pages 528-533,
                    May 15, 1844.

The excitement and exuberance of the presidential campaign shortly afterward gave way to nightmarish fear and
sorrow. Assassination terminated abruptly Joseph and
Hyrum Smith's dreams and aspirations, and brought the
church to a leadership crisis that no one had been able to
anticipate.

LATE NAUVOO

The tragic circumstances of June 27, 1844, were precipi-
tated by the appearance in Nauvoo of an unwelcome rival
newspaper. A trusted church leader, William Law, broke with
the prophet, and in association with several other disaffected
members set about to publish the *Nauvoo Expositor*. In the
first issue of this paper several charges were made against
Joseph Smith and other prominent church leaders concerning
the introduction of a "spiritual marriage" system involving a

plurality of wives. The city council met three days after the appearance of the *Expositor*. Ironically, it was W. W. Phelps, who knew firsthand the horror of violent action against a minority-opinion press, who sponsored a resolution declaring the *Expositor* a public nuisance and urging the destruction of the press. Joseph Smith, as mayor of the city, issued the executive order that sent some Nauvoo Legionnaires to suppress the rival printing firm. Little did the prophet anticipate the public outcry against this act. Mobs began forming and arming themselves in the nearby towns of Quincy and Carthage. A summons was expedited for the arrest of the church's leaders. The rest of the story is told to the readership of the *Times and Seasons* in the July 1, 1844, issue. At the conclusion of that issue, Eliza R. Snow adds her eloquent voice to the protest against the infamy of the mob action.

Awful assassination of JOSEPH AND HYRUM SMITH:— The pledged faith of the state of Illinois stained with innocent blood by a Mob!

On Monday the 24th inst., after Gov. Ford had sent word, that those eighteen persons demanded on a warrant, among whom were Joseph Smith and Hyrum Smith *should be protected,* by the militia of the State, they in company with some ten or twelve others, started for Carthage. Four miles from that place, they were met by Capt. Dunn, with a company of cavalry, who had an order from the Governor for the *"State Arms."* Gen Smith endorsed his acceptance of the same, and both parties returned to Nauvoo to obtain said arms. After the arms were obtained, both parties took up the line of march for Carthage, where they arrived about five minutes before twelve o'clock at night. Capt. Dunn nobly acquiting himself, landed us safely at Hamilton's Hotel

In the morning we saw the Governor, and he *pledged the faith of the State,* that we should be protected. Gen Smith and his brother Hyrum were arrested by a warrant founded upon the oaths of H. O. Norton and Augustine Spencer for *treason.* Knowing the threats from several persons, that the two Smiths should never leave Carthage *alive*, we all began to be alarmed for their personal safety. The Gov and Gen. Deming conducted them before the McDonough troops and introduced them as *Gen. Joseph Smith and Gen. Hyrum Smith.*—This manoeuvre came near raising a mutiny among the "Carthage Greys," but the Governor quelled it.

360

In the afternoon, after great exertions on the part of our counsel, we dispensed with an investigation, and voluntarily gave bail for our appearance to the Circuit Court, to answer in the case of abating the Nauvoo Expositor, as a nuisance.

At evening the Justice made out a mittimus. without an investigation, and committed the two Gen. Smiths to prison *until discharged by due course of law,* and they were safely guarded to jail. In the morning the Governor went to the jail and had an interview with these men, and to every appearance all things were explained on both sides.

The constable then went to take these men from the jail, before the Justice for examination, but the jailer refused to let them go, as they were under his direction *"till discharged by due course of law;"* but the Governor's troops, to the amount of one or two hundred, took them to the Court House, when the hearing was continued till Saturday the 29th, and they were remanded to jail. Several of our citizens had permits from the Governor to lodge with them, and visit them in jail. It now began to be rumored by several men, whose names will be forthcoming in time, *that there was nothing against these men, the law could not reach them, but powder and ball would!* The Governor was made acquainted with these facts, but on the morning of the 27th, he disbanded the McDonough troops, and sent them home; took Captain Dunn's company of Cavalry and proceeded to Nauvoo, leaving these two men and three or four friends, to be guarded by *eight men* at the jail; and a company in town of 60 men, 30 or 100 rods from the jail, as a corps in reserve.

About six o'clock in the afternoon the guard was surprised by an armed Mob of from 150 to 250, painted red, black and yellow, which surrounded the jail, forced in—poured a shower of bullets into the room where these unfortunate men were held, "in durance vile," to answer to the laws of Illinois; under the solemn pledge of the faith of the State, by Gov. Ford, *that they should be protected!* but the mob ruled!! They fell as Martyrs amid this tornado of lead, each receiving four bullets! John Taylor was wounded by four bullets in his limbs but not seriously. Thus perishes the hope of law; thus vanishes the plighted faith of the state; thus the blood of innocence stains the constituted authorities of the United States, and thus have two among the most noble martyrs since the slaughter of Abel, sealed the truth of their divine mission, *by being shot by a Mob for their religion!*

Messengers were dispatched to Nauvoo, but did not reach there till morning. The following was one of the letters:

12 o'clock at night, 27th June,
Carthage, Hamilton's Tavern.

TO MRS. EMMA SMITH,
AND MAJ. GEN. DUNHAM, &C–

The Governor has just arrived; says all things shall be inquired into, and all right measures taken.

I say to all the citizens of Nauvoo, my brethren, be still, and know that *God reigns. Don't rush out of the city*–don't rush to Carthage; stay at home, and be prepared for an attack from Missouri mobbers. The Governor will render every assistance possible–has sent out orders for troops–Joseph and Hyrum are dead, but not by the Carthage people–the guards were true as I believe.

We will prepare to move the bodies as soon as possible.

The people of the county are greatly excited, and fear the Mormons will come out and take vengeance–I have pledged my word the Mormons will stay at home as soon as they can be informed, and no violence will be on their part, and say to my brethren in Nauvoo, in the name of the Lord–be still–be patient–only let such friends as choose come here to see the bodies–Mr. Taylor's wounds are dressed & not serious–I am sound.

WILLARD RICHARDS,
JOHN TAYLOR,
SAMUEL H. SMITH.

–Volume 5, pages 560-561,
July 1, 1844.

TO THE CHURCH OF JESUS CHRIST OF
LATTER DAY SAINTS.

Deeply impressed for the welfare of all, while mourning the great loss of President *Joseph Smith,* our "prophet and seer," and President *Hyrum Smith,* our "patriarch," we have considered the occasion demanded of us a word of consolation. As has been the case in all ages, these saints have fallen martyrs for the truth's sake, and their escape from the persecution of a wicked world, in blood to bliss, only strengthens our faith, and confirms our religion, as pure and holy. We, therefore, as servants of the Most High God, having the Bible, Book of Mormon and the book of Doctrine and Covenants; together with thousands of witnesses, for Jesus Christ; would beseech the Latter Day Saints in Nauvoo, and elsewhere, to hold fast to the faith that has been delivered to them in the last days, abiding in the perfect law of the gospel. Be peaceable, quiet citizens, doing the works of righteousness, and as soon as the ,"Twelve" and other authorities can assemble, or a majority of them, the onward course to the great gathering of Israel, and the final consummation of the dispensation of the fulness of times, will be pointed out; so that the murder of Abel; the assassination of hundreds; the righteous blood of all the holy prophets, from Abel to Joseph, sprinkled with the best blood of the Son of God, as the crimson sign of remission, only carries conviction to the business and bosoms of all flesh, that the cause is just and will continue; and blessed are they that hold out faithful to the end, while apostates, consenting to the shedding of innocent blood, have no forgiveness in this world nor in the world to come. Union is peace, brethren, and eternal life is the greatest gift of God. Rejoice then, that you are found worthy to live and die for God: men may kill the body, but they *cannot* hurt the soul, and wisdom shall be justified of her children: Amen.

W. W. PHELPS,
W. RICHARDS,
JOHN TAYLOR.
July 1, 1844.

—Volume 5, page 568,
July 1, 1844.

THE ASSASSINATION OF GEN'LS JOSEPH SMITH AND HYRUM SMITH, FIRST PRESIDENTS OF THE CHURCH OF LATTER DAY SAINTS: WHO WERE MASSACRED BY A MOB, IN CARTHAGE, HANCOCK COUNTY, ILL, ON THE 27TH JUNE, 1844;

BY MISS ELIZA R. SNOW.

"And when he had opened the fifth seal, I saw under the altar, the souls of them that were slain for the word of God, and for the testimony which they held.

And they cried with a loud voice, saying, How long, O Lord, holy and true, dost thou not judge and avenge our blood on them that dwell on the earth?

And white robes were given unto every one of them; and it was said unto them, that they should rest yet for a little season, until their fellow servants also, and their brethren, that should be killed as they were, should be fulfilled."—Rev. 6:—9, 10, 11.

Ye heav'ns attend! Let all the earth give ear!
Let Gods and seraphs, men and angels hear—
The worlds on high—the universe shall know
What awful scenes are acted here below!
Had nature's self a heart, her heart would bleed;
For never, since the Son of God was slain
Has blood so noble, flow'd from human vein
As that which now, on God for vengeance calls
From "freedom's ground"—from Carthage prison walls!

Oh! Illinois! thy soil has drank the blood
Of prophets martyr'd for the truth of God.
Once lov'd America! what can atone
For the pure blood of innocence, thou'st sown?
Were all thy streams in teary torrents shed
To mourn the fate of those illustrious dead;
How vain the tribute, for the noblest worth
That grac'd thy surface, O degraded Earth!

Oh wretched murd'rers! fierce for human blood!
You've slain the prophets of the living God,
Who've borne oppression from their early youth.
To plant on earth, the principles of truth.

Shades of our patriotic fathers! Can it be,
Beneath your blood-stain'd flag of liberty:
The firm supporters of our country's cause,
Are butcher'd while submissive to her laws?
Yes, blameless men, defam'd by hellish lies
Have thus been offer'd as a sacrifice
T'appease the ragings of a brutish clan,
That has defied the laws of God and man!
'Twas not for crime or guilt of theirs, they fell—
Against the laws they never did rebel.
True to their country, yet her plighted faith
Has prov'd an instrument of cruel death!

Where are thy far-fam'd laws—Columbia! where
Thy boasted freedom—thy protecting care?
Is this a land of rights? Stern-facts shall say
If legal justice here maintains its sway;
The official pow'rs of State are sheer pretence
When they're exerted in the Saints' defence.

Great men have fall'n and mighty men have died—
Nations have mourn'd their fav'rites and their pride;
But two, so wise, so virtuous, great and good,
Before on earth, at once, have never stood
Since the creation—men whom God ordain'd
To publish truth where error long had reigned;
Of whom the world, itself unworthy prov'd:
It knew them not; but men with hatred mov'd
And with infernal spirits have combin'd
Against the best, the noblest of mankind!

Oh, persecution! shall thy purple hand
Spread utter destruction through the land?
Shall freedom's banner be no more unfurled?
Has peace indeed, been taken from the world?

Thou God of Jacob, in this trying hour
Help us to trust in thy almighty pow'r;
Support thy Saints beneath this awful stroke—
Make bare thine arm to break oppression's yoke.
We mourn thy Prophet, from whose lips have flow'd
The words of life, thy spirit has bestow'd—
A depth of thought, no human art could reach
From time to time, roll'd in sublimest speech,
From the celestial fountain, through his mind,
To purify and elevate mankind:
The rich intelligence by him brought forth,
Is like the sun-beam, spreading o'er the earth.

Now Zion mourns—she mourns an earthly head
The Prophet and the Patriarch are dead!
The blackest deed that men or devils know
Since Calv'ry's scene, has laid the brothers low!
One in their life, and one in death—they prov'd
How strong their friendship—how they truly lov'd
True to their mission, until death, they stood,
Then seal'd their testimony with their blood.
All hearts with sorrow bleed, and ev'ry eye
Is bath'd in tears—each bosom heaves a sigh—
Hart broken widows agonizing groans
Are mingled with the helpless orphans' moans!

Ye Saints! be still, and know that God is just—
With steadfast purpose in his promise trust.

Girded with sackcloth, own his mighty hand,
And wait his judgments on this guilty land!
The noble martyrs now have gone to move
The cause of Zion in the courts above.
Nauvoo, July 1, 1844.

—Volume 5, page 575,

July 1, 1844.

After the funeral, the bodies of the slain prophet and his brother were first buried in the basement of the Nauvoo House, then later reinterred in a secret grave in order to thwart any attempts to desecrate the bodies. Though in a state of shock for several days, the citizenry of Nauvoo began to pick up the threads of their lives and to think once more about their present predicament and their uncertain future. The question that was uppermost in everyone's mind was, Who would lead the church now that the prophet of the Lord had been taken from their midst? In the July 15 *Times and Seasons*, four beloved church leaders, including two who had been with the brothers at the time of their martyrdom, composed a joint epistle addressed "To the Saints Abroad." The intention of the letter was to remind the Saints that God was still in control of his world and still the Lord of his church. The counsel, then, was not to panic, nor to be divided in their loyalty to church leadership.

Dear Brethren;
On hearing of the martyrdom of our beloved prophet and patriarch, you will doubtless need a word of advice and comfort, and look for it from our hands. We would say, therefore, first of all, be still and know that the Lord is God; and that he will fulfill all things in his own due time; and not one jot or tittle of all his purposes and promises shall fail. *Remember,* remember that the priesthood, and the keys of power are held in eternity as well as in time; and, therefore, the servants of God who pass the veil of death are prepared to enter upon a greater and more effectuul work, in the speedy accomplishment of the restoration of all things spoken of by his holy prophets.
Remember that all the prophets and saints who have existed

since the world began, are engaged in this holy work, and are yet in the vineyard, as well as the laborers of the eleventh hour: and are all pledged to establish the kingdom of God on the earth, and to give judgement unto the saints; therefore, none can hinder the rolling on of the eternal purposes of the Great Jehovah. And we have now every reason to believe that the fulfilment of his great purposes are much nearer than we had supposed, and that not many years hence, we shall see the kingdom of God, coming with power and great glory to our deliverance.

As to our country and nation, we have more reason to weep for them, than for those they have murdered; for they are destroying themselves and their institutions and there is no remedy: and as to feelings of revenge, let them not have place for one moment in our bosoms, for God's vengeance will speedily consume to that degree that we would fain be hid away and not endure the sight.

Let us then humble ourselves under the mighty hand of God, and endeavor to put away all our sins and imperfections as a people, and as individuals, and to call upon the Lord with the spirit of grace and supplication; and wait patiently on him, until he shall direct our way.

Let no vain and foolish plans, or imaginations scatter us abroad, and divide us assunder as a people, to seek to save our lives at the expense of truth and principle, but rather let us live or die together and in the enjoyment of society and union. Therefore, we say, let us haste to fulfill the commandments which God has already given us. Yes, let us haste to *build the Temple of our God,* and to gather together thereunto, our silver and our gold with us, unto the name of the Lord; and then we may expect that he will teach us of his ways and we will walk in his paths.

We would further say, that in consequence of the great rains which have deluged the western country, and also in consequence of persecution and excitement, there has been but little done here, either in farming or building this season; therefore there is but little employment, and but little means of subsistence at the command of the saints in this region—therefore, let the saints abroad, and others who feel for our calamities and wish to sustain us, come on with their money and means without delay, and purchase lots and farms, and build buildings, and employ hands, as well as to pay their tythings into the Temple, and their donations to the poor.

We wish it distinctly understood abroad, that we greatly need the assistance of every lover of humanity whether members of the church or otherwise, both in influence and in contributions for our aid, succor, and support. Therefore, if they feel for us, now is the time to show their liberality and patriotism towards a poor and persecuted, but honest and industrious people.

Let the elders who remain abroad, continue to preach the gospel in its purity and fullness, and to bear testimony of the truth of these things which have been revealed for the salvation of this generation.

P. P. PRATT,
WILLARD RICHARDS,
JOHN TAYLOR,
W. W. PHELPS.

Nauvoo, July 15, 1844.

—Volume 5, pages 586-587,

July 15, 1844.

Two of the epistle's cosigners expressed their grief over the tragedy by penning poetic tributes to the prophet. Brother Phelps wrote:

Praise to the man who commun'd with Jehovah,
   Jesus' anointed "that Prophet and Seer,"
Blessed to open the last dispensation;—
   Kings shall extol him, and nations revere.

CHORUS—Hail to the Prophet, ascended to heaven,
          Traitors and tyrants now fight him in vain,
          Mingling with Gods, he can plan for his brethren,
          Death cannot conquer the hero again.

Praise to his mem'ry, he died as a martyr;
   Honor'd and blest be his ever great name;
Long shall his blood, which was shed by assassins,
   Stain Illinois, while the earth lauds his fame.

CHORUS—Hail to the Prophet, &c.

Great is his glory, and endless his priesthood,
   Ever and ever the keys he will hold;
Faithful and true he will enter his kingdom,
   Crown'd in the midst of the prophets of old.

CHORUS—Hail to the Prophet, &c.

Sacrifice brings forth the blessings of heaven;
    Earth must atone for the blood of that man!
Wake up the world for the conflict of justice,
    Millions shall know "brother Joseph" again.

CHORUS—Hail to the Prophet, &c.

—Volume 5, page 607,

August 1, 1844.

Parley P. Pratt, in the same spirit but with more ambitious cadences, wrote:

Hark!—the sound of many voices mingling
Their feeble cries like the groans of myriads
Of expiring insects, assends the skies
In solemn music. While the wide expanse
Of Heavens' courts re echoes with the sound:
Its strains, tho' mournful, sad, and solemn are
Powerful and mighty, and dignified,
And grand, and sublime: and fill all heaven,
As the sound of many waters; or as
The voice of a great thunder; rending the
Skies; startling the angels; and penetrating
The hearts of the Gods: thrilling every nerve
And kindling the flame of justice in each
Holy bosom.—And whose voices are these?

They are the voices of ancient martyre
Who were slain for the witness of Jesus;
And for the word of their testimony.
Yes—crucified, beheaded, sawn asunder,
Burned, torn by wild beasts; betrayed, shot,
Hung, boiled, roasted, imprisoned, starved, and
Tortured in ten thousand nameless ways.

And who, so cruel, or so hard in heart
As to afflict these blessed martyrs thus?
Perchance some demon from the courts of Hell
In human form arrayed, alone performed it?
Or if by human aid it must have been
Some low degraded heathen—cannibal,
Trained from his youth to feed on human flesh.
Or tell me, where such wretches could be found?

Alas, I blush to own the truth, and yet
Myself a man. These were their PRAYING FRIENDS;
Their fathers, mothers, brothers, sisters, sons,
And neighbors. Ah, too oft their fellow christians,
In name, but not in spirit. Yes, pious
Priests, and praying friends, too oft betrayed them.
But how could these in concience kill such men,
And all for their religion and their faith:
Ah, this, (themselves the judge) they never did.
They first accused them, charged with various
Crimes, belied and slandered; then, for justice
Cried: and thus distroyed them, in holy zeal for God;
And vainly thought to do him service.

    But hark.—That piercing cry still tingles in
My ears, and fills my very heart with grief
What are their words that burn, with might and power
To pain both heaven and earth and all that hear?
    "How long, O Lord! holy and true, dost thou
Not judge and avenge our blood on them that
Dwell on the earth?"
    Are these the awful words? And what reply
Is given by the avenging heavens?
    BE PATIENT—O ye martyred souls and wait
Till your fellow servants who are to be
Killed in like manner shall be fulfilled.
    WAIT—till Missouri's plains are soaked in blood
Of innocence, and the souls of Latter day Saints
Mingle their cries with yours for vengeance on
The earth. Wait, till the plains of Illinois,
And the walls of Carthage, are soaked with
The blood of martyred prophets, whose cries
Ascend to heaven for vengeance on a mob.
    Wait—till the last vestige of civil and
Religious liberty shall expire in
The bosom of a boasting nation, whose
Rulers mock the cries of justice,
And laugh at the prayers of the oppressed.
Wait till then; but wait no longer.—You have
The answer.

—Volume 5, page 639,

September 2, 1844.

370

WHO IS JOSEPH'S SUCCESSOR?

Soon after arriving in Nauvoo from Pittsburgh, Sidney Rigdon began making claims to leadership as the only surviving member of the First Presidency. He called a conference for August 6 in which his claims could be placed before the people. Unfortunately for him, the conference was postponed for a few days, allowing time for Brigham Young, president of the Council of Twelve, to arrive home from Boston, where he had been campaigning on behalf of the prophet. Young frustrated Rigdon's plan by pitting Rigdon, who had not enjoyed the full measure of the prophet's confidence for several years, against the Twelve. The reading public of the *Times and Seasons* away from Nauvoo was to find out the details of the confrontation between the two men later as the information was prepared for publication under the supervision of John Taylor, a member of the Twelve.

In the August 15 issue, "An Epistle of the Twelve to the Church of Jesus Christ of Latter Day Saints, in Nauvoo and all the world," was presented over Brigham Young's signature.

Beloved Brethren:—Forasmuch as the Saints have been called to suffer deep affliction and persecution, and also to mourn the loss of our beloved Prophet and also our Patriarch, who have suffered a cruel martyrdom for the testimony of Jesus, having voluntarily yielded themselves to cruel murderers who had sworn to take their lives, and thus like good shepherds have laid down their lives for the sheep, therefore it becomes necessary for us to address you at this time on several important subjects.

You are now without a prophet present with you in the flesh to guide you; but you are not without apostles, who hold the keys of power to seal on earth that which shall be sealed in heaven, and to preside over all the affairs of the church in all the world; being still under the direction of the same God, and being dictated by the same spirit, having the same manifestations of the Holy Ghost to dictate all the affairs of the church in all the world, to build up the kingdom upon the foundation that the prophet Joseph has laid, who still holds the keys of this last dispensation, and will hold them to all eternity, as a king and priest unto the most high God, ministering in heaven, on earth, or among the spirits of the departed dead, as seemeth good to him who sent him.

Let no man presume for a moment that his place will be filled by another; for, *remember he stands in his own place,* and always will; and the Twelve Apostles of this dispensation stand in their own place and always will, both in time and in eternity, to minister, preside and regulate the affairs of the whole church.

How vain are the imaginations of the children of men, to presume for a moment that the slaughter of one, two or a hundred of the leaders of this church could distroy an organization, so perfect in itself and so harmoniously arranged that it will stand while one member of it is left alive upon the earth. Brethren be not alarmed, for if the Twelve should be taken away still there are powers and offices in existence which will bear the kingdom of God triumphantly victorious in all the world. This church may have prophets many, and apostles many, but they are all to stand in due time in their proper organization, under the direction of those who hold the keys.

On the subject of the gathering, let it be distinctly understood that the City of Nauvoo and the Temple of our Lord are to continue to be built up according to the pattern which has been commenced, and which has progressed with such rapidity thus far. . . .

The United States and adjoining provinces will be immediately organized by the Twelve into proper districts, in a similar manner as they have already done in England and Scotland, and high priests will be appointed over each district, to preside over the same, and to call quarterly conferences for the regulation and representation of the branches included in the same, and for the furtherance of the gospel; and also to take measures for a yearly representation in a general conference. This will save the trouble and confusion of the running to and fro of elders; detect false doctrine and false teachers, and make every elder abroad accountable to the conference in which he may happen to labor.— Bishops will also be appointed in the larger branches, to attend to the management of the temporal funds, such as tythings, and funds for the poor, according to the revelations of God, and to be judges in Israel.

The gospel in its fulness and purity, must now roll forth through every neighborhood of this wide-spread country, and to all the world; and millions will awake to its truths and obey its precepts; and the kingdoms of this world will become the kingdoms of our Lord and of his Christ.

As rulers and people have taken counsel together against the Lord; and against his annointed, and have murdered him who would have reformed and saved the nation, it is not wisdom for the Saints to have any thing to do with politics, voting, or president-making, at present.—None of the candidates who are now before the public for that high office, have manifested any disposition or intention to redress wrong or restore right, liberty or law; and therefore, wo unto him who gives countenance to corruption, or partakes of murder, robbery or other cruel deeds. Let us then stand aloof from all their corrupt men and measures, and wait, at least, till a man is found, who, if elected, will carry out the enlarged principles, universal freedom, and equal rights and protection, expressed in the views of our beloved prophet and martyr, General Joseph Smith.

We do not, however, offer this political advise as binding on the consciences of others; we are perfectly willing that every member of this church should use their own freedom in all political matters; but we give it as our own rule of action, and for the benefit of those who may choose to profit by it.

Now, dear brethren, to conclude our present communication, we would exhort you in the name of the Lord Jesus Christ, to be humble and faithful before God, and before all the people, and give no occasion for any man to speak evil of you; but preach the gospel in its simplicity and purity, and practice righteousness, and seek to establish the influence of truth, peace and love among mankind, and in so doing the Lord will bless you, and make you a blessing to all people.

You may expect to hear from us again.

BRIGHAM YOUNG,
President of the Twelve.

Nauvoo, August 15th, 1844.

—Volume 6, pages 618-620,

August 15, 1844.

The first news of serious dissension concerning the leadership of the church appeared in a brief notice of excommunication in the September 2 issue.

TO THE SAINTS.

Whereas Elders James J. Strang and Aaron Smith have been circulating a "revelation," (falsely called) purporting to have been received by Joseph Smith on the 18th of June, 1844: and through the influence of which they have attempted and are attempting to establish a stake, called Voree, in Wisconsin Territory, thereby leading the saints astray: therefore, the said James J. Strang and Aaron Smith are cut off from the church of Jesus Christ of Latter-day Saints, this 26th day of August, 1844.

By order of the Council of the Twelve.

W. RICHARDS, Clerk.

—Volume 5, page 631,

September 2, 1844.

Immediately following this notice, an editorial comment is made:

Great excitement prevails throughout the world to know "who shall be the successor of Joseph Smith?"

In reply, we say, be patient, *be patient* a little, till the proper time comes, and we will tell you all. "Great wheels move slow." At present, we can say that a special conference of the church was held in Nauvoo on the 8th ult., and it was carried *without a discenting voice,* that the "Twelve" should preside over the whole church, and when any alteration in the presidency shall be required, seasonable notice will be given; and the elders abroad, will best exibit their wisdom to all men, by remaining silent on those things they are ignorant of.—Bishops Whitney and Miller have been appointed trustees, to manage the financial concerns of the church, and will soon enter on the duties of their calling.

—Volume 5, page 632,

September 2, 1844.

Later in this same issue the proceedings at a "special meeting" are described.

On the 8th of August, 1844, at a special meeting of the Church of Jesus Christ of Latter Day Saints, convened at the stand in the city of Nauvoo, President Brigham Young called the audience to order, and arranged the several quorums according to their standing, and the rules of the church. The meeting had been previously called, as stated, to choose a guardian, or trustee for said church.

374

Elder Phelps opened the meeting by prayer, and President Young then proceeded to speak, and gave his views of the present situation of the church, now that the prophet and patriarch were taken from our midst by the wickedness of our enemies. For the first time since he became a member of the church; a servant of God, a messenger to the nations in the nineteenth century; for the first time in the kingdom of God, the Twelve Apostles of the Lamb, chosen by revelation, in this last dispensation of the gospel for the winding up scene, present themselves before the saints, to stand in their lot according to appointment. While the prophet lived, we all walked by 'sight;' he is taken from us and we must now walk by 'faith.' After he had explained matters so satisfactorily that every saint could see that Elijah's mantle had truly fallen upon the 'Twelve,' he ashed the saints what they wanted. Do you want a guardian, a prophet, a spokesman, or what do you want? If you want any of these officers, signify it by raising the right hand. Not a hand was raised.

He then gave the saints his views of what the Lord wanted. Here are the 'Twelve,' appointed by the finger of God, who hold the keys of the priesthood, and the authority to set in order and regulate the church in all the world. Here is elder Amasa Lyman and elder Sidney Rigdon; they were councillors in the first presidency, and they are councillors to the Twelve still; if they keep their places; but if either wishes to act as 'spokesman' for the prophet Joseph, he must go behind the veil where Joseph is. He continued his remarks nearly an hour, opening by the spirit of God, the eyes, ears and hearts of the saints to the subject before them, and to their duty and the glory of God. . . .When the whole subject was properly explained and understood, and counsellor Rigdon refused to have his name voted for as a spokesman or guardian, the question was put, 'all in favor of supporting the Twelve in their calling, (every quorum, man and woman,) signify it by the uplifted hand;' and the vote was unanimous, no hand being raised in the negative. The next vote was that the Twelve should select and appoint two bishops to act as trustees for the church, according to law. This vote was unanimous also. Another unanimous vote was passed to use every exertion to forward the building of the Temple, and to strengthen the hands of the committee. The revelation in relation to tithing was referred to, and the manifestation of every saint seemed to be, *we* will do as the Lord hath commanded; and the assembly was dismissed with the blessings of the Lord.

NOTICE.

Fellowship was, last evening, withdrawn from Elders Sidney Rigdon, James Emmet, and Zachariah Wilson, by the Counsel of the Twelve, and on Sunday next the matter will be laid before the church for their action.

—Volume 5, pages 637-639,

September 2, 1844.

The minutes of the trial of Sidney Rigdon on September 8 are reported in two issues of the *Times and Seasons*, including remarks spoken in Rigdon's defense by William Marks, president of the Nauvoo Stake. It is evident from these proceedings that the Council of Twelve was firmly in control. Sidney Rigdon and those who favored his claims were condemned. "Elder Young arose and delivered Sidney Rigdon over to the buffetings of Satan, in the name of the Lord, and all the people said, amen."

At the October conference, the Twelve further entrenched their position by discrediting all rival claimants to ecclesiastical authority. This was the first general conference in which the Saints did not have their prophet to lean on when "instruction from the Lord" seemed desperately needed.

City of Nauvoo, Oct. 6, 1844.

Thousands having arrived on the ground by ten o'clock A. M. Elder P. P. Pratt called the people to order Singing by the choir.—Prayer by Elder Phelps. Some instructions were given by Elder Pratt, when President B. Young having arrived, arose to lay before the brethren the matters to be attended to during the conference: This day will be devoted to preaching and instruction, and we will attend to business to-morrow. If the Twelve could have had their desires when they returned home, they would have set their houses in order, and devoted themselves to fasting and prayer. It has not been the Twelve who desired to have business which pertains to this conference, transacted previous, it was others who urged it on. Some elders who have known the organization of the church from the beginning, have faultered and become darkened. We feel to give the necessary instruction pertaining to the church, and how it has been led &c. It is necessary that the saints should also be instructed relative to building the temple, and spreading the principles of truth from sea to sea, and from land to land until it shall have been preached

376

to all nations, and then according to the testimony of the ancients, the end will come. When the Lord commences to work upon the earth he always does it by revealing his will to some man on the earth, and he to others. The church is built up by revelation, given from day to day according to the requirements of the people. The Lord will not cease to give revelations to the people, unless, the people trample on his laws and forsake and reject him. I request that the Latter-day Saints may pray that we may have the outpouring of the spirit that we may hear, and I wish them to pray for me that I may have strength, and that I may make every principle I speak upon, so perfectly plain, that we may all understand as quick as when we talk together upon our daily matters.

This church has been led by revelation, and unless we forsake the Lord entirely, so that the priesthood is taken from us, it will be led by revelation all the time. The question arises with some who has the right to revelation? I will not ascend any higher than a priest, and ask the priest what is your right? You have the right to receive the administration of angels. If an angel was to come to you and tell you what the Lord was going to do in this day, you would say you had a revelation. The president of the priests have a right to the Urim and Thummim, which gives all revelation. He has the right of receiving visits from angels. Every priest then in the church has the right of receiving revelations. Every member has the right of receiving revelations for themselves, both male and female. It is the very life of the church of the living God, in all ages of the world. The spirit of truth is sent forth into all the world to reprove the world of sin and righteousness, and of a judgment to come. . . .It is the right of an individual to get revelations to guide himself. It is the right of the head of a family to get revelations to guide and govern his family. It is the right of an elder when he has built up a church to get revelations to guide and lead that people until he leads them and delivers them up to his superiors. An elder will always be a little in advance of those whom he has raised up if he is faithful.

He next showed how the saints are delivered up in their progress from those who give them up to the High Council, and from the High Council to the prophet, and from the prophet to the son, the elder brother, and from the son to his father. Is the keys of the kingdom taken from Joseph? Oh no; well then he still lives. He that believes in Jesus as Joseph did, they will never die. They may lay down their lives, but they still hold the keys. You are not going to be led without revelation. The prophet has stepped behind the vail and you have the right to obtain revelations for your own salvation. Who stood next to the prophet when he was here. You have all acknowledged that the Twelve were the presidents of the whole church when Joseph was not; and now he has stepped behind the vail, he is not here, and the Twelve are the presidents of the whole church. When did Joseph become a prophet? I can tell you, when he became an apostle. Years and years before he had the right of holding the keys of the Aaronic priesthood, he was a prophet, even before he was baptised. There has been a perfect flood of revelation poured from this stand all the time and you did not know it. Every spirit that confesses that Joseph Smith is a prophet, that he lived and died a prophet and that the Book of Mormon is true, is of God, and every spirit that does not is of anti-christ.

It is the test of our fellowship to believe and confess that Joseph lived and died a prophet of God in good standing; and I dont want any one to fellowship the Twelve who says that Joseph is fallen. If you dont know whose right it is to give revelations, I will tell you. It is I. There never has a man stood between Joseph and the Twelve, and unless we apostatize there never will. If Hyrum had lived he would not have stood between Joseph and the Twelve but he would have stood for Joseph.—Did Joseph ordain any man to take his place? He did. Who was it? It was Hyrum, but, Hyrum fell a martyr before Joseph did. If Hyrum had lived he would have acted for Joseph, and then when we had gone up, the Twelve would have set down at Joseph right hand, and Hyrum on the left hand. The bible says God hath set in the church, first apostles, then comes prophets, afterwards, because the keys and power of the apostleship are greater than that of the prophets. Sidney Rigdon cannot hold the keys without Joseph, if he had held the keys with Joseph and been faithful he would have been with us. If the Twelve do not apostatize they carry the keys of this kingdom wherever they go. He concluded by requesting all the brethren to tarry with us until all the business is through. . . .

The first business that we shall attend to, will be to present the several quorums before the conference, for the purpose of taking an expression of the brethren and sisters, whether they will sustain the officers according to their several appointments.

I shall therefore give way, and I am to hear motions and present them to the conference for their action: wherefore,

It was motioned by Elder Heber C. Kimball, that we as a church endeavor to carry out the principles and measures heretofore adopted and laid down by Joseph Smith as far as in us lies, praying Almighty God to help us to do it.—This motion was put to the conference by President Young and carried unanimously.

President Young said by way of explanation, that, this is as much as to say that we receive and acknowledge Joseph Smith as a Prophet of God; being called of God and maintaining his integrity and acceptance until death.

Elder H. C. Kimball then moved that we carry out all the measures of Hyrum Smith, the Prophet and Patriarch of the church, so far as in us lies, by the help of God.

This motion was also carried unanimously.

President Young said, this is an acknowledgement that he lived approved of God and died a martyr for the truth.

Elder W. W. Phelps moved that we uphold Brigham Young the president of the quorum of the Twelve, as one of the Twelve and first presidency of the church

This motion was duly seconded, and put to the church by Elder John Smith and carried unanimously. . . .

President John Smith moved that William Marks be sustained in his calling as president of this stake.

Elder W. W. Phelps objected inasmuch as the High Council had dropped him from their quorum.

Elder S. Bent explained and said the reason why the High Council dropped Elder Marks, was because he did not acknowledge the authority of the Twelve, but the authority of Elder Rigdon.

President Young said that a president of a stake could be dropped without taking his standing from him in the church. But not so with the first presidency or the Twelve. A president of a stake is only called for the time being, if you drop him he will fall back into the High Priests quorum.

The motion was then put, but there was only two votes. The contrary vote was put and carried by an overwhelming majority.

Elder H. C. Kimball moved that Elder John Smith stand as the president of this stake.—Carried unanimously. . . .

Elder G. A. Smith moved that all in the elder's quorum under the age of thirty-five should be ordained into the seventies', if they are in good standing, and worthy, and will except it. The motion was seconded and carried unanimously.

Elder H. C. Kimball stated that President Joseph Young's wife was very sick and he wished to have her blessed, that brother Young might tarry and perform the duties of his office, and if the congregation would bless her let them say amen, and all the congregation said, amen.

He then recommended all those elders who are under the age of thirty-five, and also all the priests, teachers deacons, and members, who are recommended to be ordained, to withdraw and receive an ordination into the seventies, which was done. . . .

President B. Young then said that the elders, young men who are capable of preaching, will be ordained; but do not be anxious. You must now magnify your calling. Elders who go to borrowing horses or money, and running away with it, will be cut off from the church without any ceremony. They will not have as much lenity as heretofore. The seventies will have to be subject to their presidents and council. We do not want any man to go to preaching until he is sent. If an elder wants to go to preaching, let him go into the seventies. You are all apostles to the nations, to carry the gospel; and when we send you to build up the kingdom, we will give you the keys, and power and authority. If the people will let us alone we will convert the world, and if they persecute us we will do it the quicker. I would exort all who go from this place to do right and be an honor to the cause. Inasmuch as you will go forth and do right you shall have more of the spirit than you have heretofore.—We have had a good conference; we have had beautiful weather and no accidents; and if you will go and do honor to the Lord for this, say amen; and all the people, said amen.

—Volume 5, pages 682-684, October 15, 1844;
pages 691-692, November 1, 1844;
pages 695-697, November 1, 1844.

An editorial entitled "The City of Nauvoo" sought to reassure the Saints that the church and the community were still intact and in good hands. In spite of some near hysteria at the time of the martyrdom, calm and stability, it was affirmed, had returned to bless the community once more.

Since the death of our beloved Prophet and Patriarch, many have supposed that our city would be laid desolate, or, at least that it would cease to prosper, that Mormonism would die, with its great leader, and that the Latter-day Saints would be scattered to the four winds.—The editors of the day, with few exceptions, have come to this conclusion, and some few in our midst, not being better informed, or wayward in their dispositions, have essayed to believe this egregious folly. Some few families have left us and gone to Pittsburgh, some few to the Pine Country, and a few have gone west: but since this occurrence we should think that twice as many have been added to our numbers, as those that have left, as emigration has been pouring in all the time. It is true that a momentary panic ensued immediately after that tragical event; humanity shuddered at the perpetration of so horrid a deed, a temporary gloom overspread the minds of the Saints; they felt that every principle of humanity was violated, and that they were living among a horde of savage barbarians, who were reckless alike of faith, honor and human life; their finer feelings were for a moment stunned; they considered themselves degraded, and their national honor laid prostrate in the dust, and that their nation was damned in the eyes of all nations, by such diabolical acts as had never degraded any other soil.

They felt also to mourn over the bodies of their martyred chiefs, to hang their harps upon the willows, and in their overwhelming grief to cease for a while from the common avocations of life. Their feelings over, and they awoke from their stupor, they started again into life, and every where might be seen the mechanic, the laborer, and the husbandman, following with their wonted alacrity all the various avocations of life.

Great numbers of brick houses have been, and are being put up; various branches of manufactures have been started, and every thing wears the aspect of industry, content, and prosperity.

The Temple has progressed with greater rapidity since the death of Joseph and Hyrum than ever it has done before; and things in this city never looked more prosperous.

As it regards the church, there never was more faith manifested, nor a greater degree of union than exists at the present time; the church has been more perfectly organized lately in its different quorums, there are fewer dissatisfied spirits in our midst; and peace and harmony universally prevail.

The idea of the church being disorganized and broken up because of the Prophet and Patriarch being slain, is preposterous, This church has the seeds of immortality in its midst. It is not of man, nor by man—it is the offspring of Deity: it is organized after the pattern of heavenly things, through the principles of revelation; by the opening of the heavens, by the ministering of angels, and the revelations of Jehovah. It is not affected by the death of one or two, or fifty individuals; it possesses a priesthood after the order of Melchisedec, having the power of an endless life, "without beginning of days, or end of years." It is organized for the purpose of saving this generation, and generations that are past; it exists in time and will exist in eternity. This church fail? No! Times and seasons may change, revolution may succeed revolution, thrones may be cast down, and empires be dissolved, earthquakes may rend the earth from centre to circumference, the mountains may be hurled out of their places, and the mighty ocean be moved from its bed; but amidst the crash of worlds and the crack of matter, truth, eternal truth, must remain unchanged, and those principles which God has revealed to his Saints be unscathed amidst the warring elements, and remain as firm as the throne of Jehovah.

—Volume 5, pages 743-744,

December 15, 1844.

Some Saints wondered whether Apostle William Smith, the only surviving brother of the prophet, would support Brigham Young or claim his brother's prophetic mantle for himself. For months nothing was heard from him. Then, in the December 1 issue, Editor and Apostle John Taylor was pleased to announce:

> We have just received a communication from Elder William Smith, the only surviving brother of Joseph, and one of the Quorum of the Twelve. He would have been here some time ago had it not been for the sickness of his wife: he went to the east for the purpose of recruiting her health, which, we are sorry to be informed, is fast failing. He has been laboring for some time among the eastern churches, and purposes returning here as soon as circumstances will permit.
>
> It will be his privilege when he arrives, to be ordained to the office of patriarch to the church, and to occupy the place that his brother Hyrum did, when living; and he will stand in the same relationship to the Twelve, as his brother Hyrum did to the First Presidency, after he was ordained patriarch.
>
> We sincerely sympathise with him in the loss of his brothers, and in the sickness of his family; and although he may find himself loney and desolate on his return, having lost three brothers since his departure, three of the best men in the world—yet we can assure him that his old friends the Twelve have not forgotten him; he yet lives in their remembrance, and though with him they

mourn the loss of departed friends, they will rejoice to shake him again by the hand, and to enjoy his company, and share his counsels in the city of Nauvoo.

Volume 5, page 727,

December 1, 1844.

A letter from William Smith written from Bordentown, New Jersey, to W. W. Phelps on November 10 was printed in the January 1, 1845, *Times and Seasons.*

Dear Brother:—Situated as I am in this eastern land, and far from the great emporium of the west, (Nauvoo) and I might say my home, if there is any place on earth that I might with propriety call so. But, indeed, I could say with Abraham, I have no home this side the vale, but a pilgrim and sojourner here on earth; (not exactly in tents, as the good old Patriarch with flocks and herds) a stranger without purse or scrip among strangers to build up the kingdom of God, (a most unpopular theme) and bear some humble part of this last ministry to the nations of the earth?

Can you tell, dear brother, why it is, the saints of God in all ages, and especially in these last times, can have no more rest? persecuted as they are from city to city, and from place to place; I ask myself the question, is anything criminal in Mormonism—in the divine pretensions of the prophet? this cannot be, others have professed the same; there has been hundreds of prophets, true ones too, and men have declared that if they had lived in their day, they would not have killed them; and yet, what have they not done? ("for if they will do these things in the green tree, what will they do in the dry?") But, they say, none of these signs have followed and proven him a prophet, that followed and proved them of old. What say ye, can you answer this? . . .

But it is said in Mormonism there is a charm a mystery that the world cannot explain; I admit it; it has a charm more inviting than all the magicians and sooth sayers of Egypt, and a mystery that sectarians cannot unravel. Why? Because they have not the spirit of Christ, which is the spirit of prophecy. Mormonism has inferiors, but no superiors; it acknowledges no twin-sister but heaven; no superior but God; no king but Jesus: with unparalleled

383

rapidity it has rolled on, "out-vied the muttering crowd," and accumulated its thousands, who are now rejoicing in the fulness of the gospel revealed and brought to light by the prophet Joseph.

If it should be asked, then, is Mormonism true? a thousand intelligent voices reverberate yes! yes! yes!

Again, who has gathered their thousands? built a city? two temples? and embodies a code of morals garbed with immortality, that has made its way do the imperial thrones of the earth, embosomed itself in the golden rays and unbounded glories of heaven, crowned with never fading laurels, (is it not Joseph?) Men of sound minds (not Millerites nor bigots) of all ranks, from all societies, of all the intelligence of the earth; combined in one word, the cream and salt of the same, and virtue of heaven; can this be, and Joseph Smith a false prophet?—again is heard from a thousand voices, no! no! no! . . .

I must say, I wish I could think more of Nauvoo than I do, yet it is not Nauvoo! for when I reflect that there lie the silver locks of an aged and martyred father, martyred by a Missouri persecution, in the grave, numbered with the dead; and four brothers, two of whom in my vision appear with mangled bodies, and garments red with crimson gore. Oh! the fatal steel and barbarous murder! Their blood is still unavenged, and the cruel murderers are lounging about seeking for more; what have others to expect? Yet Nauvoo contains almost all that is near to me. My poor old mother, almost worn out with years and trouble, and three sisters that remain, with myself, are all of that family, who were the founders of Mormonism and the church of Christ in these last days, through great persecution and trouble, having borne the heat of the day; and how long the rest may be spared, God only knows.

Brother Phelps, will you call and see my mother, and give her a word of consolation from me. I hope she will live till I can get to see her. She may live to see all her sons laid in the grave. Remember me also to my sisters Sophronia, Catherine, Lucy and their husbands, and the martyrs' widows—God bless them all for ever is my prayer. I wish also to be remembered to all the saints in Nauvoo, give them my prayer, that God may sustain them in all their trials, for truly they are great, and tell them to think of me their brother in affliction, and my sick family, which has kept me from their society in this their time of peril; and if the Lord does not interpose, they must ere long be numbered with the dead. Oh! that God would have mercy upon me and my sick family!

Will you pray for us, dear brethren at Nauvoo? Remember me to your family. Mrs Smith sends her love to your wife, and wishes to be remembered to all her friends in that country, as it will be a miracle if she ever sees them again. Write to me immediately.

With sentiments of respect and esteem I subscribe myself, your friend and brother in the gospel of Christ.

WM. SMITH.

—Volume 5, pages 755-757,

January 1, 1844.

Under the title "Patriarchal," William Smith addressed the church in the May 15, 1845, *Times and Seasons*. W. W. Phelps, a "junior editor" at the time, adds a lengthy note giving his view of the role of the patriarch. One particular phrase, "patriarch over the whole church," led some readers to ask whether this suggested that the patriarch should preside over the whole church, a function then being fulfilled by the Council of Twelve. A correction is published in the next issue. Here are some excerpts from Smith's original remarks, Phelps's editorial addendum, and the correction written by Editor Taylor:

Only fifteen years have passed away since the organization of the church of God in the last days: but, those years have been as ages (in suffering) to the hapless family, who were its founders. Forced to flee from their homes, they settled in Ohio, driven from thence, they founded a city in Missouri; and, banished from that land of *freedom,* they have, at last, built up a beautiful city, upon the banks of the majestic Mississippi, under the banners of Illinois; but, again have they been deceived, in this boasted land of liberty; and they have now paid the last penalty of their adherence to the commands of God. Through all these scenes the great object of their lives has continued to roll onward; cities have been built up; countries have been settled; the wilderness has been converted into a fruitful field; the desert has been made to blossom as the rose; the church has increased from six, till it now numbers two hundred thousand members; and, though all but one have sealed their testimony with their blood, yet, their works remain as a monument of their indomitable perseverance, their faith, their wisdom and their greatness.

After having myself passed through all these scenes of affliction, and seen my father and brothers laid beneath the cold sod, in consequence of the unhallowed persecutions of an inhuman mob; after having been beaten, driven, and persecuted for a long series of years; after having been compelled, so many times, by mobs, to sacrifice all this world's goods—though fifteen years of my life have been spent in the service of my fellow-men, and in the building up of the kingdom of God; though reduced to poverty and distress; and though I have suffered the loss of all I hold dear, yet, I do not complain; my trust is in the God of Israel, who will make all things work together for the good of his Saints.

Brethren, I have now settled among you—the last of the family. Shall I be sustained by this community? My health, my strength, my time and my talents have been freely spent in your service; and I am ready to do the same again, if required. Having passed the last two or three years among the eastern churches, in setting them in order, and organizing them according to the pattern laid down; and after having labored diligently in teaching them the true principles of virtue and morality, and building them up in the most holy faith, I have now returned to this city, and intend to take up my abode in your midst. As to my presidency over the eastern churches, I am confident that my precept and example have been unexceptionable in the eyes of all good Saints; my counsel both to elders and members, will, if followed out, lead them to the most exalted glory in the kingdom of God, and no individual, whether he be prophet, priest, or Pharisee, can in *truth* say aught to the contrary. My advice to all, without respect of persons, is the same now that it was then. Support and uphold the proper authorities of the church—when I say authorities, I mean the whole, and not a part; the *Twelve*, and not one, two, six, eight, ten, or eleven, but the whole *Twelve;*—follow me as I follow Christ, God being our judge. It was in accordance with the counsel and advice of my brethren, and in obedience to the calls of my old friends, that I have now settled among you. It is for you to say, whether base intriguers and vile slanderers shall deprive me of my home, my friends, and my city; it is to you I look for protection, and it is by you that I expect to be sustained. The cause of Zion, for which my brethren died, lies near my heart; its prosperity is my glory and my theme; and would to God I could see Zion arise, put on her beautiful garments, and become the glory of the earth.

My residence is on Water street, in the house formerly occupied by Mr. William Marks, where I am ready to receive the
calls of the Saints, and bestow upon them their patriarchal blessings according to the order of the priesthood.

WM. SMITH.

The office of Patriarch over the whole church is to be a father
to the church, and to confer blessings on its members, according
to the order handed down from the first of Patriarchs to the
present. By some of these, great and most marvellous events have
been predicted, which have received their fulfilment after many
generations have passed away: for instance: Jacob blessing his son
Joseph. Moses blessing the tribes of Israel, &c, &c.

Father Smith, the first Patriarch and Hyrum his successor conferred many blessing upon the Saints that made their hearts glad.
But they, in the wisdom of God, have been called away, and
William the son and brother succeeds them. How many, now will
say, I wish I had my patriarchal blessing? This has been the
lamentation of many since the death of Joseph and Hyrum. William is the last of the family, and truly inherits the blood and
spirit of his father's house, as well as the priesthood and patriarchal office from his father and brother, legally, and by heredi-
tary descent.

It may not be amiss to give the readers of the Times and
Seasons, a few ideas relative to the office of a patriarch. The
sectarian world without a priesthood, are, of course, with a
patriarch just as they are without the power to administer in
spiritual blessing; but in all churches holding the keys of the
everlasting priesthood, a patriarch is set apart to bless the people;
and his descent, according to right of lineage, by blood and birth-
right, is from father to son. . . .

—Volume 5, pages 904, 905,

May 15, 1845.

PATRIARCHAL

Since the publication of the last *Times and Seasons,* we have
frequently been interrogated about the meaning of some remarks
made by Eld. Wm. Smith in an article headed patriarchal, and also
concerning some expressions in the editorial connected therewith;

and as the nature of the office of Patriarch, does not seem to be fully understood, we thought a little explanation on this point might not be amiss.

So far as the editorial is concerned it was written rather hastily by our junior editor, W. W. Phelps, and did not come under our notice until after it was published. There are some expressions contained in it, which might have been worded better and have rendered it less subject to criticism; but he assures us that no such intention was intended to be conveyed as that which is conceived by some. And concerning Brother Wm. Smith, we are better acquainted with him, and with his views, than to believe that he intended to convey any such idea as the one which some persons would put upon, or gather from his sayings.

In regard to the office of Patriarch, William Smith has been ordained Patriarch to the church; but he is not the only Patriarch, but would act as a senior Patriarch, holding the keys of that priesthood; and his labors would be more especially connected with the church in Zion; and he would take the lead, priority, or presidency of the Patriarchal office in this place; and in this capacity if there should be a council of Patriarchs, he as a matter of course would preside by right of office—But every legally ordained Patriarch has the same right to bless that he has, and their administrations are just as legal as his are. . . .

We have been asked, "Does not patriarch *over* the *whole* church" place Brother William Smith at the head of the whole church as president?

Ans. No. Brother William is not patriarch *over* the *whole* church; but patriarch to the church, and as such he was ordained. The expression "over the whole church," is a mistake made by W. W. Phelps. He is patriarch to the church of Jesus Christ of Latter-day Saints. The Twelve are commanded to ordain evangelical ministers in all large branches of the church abroad, and who has charge over them, the patriarch? No. Those who ordained them, and to whom is committed the power and authority to regulate all the affairs of the churches abroad. And who has the charge of the whole priesthood here? Ans. The presidency of the church; and not the patriarch. . . .

The president of the church presides over all patriarchs, presidents, and councils of the church; and this presidency does not depend so much upon genealogy as upon calling, order, and seniority. James and Joses were the brothers of Jesus, and John was his beloved disciple, yet Peter held the keys and presided over all the church. Br. William was in the Quorum of the Twelve yet he was not president of the Twelve during his brother's lifetime, nor since; and if being ordained a patriarch would make him president of the church, it would have made Father Joseph Smith and Hyrum Smith, presidents over the church instead of Joseph.

Br. William understands the matter, and were it not for the folly of some men there would be no necessity for these remarks.

A Patriarch is what is termed in scripture an evangelist, and Br. William acts in that capacity, and God placed in the church "first apostles," not first evangelists, but the president stands in the same relationship to the church as Moses did to the children of Israel, according to the revelations.

Again, who ordained Father Smith to the office of patriarch? His son Joseph: and Father Smith ordained Hyrum, and the Twelve (of whom Br. William is one) ordained him.—Who are appointed to ordain evangelical ministers? (See page 104 D. C.) Can a stream rise higher than its fountain? No. Says Paul, "verily the less is blessed of the better."

We think that every one will see that Br. William Smith's patriarchal office will not exalt him higher in regard to priesthood than he was before, as one of the Twelve; but will rather change the nature of his office.

But will it take any thing from his priesthood? it may be asked. No. You cannot take any man's priesthood away without transgression. Br. William will still retain the same power, priesthood and authority that he did before, and yet will hold in connexion with that the patriarchal office and the keys of that priesthood, and as one of the Twelve must maintain his dignity as one of the presidents of the church, of whom President Brigham Young is the president and head, and presides over all patriarchs, presidents and councils of the church.

—Volume 6, pages 920-922,

June 1, 1845.

The last chapter in William Smith's tenuous relationship to the church leadership at Nauvoo was written at the general conference in October of 1845.

> It was next moved, that William Smith be continued and sustained as one of the Twelve Apostles; seconded. Whereupon Elder Pratt arose and said, I have an objection to Brother William continuing in that office. I feel, as an individual, that I cannot, conscientiously, uphold and sustain Brother William as one of the Twelve Apostles, until he thinks different from what he does now. I have many reasons for this, but I will merely mention one or two, which must suffice for the present. In the first place, I have proof positive that he is an aspiring man; that he aspires to uproot and undermine the legal Presidency of the church, that he may occupy the place himself. This he has avowed openly in the east, which I can prove by good and substantial witnesses. In the second place, while Brother William was in the east, to my certain knowledge, his doctrine and conduct have not had a savory influence; but have produced death and destruction wherever he went. This also I am well prepared to prove. I have been waiting in all long suffering, for an alteration in Brother William's course, but up to the present time, I have been disappointed. For these two reasons, I would plead for one, that we no longer sustain him in his office, till a proper investigation can be had, and he make satisfaction. I do this individually; I leave others to do as they please. The motion being seconded, a vote was then taken to sustain him, but was lost unanimously.

> —Volume 6, page 1008,
>
> November 1, 1845.

William Smith later attempted to set up his own church and for a while was also associated with James J. Strang's movement. Never again was William to command the loyalty of large numbers of Latter Day Saints. For some observers William Smith became one of the most tragic figures in an era of church history marked by dissension and division.

The position of Brigham Young as leader of the majority body of Saints at Nauvoo was recognized by the poetic affirmation of Eliza R. Snow, who was later to become one of President Young's wives.

TO PRESIDENT BRIGHAM YOUNG.

BY MISS ELIZA R. SNOW

An important station is truly thine,
And the weight of thy calling can none define:
Being call'd of the Lord o'er the Twelve to preside,
And with them over all of the world beside.

Like Elisha of old, when Elijah fled
In a chariot of fire, thou hast lost thy head;
Lost thy head? O no! thou art left to prove
To the gods, thy integrity, faith, and love.

Thou hast gain'd, like Elisha, a rich behest,
For the mantle of Joseph seems to rest
Upon thee, while the spirit and pow'r divine,
That inspir'd his heart, is inspiring thine.

The great work which he laid the foundation to
Is unfinished, and resting on thee to do—
With thy brethren, the Twelve, thou wilt bear it forth
To the distant nations of the earth.

Kings, princes, and nobles will honor thee.
And thy name will be great on the isles of the sea—
The pure light of intelligence thou wilt spread
Will exalt the living and save the dead.

The great spirit of truth, will direct thy ways,
Generations to come, will repeat thy praise—
When thy work is completed on earth, thou'll stand
In thy station appointed at God's right hand.

—Volume 6, page 815,

February 15, 1845.

DOCTRINAL DEVELOPMENTS

During the April general conference of 1844, a funeral sermon in memory of Elder King Follett was preached by Joseph Smith. A report of his remarks was published in the August 15, 1844, *Times and Seasons.* Some distinctive notions of the nature of God and man were presented in the report, as can be seen from the following:

> The president having arrived; the choir sung a hymn. Elder A. Lyman offered prayer.
>
> The president then arose and called the attention of the congregation upon the subjects which were contemplated in the fore part of the conference. As the wind blows very hard, it will be hardly possible for me to make you all hear unless there is profound attention. It is of the greatest importance, and the most solemn of any that can occupy our attention, and that is, the subject of the dead; on the decease of our brother Follett, who was crushed to death in a well, I have been requested to speak by his friends and relatives, and inasmuch as there are a great many in this congregation who live in this city, as well as elsewhere, and who have lost friends, I feel disposed to speak on the subject in general, and offer you my ideas so far as I have ability, and so far as I shall be inspired by the Holy Spirit to dwell on this subject. I want your prayers and faith, the instruction of Almighty God and the gift of the Holy Ghost, that I may set forth things that are true, that can easily be comprehended, and shall carry the testimony to your hearts; pray that the Lord may strengthen my lungs, stay the winds and let the prayers of the saints to heaven appear, that it may enter into the ear of the Lord of Sabaoth; for the effectual prayers of righteous men availeth much, and I verily believe that your prayers shall be heard before I enter into the investigation fully of the subject that is laying before me. Before entering fully into the investigation, I wish to pave the way: I will make a few preliminaries, in order that you may understand the subject when I come to it. I do not calculate to please your ears with superfluity of words or oratory, or with much learning; but I calculate to edify you with the simple truths from heaven. In the first place, I wish to go back to the beginning of creation; there is the starting point, in order to be fully acquainted with the mind, purposes, decrees, &c. of the great Eloheim, that sits in yonder

heavens, it is necessary for us to have an understanding of God himself in the beginning. If we start right, it is easy to go right all the time; but if we start wrong, it is a hard matter to get right. There are a very few beings in the world who understand rightly the character of God. They do not comprehend any thing, that which is past, or that which is to come; and consequently, but little above the brute beast. If a man learns nothing more than to eat, drink, sleep, and does not comprehend any of the designs of God, the beast comprehends the same thing; it eats, drinks, sleeps, knows nothing more; yet knows as much as we, unless WE are able to comprehend by the inspiration of Almighty God. I want to go back to the beginning, and so lift your minds into a more lofty sphere, a more exalted understanding; that what the human mind generally understands. I want to ask this congregation, every man, woman and child, to answer the question in their own heart, what kind of a being is God? ask yourselves. I again repeat the question, what kind of a being is God?

First, God himself, who sits enthroned in yonder heavens, is a man like unto one of yourselves, that is the great secret. If the vail was rent to-day, and the great God, who holds this world in its orbit, and upholds all things by his power; if you were to see him to-day, you would see him in all the person, image and very form as a man; for Adam was created in the very fashion and image of God; Adam received instruction, walked, talked and conversed with him, as one man talkes and communes with another.

In order to understand the subject of the dead, for the consolation of those who mourn for the loss of their friends, it is necessary they should understand the character and being of God, for I am going to tell you how God came to be God. We have imagined that God was God from all eternity. These are incomprehensible ideas to some, but they are the simple and first principles of the gospel, to know for a certainty the character of God, that we may converse with him as one man with another, and that God himself; the Father of us all dwelt on an earth the same as Jesus Christ himself did, and I will show it from the Bible. I wish I had the trump of an arch angel, I could tell the story in such a manner that persecution would cease forever; what did Jesus say? (mark it elder Rigdon;) Jesus said, as the Father hath power in himself, even so hath the Son power; to do what? why what the Father did, that answer is obvious; in a manner to lay down his body and take it up again. Jesus what are you going to do? To lay down my life, as my Father did, and take it up again.—If you do not believe it, you do not believe the Bible; the scriptures say it, and I defy all the learning and wisdom, all the combined powers of earth and hell together, to refute it. Here then is eternal life, to know the only wise and true God. You have got to learn how to be Gods yourselves; to be kings and priests to God, the same as all Gods have done; by going from a small degree to another, from grace to grace, from exaltation to exaltation, until you are able to sit in glory as doth those who sit enthroned in everlasting power; and I want you to know that God in the last days, while certain individuals are proclaiming his name, is not trifling with you or me; it is the first principles of consolation. How consoling to the mourner, when they are called to part with a husband, wife, father, mother, child or dear relative, to know, that although the earthly tabernacle shall be dissolved, that they shall rise in immortal glory, not to sorrow, suffer or die any more, but they shall be heirs of God and joint heirs with Jesus Christ. What is it? to inherit the same glory, the same power and the same exaltation, until you ascend the throne of eternal power the same as those who are gone before. . . .

I suppose I am not allowed to go into an investigation of any thing that is not contained in the Bible, and I think there are so many wise men here, who would put me to death for treason; so I shall turn commentator to-day; I shall comment on the very first Hebrew word in the Bible; I will make a comment on the very first sentence of the history of creation in the Bible, *Berosheit*. I want to analyze the word; *baith*, in, by, through, in, and every thing else. *Rosh*, the head. *Sheit*, gramatical termination. When the inspired man wrote it, he did not put the *baith* there. A man, a Jew without any authority, thought it too bad to begin to talk about the *head*. It read first, 'The head one of the Gods brought forth the Gods,' that is the true meaning of the words. *Baurau*, signifies to bring forth. If you do not believe it, you do not believe the learned man of God. No man can learn you more than what I have told you. Thus the head God brought forth the Gods in the grand council. I will simplify it in the English language. Oh ye lawyers! ye doctors! who have persecuted me; I want to let you know that the Holy Ghost knows something as well as you do. The head God called together the Gods, and set in grand council. The grand counsellors sat in yonder heavens, and contemplated the creation of the worlds that were created at that time. When I say doctors and lawyers, I mean the doctors and lawyers of the scripture. I have done so hitherto, to let the lawyers flutter, and every body laugh at them. Some learned doctor might take a notion to say, the scriptures say thus and so, and are not to be altered, and I am going to show you an error. I have an old book of the New Testament in the Hebrew, Latin, German and Greek. I have been reading the German and find it to be the most correct, and it corresponds nearest to the revelations I have given for the last fourteen years. . . .

I have another subject to dwell upon and it is impossible for me to say much, but I shall just touch upon them; for time will not permit me to say all; so I must come to the resurrection of the dead, the soul, the mind of man, the immortal spirit. All men say God created it in the beginning. The very idea lessens man in my estimation; I do not believe the doctrine, I know better. Hear it all ye ends of the world, for God has told me so. I will make a man appear a fool before I get through, if you dont believe it. I am going to tell of things more noble—we say that God himself is a self existing God; who told you so? it is correct enough, but how did it get into your heads? Who told you that man did not exist in like manner upon the same principles? (refers to the old Bible,) how does it read in the Hebrew? It dont say so in the Hebrew, it says God made man out of the earth, and put into him Adam's spirit, and so became a living body.

The mind of man is as immortal as God himself. I know that my testimony is true, hence when I talk to these mourners; what have they lost, they are only seperated from their bodies for a short season; their spirits existed coequal with God, and they now exist in a place where they converse together, the same as we do on the earth. Is it logic to say that a spirit is immortal, and yet have a beginning? Because if a spirit have a beginning it will have an end; good logic. I want to reason more on the spirit of man, for I am dwelling on the body of man, on the subject of the dead. I take my ring from my finger and liken it unto the mind of man, the immortal spirit, because it has no beginning. Suppose you cut it in two; but as the Lord lives there would be an end.—All the fools, learned and wise men, from the beginning of creation, who say that man had a beginning, proves that he must have an end and then the doctrine of annihilation would be true. But, if I am right I might with boldness proclaim from the house tops, that God never did have power to create the spirit of man at all. God himself could not create himself: intelligence exists upon a self existent principle, it is a spirit from age to age, and there is no creation about it. All the spirits that God ever sent into the world are susceptible of enlargement. The first principles of man are self existent with God; that God himself finds himself in the midst of spirits and glory, because he was greater, and because he saw proper to institute laws, whereby the rest could have a privilege to advance like himself, that they might have one glory upon another, in all that knowledge, power, and glory, &c., in order to save the world of spirits. I know that when I tell you these words of eternal life, that are given to me, I know you taste it and I know you believe it. You say honey is sweet and so do I. I can also taste the spirit of eternal life; I know it is good, and when I tell you of these things, that were given me by inspiration of the Holy Spirit, you are bound to receive it as sweet, and I rejoice more and more.

I want to talk more of the relation of man to God. I will open your eyes in relation to your dead; all things whatsoever God of his infinite wisdom has seen proper to reveal to us, while we are dwelling in mortality, in regard to our mortal bodies, are revealed to us in the abstract and independent of affinity of this mortal tabernacle; but are revealed to us as if we had no bodies at all, and those revelations which wil save our dead will save our bodies; and God reveals them to us in view of no eternal dissolution of the body; hence the responsibility, the awful responsibility, that rests upon us in relation to our dead: for all the spirits who have not obeyed the gospel in the flesh, must either obey the gospel or be damned. Solemn thought, dreadful thought. Is there nothing to be done; no salvation for our fathers and friends who have died and not obeyed the decrees of the Son of Man? Would to God that I had forty days and nights to tell you all, I would let you know that I am not a fallen prophet. What kind of characters are those who can be saved although their bodies are decaying in the grave? When his commandments teach us, it is in view of eternity. The greatest responsibility in this world that God has laid upon us, is to seek after our dead.—The apostle says, they without us cannot be made perfect. . . .

We have reason to have the greatest hope and consolations for our dead, for we have aided them in the first principles; for we have seen them walk in our midst, and seen them sink asleep in the arms of Jesus. And hence is the glory of the sun. You mourners have occasion to rejoice; (speaking of the death of Elder King Follett,) for your husband is gone to wait until the resurrection; and your expectations and hope are far above what man can conceive: for why has God revealed it to us? I am authorised to say by the authority of the Holy Ghost, that you have no occasion to fear, for he is gone to the home of the just. Don't mourn: don't weep. I know it by the testimony of the Holy Ghost that is within me. Rejoice O Israel! your friends shall triumph gloriously, while their murderers shall welter for ages. I say this for the benefit of strangers. I have a father, brothers, and friends who are gone to a world of spirits. They are only absent for a moment; they are in the spirit, and when we depart we shall hail our mothers, fathers, friends, and all whom we love.—There will be no fear or mobs, &c., but all will be an eternity of felicity. Mothers you shall have your children, for they shall have eternal life: for their debt is paid, there is no damnation awaits them, for they are in the spirit.—As the child dies, so shall it rise from the dead and be forever living in the learning of God, it shall be the child, the same as it was before it died out of your arms. Children dwell and exercise power in the same form as they laid them down. The baptism of water without the baptism of fire and the Holy Ghost attending it is of no use: they are necessary. He must be born of water and the spirit in order to get into the kingdom of God.

I have intended my remarks to all; both rich and poor, bond and free, great and small. I have no enmity against any man. I love you all. I am your best friend, and if persons miss their mark, it is their own fault. If I reprove a man and he hates me, he is a fool, for I love all men, especially these my brethren and sisters. I rejoice in bearing the testimony of my aged friends. You never knew my heart; no man knows my history; I cannot tell it. I shall never undertake it; if I had not experienced what I have I should not have known it myself. I never did harm any man since I have been born in the world. My voice is always for peace, I cannot lie down until all my work is finished. I never think any evil, nor any thing to the harm of my fellow man.—When I am called at the trump of the ark-angel, and weighed in the balance, you will all know me then. I add no more. God bless you all. Amen.

—Volume 5, pages 612-617,

August 15, 1844.

This kind of theological reflection received support from other sources in the *Times and Seasons*, although most of the doctrinal material in later issues appears to be more in the traditional style and thought world of the earlier statements of faith. Note, however, how these two poems seem grounded in the theological orientation developed in the King Follett funeral sermon.

POETRY.

Tune—'*The rose that all are praising.*'
The God that others worship is not the God for me;
He has no parts nor body and cannot hear nor see;—
    But I've a God that lives above—
    A God of power and of love,—
A God of Revelation—O, that's the God for me:
O, that's the God for me; O, that's the God for me.

A church without Apostles is not the church for me;
It's like a ship dismasted, afloat upon the sea.
    But I've a church that's always led,
    By the twelve stars around her head;—
A church with good foundations—O, that's the church for me—
O, that's the church for me, &c.

A church without a Prophet is not the church for me;
It has no head to lead it, in it I would not be;—
    But I've a church not built by men,
    Cut from the mountain without hands;
A church with gifts and blessings—O, that's the church for me. &c.

The hope that Gentiles cherish is not the hope for me;
It has no faith nor knowledge, far from it I would be.
    But I've a hope that will not fail,
    That reaches safe within the veil,—
Which hope is like an anchor—O, that's the hope for me, &c.

The heaven of sectarians is not the heaven for me;
So doubtful its location, neither on land nor sea.
    But I've a heaven on the earth—
    The land and home that gave me birth.—
A heaven of light and knowledge—O, that's the heaven for me, &c.

A church without a gathering is not the church for me;
The Savior would not own it, wherever it might be.
    But I've a church that's called out,
    From false traditions, fears and doubts,
A gathering dispensation—O, that's the church for me, &c.

—Volume 6, page 799,

February 1, 1845.

MY FATHER IN HEAVEN;

BY MISS ELIZA R. SNOW

O my Father, thou that dwellest
  In the high and glorious place:
When shall I regain thy presence,
  And again behold thy face?
In thy holy habitation
  Did my spirit once reside?
In my *first* primeval childhood
  Was I nurtur'd near thy side?

For a wise and glorious purpose
  Thou hast plac'd me here on earth,
And withheld the recolleection
  Of my former friends and birth:
Yet oft times a secret something
  Whispered you're a stranger here;
And I felt that I had wandered
  From a more exalted sphere.

I had learn'd to call thee father
  Through thy spirit from on high;
But until the key of knowledge
  Was restor'd, I knew not why.
In the heav'ns are parents single?
  No, the thought makes reason stare;
Truth is reason—truth eternal
  Tells me I've a mother there.

When I leave this frail existence—
  When I lay this mortal by,
Father, mother, may I meet you
  In your royal court on high?
Then, at length, when I've completed
  All you sent me forth to do,
With your mutual approbation
  Let me come and dwell with you.

City of Joseph, Oct. 1845.

—Volume 6, page 1039,

November 15, 1845.

Funeral sermons and conference talks are perhaps the most fruitful areas for study when attempting to determine what was being discussed and believed among the Saints, since the typical doctrinal article in the church publications was written with a nonmember clientele in mind and was carefully worded so as to avoid offending their theological sensitivities. We shall look, then, at another example of doctrinal exposition via a funeral sermon. Caroline Smith, wife of William Smith, died on May 24, 1845. Orson Pratt, later to gain fame as one of the most scholarly defenders of the Mormon faith, preached the funeral message.

> At half past 9 o'clock A. M., on Saturday the 24th ult., a lengthy procession of carriages was formed in front of the residence of Mrs. Emma Smith, widow of the martyred Joseph Smith, at the front of which rested, upon a hearse, the coffin that contained the lifeless remains of Mrs. Caroline Smith, deceased wife of Elder William Smith, of the quorum of the Twelve.
>
> At 7 o'clock P. M., of Thursday previous, her spirit took its flight to the spirit world, leaving her companion, two daughters, and numerous relatives and friends to mourn her loss.
>
> The procession moved on slowly and majestically, and arrived at the stand east of the Temple, where it halted. The corpse was conveyed in front of the stand; the mourners were seated around it, and at 10 o'clock the services were opened by prayer from Elder Page.
>
> After singing, Elder Orson Pratt arose and delivered an address, of which the following is the substance:—
>
> "We will read a few passages of scripture contained in the seventh chapter of the revelations of St. John, commencing at the ninth verse. [He read the remainder of the chapter.]
>
> The words of our text, which will be a foundation upon which to predicate some remarks upon the present occasion, will be found in the forty-fourth verse of the fifteenth chapter of Paul's Epistle to the Corinthians: 'It is sown a natural body; it is raised a spiritual body. There is a natural body, and there is a spiritual body.'
>
> Brethren, sisters and friends,—we have assembled ourselves together, this morning, upon this solemn and important occasion, to pay our last earthly respects so a beloved sister, whose remains now lay before us. It is a custom among the nations of the earth

to witness their respect for deceased friends by following them to the place of interment, and it is also a custom with the Saints of the Most High God, to assemble themselves together to hear a word of consolation and instruction upon such occasions.

It may not be amiss to make a few remarks, this morning, upon the subject of the resurrection of the dead. In reflecting upon this subject, the mind is led to inquire: why is it that the human family are subject to death, to a separation of soul and body? Why is it that the plan of the resurrection was devised? These are questions of vast importance, and are gratifying to be understood.

Death is no part of the original plan of salvation; that is, the Almighty did not decree it from before the foundation of the world, independent of the agency of man. But it has been entailed upon us as a curse; not in consequence of our own transgressions, but in consequence of the transgression of our first parents in the garden of Eden.

In the morning of creation all things were pronounced good by the Creator, as they rolled into organized existence unsullied and without a curse. Man, the last and noblest of God's creation was placed in the garden of Eden, being goverened by laws and restricted by commandments, not being subject to sickness, disease, or death. Adam was placed upon the earth an immortal being. He was placed in the garden to dress, beautify and adorn it, and to hold the supremacy of power over all the things of God's creation.

Instead of our first parents eating animal food, they subsisted upon herbs and the fruits of the earth, which were originally designed for the food of man, and had they not transgressed they would have both been living upon the earth at the present day, as fair, as healthy, as beautiful and as free from sickness and death, as they were previous to the transgression. What was that transgression? It was violating a single commandment of God, and disregarding the counsel of those immortal beings who stood above them in authority. The Creator placed in the garden a certain tree and warned Adam that in the day he eat the fruit thereof he should surely die. He commanded him not to eat the fruit. His was a simple commandment; but the violation of it subjected Adam to a fall from his exalted station in the favor of God. Consequently a curse was passed upon all created things, and in the posterity of Adam were sown the seeds of dissolution. . . .

Having examined briefly the origin and extent of the curse, let us now examine the extent of its duration, and see if any way has been devised by which it will ever be removed. For if there has not been a plan devised, then there is no resurrection of the dead; for the effect of the curse upon Adam and his posterity was a final and complete destruction of the body. When death ensued, the spirit took its departure from the body, never to be united with it again.—This was to be the deplorable condition of the human family, and this would have been their fate, had not an atonement been made, and a plan of redemption been devised. But, thanks be to the great Ruler of heaven and earth, an atonement has been made and a plan has been devised, by which the human family will be redeemed from the curse and be brought up from their graves in a state of immortality and eternal life. Dry up your tears, brethren and sisters; let your hearts rejoice with the assurance that we soon shall meet with those for whom we mourn, never more to be separated by death—Were it not for this atonement, it would be far better for our spirits had they never taken tabernacles. Deplorable would have been our condition to all eternity.

The spirit of the Savior, from the eternal world, looked down upon the condition of the human family, and in order that they might be redeemed he offered to come into the world, take a tabernacle and lay down his life as an atonement for the transgression of Adam. His was a pure and holy Spirit, having never been sullied by the commission of sin, therefore the grave could not retain him. He came and did the will of the Father, lived without the commission of sin, laid down his life for the sins of the world; therefore was the atonement complete and the redemption universal.

What is to be understood by the terms spiritual body? I am aware that this is a difficult question to answer. The sectarian would suppose that a spirit is something capable of being every where present; that it can fly away beyond the bounds of time and space,' and be present there at the same time that it is present with us here. But as for the Saints of the Most High God, we do not believe in the existence of any place or thing 'beyond the bounds of time and space,' neither do we believe in any immateriality, being connected with any of the creations of God. We believe that spirit is as much a substance as the earth on which we move, yet it is of a more refined substance and nature;—so refined that mortal eyes cannot behold; but when our sight becomes celestialized and strengthened, then can we behold spirit as distinctly as we now can behold one another.—What did Paul mean when he said it should be raised a spiritual body? Did he mean that the flesh and bone that would be raised would be spirit? No: But he meant that after bone had come together to its bone, and flesh and sinews had come upon the bones and they had been covered with skin, according to Ezekiel, that the form would be quickened to life by the spirit of God, which would constitute it a spiritual body.

Some people suppose that when a person dies his spirit enters immediately into those high degrees of glory, designed for them from before the foundation of the world. This is a mistaken idea. If you will examine the Bible, the Book of Mormon and the Book of Doctrine and Covenants, you will find that there is but very little recorded relative to the situation of the spirit after it leaves the body, before it again unites with the same. But it is revealed in the Book of Mormon that the spirit goes back to the Father of all spirits, and finds a place of rest, where it will remain until the resurrection, when it will again possess the body that it laid down in consequence of the curse, and thus be prepared to enter upon higher exaltations and glories in the eternal world. During the period of this separation the sprit will not be employed in ministering to beings of flesh and bone; but they will minister to their own kind; they will be ministers to the world of spirits, preaching the gospel to those who did not embrace it previous to their separation from their bodies. How do you think the spirit of the Savior spent the three days that intervened between his crucifixion and his resurrection? Did he sit down in his Father's kingdom and do nothing but slap his hands and sing praises? His Father unfolded to him the world of spirits. He looked upon them and saw that they were his lawful, legitimate brothers and sisters in the spirit, that they all descended from the same Father, and he possessed the natural feeling of anxiety to redeem his kindred from their situation. The Father commissioned him to preach the gospel to them and show them the plan by which they could be brought up in the resurrection and prepare themselves for higher glories. This is the way that he spent the time, and this is the way that every person who holds the priesthood will spend the time that intervenes between his death and his resurrection. The spirits of men are not all that will be employed in this delightful task; but you too, my sisters, will take a part therein, for you will hold a portion of the priesthood with your husbands, and you will thus do a work, as well as they, that will augment that glory which you will enjoy after your resurrection. . . .

Our beloved sister, whose remains are now before us, has fallen
asleep with the assurance of a glorious resurrection, and she will
come up, being numbered with those who have washed their
robes and made them white in the blood of the Lamb, having
passed through great tribulations. She has a right to this honor.
She passed through the Missouri persecutions, with her companion, and was ever faithful and true to the cause of God. Her
constitution was destroyed in consequence of the hardships she
there endured. Soon after she came to Illinois, she was taken sick
with the dropsy, which continued to prey upon her system, and
something like two years ago, through the advice and counsel of
her friends, she went with her husband to the east, for the purpose of recovering her health. Some two weeks ago she returned
to this city. Every exertion was made to restore her to health; but
her disease was of so long standing, and had become so settled
upon her system, that it was impossible to restore her, and her
spirit was called back to the world of spirits, to await that period
when she shall be called forth from her grave by the power of the
priesthood, to join again with her companion and friends in a
state of immortality, to be crowned with celestial honors in the
kingdom of our God."

—Volume 6, pages 918-920,

June 1, 1845.

A conference sermon that the editor felt merited publication in full was Brigham Young's address on baptism for the
dead and temple work, given at the April 1845 conference.

SPEECH

*Delivered by President B. Young, in the City of Joseph, April 6th
1845.*

I hope there may be faith enough in this congregation of
Saints to still the wind, and strengthen me so that I may be heard
by all of this vast assemblage of people; and in order that my
voice may extend, and be heard by all it will be necessary for the
brethren and sisters to be as quiet as possible, and I will do my
best to speak that you may all hear and understand.

We shall devote this day to preaching—exhoration—singing—
praying and blessing children. (such as have not been blessed,)
and all those who have not been able to come to meeting: such

women may be, who have not had their children blessed, and have the privilege this afternoon.

Last Sunday I proposed to the Saints, to speak to day on the subject of the baptism for the dead in connexion with other items, that the Saints may be satisfied—that all doubt and darkness may be removed with regard to certain principles of the doctrine of redemption.

But before I undertake to explain or give correct views upon this important subject, I would say to all those who are satisfied with all the knowledge they have, and want no more: to you I do not expect to be an apostle this day; but for those who are hungering and thirsting after righteousness, I pray, that they may be filled and satisfied with the intelligence of God, even his glory.

What I have stated in the winter past relative to the baptism for the dead, has been a matter of discussion among the elders, and among the brethren and sisters in general, but I will endeavor to show to this congregation of Saints the propriety of it; and that the people could not run at hap-hazard, and without order to attend to this ordinance and at the same time it be valid, and recognized in heaven.

We are building a house at present unto the Lord in the which we expect to attend to the fulfilment of this doctrine; you all believe that this is a doctrine revealed by God to his servant Joseph. Admitting this to be the fact, that he has revealed through him a plan by which we may bring to life the dead, and bless them with a great and glorious exaltation in the presence of the Almighty with ourselves; still we want to know how to do these things right; to do them in a manner that shall be acceptable to the Almighty, if otherwise he will say unto us at the last day, "ye have not known me right, because of your slothfulness and your wickedness depart from me for I know you not." O ye Latter-day Saints! I don't want one of you to be caught in that snare, but that you may do things right, and thus be enabled to make your calling and election sure. I might say the plan of salvation is perfect of itself—it is a system that can save, redeem, honor and glorify all who are willing to apply themselves to it according to the pattern—it is a plan of salvation to all men both male and female: it has been handed down, and known from the days of Adam, and those who will open heir eyes to see, their ears to hear, and their hearts to understand, they will acknowledge at once that it is a perfect system; but those whose eyes, ears and hearts are shut up by incorrect tradition and prejudice, they acknowledge by their lives, by their practices, by their walk and conversation, and by their actions in general, that they do not understand it, yet they plead the atonement, and say we believe the atonement is sufficient for all—only believe and he will save you; yet at the same time the bible, reason, common sense and every other righteous principle positively testifies that there must be means made use of to put you in possession of the blessings of the atonement, as well as any other blessing. . . .

I do not say that you have not been taught and learned the principle; you have heard it taught from this stand from time to time, by many of the elders, and from the mouth of our beloved and martyred prophet Joseph; therefore my course will not be to prove the doctrine, but refer to those things against which your minds are revolting. Consequently I would say to this vast congregation of Saints, when we enter into the Temple of God to receive our washings, our anointings, our endowments and baptisms for the saving of ourselves, and for the saving of our dead; that you never will see a man go forth to be baptized for a woman, nor a woman for a man. If your minds should be in any dubiety with regard to this, call to mind a principle already advanced, that when an infinite being gives a law to his finite creatures, he has to descend to the capacity of those who receive his law, when the doctrine of baptism for the dead was first given, this church was in its infancy, and was not capable of receiving all the knowledge of God in its highest degree; this you all believe. I would keep this one thing in your minds, and that is, that there is none, no not one of the sons and daughters of Adam and Eve, that ever received the fullness of the celestial law at the first of the Lord's commencing to reveal it unto them.

The doctrine of baptism for the dead you have been taught for some time, and the first account that I heard of it was while I was in England; It was there I got the glad tidings that the living could go forth and be baptised for those who had fallen asleep. This doctrine I believed before anything was said or done about it in this church; it made me glad when I heard it was revealed through his servant Joseph, and that I could go forth, and officiate for my fathers, for my mothers, and for my ancestors, to the latest generation who have not had the privilege of helping themselves; that they can yet arise to the state of glory and exaltation as we that live, have a privilege of rising to ourselves. The next year I came home and requested Brother Joseph to preach upon the subject, which he did, I also heard many of the elders preach upon the same subject. . . .

Joseph in his life time did not receive every thing connected with the doctrine of redemption, but he has left the key with those who understand how to obtain and teach to this great people all that is necessary for their salvation and exaltation in the celestial kingdom of our God. We have got to learn how to be faithful with the few things, you know the promise is, if we are faithful in a few things we shall be made rulers over many things. If we improve upon the small things, greater will be given unto us.

I have said that a man cannot be baptized for a woman, nor a woman for a man, and it be valid. I have not used any argument as yet; I want now to use an argument upon this subject, it is a very short one; and I will do it by asking this congregation, if God would call a person to commence a thing that would not have power and ability to carry it out? Would he do it? (no.) Well then, what has been our course on former occasions? Why, here goes our beloved sisters, and they are baptised in the river or in the fount for their uncles, for their fathers, for their grand-fathers and great grandfathers.

Well, now I will take you and confirm you for your uncles, for your fathers, for your grandfathers, and for your great grand-fathers, and let you go; after a while here comes our beloved sisters, saying, I want to be ordained for my uncle, and for my father, and for my grandfather, and great grand-father; I want my father ordained to the high priesthood, and my grandfather, I want to be patriarch, and you may ordain me a prophet for my uncle! What would you think about all that, sisters, come now you have been baptised and confirmed for your father, wont you be ordained for him? You could cast on a stocking and finish it.—You could take wool and card and spin it and make it into cloth, and then make it into garments A person that commences a work and has not ability and power to fiinish it, only leaves the unfinished remains as a monument of folly. We will not commence a work we cannot finish; but let us hearken to the voice of the spirit and give heed to his teachings and we will make ourselves perfect in all things.

I would now call your attention to some of the sayings of the apostle Paul. I hope you will not stumble at them. Paul says, "nevertheless, neither is the man without the woman, neither the woman without the man, in the Lord, for as the woman is of the man, even so is the man also by the women, but all things of God." The same Apostle also says, "The woman is the glory of the man." Now brethren, these are Paul's sayings, not Joseph Smith's spiritual wife system sayings.

And I would say, as no man can be perfect without the woman, so no woman can be perfect without a man to lead her, I tell you the truth as it is in the bosom of eternity; and I say so to every man upon the face of the earth: if he wishes to be saved he cannot be saved without a woman by his side. This is spiritual wife *ism,* that is, the doctrine of spiritual wives.

Lest these my sisters should think I give power into the hands of their husbands to abuse them, I would say there is no man has a right to govern his wife and family unless he does it after the order of the church of Christ, unless he does it upon this principle he need not expect to receive a celestial glory. He that does not govern as Jesus governs his church, breaks his bonds and solemn obligations to his family.

Now ye elders of Israel will you go and beat your wives? will you neglect and abuse them? You may ask, is that anything about being baptised for the dead, or the laws of the celestial kingdom? . . .

The religion of heaven teaches us to give every man and every woman their due, that rightly belongs to them. And he that walks up to his privilege and duty, he has honor and glory, and shall never be removed out of his place.

I have shown to the brethren and sisters that Brother Joseph did not tell them all things at once, consequently you may expect to hear and see many things you never thought of before. One thing is that we have taken down the wooden fount that was built up by the instructions of Brother Joseph. This has been a great wonder to some, and says one of the stone-cutters the other day, "I wonder why Joseph did not tell us the fount should be built of stone." The man that made that speech is walking in darkness. He is a stranger to the spirit of this work, and knows nothing. In fact he does not know enough to cut a stone for the house of God. There is not a man under the face of the heavens that has one particle of the spirit about him, but knows that God talks to men according to their circumstances. God knew that old Abraham could not build a temple, therefore he said unto him, go to the mountain I shall tell thee of, and there offer up your sarifice. He tells us to build an house here in this place, according to our means. And when we get a little more strength, he will say, go now and execute your means upon the next house we have got to build, and it is just to stretch our faith until it shall become exceeding great, that we can command the elements and they will obey. And when we get into Jackson county to walk in the courts of that house, we can say we built this temple: for as the Lord lives we will build up Jackson county in this generation, (cries of amen,) and we will be far better off with regard to temporal things, when we have done, than ever we were before. If we had the means to build a fount in that house, say one of marble, the Lord would just as like as not tell us to cover it with gold just to stretch our faith. Brother Joseph said to me with regard to the fount, "I will not go into the river to be baptised for my friends, we will build a wooden fount to serve the present necessity; brethren does that satisfy you? This fount has caused the Gentile world to wonder, but a sight of the next one will make a Gentile faint away. This brings to my memory a circumstance that transpired in the temple at Kirtland. A very pious lady came to see the temple, she walked up and down in the house, with her hands locked together, and after the escape of one or two of the sectarians most sanctified groans, she exclaimed, "The Lord does not like such extravagance." Poor thing, I wonder how she will walk upon the streets when they are paved with gold; she could not bear to see the temple of God adorned and beautified, and the reason was because she was *full of the devil.*

I would put you on your guard against those who wear a long face, and pretend to be so holy, and so much better than every body else—They cannot look pleasant because they are full of the devil. Those who have got the forgiveness of their sins have countenances that look bright, and they will shine with the intelligence of heaven. If you dont believe it, try yourselves and then look up into the glass.

We will have a fount that will not stink and keep as all the while cleansing it out; and we will have a pool wherein to baptise the sick, that they may recover. And when we get into the fount we will show you the priesthood and the power of it; therefore, let us be diligent in observing all the commandments of God. Put away all fears of mobs, let not these things trouble you, for I say to the people I believe myself we shall have a healthy season, and that we shall have a summer of peace—The devils will growl without, and if they could get in here they would growl, but if they do they must look out. And I dare venture to say, that there could not be found as healthy a looking congregation in all the United States as I see here this day.

Brethren and sisters, for the sake of your dead and for the sake of yourselves, be faithful and have no feelings in your hearts against one another, but learn to suffer wrong rather than do wrong, and by so doing we will outstrip all our enemies and conquer the evil one, for know ye not that here is Zion? know ye not that the millennium has commenced? We have had Zion upon the earth this fourteen years. Peace reigns among this people which is Zion. Union and true charity dwells with this people: this is the most orderly and peaceable people upon the face of the whole earth. Well, this is Zion, and it is increasing and spreading wider and wider, and this principle of Zion, which is peace, will stretch all over the earth; that is the millennium.

The saints will increase, and continue to increase, and virtue, love, holiness and all good principles, will continue to spread and spread, and will rule the nations of the earth, and who is there that can stop its progress? None, but it will roll until there is no room for the devil; then he will be bound and shut up. The principles of the kingdom of God will prevail, from city to city, from nation to nation, until the devil shall be bound and there is no place for him. They killed the prophet Joseph for fear he would spread this principle, but it will go and fill the whole earth; this is true and will come to pass as the Lord lives. Amen.

—Volume 6, pages 953-957,

July 1, 1845.

LIFE IN NAUVOO

Much activity during the final days at Nauvoo focused on completing the construction of the temple. In an apostolic epistle dated January 14, 1845, Brigham Young made a progress report to the church at large.

Beloved Brethren:—
As the purposes of God roll forth and the work of the Lord hastens to its accomplishment, it is necessary that we, as watchmen upon the towers of Zion, communicate with you from time to time, and put you in possession of such information as may be deemed necessary for your welfare, for the furtherance of the cause of God, and for the fulfilling of those great purposes which our heavenly father has designed in the rolling forth of the dispensation of the fulness of times, 'spoken of by all the prophets since the world was.'

The Temple has progressed very rapidly since the death of our beloved Prophet and Patriarch. The diligence of those employed, and the willingness of the saints to contribute, have brought it to a state of forwardness, which has far exceeded our most sanguine expectations. You have already been informed that the capitols of the columns were all on; we have now to announce to you that by the time the spring opens we expect that every stone will be cut to complete the Temple, and it will not take long to lay them, when they are all prepared. . . .

We wish all the young, middle aged, and able bodied men who have it in their hearts to stretch forth this work with power, to come to Nauvoo, prepared to stay during the summer; and to bring with them means to sustain themselves with, and to enable us to forward this work; to bring with them teams, cattle, sheep, gold, silver, brass, iron, oil, paints and tools; and let those who are within market distance of Nauvoo bring with them provisions to sustain themselves and others during their stay. And let all the churches send all the money, cloth, and clothing, together with the raw matereal for manufacturing purposes; such as cotton, cotton yarn, wool, steel, iron, brass &c., &c., as we are preparing to go into extensive manufacturing operations, and all these things can be applied to the furtherance of the Temple.

There was a font erected in the basement story of the Temple, for the baptism of the dead, the healing of the sick and other purposes; this font was made of wood, and was only intended for the present use; but it is now removed, and as soon as the stone cutters get through with the cutting of the stone for the walls of the Temple, they will immediately proceed to cut the stone for and erect a font of hewn stone. This font will be of an ovel form and twelve feet in length and eight wide, with stone steps and an iron railing; this font will stand upon twelve oxen, which will be cast of iron or brass, or perhaps hewn stone; if of brass, polished; if of iron, bronzed:—upon each side of the font: there will be a suit of rooms fitted up for the washings. In the recesses, on each side of the arch, on the first story, there will be a suit of rooms or ante-chambers, lighted with the first row of circular windows. As soon as a suitable number of those rooms are completed we shall commence the endowment.

Brethren, inasmuch as you have long desired blessings, come up to the help of the Lord, and help to forward the work that we are engaged in; for we trust that these rooms will be finished by the first of December next, so that you may enter therein and receive wisdom, knowledge, understanding, and the power of the priesthood, which you have so long desired; that you may be prepared to go forth to the nations of the earth and build up the kingdom in all parts of the world; gather up Israel, redeem Zion; rebuild Jerusalem; and fill the whole earth with the knowledge of God. . . .

There is now in the city eight of the Twelve all in good health and spirits; our city is progressing, and the work of the Lord is rolling forth with unprecedented rapidity.

Thus, dear brethren, we have given you, in part, some of the measures and calculations, which we mean to carry into effect for your salvation, and for the furtherance of the salvation of the world. We have commenced a new year, and, as the Lord says; "All victory and glory is brought to pass unto you through diligence, faithfulness and prayers of faith," so we cannot but hope, that you will renew your exertions, your prayers, and your tithings, for the benefit of Zion, that she may arise and shine, for the good of all people.

We cannot say every thing in one short epistle, therefore, from time to time, as the Lord puts into our hearts instructions, we shall give them unto you; solemnly praying that you will increase your faith, double your diligence, walk by light and obedience, and be instant in season, to do the will of our Father in heaven:— Beware of ungodly men, who creep among you unawares; they are clouds without water, driven about by winds, and will finally be blown into outer darkness.

Our counsel to the travelling Elders abroad is for them to return to Nauvoo by the 6th of April, to Conference, or as soon as possible afterwards, and before they leave, it will be necessary for them to ordain good and wise men to preside over the branches during their absence.

May the grace of our Lord Jesus Christ, a veneration for the names of the first martyrs, first elders, and first prophets of the nineteenth century, inspire your hearts, to hear counsel, to keep counsel, to practice holiness, live the life of Saints, and "die the death of the righteous, that your last end may be like his."

Done in council, at Nauvoo, this 14th day of January 1845.

BRIGHAM YOUNG, *Pres't.*

Willard Richards, *Clerk.*

—Volume 6, pages 779-780,

January 15, 1845.

412

The report of the laying of the temple's capstone appeared in the June 1, 1845, issue.

> After a little more than four years of hard labor, in truly troublesome times, and not, too, without the loss of the best blood in the church, on the morning of the 24th ult. at a little past 6, a goodly number of Saints had the honor, and glory to witness *the Capstone of the Temple laid in its place.* The morning was cool, clear, and beautiful: the Saints felt glorious, the band upon the top of the walls, played charmingly and when the stone was placed, there was a united *Hosanna to God and the Lamb, amen and amen* shouted three times, which not only gave joy on earth, but filled the heavens with gladness!
>
> The "Twelve," and other authorities of the church, were present to witness and conduct this interesting scene. Like the event when God finished his work and rested, (so said President Young,) as it was the seventh day of the week, the Saints might do the same.
>
> A new hymn was sung, and as the prophets have written for our instruction, so the "head stone" was brought forward with shouting—grace, grace unto it:—and may the God of Israel, with his Almighty power, grant that the Saints may have peace to obtain their endowment therein. Amen.

W. W. Phelps commemorated the occasion with a poem, appropriately entitled "The Cap Stone."

> Have you heard the revelation,
> Of this latter dispensation,
> Which is unto every nation,
> O! prepare to meet thy God?
> CHORUS—We are a band of brethren,
> And we've rear'd the Lord a temple,
> And the cap stone now is finish'd,
> And we'll sound the news abroad.
>
> Go and publish how Missouri,
> Like a whirlwind in its fury,
> And without a judge or jury,
> Drove the saints and spilt their blood.
> CHORUS—We are a band of brethren, &c.

Illinois, where satan flatters,
Shot the prophets too, as martys,
And repeal'd our city charters,
   All because we worship'd God.
CHORUS—We are a band of brethren, &c.

Bennett, Law and many others,
Have betray'd our honest brothers,
To destroy our wives and mothers,
   As a Judas did the Lord.
CHORUS—We are a band of brethren, &c.

And their chief is Sidney Rigdon,
Who's a traitor, base, intriguing,
And will fight at Armageddon,
   When the fire comes down from God.
CHORUS—We are a band of brethren, &c.

While the devil such men jostles,
With his "keys of conquest morsels,
We'll uphold the Twelve apostles,
   With authority from God.
CHORUS—We are a band of brethren, &c.

And we'll give the world a sample,
Of our faith and works most ample,
When we've finish'd off the temple,
   As a dwelling for the Lord.
CHORUS—We are a band of brethren, &c.

And we'll feed the saints that's needing,
And improve our hearts by weeding,
Till we make Nauvoo as Eden,
   Where the saints can meet the Lord.
CHORUS—We are a band of brethren, &c.

—Volume 6, page 991,

August 1, 1845.

414

Mother Smith as a mother in Israel, signify it by saying yes!—One universal "yes" rang throughout.)...I feel as though God was vexing this nation a little, here and there, and I feel that the Lord will let Brother Brigham take the people away. Here, in this city, lay my dead; my husband and children; and if so be the rest of my children go with you, (and I would to God they may all go,) they will not go without me; and if I go, I want my bones brought back in case I die away, and deposited with my husband and children. (Mother Smith said many more good things, but the rest being inaudible to the reporters, they are lost.

President Brigham Young then arose and said he wanted to relate to the congregation the last closing remarks of Mother Smith; inasmuch as she could not be heard by all.

Mother Smith proposes a thing which rejoices my heart: she will go with us. I can answer for the authorities of the church; we want her and her children to go with us; and I pledge myself in behalf of the authorities of the church, that while we have any thing, they shall share with us. We have extended the helping hand to Mother Smith. She has the best carriage in the city and while she lives, shall ride in it when and where she pleases.

When William came here we furnished him a span of horses, and a carriage and a house, and Brother Kimball became responsible for the rent of it. He has run away in a time of trouble; but I suppose will come back when it is peace, and we mean to have him with us yet. . . .

President B. Young continued; we are determined also to use every means in our power to do all that Joseph told us. And we will petition Sister Emma, in the name of Israel's God, to let us deposit the remains of Joseph according as he commanded us. And if she will not consent to it, our garments are clear.—Then when he awakes in the morning of the resurrection, he shall talk with them, not with me; the sin shall be upon her head, not ours.

Elder W. W. Phelps said; as a people we are fast approaching a desired end, which may literally be cllaed a beginning. Thus far, we crnnot be reproached with being backward in instruction. By revelation, in 1831, I was appointed to "do the work of printing, and of selecting and writing books for schools in this church, that little children might receive instruction;" and since then I have received a further sanction. We are preparing to go out from among the people, where we can serve God in righteousness; and the first thing is, to teach our children; for they are as the Israel of old. It is our children who will take the kingdom and bear it off to all the world. The first commandment with promise to Israel was "Honor thy father and thy mother, that thy days may

William B. Smith in his later years

Apostle Brigham Young (1801-1877)

be long in the land, which the Lord thy God giveth thee." We will instruct our children in the paths of righteousness; and we want that instruction compiled in a book.

Moved, that W. W. Phelps write some school books for the use of children; seconded and carried.

Elder G. A. Smith said; the next item was of very great importance: there has been more powder and ball wasted within the last two weeks, than would supply all the people with meat for three months, if they were in a game country. What is the use of this waste? You cannot wake up in the night, but you hear them cracking away. You can hardly walk the street, but sometimes a bullet will whistle over your head. Men say they are afraid their guns won't go off, it is wet; then I am in favor of getting something to draw them: I hope there will be no more firing. If there was a mob in sight, you have time enough to load your guns and fire on them. I want the powder and lead saved, so that when you get to your journey's end, you can sustain yourselves with food.—*Save your powder, caps, and lead.* I move that this conference discountenance all firing in the city, by any man, by night or by day, in every possible manner; seconded and carried.

Elder H. C. Kimball said; there are a good many complaints of late, and I am sorry to hear it, of some of the neighbors having had their cattle shot. Bro. John Benbow has had fifteen wounded. I am ashamed of a man who will do such things. The man that will destroy his neighbor's property in that way, I will prophesy that the hand of God will be upon him until he makes restitution, and he will not prosper.

Moved, that all persons who have been guilty, or may be hereafter, of shooting cattle, shall be cut off from the church, unless they make restitution; seconded and carried.

Moved, that all persons, who will not take care of their unruly cattle, shall be cut off from the church; seconded and carried.

—Volume 6, page 1016,

November 1, 1845.

During this difficult period, when the future of the Nauvoo community seemed so bleak in light of the continuing hostility of the residents of neighboring towns, the *Times and Seasons* continued publishing a variety of news, editorials, features, letters, and mission reports. It is to the editor's credit that the somber gloom that at times enshrouded

Nauvoo did not unduly pervade the pages of the paper. Enthusiastic reports of missionary work, particularly those from the South Sea Islands, graced the pages of the *Times and Seasons*, bringing joy and comfort to a people who had lately known much of tears and bitterness.

On occasion, a little levity shone through, as in the case of a full page reproduction of Matthew 24 in the Tahitian language, printed with the instructions to the American Saints, "Read and reflect" (found in February 1, 1846, issue, pages 1115, 1116).

A series of "Mormon Proverbs" reprinted from the *New York Prophet* appeared in the May 15, 1845, *Times and Seasons*. Some of these may be nothing more than the miscellaneous sayings of W. W. Phelps or P. P. Pratt. Others are quotations from Joseph's documents as printed in the Doctrine and Covenants.

> The globe lamp, suspended in the heavens is the best and cheapest light in the world.
> A wise man will prefer it to any other; but a fool will sleep while the morning sun shines, and light a lamp when it goes down.
> This is like cutting cloth from one end of a piece, and sewing it on to the other to make it longer.
> He that sleeps when the sun shines, and lights his lamp when it does not, despises the lamp of the Lord, and taxes his eyes and purse for nought.
> Industry goes hand in hand with godliness.—It is an houor to be an agriculturist, for such was our Father in heaven. He performed the first planting on this earth.
> It is good also to be a tailor, for our Father in heaven was the first tailor on this planet.—He made coats for Adam and Eve, when they were young and inexperienced, and thus clothed them.
> It is good also, to write, for our Father in heaven was a writer. He wrote with his own finger on the tables of stone.
> To build ships, temples and houses, is also godliness, for God was master workman in all these branches of industry. He gave the pattern of the first ship to Noah; and he was the architect of the tabernacle of Moses, and of the temple of Solomon.
> A wise man will pattern after his order; but fools will erect synagogues after the imagination of their own heart.

Great is the mystery of iniquity, and error; but all truth is simple, and easy to be understood.

"Truth is a knowledge of things as they are and were, and are to come."

All truth is independent in its own sphere.—Its laws are omnipotent, eternal, and unchangeable.

"Intelligence, or the light of truth never was created, neither indeed can be."

Truth is light—light is spirit—spirit is life. Truth, light, spirit, is the law of life and motion, by which all things are governed, and by which they move and have a being.

Truth will justify.

Truth will sanctify.

Truth will purify.

Truth will exalt man to the throne of heaven and crown him with eternal life and dominion in the presence of Jehovah.

The truth comes to man by means of higher intelligences; by the voice of God—by the ministering of angels, and by the Holy Spirit of prophecy and revelation.

In all your gettings, get truth, for this will give you everlasting life, and crown you with riches and honors, which shall never fade away.

—Volume 6, page 900,

May 15, 1845.

An editorial on December 1, 1845, described the situation in Nauvoo. The church members were at that time using the temple for special ordinances and looking toward abandoning the city sometime during the next spring.

THE PROSPECT.

Peace and union reign at Nauvoo, and as to business, every saint that means to keep the commandments of the Lord, and prepare for the revelation of Jesus Christ, is earnestly employed in fitting out for the intended removal next spring: or, as a willing and obedient people many are engaged upon the Temple—determined to finish that glorious structure of Latter-day Saints' faith and works, as a monument, that they were industrious, noble minded, and sincere.

It is now the first of December, and the suit of rooms in the attic story for the accommodation of the Priesthood, in the ordinances of washings, anointings, and prayer, are nearly ready for use; so that the faithful saints begin to rejoice in the Holy one of Israel. The tithings of good men; the widow's mite; the blood of the martyrs, and the tears of the fatherless, have not been unavailing, but, like the prayers of the saints which are bottled up in Heaven for the gratification of holy beings, they sparkle before the Lord, as monuments of virtue, union, perseverence and religion unknown to the world. We have great reason to rejoice, for the Lord is with us.

The mob, as usual, are busy in manufacturing lies about the Saints; and what they lack, is gratuitously supplied by apostates, who naturally drop down among the dregs of society, as a fall from a slaughter house, and are devoured up by beasts of prey. We believe also, that the mob keep up the old system of plundering and crying *mad-dog* in order to prejudice the community against the saints, but God, who never fails to bless the righteous, is our friend, and *we live,* and blessed be his name.

We can say in the voice of truth; brethren; be just—be wise—be watchful—be prayerful—and put away all evil, and he that said to the raging waves; "peace, be still," will say, *well done good faithful servants, enter into the joys of your Lord.*

—Volume 6, page 1050,

December 1, 1845.

More details concerning the planned migration arose out of a circular prepared by the High Council the following month.

TO THE MEMBERS OF THE CHURCH OF JESUS CHRIST OP LATTER DAY SAINTS, AND TO ALL WHOM IT MAY CONCERN: GREETING.

Beloved Brethren and Friends;— We, the members of the High Council of the Church, by the voice of all her authorities, have unitedly and unanimously agreed, and embrace this opportunity to inform you, that we intend to send out into the Western country from this place, some time in the early part of the month of March, a company of pioneers, consisting mostly of young, hardy men, with some families. These are destined to be fur-

423

nished with an ample outfit; taking with them a printing press, farming utensils of all kinds, with mill irons and bolting cloths, seeds of all kinds, grain &c.

The object of this early move, is, to put in a spring crop, to build houses, and to prepare for the reception of families who will start so soon as grass shall be sufficiently grown to sustain teams and stock. Our pioneers are instructed to proceed West until they find a good place to make a crop, in some good valley in the neighborhood of the Rocky Mountains, where they will infringe upon no one, and be not likely to be infringed upon. Here we will make a resting place, until we can determine a place for a permanent location. In the event of the President's recommendation to build block houses and stockade forts on the rout to Oregon, becoming a law, we have encouragements of having that work to do; and under our peculiar circumstances, we can do it with less expense to the Government than any other people. We also further declare for the satisfaction of some who have concluded that our grievances have alienated us from our country; that our patriotism has not been overcome by fire—by sword—by daylight, nor by midnight assassinations, which we have endured; neither have they alienated us from the institutions of our country. Should hostilities arise between the Government of the United States and any other power, in relation to the right of possessing the territory of Oregon, we are on hand to sustain the claim of the United State's Government to that country. It is geographically ours; and of right, no foreign power should hold dominion there: and if our services are required to prevent it, those services will be cheerfully rendered according to our ability. We feel the injuries that we have sustained, and are not insensible of the wrongs we have suffered; still we are Americans, and should our country be invaded we hope to do, at least, na much as did the conscientious Quaker who took his passage on board a merchant ship, and was attacked by pirates. The pirate boarded the merchantman, and one of the enemies' men fell into the water between the two vessels, but seized a rope that hung over and was pulling himself up on board the merchantman. The conscientious Quaker saw this, and though he did not like to fight, he took his jack-knife and quickly moved to the scene, saying to the pirate, "if thee wants that piece of rope I will help thee to it." He cut the rope asunder—the pirate fell—and a watery grave was his resting place.

Much of our property will be left in the hands of competent agents for sale at a low rate, for teams, for goods and for cash. The funds arising from the sale of property will be applied to the removal of families from time to time as fast as consistent, and it now remains to be proven whether those of our families and friends who are necessarily left behind for a season to obtain an outfit, through the sale of property, shall be mobbed, burnt, and driven away by force. Does any American want the honor of doing it? or will Americans suffer such acts to be done, and the disgrace of them to rest on their character under existing circumstances? If they will, let the world know it. But we do not believe they will.

We agreed to leave the country for the sake of peace, upon the condition that no more vexatious prosecutions be instituted against us.—In good faith have we labored to fulfil this engagement. Governor Ford has also done his duty to further our wishes in this respect.—But there are some who are unwilling that we should have an existence any where. But our destinies are in the hands of God, and so also is theirs.

We venture to say that our brethren have made no counterfeit money: And if any miller has received fifteen hundred dollars base coin in a week, from us, let him testify. If any land agent of the General Government has received wagon loads of base coin from us in payment for lands, let him say so. Or if he has received any at all from us, let him tell it.—Those witnesses against us have spun a long yarn: but if our brethren had never used an influence against them to break them up, and to cause them to leave our city, after having satisfied themselves that they were engaged in the very business of which they accuse us, their revenge might never have been roused to father upon us their own illegitimate and bogus productions.

We have never tied a black strap around any person's neck, neither have we cut their bowals out, nor fed any to the "Catfish." The systematic order of stealing of which these grave witnesses speak, must certainly be original with them. Such a plan could never originate with any person, except some one who wished to fan the flames of death and destruction round us. The very dregs of malice and revenge are mingled in the statements of those witnesses alluded to by the 'Sangamo Journal.' We should think that every man of sense might see this. In fact, many editors do see it, and they have our thanks for speaking of it.

We have now stated our feelings, our wishes, and our intentions: And by them we are willing to abide; and such Editors as are willing that we should live and not die; and have a being on the earth while heaven is pleased to lengthen out our days, are respectfully requested to publish this article. And men who wish to buy property very cheap, to benefit themselves, and are willing

to benefit us; are invited to call and look: and our prayer shall
ever be that justice and judgement—mercy and truth may be exalted, not only in our own land, but throughout the world, and
the will of God be done on earth as it is done in Heaven.

Done in Council at the City of Nauvoo, on the 20th day of
January, 1846.

> SAMUEL BENT,
> JAMES ALLRED,
> GEORGE W. HARRIS,
> WILLIAM HUNTINGTON,
> HENRY G. SHERWOOD,
> ALPHEUS CUTLER,
> NEWEL KNIGHT,
> LEWIS D. WILSON,
> EZRA T. BENSON,
> DAVID FULLMER,
> THOMAS GROVER,
> AARON JOHNSON.

—Volume 6, pages 1096-1097,

January 20, 1846.

A final note of readiness is sounded in a short editorial in
the second to the last *Times and Seasons*:

All things are in preparation for a commencement of the great
move of the Saints out of the United States;—(we had like to have
said, beyond the power of Christianity,) but we will soften the
expression, by merely saying, *and back to their "primitive possessions,"* as in the enjoyment of Israel. It is reduced to a solemn
reality, that the rights and property, as well as the lives and
common religious belief of the church of Jesus Christ of Latter-
day Saints, *cannot be protected* in the realms of the United
States, and, of course, from one to two hundred thousand souls,
must quit their freedom among freemen, and go where the land,
the elements, and the worship of God *are free.*

About two thousand are ready and crossing the Mississippi to
pioneer the way, and make arrangements for summer crops at
some point between this and the "Pacific," where the biggest
crowd of good people, will be the old settlers.

426

To see such a large body of men, women and children, compelled by the inefficiency of the law, and potency of mobocracy, to leave a great city in the month of February, for the sake of the enjoyment of *pure religion,* fills the soul with astonishment, and gives the world a sample of fidelity and faith, brilliant as the sun, and forcible as a tempest, and as enduring as eternity.

May God continue the spirit of fleeing from false freedom, and false dignity, till every Saint is removed to where he "can sit under his own vine and fig tree" without having any to molest or make afraid. *Let us go—let us go.*

—Volume 6, page 1114,

February 1, 1846.

The final issue of the *Times and Seasons* is closed by two poems. One poem, for which no author is credited, was entitled the "Song of Life." It presented joyous, life-affirming sentiments that must have mocked those who felt that they were crushing the spirit of life and the will to survive in the Latter Day Saints by driving them again into the wilderness. The last stanza reads:

> All things which meet the wand'ring eye,
> From flowery earth to starry sky;
> The joy of morn, the calm of even,
> All on the earth, in air, in heaven,
> All which a bounteous God hath given—
> Doth sing of life;
> Doth sing of life.

—Volume 6, page 1135,

February 15, 1846.

The concluding poem by W. W. Phelps celebrated the termination of work on the temple.

DEDICATION HYMN.

> Ho, ho, for the Temple's completed,—
> The Lord hath a place for his head,
> And the priesthood, in power, now lightens
> The way of the living and dead!

427

See, see, mid the world's *dreadful splendor*
    Christianity, folly and sword,
The Mormons, the diligent Mormons,
    Have rear'd up this house to the Lord!

By the spirit and wisdom of Joseph,—
    (Whose blood stains the honor of State,)
By tithing and sacrifice daily,
    The poor learn the way to be great.

Mark, mark, for the Gentiles are fearful
    Where the work of the Lord is begun;
Already this monument finish'd,
    Is counted—*one miracle done!*

Gaze, gaze, at the flight of the righteous,
    From the "fire show r of ruin" at hand,
Their pray'rs, and their suff'rings, are wrathing
    Jehovah to sweep off the land!

Sing, sing, for the hour of redemption,
    The day for the poor Saint's reward,
Is coming for temp'ral enjoyment,
    All shining with crowns from the Lord!

Watch, watch, for the blessing of Jesus,
    Is richer the farther it's fetch'd;—
The wonderful chain of our union
    Is tighten'd the longer it's stretch'd!

Shout, shout, for the armies of heaven,
    Will purify earth at a word,
And the "Twelve, with the Saints that are faithful,
    "ENTER INTO THE JOYS OF THEIR LORD!"

—Volume 6, page 1135,

February 15, 1846.

This last issue was published a few days after the westward exodus had begun. In a period of six years, 131 issues of the *Times and Seasons* had been published, about 2,100 pages in all. This paper chronicled the growth and decline of Nauvoo, called by many Saints the "City of Joseph." It is not definitely known what became of the press. It was probably sold to nonmember interests during the exodus in early 1846.

The Saints once again had been scattered by misfortune. Some were convinced that their destiny lay somewhere to the west high in the mountain ranges beyond the borders of the United States, and that conviction produced one of the great westward migrations of American history. Others felt that their fortune lay in remaining in the midwest region, witnessing of the restored gospel and waiting patiently all the while for God to call his flock together again.

Capstone of Nauvoo Temple

Modern view of Old Nauvoo as viewed from the air

430

Chapter 7

LIVING WITH OUR PAST

For several generations of Americans, one of the most romantic and glorious eras in the nation's history was the taming and development of the Wild, Wild West. Our cultural hero images include the brave cowboy and his faithful horse, the undaunted sheriff and his trusty six-shooter, the cavalry officer mustering his strength to fend off a blood-thirsty Indian attack.

Colin Rickards, noted Western historian, refuses to let us hold our cherished myths about the Wild, Wild West without critical examination. He calls to our attention a few myth-shattering facts, as he points out, for example, that Dodge City, the town that Hollywood has made the most glamorous in the West, was in fact a shapeless sprawl of stockyards, clapboard stores, saloons, lodging houses, and brothels. For much of the year the apology for a main street was a muddy quagmire.

Hollywood's smooth-shaven, clean-limbed, tall-in-the-saddle Western heroes with their clean shirts, low-crowned hats and tied-down guns are a far cry from their Old West prototypes, Rickards notes. Most of them, in fact, were heavily moustached, shabby men with oversized hats and scuffed boots, and they wore their gun belts high for comfort and to hold up their trousers.

As for the image of Western cavalry, death and defeat contributed to making George Armstrong Custer into a national hero and into Hollywood's prototype for the United States Cavalry. If Custer had been victorious over the Sioux and Cheyenne at the Battle of the Little Big Horn, he would probably have been dismissed by historians as a dandified, self-seeking braggard. On June 25, 1876, Custer's scouts located an Indian village on the Little Big Horn River in Montana. They warned that it was far too large for his force of about two hundred men and they urged him to await reinforcements a mere day's march away. But Custer was still smarting under a stinging rebuke which had been administered after he had testified at a court of inquiry where he had made unfounded allegations against President Grant's family. He needed a brilliant victory over the Indians to put him back in official graces. He therefore ignored the warning of his scouts and led his men down the valley. Suddenly they were surrounded by more than three thousand Sioux, Cheyenne, and Arapahoe warriors. It was all over in less than three hours. According to Indian witnesses, many of the soldiers had whiskey in their canteens and were half-drunk by the end of the skirmish.

What would a group of young people do with this kind of information that debunks tradition-ladened myths? To answer this question, a young people's High School of Religion class studying church history was confronted with the article written by historian Rickards. These students proved themselves to be astute, level-headed, and rather sophisticated about the whole matter of historical myth. Out of the class discussion the group determined that our view of the Wild West is distorted in several ways. For example, the "cowboy period" depicted in so many movies and on TV lasted only fifteen or twenty years although it might seem interminable in light of the quantity of shoot-em-up tales it has spawned. In the movies the developing of the West is almost always seen from the perspective of the cowherders rather than from that of the sheepmen, a perspective as different as night from day.

Much folklore is mixed in, including the stories concerning Matt Dillon, a Dodge City marshal who never really existed, and fanciful stories about characters, especially outlaws (those who wear the black hats) who did live but not nearly such exciting lives as we have been led to believe. Jesse and Frank James, Jim and Bob Younger, and Billy the Kid all had off

432

days when life seemed but a series of monotonous chores. We have whitewashed the heroes (those who wore white hats) such as Wyatt Earp. Mr. Earp never did "clean up" any frontier town although he did work as a lawman for a brief period in Wichita and Dodge City.

Some aspects of western history have been all but ignored, such as the contribution of Negro cowboys, many of whom headed west after the Civil War to make a new life for themselves in the development of the western frontier. Following the precedent of some whites, some black men decided that outlawing was more exciting and more remunerative than abiding by the law. A black rustler by the name of George Washington rode with Billy the Kid. Cherokee Bill, a mulatto, was one of the most feared of renegades, having killed nineteen men before he was twenty-one years old. Only recently have blacks been depicted in western movies or TV shows, and then mostly as a result of pressure from Black Power groups rather than out of any concern for historical accuracy.

So impressive was this youth group's ability to deal responsibly with historical data that we asked them to apply the principles learned from this excursion in Wild West history to the history of their country as a whole. From them we learned the following:

1. Our American history, as it is generally conveyed to us, is slanted. It has a definite bias in that it was written from the white settlers' point of view. How would American history read if it were interpreted by an American Indian or an Afro-American, both of whose predecessors have been victimized by the European colonists?

2. The leading characters tend to be whitewashed or blackwashed, depending on whether they are hero or villian to us. How many negative reports are ever voiced about George Washington, the nation's first president, or, in the North at least, Abraham Lincoln? Their characters are usually depicted as somewhat saintly. For one to suggest

433

that Washington was power-hungry or that Lincoln could outswear any boisterous sea sailor would seem to be almost unpatriotic, if not treasonous. And who has ever heard a good word about Benedict Arnold? So what if he was merely being true to his conscience when he finally decided to throw in his lot with the British command after a long, soul-searching struggle, and after a very valuable contribution to the American colonial cause? Our personal experience tells us that the people we know, including ourselves, are a mixture of rational morality and irrational impulses, good and bad, kindness and indifference. Many of the media that treat historical personages focus on them, however, as one-dimensional characters that either bestow unmixed good or bequeath undiluted evil to their associates.

3. Some folklore may become mixed with historical fact. George Washington and the cherry tree, and the Devil and Daniel Webster are two legends that do much to inform us of the characters of these men, but few informed persons would take these stories literally. Even where legend is not operative, we can expect that exaggeration, repression of uncomplimentary facts, or patriotic pride or sectional vindictiveness help to shape the kinds of information mediated to us by those who relay the tales.

4. There may occur a distortion of the time sequence. For example, in their understanding of American history many students tend to telescope the events during the colonial period from the founding of Jamestown in 1607 until the Revolutionary War. The period from the Revolution is studied avidly up till the period of Reconstruction after the War between the States, which is approximately where the typical American history class terminates as summer vacation arrives. It is therefore hard to imagine that the colonial period was almost as long as the postcolonial period up to the present day. For some it is even more difficult to realize that the founding of Jamestown

didn't occur until over a century after America was discovered by Columbus.

5. As part of the general bias mentioned earlier, there is a tendency to hold a specialization of perspective or focus, such as economic, political, or military, so that a restrictive selection of data occurs. For example, most would see the American Revolution as a political phenomenon in which men were seeking a fuller measure of freedom with which to exercise their citizenship. Others would tend to focus on the economic factors that caused the American merchants and businessmen to want to be free in the economic realm to develop to the full their natural resources. Of course, a multidimensional, comprehensive view that involves all spheres of influence is safer but less easily come by and less easily employed.

The next question for the youth group was whether similar principles for historical interpretation apply to church history as well. The young people thought that they most certainly must. Together during the course, as we explored the familiar and not so familiar episodes of the Restoration saga, we continually considered these questions:

1. Is the reporting of church history slanted? If so, in what direction? The general public first became aware of the Latter Day Saints, we discovered, by means of books written by those outside the fold or by those once affiliated with the church but later "apostatized." Most influential of the early anti-Restoration books were the following:

Campbell, *Delusions: An Analysis of the Book of Mormon, 1832*

Howe, *Mormonism Unvailed* (sic) 1834

McChesney, *An Antidote to Mormonism,* 1838

Bachelor, *Mormonism Exposed,* 1838

Lee, *The Mormons; or Knavery Exposed*, 1841

Bennett, *The History of the Saints; or an Exposé of Joe Smith and Mormonism*, 1842

Kidder, *Mormonism and the Mormons*, 1842

Turner, *Mormonism in All Ages*, 1842

Clarke, *Mormonism Unveiled*, 1842

These books vilified the Prophet and other church leaders and represented the Saints either as innocent, ignorant dupes, as raving lunatics, or as malicious scoundrels.

The first references to the origin and development of the movement from the faithful insiders' point of view came in the pages of the early periodicals, particularly in Oliver Cowdery's letters in the *Messenger and Advocate* and Joseph Smith's own personal history as written for the *Times and Seasons*. Our diet of church history today consists largely of interpretation of selected portions of accounts written by those who were sympathetic to, though not necessarily directly involved in, the unfolding events themselves. In our later editing of the various accounts from which we have drawn our popular accounts of church history, we have sometimes wanted to smooth out the wrinkles and iron down the rough edges to present the best view imaginable of what went on in the early Restoration movement. Often out of the best of motives—the desire to attract potential converts and to strengthen new members—we have sometimes omitted from our accounting any mention of human failings or mistakes. In doing this we have in a sense acted like the overprotective parents who keep their children penned up in the house all the time to avoid the danger of accidents from automobiles and falling meteorites. Safety under these conditions is a worse fate than the possible dangers of roaming freely in the outside world.

An example of the exercise of our bias is our uncanny ability to read about the Saints being driven from Jackson County, Clay County, and Caldwell County in Missouri, from Kirtland, and finally from Nauvoo, all the time one-sidedly placing the blame on the Saints' opponents. Very rarely do we think to ask what the Saints were doing that could excite such hostility. Why should the Saints be welcomed to Illinois with open arms in 1839 and driven from the state with such vindictiveness only seven years later? Naturally, the issues are complex and no easy answers can be given. But we would do well to recognize that every feud and every argument has two sides, passionately believed in and valiantly fought for by honest persons on both sides of the issues. What would a non-Latter Day Saint gentleman in early Independence, a man of honesty and honor (and there were such persons in the community), tell us of the conflicts that developed between the original settlers and the new "mormon" immigrants? We who are so accustomed to hearing only one explanation of problems and difficulties need to search out a more balanced view of the issues from every source available. Then and only then can our judgments be considered to be on sound ground.

2. Have we told the whole story about the early church leaders, or have we tended to emphasize one element of their characters at the expense of other quite human characteristics? One of the best ways to sense the humanity of prophets is to read about them in the Old Testament. Amos apparently was a crude, uncouth shepherd fresh out of the hills of Tekoa, called upon to address the "high society" at Bethel. If his hearers had rejected him out of hand merely because he didn't fulfill their expectatioons of what a prophet should be and do,

we would not have had his magnificent oratory preserved for us. Hosea knew firsthand the experience of a broken home. His wife left him to follow a life of prostitution, reason enough for "good people" with their own house set in order to ignore his ministry. But Hosea used his own personal tragedy to teach a much needed lesson on God's unquenchable love for his faithless people. Then there were several great spokesmen for Yahweh who by present-day standards would probably be judged incurable neurotics. Elijah wore a garment of heavy animal fur. Isaiah walked naked and barefoot for three years. Jeremiah had tremors "like a drunken man." Ezekiel lay on his side eighty days, and cut off all his hair. All the prophets have been men of their times who wrote or spoke out of the context of the world they knew and were called to serve.

Thus it should be no surprise to discover that the prophets and apostles of the Restoration movement have been *people* too, with insights, opportunities, temptations, wrong judgments, challenges, dreams, and personal idiosyncracies just like everyone else. And so, as a matter of general principle, when we read an expose of "that scoundrel Joe Smith," we should instinctively realize that Joseph Smith can't be all that bad. Similarly when we listen to an overenthusiastic church school teacher mustering support for Doctrine and Covenants 113:3a, which states, "Joseph Smith, the prophet and seer of the Lord, has done more (save Jesus only) for the salvation of men in this world, than any other man that ever lived in it," we can perhaps with accuracy respond, "but surely no one can be all that good." Joseph Smith, Jr., has become a sanctimonious symbol—unblemished, untarnished—for some Latter Day Saints, rather than a man of flesh and blood. This unearthly canonization of the prophet is not fair to him.

438

Reading some popular church history accounts emanating from Utah would suggest how brave, loyal, noble, and true the president of the Twelve, <u>Brigham Young</u>, was in his contributions to the early Restoration movement. Some Reorganized Church sources, however, tend largely to ignore him before 1844 and then gleefully point to his demonic lust for power and penchant for swaying and deceiving the people of the church. Surely no one can be all that good or all that bad. Perhaps somewhere in between, somewhere in the gray, shadowy areas where men live most of their lives, these two church leaders could generally be found, at times responding magnificently to new opportunities to give creative leadership, at other times muffing their chance to excel by allowing personal prerogatives and selfish concerns to dictate their action or lack of action on crucial issues.

3. Has folklore infiltrated our understanding of church history? On occasion, it undoubtedly has. I remember vividly a campfire experience in which a storyteller informed a group of young, impressionable people around the campfire that Joseph Smith had the strength of ten men. On one occasion, when an enemy of the church was mocking him, we were told, Joseph picked up that man and hurled him like a javelin through the air. Now it is a well-known fact that Joseph enjoyed competing in wrestling matches and often proved himself to be in excellent physical condition by besting his opponent, but any suggestion that Joseph was Hercules moves us into the realm of imagination rather than fact.

During the early days of Nauvoo, malaria and perhaps typhoid fever visited the town in an epidemic that spread misery and death in its wake. The winter had been a bitterly cold season for which the new settlers were unprepared, the swamp upon which part of the city was being built had not yet been fully reclaimed, and there were not yet sufficient sanitation facilities to care for the physical needs of a burgeoning town. At the height of the sickness, the Smith family gave its home over as a make-shift hospital and lived in a tent in the yard so that those most severely infected could have the benefits of a dry, enclosed dwelling. The Prophet spent much time visiting among the sick, who seemed to take cheer and comfort from his presence. No healings were described in Joseph's personal journal, but the word got around that Joseph had been able to heal certain persons. Perhaps the Prophet remained silent himself because for every "healing" there were countless individuals who did not recover quickly or who did not recover at all. Almost every family lost at least one family member to the ravages of the disease. Eventually the epidemic dissipated, but later on the stories of Joseph's healing ministries grew in number and were embellished with flamboyant detail. It was reported that Joseph's handkerchief was blessed for the purpose of healing and was carried about by Wilford Woodruff, who healed many persons merely by wiping their faces with the consecrated cloth. What actually happened here? Is this a matter of a modern legend growing up around the skeleton of a historical happening? It is difficult to reconstruct with accuracy the minute details of any happening in early Nauvoo, and so we must once again exercise our judgment. If we enjoy tales of the mysterious and the miraculous, perhaps we will want to accept the handkerchief account with some measure of credulity.

4. Have we had a tendency to distort the time sequences of church history? Most RLDS members tend to visualize church history as three periods—the days of Joseph Smith, Jr., the "dark and cloudy day" when the Saints were scattered, and the period of the Reorganization. Most of our time spent on church history study focuses on the first period, causing these earliest episodes to play a tremendous role in the self-understanding of our people. What we sometimes fail to recognize is that the second period, from the martyrdom of the Smith broth-

ers in 1844 until the coming of Young Joseph to the Amboy Conference in 1860, is chronologically a longer period than the 1830-1844 experience of the church. Most of our knowledge about church history dates and names and places in all likelihood falls into the first period rather than into the second or third period, the last of which spans more than a century. Joseph Smith III was president of the church for fifty-four years as compared to his father's tenure of fourteen years, and yet few of our members have much awareness of the important developments that occurred during Joseph III's presidency. To be sure, quantity of time should not be equated with criterian for historical importance, yet the student of history should not ignore time scales either.

5. Has most of our history come to us from one particular perspective with a resultant lack of comprehensiveness of approach? Almost every major treatment of Joseph Smith has centered on his ''religious'' experiences—his mystical grove experience, angelic visitations, organizing a church, prophesying in the name of the Lord, and finally martyrdom for the Cause of the Kingdom. But Joseph was an individual with an enormous amount of interest in many facets of life's experience. In 1965 Robert Flanders, a professor of history and a high priest in the church, published his book *Nauvoo: Kingdom on the Mississippi.* Some of the "faithful" were disturbed because the traditional approach to the biographical reporting of Joseph Smith was not followed. Flanders writes in his preface:

> The account of Smith [in this book] is not a balanced one if for no other reason than that it does not treat him as a great religious teacher, evangelist, and lawgiver, though it is this facet of his career that has been most revered by successive generations of Latter-day Saints. The image which emerges in the following pages is of a man of affairs—planner, promoter, architect, entrepreneur, executive, politician, filibusterer—matters of which he was sometimes less sure than he was those of the spirit. Such an image is inevitable however in a study of Nauvoo. Central to

Smith's religious vision was the conviction that the men of God must be men of affairs, fashioning the Kingdom of Heaven into a kingdom of this world.

Needed today are more persons within the church able to examine our spiritual forebears in their nonchurchly roles without feeling that these men of God have somehow violated their calling by giving themselves to non-ecclesiastical pursuits. God's call to us is to be Christians in the world, serving this world which God loved to such an extent that he was willing to give his Son on its behalf. Service in and to the world can take many forms and shapes which cannot always be labeled in terms of churchly categories.

Jews can look at Abraham and confess that he was a polygamist, a man willing to give his wife over to the lustful desires of Pharaoh, and potentially a child sacrificer. Roman Catholics can look at Peter, whom they consider the first Bishop of Rome, and admit that he was on occasion a coward, a liar, and an impetuous buffoon. Protestants can look at Martin Luther and recognize that he was a beer guzzler, and anti-Semite, and at times a poor adviser. (He once consented to allow Landgrave Philip of Hesse to take a second wife and then when the bigamist relationship was uncovered, Luther counseled a "good strong lie.") Why then should Latter Day Saints be so protective of the reputations of their first founders? Were they not men as other men? Were they not entitled to learn by making mistakes? Does our faith today depend so very much upon what our church leaders of a century ago believed and said and did?

Today in the church there seems to be manifest an increasing openness to the spirit of inquiry which favors frank discussion within the community of faith. Many of today's church members feel an urgent mandate to be honest with themselves and an impetus toward refusing to compartmentalize life in churchly and nonchurchly realms. Only within the limits of this honesty and comprehensiveness of view can proper historical studies be conducted. History is an interpretation of extremely complex phenomena. We owe our church leaders of the past a careful consideration, though not necessarily blind acceptance, of what they said and did. We should strive to see past performance in light of what they were intending to say to the men and women of those past days. But then we must make our present judgments based on what our forebears knew *plus* what we have learned in the interim. As always, hindsight is better than foresight. Much that our spiritual ancestors said and did at Kirtland, Far West, and Nauvoo we would decidedly not say or do. We have been able to see in historical perspective the effects of those preachments and actions, and in light of those effects we have at times judged certain of those actions to have been unwise.

Values shift and change with the passage of time, bringing new resources and insights to succeeding generations. Members of the early church saw themselves as alienated and isolated from the world in which they lived. We, however, see them as related to that world of the 1830's and 1840's more than they could ever know. Many then saw the Restoration as a once-and-for-all recovery of something that had been lost to Christianity hundreds of years previously. Today we tend to view the Restoration as a process involving free, creative, open-ended responsiveness to whatever God brings to us day by day, year by year.

If faithfulness to the Restoration movement means recapturing in minute detail the worldview of the 1830's, then the imperative is a futile one, for the 1830's no longer exist. God is now calling us to respond with faithful concern and prophetic insight to the 1970's and the challenges, opportunities, issues, and problems that the latter half of the twentieth century present to us.

We cannot change the past, to be sure, but we can learn from it today to build for the future. Tomorrow's past is happening now, and our stewardship involves being aware of those historical circumstances that have brought us to this day. Only then can the history we are forging be created in the light of the best wisdom we can muster.